Don't Sweat the Technique

Don't Sweat the Technique

A Performer's Guide to Hip-Hop and Rap

Melissa L. Foster

ROWMAN & LITTLEFIELD
Lanham • Boulder • New York • London

Published by Rowman & Littlefield
An imprint of The Rowman & Littlefield Publishing Group, Inc.
4501 Forbes Blvd., Ste. 200
Lanham, MD 20706
www.rowman.com

86-90 Paul Street, London EC2A 4NE

Copyright © 2024 by The Rowman & Littlefield Publishing Group, Inc.

All rights reserved. No part of this book may be reproduced in any form or by any electronic or mechanical means, including information storage and retrieval systems, without written permission from the publisher, except by a reviewer who may quote passages in a review.

British Library Cataloguing in Publication Information Available

Library of Congress Cataloging-in-Publication Data

Library of Congress Cataloging-in-Publication Data
Names: Foster, Melissa L., 1974- author.
Title: Don't sweat the technique : a performer's guide to hip-hop and rap / Melissa L. Foster.
Description: Lanham : Rowman & Littlefield Publishers, 2023. | Includes bibliographical references and index.
Identifiers: LCCN 2023030231 (print) | LCCN 2023030232 (ebook) | ISBN 9781538167168 (cloth) | ISBN 9781538167175 (paperback) | ISBN 9781538167182 (epub)
Subjects: LCSH: Rap (Music)--Instruction and study. | Rap (Music)—History and criticism. | Rap musicians—Interviews.
Classification: LCC MT869 .F67 2023 (print) | LCC MT869 (ebook) | DDC 782.421649—dc23/eng/20230705
LC record available at https://lccn.loc.gov/2023030231
LC ebook record available at https://lccn.loc.gov/2023030232

To Matt and Vivian Boresi. You both made this book possible by wearing countless hats: you have been my unwavering cheerleaders, dedicated research assistants, reliable accountability agents, tireless caffeine suppliers, meticulous editors, creative brainstormers, and invaluable critical listeners. Thank you for being the best part of my world.

Contents

Acknowledgments *ix*

Introduction *1*

Part I. History and Influence *9*

1. *Black Reign* (Queen Latifah): The Birth of Hip-Hop *11*
2. *Back 'n the Day* (Dr. Dre): A History of Hip-Hop as a Culture, 1973–1999 *33*
3. "Harder, Better, Faster, Stronger" (Daft Punk, The Neptunes): An Examination of the Master Producers *67*
4. "Top Notch" (City Girls Featuring Fivio Foreign): Hip-Hop's Rise to the Top, 2000–Present *79*
5. *The Big Bang* (Busta Rhymes): A Roadmap to Rap Styles *89*
6. *Masterpiece Theatre* (En Vogue): *Hamilton*—Why This, Why Then, and Why Now? *115*
7. *Stakes Is High* (De La Soul): The Need for Authenticity *127*

Part II. Vocal Technique *141*

8. *Strictly Business* (EPMD): The House is Built on This Foundation *143*
9. "Let Your Backbone Slide" (Maestro): Posture and its Relationship to Movement *155*
10. "Lose My Breath" (Destiny's Child): Breath, Inhalation, and Supporting Your Sound *167*

11. "Protecting My Energy" (Jackboy): Pitch, Tone Quality, and Resonance   183

12. "Hustle & Flow" (Ro Diddy): Rhythm and Flow   201

13. "Runnin' Your Mouth" (Notorious B.I.G.): Diction—Articulators and Articulation   223

14. "Express Yourself" (Ice Cube): The Art and Authenticity of Storytelling   249

15. "Protect Ya Neck" (Wu-Tang Clan): Vocal Health   265

16. "Roc the Mic" (Freeway, Beanie Sigel, Nelly, Murphy Lee): Microphone Techniques   275

17. *Beats, Rhymes, and Life* (A Tribe Called Quest): What to Prioritize and Other Things to Consider   293

18. *Shoot for the Stars, Aim for the Moon* (Pop Smoke): Interviews   307

Select Bibliography   345

Index   349

About the Author   367

Acknowledgments

"Rap is something you do. Hip-hop is something you live."

—KRS-One

This book would not have been possible without the support, mentorship, guidance, expertise, and continuous support of so many people who have not only helped me with this process but also made me the teacher and person that I am. I would like to thank:

My colleagues and friends who read rough drafts and gave me thoughtful and honest feedback: all made time in their immensely packed schedules to read and lend thoughts to parts of this book, and I am so grateful: Typhanie Monique, AJ Wester, Nadine Gomes, Ruth Ellis, Jonathan Baker, Jon Belonio, Adam Schlipmann, Claire Donovan Scane, and Mark Stewart.

Students past and present: thank you for contributing your time, expertise, patience, and creativity throughout this process: Luke Jordan, Ethan Weihl, Kate Jarecki, Lucia Katz, Ruby Gibson, Tom Avery, Matheus Barbee, Maddie Mazella, Nolan Robinson, Idaya Chambers, Jay Towns, Dan Calderon, and finally, Andy Hartman, who read every word of this book, even through the roughest of the rough drafts, offering edits, organizational life rafts, and encouragement. Thank you for being an incredible research assistant every step of the way. It is not an understatement to say this book would not exist without you.

All of my esteemed colleagues in the Musical Theatre Area at Northwestern University: your passion for the future of the art form is a marvel and I am grateful to teach alongside you.

Karen Olivo and Amanda Dehnert, thank you for helping me pick up the pieces while I juggled (and dropped plates) throughout this process. Sarah Smith Inendino, thank you for teaching my voice studio and for being my NU lifeline while I was on writing sabbatical. Chair extraordinaire, Henry Godinez, you allow me to dream, lift me up, and put up with my being 'a lot.' Rives Collins, you have been my earliest cheerleader and support system and put all of this into motion. Finally, to Dean E. Patrick Johnson for supporting this project from start to finish.

Colleagues in the industry that inspire me and are so generous with their knowledge and kindness; this fountain of knowledge keeps my synapses firing, keeps me learning and growing: Matt Edwards, Tom Burke, Shannah Rae, Raymond Sage, Edrie Means Weekly, Jared Trudeau, Chris York, Gwen Walker, Trinice Martin, Kathryn Green, Jess Baldwin, Edrie Means Weekly, Mary Saunders Barton, Dale Cox, Alisa Hauser, Ronve O'Daniel, Corinne Ness, Colleen Brooks, Maddy Tarbox, Gary Kline, Todd Simpkins, Deonte Warren, Rose Van Dyne, Claudia Barnick, Sunny Joy Langton, Steven Chicurel, Elizabeth Benson, Kikau Alvero, Matthew Teague Miller, Steven Gross, Matthew Ellenwood, John Nix, Leda Scearce, Kurt Hansen, Terri Branccachio, Heather Arani, Megan Elk, Tarah Durnbaugh, Lori Sonnenberg, Nathan Waller, The Bastian Institute, Dr. Robert Sims, Allen Henderson, The National Association of Teachers of Singing, The CCM Vocal Pedagogy Institute, The Musical Theatre Educators' Alliance, and each of the forty rap artists who were interviewed for this book.

Ann Hines and Common. My incredible editor, Michael Tan.

My family and friends, who haven't seen that much of me during this process—but for always saving my seat and catching me up. For making me take breaks, for keeping my head above water; thank you for being my community. You believed I could do this even when I didn't believe I could do this. Mommy and Popsicle, you are the world's best parents, full stop. I am so lucky to be your daughter. Vivian, you are a star—I won the kid lottery. Thank you for being you, because you bring me happiness every single day. P.S. I love that now I am waking up to you asking Alexa to play rap songs. Finally, and most importantly, thank you to my wonderful husband Matt. You are my support system, confidante, sounding board, and editor supreme. Despite having numerous commissions and deadlines of your own, you somehow found time to walk with me through every step of this endeavor. Thank you, thank you, thank you.

Scan the QR code or go to https://biolink.info/dontsweatthetech to access a playlist of songs featured in the book.

Introduction

"The question of do I think understanding the history of hip-hop is important to being an artist today. . . . I really believe that the history of hip-hop is so important to history, American history, world history, because it tells so much about people, which is a culture of Black and Latino people at a certain time period that really didn't have a way to express themselves in the purest way. I mean, when I say that, I mean a lot of the things that we were being able to express ourselves through were produced and created or were controlled by the masses, or by white power in many ways. And you know, the actual networks and stations that weren't ours—it wasn't like us being able to tell our stories, so hip-hop became that way of us telling our stories. It was our news, it was our love letters to ourselves, it was our mirrors where we got to see ourselves and be like 'Oh, this is how I feel and now here's somebody talking about it!' It was our therapy, it was our joy . . . so the history of it is so important because it really tells about who we were at that time and it also informs who we are now, because, you know, if you're entering into any art form or if you're studying—if you're studying a craft or a profession, it's great and I think it's very important to know the origin of it and know where it comes from . . . who these people are, this is what the standard of great was at that time. Whether you love it or not is not even important. It's important just to know where this comes from and how this evolved and what was noted as great. You can see the things that have lasted in hip-hop through generations, things like—like I've done this thing in comparison and parallel, I did that in films when I started studying acting. I went back and watched all these classic films that my teachers would tell me to watch. And some of them I didn't love, but I was

like okay, I see when people reference this, when people talk about this actor . . . you know, and I learned a lot from that. So I think just studying the history of hip-hop and being aware of it—it gives you so many reference points, it gives you standards and levels that you can achieve and it gives you what is timeless, and it also can inform you and inspire you if you are an artist or a creator. Or, if you're just a listener, to know what—where does this come from. I think that applies to so many things in life, just knowing the history. I need that, you know, that's why we as a people—it's been important for us to know our history, and I think knowing hip-hop history is just as important."

—*Common*

The author with Common.

I am going to open this introduction with a bold statement: hip-hop is today's pop culture. It is the American culture of today. Some of you are now saying "hell yeah!" and some of you are probably raising an eyebrow. But my belief in that, and how it relates to who I am, what I study, and how I teach is why I not only chose, but felt that I needed, to write this book.

The quote is from an exclusive interview with Common, and yes, I'm still a bit on cloud nine from getting to meet with him. *Don't Sweat The Technique: A Performer's Guide to Hip-Hop and Rap* is about both the history and the pedagogy of hip-hop, and one needs the other. When answering the question, "why is hip-hop history important to an artist today?" Common brilliantly connects the dots between the centrality of hip-hop to the last fifty years of American history and the necessity of understanding this history to find your unique voice and skill as a hip-hop artist and listener. He poetically explains a belief that he and I share. This book is structured on the pillars of both history and technique, because they are intertwined. As soon as I heard him say those words, I decided that it would be my honor to have this statement open my book.

In June 2020, I was working on my porch. We were in the midst of a pandemic, vaccines weren't available yet, and, being someone who has a compromised immune system, I wasn't really leaving the house. So, there I was, housebound, working on my porch to get some fresh air, and my phone started blowing up with alerts from a Facebook group I'm in. Heated words were being exchanged between a Black member and a white member of the group due to the fact that the latter was seemingly using the Black Lives Matter hashtag to make a personal profit. It got pretty ugly. I knew both of the people, and I was watching my white friend dig himself into a cavernous hole because he was offended for being "called out." White folks were, and still are, learning how to be allies after the brutal and devastating deaths of Ahmaud Arbery, Breonna Taylor, and George Floyd shook our nation to its core. That argument on Facebook was just one of dozens I was witnessing involving Black voices trying to portray the current-day Black experience, and desperately trying to be heard, but how? It got me thinking . . . and those thoughts took me to hip-hop.

One of my all-time favorite hip-hop groups, A Tribe Called Quest, is labeled as "conscious rap." This term means that their songs intentionally put a spotlight on cultural or socio-political issues that the Black community faces. But a rapper doesn't have to be labeled as a "socially conscious rapper" to raise awareness of issues. When I mention conscious rap, you might think "okay, she means Public Enemy's 'Fight The Power,' or Queen Latifah's 'U.N.I.T.Y.,' or Kendrick Lamar's 'How Much a Dollar Cost.'" But then you think, "well, maybe she means Benny The Butcher's 'New Streets,' or Blackstar's 'Thieves In The Night,' or KRS-One's 'Know Thyself,' or Talib Kweli's 'The Proud.'" But then you say, "wait though, she *must* be talking about J. Cole's 'Snow on the Bluff' and Childish Gambino's 'America.'" Or you're thinking, "maybe she means Lil Baby's 'The Bigger Picture' or Lupe Fiasco's 'Deliver,' or even Tupac's 'Changes'?" The answer is yes and yes and yes and yes. I mean all of it, yes. Hip-hop gives us a voice—it is a way for an authentic voice to be heard. It makes me think of a quote I read: "Hip hop is much more active, much more aggressive, much more militant. . . . It uses language as a weapon—not a weapon to violate or not a weapon to offend, but a weapon that pushes the envelope that provokes people, makes people think."[1]

Hip-hop culture is in everything we do. It's in the television shows and movies we watch, the way we speak, and the way we see the world. You can see it in TikTok dances and feel it in almost every major city in the United States, from New York to Miami to Los Angeles. Yet, people don't always seem to see this massive influence—they love listening to the music and doing the dances, but they don't always understand the deep cultural elements that inspire the pop culture we all know and love.

Take a place like New York City, the birthplace of hip-hop. Walking down the street in Times Square, you might look up and see a billboard advertising Megan Thee Stallion's most recent rap album *Traumazine*. Next, you can visit the Forever 21 or H&M stores, full of styles directly influenced by hip-hop MCs, rappers, and dancers. Down the street, there is a Broadway theatre showing "& Juliet," a musical filled to the brim with hip-hop–influenced music and dance. Walk a few more steps and you'll undoubtedly see street graffiti art, another expression of hip-hop culture.

You'll probably even see a breakdance group busking for tips. All of these elements make New York City the amazing place that it is. Without them, Times Square would be bland, quiet, and definitely not the center of the greatest city in the world. Hip-hop culture is responsible for all these parts of our daily lives that make up America.

However, not everyone recognizes that many of our favorite art forms and mediums are a part of hip-hop culture. And, more importantly, most people do not see how African American culture, the lifeblood of hip-hop culture, is responsible for most elements of our pop culture.

I'm a college professor. I teach voice in the musical theatre area at Northwestern University. I specialize in pop singing styles, and that includes rap. Y'all, rapping is hard work. Doing it well takes an incredible amount of skill. I have a lot of students that are intimidated by rapping, especially white students. They love rap but don't think they could or *should* rap. I think that rap is for anyone and everyone that loves to rap, and I wanted to develop an organized approach studying the craft of rapping. There are so many books on singing. Do you want to read about opera pedagogy? Or how about how to sing jazz? There are shelves of books about those topics. But if you are trying to learn to rap, well, it's harder to find a book that talks about that.

Personally, I grew up with older siblings that love hip-hop, and I snuck into their rooms when they weren't home and played their albums (shh—let's keep that our little secret, they'd kill me if they found out). My favorite memories of college are all of those Saturday nights spent at parties thrown by either Kappa Alpha Psi or Alpha Phi Alpha, and dancing with my friends Nishea, Tara, and Stacy to Black Sheep's "The Choice Is Yours." I'm also a Black woman living in America. I wanted to write this book because all of these parts of my identity intersect with both hip-hop and my excitement in helping you both hone your technical skills and find your authentic rap voice.

This book will help you become a better rapper via a multifaceted approach. Through an organized method of practice, you'll build your techniques and skills and will unlock solutions to stumbling blocks that have been holding you up—the blocks that have been making you afraid to get out there and rap. This book also has exclusive advice from dozens of MCs in the industry, as well as interviews with those MCs. They will share their approaches and techniques, giving you insight into how they mastered the craft.

Researching this book required a multipronged approach. While this is a book for performers, including beginning performers, I would have been remiss in not reading scholarly material. Hip-hop is a relatively new phenomenon, though, and while, at fifty years old, it can expect to get its AARP card in the mail any day now, forms like opera are over four hundred years old! You can spill a lot of scholarly ink in four centuries. Add to that the way hip-hop has been stigmatized by both its newness, its popularity, and its association with marginalized groups, and there aren't infinite hip-hop studies PhDs in this world. A lot of fine scholarship does exist, however, and it warranted exploration. All authors stand on the shoulders of those who came before. There are also many popular books (and even comic books) on hip-hop history, and they, too, deserved a read.

Learning about the history of hip-hop, the how and why it was born, and tracing its fifty-year timeline takes time and investment, but it's worth it. It directly affects why rap sounds the way it does. It affects the sound of each subgenre of rap. Knowing this info will change how you rap. How? This book will help you understand the history of hip-hop and how it reflects the African American experience and culture. That understanding will enable you to better understand this artform and how you fit into it, helping you to rap using your authentic voice and soul, your story, your authenticity. Not only will you be a better rapper, but you'll have something to say that makes people want to listen.

Then there's the music itself. While much of hip-hop's history fits within my lifetime, I certainly haven't heard all of it. Despite working on this book for many years, I haven't heard even a fraction of the hip-hop that exists in the world. Hip-hop can sometimes seem like the most accessible form in the world—I mean, it's party music that every child now bops along to. But sometimes it also seems like such an overwhelming tsunami of music that it's terrifying to wade into the waters. Regional, political, complex, controversial; all of these are common descriptors of hip-hop, and all are accurate. My own taste in hip-hop has improved and expanded a great deal in the course of putting this book together. Are you old enough and west coast enough to know that G-funk was heavily influenced by something called hyphy? You might be from Chicago and remember Chief Keef, but did you know that Drill got a passport and became UK Drill? Did you know that there are legendary cursed rap tapes floating around Memphis? That soulless artificial intelligences are pumping out LoFi beats for streaming services? Fifty years of hip-hop: there is always more to hear and more to learn.

What I brought of myself, besides my love of The Native Tongues, is my own knowledge of vocal pedagogy. As an experienced teacher of pop, Broadway, and commercial singing forms, much of my research for this book involved pointing my expertise at hip-hop vocal performance and deconstructing it the way other vocal performance styles have already been deconstructed, so that you, dear reader, can approach performing hip-hop systematically and efficiently. This involved not just watching and listening to hip-hop performance, but breaking functional training down to a component level as it applies to hip-hop, and then determining how those components can be healthfully and reliably reconstructed by you, the performer.

This book is purposefully written in simple and direct language. It's easily digestible, in a non-textbook kind of way. Hip-hop is the voice of the people. The entire point of hip-hop is accessibility. So this book is accessible, whether you are sixteen or sixty-one. Read it a few pages at a time or all in one sitting. Come back to the exercises again and again to help you strengthen your skills.

Don't Sweat The Technique: A Performer's Guide to Hip-Hop and Rap consists of two sections.

The first section walks you through the history of hip-hop in a bite-size, very conversational way. It is purposefully written in the way you might talk to a friend, and it works to break down any barriers between you and the fifth pillar of hip-hop: knowledge. You will learn:

- How hip-hop was born
- How hip-hop became the pop music of today
- The major influencers in the industry
- The different sub genres of rap
- Rap in musical theatre
- Some gut check points toward finding your authentic self in rap
- . . . and more!

You'll also find valuable advice and anecdotes from actual MCs on how they approach the art of rapping. Dozens of MCs were interviewed exclusively for this book, and their knowledge and know-how is passed directly on to you, the reader.

The second section provides an introduction to the nuts and bolts of rapping and is intended for anyone who is interested in learning how to rap, including singers and performers who are new to rap:

- Breath support
- Posture
- Diction and articulation
- Rhythm and counting
- Essential vocabulary
- Storytelling and delivery techniques
- Mic technique
- Keeping your voice healthy
- . . . and more!

Why did hip-hop become a world changing phenomenon? Where do you, the listener and artist, fit into the story of hip-Hop . . . a story that's still being written? And if you're going to rap, how do you do it healthfully, honestly, and effectively? Relax, read on, and enjoy.

Note

1. Simon, S. (2003, March 1). Hip Hop: Today's Civil Rights Movement? *NPR*. Retrieved March 19, 2023, from https://www.npr.org/2003/03/01/1178621/hip-hop-todays-civil-rights-movement

Part I
HISTORY AND INFLUENCE

One

Black Reign (Queen Latifah)
The Birth of Hip-Hop

Hip-Hop *Is* Pop Culture

Then-Beatle John Lennon got himself in a lot of hot water in a 1966 interview when he stated that the Beatles were "more popular than Jesus now." There was a huge backlash, especially in the South; radio stations stopped playing their songs, some fans were even burning records . . . oh, it was a hot mess! But, of course, the Beatles weathered that storm, and today they are still, perhaps more than ever, well, the Beatles that everyone knows and loves. I feel like people might similarly wet their pants today if you were to say: "hip-hop is more popular than the Beatles now." Many people would argue that this is absolutely impossible. And yet, here we are, with Drake claiming exactly that in his feature on Meek Mill's "Goin' Bad," and there was also a recent study at Queen Mary University, Imperial College London showing that hip-hop and rap's emergence as a dominant musical form in the early 1990s was more influential to popular music than the British Invasion.[1]

The study analyzed audio features (not lyrics) like chord patterns and tonal shifts on seventeen thousand songs from the US pop charts from the years 1960 and 2020 and found the boulder of hip-hop thrown into pop music's lake made more ripples than other major events and movements over that same time. Listen to nearly any pop song these days and you'll either hear a song that is obviously and explicitly hip-hop–based, or you'll at least hear some of the beats, rhythms, production elements, swagger, and sexuality of hip-hop. "Bussin!" by Yung Gravy? "N95" by Kendrick Lamar? "No Merci" by Little Simz? Of course, they're hip-hop. But: "I'm

Good" by David Guetta and Bebe Rexha? "Left and Right" by Charlie Puth, Jung Kook, and BTS? "No" by Meghan Trainor? These pop hits aren't just influenced by hip-hop—they wouldn't exist without hip-hop. Just as popular music evolved over the early and mid-twentieth century from being primarily based in ragtime to jazz to rock and R&B, nearly all pop music is hip-hop now.

While over-worried moms, academics, and rock and roll museums might wring their hands about the influence of rap, it's not even a new phenomenon. For decades now, the king and queen of celebrity land have been Beyonce and Jay-Z, Kanye and Kendrick innovate, popular styles around the world from K-Pop to Latin trap to Reggaeton are all based on hip-hop, and the language of teens on social media is full of hip-hop vernacular. The rock-centered teen culture of the garage band, the heavy metal band logos ironed on the back of jean jackets, and the Nirvana blaring parking lot is mostly a memory—high school is now a land of beats and rhymes.

> "I think hip hop in general takes from jazz, funk, has pop elements as well as rock and roll elements as well."
>
> —Nezi Momodu

The New York Times described hip-hop's rise as:

> A wholesale remaking of the pop tool kit: rock ceding ground to hip-hop, hand-played instruments giving way to (or used in concert with) computer programs. We must also give a huge nod to the internet, which opened the floodgates, providing access to the masses of new sounds and styles of hip-hop. While participants in other genres were squeaking the last profits out of the old way of doing business, hip-hop relentlessly pushed forward: mixtape distribution (first out of trunks of cars, and then online), ringtones, Vine dances, a general lack of interest in traditional album cycles, and much more. Practically every significant music-internet innovation of the last 15 years took hold in hip-hop first.[2]

As hip-hop rose to the throne, it also expanded, absorbing the genres it was surpassing and developing an expansive breadth of sound, texture, statements, and appeal. Even the icon that is Rakim couldn't have predicted hipster-hop to emo rap to nerdcore and beyond. Put simply, hip-hop was not just evolution, it was a revolution. David Jacobs, a music industry lawyer stated in, of all places, the *Wall Street Journal*: "Every genre that used to exist in music, exist[s] in hip-hop."[3]

The Origin Story

Setting the Scene

So, how did this happen?

To answer that question, you'll need to look back to cultural history in America and examine the place, time, and forces under which hip-hop was born. If hip-hop were a superhero, one of its powers would be its consistency of living in the moment. Hip-hop speaks from its moment and to its moment, and to best understand the movement of the superhero that is hip-hop, you'll want to first explore its origin story.

Let's break it down a bit: hip-hop was born in the 1960s (yes, six decades ago!) and largely in the Bronx, a borough of New York City. The Great Migration of African American people from the Southern to Northern cities in the 1910s all the way through the 1950s led to an overflowing Black neighborhood in Harlem, and that population spilled over into the south and west portions of the Bronx. Unsurprisingly, this led to "white flight" (to some, that might sound like a superhero name too, but trust me, white flight was neither heroic nor was it super) to the suburbs and other neighborhoods. This, in combination with the creation of ample middle-class housing (such as the hulking Co-Op City buildings) in the central portions of the Bronx left the western and southern portions of the borough predominantly Black or Latino and poor.

Wait, let's actually back up a bit further. To truly understand the origin story, we have to rewind the clock back a few more years. I'm sure you're thinking, "why do I need to read about the 1940s to learn about Gucci

Mane?" And I will reply by saying that you suffered through Jar-Jar Binks so you could learn how Anakin Skywalker became Darth Vader, didn't you? If you managed to tolerate that, you can read a couple of pages to understand how hip-hop came to be.

The shifting of demographics and economics was not merely an organic occurrence. In 1948, the infamous urban renewal developer Robert Moses designed the Cross Bronx Expressway. This wasn't just a road, folx. It was a seven-mile expressway. Its construction destroyed established communities, moving fifteen hundred families, clobbered property values, and left many neighborhoods in a deeply depressed state. Moses's project put the deliberate displacement of neighborhoods above even efficiency and cost,[4] and made a paved moat between the North and South Bronx, leaving the southern portion and its remaining residents poised for implosion of epic proportions.

High-rise public housing, including dozens of enormous, bleak, slab-like "tower in the park"–style projects like the Morrisiana and Crotona Park, started to emerge, with people displaced by the expressway often ending up in them. You may have heard the term "redlining," which is "a discriminatory practice that consists of the systematic denial of services such as mortgages, insurance loans, and other financial services to residents of certain areas, based on their race or ethnicity."[5] Redlining was happening all over the country, but Chicago and New York were two of the biggest offenders. When this happened, social services decreased, and the way of life deteriorated for those affected:

> As devastation spread, life for the people who remained in the South Bronx became increasingly difficult. The schools no longer served the needs of many children. Hospitals closed. Religious institutions were just starting to adapt to new populations. Many nonprofits closed. In the mid-1970s, when the South Bronx was at its lowest point and New York City was in the throes of its most serious fiscal crisis, the City's housing director, Roger Starr, proposed the radical idea of planned shrinkage. New York City could solve the problem of what to do about

its decaying poor areas by simply withdrawing City services. Resources could then be moved to more affluent areas that were worth the investment. Without police, fire stations, hospitals, and schools, the people remaining in the areas designated for shrinkage would have to leave. The land would become vacant and could be reused in future years, for industry or housing, as the economy improved.[6]

People suffered and crime was rampant as gangs took over and drug use grew more common. Per the Bronx Historical Society, "as former Hunts Point resident and later Secretary of State Colin Powell recalled, his neighborhood went 'from gang fights to gang wars . . . from marijuana to heroin.'"[7] Crime drove down property value, rents, and revenue, and landlords found themselves unable or unwilling to keep up their buildings, which led to more deterioration and more crime. "Drug induced crime, including burglaries and the robbing of tenants and shopkeepers, increased throughout the 1970s in the South Bronx and caused further exodus. Rent collections, as a result, were not sufficient for landlords to maintain their buildings. Vacant buildings invited building stripping. As properties were abandoned, or were about to be abandoned, landlords stripped their own buildings and had them burned down before others could get to them."[8] It was a death spiral. The people, the business, even the buildings of the Bronx were being forced out, squeezed out, and were poised to be literally burnt out.

With buildings deemed worthless, and tenants miserable, the Bronx fires began, in which significant portions of poor neighborhoods were destroyed by fires caused by arson. Accounts vary on who perpetrated the arson, but culprits included not just vandals but owners seeking insurance pay-outs to buildings now financially underwater. The Bronx was burning: "The extent of the fires was vast, as was the suffering. In one year, 1974, there were over thirty-three thousand fires of all types in the Bronx—structural, content, vehicle, and outdoor. That year, 140 residents and three firemen were killed, and fifteen hundred people were injured in fires."[9]

> "I think [Hip-hop] has a very important role in just shedding light on what's going on. Because a lot of people don't care or know even until it gets recorded and we get to show them what's going on."
>
> —Joseph Chilliams

The people living through this cruelty and misery rightfully needed an escape. Escape comes in many forms, but the important form in this instance were the parties. The resilience was awesome in the truest sense of the word. But, back to parties (I mean who doesn't love a good party?), those miserable high-rise buildings of the Bronx had huge courtyards. Yes, these were courtyards with room for the athletic new dances of the b-boys, courtyards with "canvas" space for the rising school of graffitos, and space for DJs to spin records and MCs to spit rhymes.

The Pillars of Hip-Hop Are Born

There is much debate regarding what falls under the umbrella of hip-hop, but I agree with the Harlem Gallery of Science which claims, "the house of Hip Hop was built with five foundational elements:[10]

1. MCing (Oral)
2. DJing (Aural)
3. Breakdance (Physical)
4. Graffiti (Visual)
5. Knowledge (Mental)"

Graffiti was already mentioned briefly earlier, and it will surface in later chapters, as will the fifth pillar, knowledge. But the other three are intermingled with one another so closely that we need to break them down and immediately connect them to the aforementioned socio-political scene.

Pillar One: DJ-ing

Hip-hop, this remarkable child of the African diaspora in the United States, was born of energies from the diaspora in the West Indies. Now that you understand what was happening in the Bronx (hopefully you can sort of picture the environment and the lives of teenagers at that time), it's only fitting to introduce you to someone you must meet: Kool Herc.

Clive "DJ Kool Herc" Campbell was born in Jamaica (the island, not Queens), and brought Jamaican traditions which would be instrumental in the development of hip-hop to the Bronx party scene. If you're wondering where we are in history, we're in 1973. Herc was a physically imposing dude with *a lot* of records (compliments of his father), a lot of sound equipment (compliments of his gig teaching for a local band), and wheels turning in his mind faster than the records spun on those turntables. Much like the five dollars that college kids will pay to get into house parties today (that five dollars gains you entrance and a red solo cup filled with a mysterious drink), the parties in 1973 were *events*—with a great DJ, an open dance floor, and an overall fun atmosphere. These parties sometimes charged for admission too, although, back then, the cost was more often than not fifty cents. (And if you are wondering, that is *not* where the rapper got his name according to my quick Google search, but wouldn't that have been cool?) At a party in August 1973, DJ Kool Herc first used the Jamaican technique of employing two turntables (and see, you have to *have* two turntables to use two turntables) and a mixer which would allow him to keep a "break" going by playing a short, dance-friendly portion of a record as long as he wanted by switching back and forth between the records. When Herc heard a break, he knew the dancers, or "b-boys," would make a meal of it— he could feed them that break longer than the original song would allow. He and his MC, MC Coke La Rock (Bronx born, but learning from Herc), brought a number of other Kingston traditions to the parties on Sedgwick Avenue, including the value of a booming bass and, perhaps most importantly, the tradition of "toasting,"[11] which is talking over records . . . not quite rapping, but it's getting close. Herc would spin the records, and MC Coke La Rock would toast. More on toasting in a moment, but first, let's talk about the phenomenon which was dancing.

Pillar Two: B-Boying

The dancers at these parties were not merely followers responding to the work of the DJs. "B-boying" (or girling) is itself an original pillar of hip-hop. Herc allegedly invented this term, although what the "b" stands for is up for debate. Break? Beat? Bronx? Burgers? (I choose to believe it's "break.") The dancing during early hip-hop breaks is probably most commonly referred to as "breakdancing" (makes sense), but that's an old catch-all term largely used to describe and market this dance style to white audiences and the mass market. By the time b-boying had been popularized by the media, for example in 1984's film *Breakin* (although I love that flick, no shame), and the backspin made its way to elementary school blacktops in the Midwest, it seemed the latest in a long line of juvenile dance fads and less a vital form of urban expression.

Author George Cassidy quotes pioneering b-boy "Cholly Rock" (Anthony Horne) as saying,[12] "some say hip hop begins with the DJ. But actually, hip hop culture itself begins with the b-boy. We're the x factor." Cholly Rock says it was Latino dancers across New York who brought these moves to rock and soul music and the parties in the Bronx, sometimes competing in dance battles in which one dancer would "burn" another with an elaborate dance topping the dance of his opponent. Given the dancer's early affiliation with gangs, the stakes of the conflict weren't just artistic in nature. The dancers would warm up with some standing footwork called the "toprock"[13] before speeding up and using hands and feet on the floor in a "downrock," adding the very recognizable "power moves" like the headspin or the windmill, and occasionally freezing to hold a position requiring firm strength and delicate balance.

Remember, hip-hop wasn't on the throne yet—at the time, disco was queen. B-boying was an answer to the growing commercial appeal of disco dance, just as hip-hop was a musical answer.

As disco grew in popularity, DJs resented its glamor and MCs its banal dancefloor sentiments. But b-boys might be the winners of the "most disgusted" award because of disco's less aggressive and athletic form of dance. Cholly Rock continues, noting, "if you were really good and you wanted to prove yourself you had to go to a Kool Herc party or a Flash party." (Grandmaster Flash being of Barbadian descent was similarly developing scratching and creating those breakbeats.) Only certain DJs played b-boy records, so if you were a b-boy you had to be at those parties. The b-boys lay claim to the term "hip-hop" itself, which dancers like Cholly Rock claim was originally a pejorative for the dancers who were alternately called "rabbits," "floor-sweepers," and more for their spirited but close-to-the-pavement dancing.

Pillar Three: MC-ing (Rapping)

And when did the MCs (short for "master of ceremonies") join the party? I think we can all agree, hip-hop is nothing without rap. Rap can most easily be thought of as rhythmic, rhyming speech, often heavy on braggadocio and traditionally, though not always, aggressive in its delivery, sometimes expressing "beef" with other rappers or personalities and sometimes even taking the form of a "rap battle" in which two MCs compete for rap supremacy through cleverness, viciousness, and virtuosity of craft. It sounds a little like the b-boys and their competitive dance-dissing, no? I'm sensing a theme here.

The Dozens

While the full spectrum of rap today includes a huge breadth of tone and content including socially conscious rap that examines socio-political themes and leans toward empowerment, party rap that primarily employs its audience to enjoy itself, and even emo rap, which enjoys swimming in the melancholy pool. That early in-your-face swaggering MCing at the parties in the Bronx grew out of "toasting" (told ya we'd get back to this) and from an African American lyrical tradition known as "The Dozens." "The Dozens" is a verbal contest in which two combatant's face off in front of a cheering (and jeering) crowd of peers and insult one another or one another's families—sometimes in rhyme—focusing their disrespect particularly on one another's mothers. For example, it might go something like: "yo Mama's so ugly, she went into a haunted house and came out with a paycheck." The Dozens have been played for decades and probably had their heyday in the 1950s and 1960s, though they persist, and were referenced in Richard Pryor's 1970s comedy special *That N*****'s Crazy*, in a recurring game show sketch on seminal 1990s Black sketch show *In Living Color*, and most definitely on my school bus rides in junior high. The Dozens can use foul language ("Dirty Dozens") or be relatively sanitized ("Clean Dozens"), but regardless, it should be whatever the person could think of to make the crowd say *dammmmmmmn!* Elijah Wald, Grammy Award winner and author of a book on the dozens, *Rap's Mama*, spoke to the *Boston Globe*, saying,

> Rap battling is really what's more like The Dozens. Because people battle and sometimes, they genuinely dislike each other, but sometimes they're really good friends. And if they're good battlers, you can't tell which you're watching, because either way they're going to say the nastiest things they can think of, and that's really how The Dozens works: It's about creativity. It's about saying something not only nasty enough so that the other guy can't think what to say, but also funny enough that the audience thinks that you've just done something smart. That's the combination at the heart of The Dozens.[14]

The leap from such rapidly improvised structures and content to the skills required for rap is a short one, and the rap battles of Old School MCs were clear descendants of the dozens.

Toasting

And "toasting"? Author Heather Augustyn landed on an interesting circular relationship here between American and Jamaican music.[15] It seems that our rhythm and blues and soul music became quite popular in Jamaica thanks to the signals from radio stations in Miami, Nashville, and New Orleans. The flashy DJs would play these songs and perform impromptu "toasts" with rhyme and percussion. Sometimes rapid-fire nonsense words, ("chick-took, chick-a-took, chick-a-took" or "pick-it-up-pick-it-up-pick-it-up") and sometimes just explosions of consonants ("ch-ch-ch-ch") are the little patterns of sound that can add a fully new texture to the music and get people on their feet. We're going to move on, but it's important to note that there's much more involved toasting: narrative poems filled with rhyming stories and boasting similar to the braggadocio found in rap. Herc picked up techniques from original Kingston toasters like DJ Count Matchuki and made it his own by adding neighborhood slang: "b-boy, b-girls, are you ready? Keep on rock steady!" Herc also called out the aliases of party goers: "Davey D is in the house / And he'll turn it out without a doubt." You can see how "pick-it-up-pick-it-up" quickly morphed into the ubiquitous. "Hip-hop, you don't stop" (a Herc original). Herc began by doing the "shout-outs'" himself, but eventually turned the duties over to Coke La Rock and another friend, Clark Kent, who became the first MC team as Kool Herc and the Herculoids.[16] From toasting, we can trace the birth of both full rap and the job of the "hype man" getting the crowd riled up and out on the dance floor.

So now you see this origin story taking shape: the environment calling for resilience, Latin dance styles emancipated from the dance halls, spinning and scratching coming from the islands, soul music borrowed from dad's record collection, clever wordplay taken from game of put-downs, all electrified by juice from the nearest streetlamp, were being forged into a glorious new cultural movement in the flames of a burning Bronx.

The Music

"There are a lot of things that a lot of people don't know originated in Africa. The drums, the music, and all of those different things. . . . It all stems from the Motherland and a lot of that culture, the break dancing, the way we move our bodies, the way we play the drums, that's where it originated from."

—*John Candyman Shaffer III,
American rapper and producer*[17]

Let's zoom in on those records on the DJs table, their labels soaked off to hide their secrets. What forces coalesced to make the music that lay under all the rapping and the breaking? To find this out, we have to get in the time machine again. (We're really doing *a lot* of traveling today. I hope you took your motion sickness meds.) We ventured way back to learn about the historical occurrences that birthed our superhero, but now let's travel back to learn about the musical forces that got us here.

African Roots

Rhythmic speech and rhythm-forward music with an all-important beat are the key components of hip-hop. Its execution is one of the greatest challenges and most satisfying elements of rap. Where does rap find its rhythms? Is it from other African American popular music like soul and funk? From folks and roots forms like blues, jazz, gospel, and spirituals? Or can it be traced all the way back to the mother continent itself? The answer to all of these questions is yes. When discussing African music traditions, rhythm is always central in the discussion concerning both instruments utilized and the incorporation of rhythm as the central component of song construction. Professor and pop music specialist Matt Edwards states, "all instruments there, including the voice, function primarily as rhythm maker."[18] These rhythmic traditions continued in America via the Africans that were forced into slavery. The transition from the instruments traditionally used in Africa into whatever could make a beat transpired when slave owners realized that communication was occurring in the percussion. On a recent trip to Nashville, I visited Belle Meade, a plantation that offers tours of the plantation through the lens of the slaves that lived there. Part of the exhibit showcased the percussion instruments that were banned by the plantation owners to prevent the slaves from communicating via the music (I'll be honest, that was a tough tour to stomach, but I'm very glad I was able to see the showcasing of the centrality that rhythm played in the African diaspora). This was a common occurrence—it wasn't just a Nashville thing—so, to combat this, the slaves communicated using percussion in their bodies and voices in religious songs as it was the only music that was condoned by the plantation owners. After many years, these eventually became what we now know as the spiritual, and our time machine will take a hop there in a short while. When discussing the African percussive roots in hip-hop, writer and poet Sherise Francis (via quoting philosopher Robert Farris Thompson) lists the intricacies of the percussive approach: "a propensity for multiple meters," "overlapping call and response," "inner pulse control," and "offbeat phrasing of melody."[19] These rhythmic descriptions are some of the central tenets of the percussive qualities in today's hip-hop.

Gospel

Just as hip-hop rose from a crumbling Bronx, each Black American music genre before it rose from some sort of tectonic social trauma, be it the fight for Civil Rights, mass migration toward work and safety, or centuries of bondage. It's a hell of a way to keep reinventing music, but here we are. The first African American music, the spiritual, was born in bondage. European hymnody met African syncopation and call and response and served a variety of essential purposes. From the "field holler" to early gospel, the spiritual kept time in the fields, helped the contents of the Bible become retainable, made torturous work bearable, made hope for a better of life in this world of the next possible, allowed an unsuppressed form of commiseration, and perhaps most importantly created a method of surreptitious communication beneath the attention of bloodthirsty masters. A spiritual could keep you going through the day, through the night, and possibly point the way to escape on the Underground Railroad.

After Emancipation, the spiritual became formally arranged, with added harmony and instrumentation, and became gospel music. There are various strings of gospel, from the Gaelic gospel of Scottish Presbyterians to a bluegrass-centered white gospel, but the most globally noted form—and the one that continues the lineage from spirituals toward hip-hop—is Black gospel with its powerful forward vocals, massive choral arrangements, improvised runs, and bursting organ accompaniment. As we continue to time travel, the stop here is important to make the similarities between the use of syncopation, runs, freestyle in the verse, and the flow of ideas back and forth between hip-hop and gospel. Explicit use of gospel trapping appears as far back as Hammer's "Pray" in 1990,[20] when the genie-pant-wearing mainstream artist tapped into his Pentecostal roots (before eventually adopting a ministry himself, but that's for another book). Kirk Franklin brought rap to church to a degree never before heard, and his 1996 crossover hit "Stomp" (featuring guest verses by Salt) was the first Gospel song to play on MTV. Puff Daddy's tribute to Biggie Smalls, "I'll Be Missing You" used vocals by Biggie's widow, the church-trained Faith Evans,[21] who incorporated part of the melody to "I'll Fly Away" into the song. Now, this did cause some huff and puff with churchgoers, but the trend has only continued. Clapping, stomping, choral harmonies, and Hammond organs appear in hip-hop numbers and 808s on the gospel charts. While Kanye's 2016 "Ultralight Beam" used countless church-born sounds, Chance the Rapper espoused Christianity within and without his music, and Nicki Minaj, T.I., Snoop, and Timbaland all charted on the Billboard's Hot Gospel charts.[22] As Kanye takes his mental-illness-driven, slow motion heel-turn, he seems to unfortunately be doing it via the church, with more and more religion and church sounds seeping into his releases. Song titles of rap hits are direct references to the church (Jay-Z's "Song Cry" or Ghostface Killah's "The Prayer," for example).[23] There is an entire subgenre of rap classified as holy hip-hop, or Christian rap.[24] We'll go into more detail about that in chapter 5, but check out LaCrae's "I'll Find You" for a taste of this subgenre. Even trap, one of the subgenres of rap most driven by life on the streets and in the drug trade, is sharing its sound with gospel music. Perhaps it makes sense for gospel to show that salvation is always available, and for rap to argue that injustice cuts right down to the essence of the spirit.

R&B

We can't talk about hip-hop without talking about R&B and its importance in the time and space before rap. R&B leapt from jazz and blues and birthed rock and roll; as a matter of fact, it's nearly impossible to determine where R&B ends and begins. Just as rhythm and blues was relabeled as such[25] (before this it was called "race music," which is such bigotry. I can't even) by Billboard editor Jerry Wexler, DJ Alan Freed repackaged the music as "rock 'n' roll," to make it more user-friendly for millions of white listeners. The difference between the styles primarily involves how much of a jazz sound is invited to the party (more in R&B), and how melismatic the singing tends to be (more so again in R&B). The umbrella of R&B has expanded over the decades to include much soul and funk music, and most sung primarily African American music, generally. All R&B is certainly not soul, funk, nor rock 'n' roll, but all soul, funk, and much rock 'n' roll could be called R&B. From the samples utilized, to the instruments incorporated, to the rhythmic two and four drive, to the vocal sound incorporated into sung hooks, and recently (in melodic rap), into the entire rap itself, R&B and rap are indubitably besties, if not close relatives.

Funk

Funk, a bass-heavy, dance-friendly, deeply sexy form of Black music existing on a blurry spectrum between soul and disco, was one of the first and most sampled types of music in hip-hop's recipe. Funk had been very commercially successful and had put large amounts of wax into Black record collections and stores. South Bronx DJs looking for records would have no trouble finding funk and soul albums in their homes and their local record shops.

The user-driven website *Who Sampled*,[26] on which hip-hop fans obsessively track and log what samples are used on what tracks, has identified the most sampled songs in history, and in the top ten alone, *five* of the songs are of the funk/soul persuasion, including most sampled song (by a lot), "Amen, Brother," a 1969 song by the relatively obscure act The Winstons. It featured a six-second section of drumming which has been sampled 5,789 times (you're not going crazy, you read that correctly), and the second most sampled song was the James Brown produced "Godmother of Soul," Lynn Collin's track "Think (About It)," sampled 3,252 times (including in 1988's "It Takes Two" by Rob Bade and DJ E-Z Rock).

Funk lent itself generously to the creation of hip-hop, and hip-hop in turn fueled a revival of funk. Music lovers young and old found not only compatible sounds but also compatible ideas and ideals. Ricky Vincent and George Clinton's *Funk: The Music, The People, The Rhythm of the One*, states:

> As the result of hip-hop artists sampling old funk records and the extensive reissues of funk albums on compact disc, [Lynn] Collins, [George] Clinton, [Maceo] Parker, [James] Brown, and others maintained modestly successful careers throughout the 1990s, touring and releasing records. . . . An intelligent youth movement in fashion, attitude, rhythm, and rhyme spread across the country through the beats of Hip Hop. . . . In almost every perceptible way, the new movement in the music, in the proud new attitude, and in the grim, bittersweet, and almost absurd ideals of change amounted to a renaissance of the funk movement of the 1970s.[27]

It's probably important to note that sampling led to some major legal debates (and continues to do so), but sampling also provided musical instruments to those that couldn't otherwise afford any. Sampling revived musical forms and made something new. Sampling endears the older generation to today's music. It's also important to know that sampling is alive and well in music today.

Disco

As we continue to time hop (no pun intended), it's important that we stop to visit disco. Hip-hop is happening concurrently with disco, so, in a way, we have arrived back where we began twenty or so pages ago. Hip-hop's relationship with disco is complicated. Hip-hop, with its DJ-oriented culture and infectious danceability, is rightly thought of these days as disco-adjacent, but it wasn't always so. Just as punk rock was disenfranchised youths' stripped-down answer to glam and prog rock (and disco), hip-hop existed for some years in opposition to disco, which was seen as an older person's glamorous and more Manhattan-friendly pastime. In discussing the rise of DJ Kool Herc's popularity at Bronx-based parties, author Joseph C. Ewoodzie asks, "Why did this music capture the attention of South Bronx youth? One potential explanation is that the music differed from disco. [Emphasis mine.] Because the most popular [Black and Latino] music of this time, the early 1970s, was composed for Manhattan disco club, the youth of the Bronx rarely identified with it. . . . It was played in venues they could not enter. So, they rejected what they were refused and declared that 'Disco sucked.'"[28]

Still, backbeats and instrumentals, particularly in extended mixes, of disco albums were *perfect* for the "breaks" of the South Bronx parties that birthed hip-hop. When Sugar Hill Gang's "Rapper's Delight" made it to a revolutionary number thirty-eight on the US Pop charts, made the top three in the United Kingdom, and went number one in Canada—making it perhaps the first song to introduce hip-hop to a wider audience (a.k.a. whiter) audience—it did so using samples from Chic's disco smash "Good Times" (which is a fantastic tune that still holds up). "Rapper's Delight" was actually recorded less than two months after "Good Times" dropped. And, while the sampling is iconic, it resulted in a lawsuit by Chic that garnered the disco outfit writing credits on Sugar Hill Gang's song. . . . See? I told you that the whole sampling thing was messy.

The Rapper (Again)

I felt like we needed to end the chapter talking about rap, so let's once again turn from the DJ to the MC. We've discussed The Dozens and toasting, but what other roots can we trace to rapping? It seems as free flowing, impulsive, intuitive, and creative as jazz . . . but do rappers agree? Influence by jazz, or at least a similarity to jazz, has certainly been an accusation regularly leveled at MCs respected for their lyrical virtuosity or accomplished rhythms: the Biggies, the Bustas, the Nases, etc. Biggie's neighbor, saxophonist Donald Harrison, claims to have introduced Biggie to jazz albums and to scat, and told him to enunciate his rhymes and work on his agility. Harrison claims to have given the young Biggie homework: scatting along

> "I think that the kids are drawn to whatever rebel music is. At the time historically, like rock and roll was rebel music, Hip-Hop when it first started was rebel music, what they call mumble rap is rebel music in today's society, and whatever the next wave of hip-hop is will just be the new form of rebel music."
>
> –Ausar

to the solos of legendary saxophonist Cannonball Adderley.[29] Give Biggie a listen—it certainly tracks. Rakim, another MC usually considered to be particularly technically skilled, claims similar influences (last night, I was sweating the technique while I was writing, and my young daughter said, "Oh I like this song." I then told her about the genius that is Rakim and how he is in a lot of people's all time top ten lists, and after fifteen minutes of my gushing I *think* she was sorry she mentioned it, but I digress): "The thing about the way I styled my rap, drawing from Coltrane and Parker or James B., and building off the flow that they had, that was because that's the music that surrounded me."[30]

Okay, yes to jazz influence. How about spoken word? Whose spoken word and which spoken word and how long ago? If we consider every spoken word poetry performance in a Black voice, then we're saying fourteenth-century West African jails and griots are early rappers. Perhaps? How about the praise poetry of the Yoruba, Zulu, and Xhosa people? Possibly? The oral traditions of enslaved people prevented from learning to write? Flash forward to the Harlem Renaissance of the 1920s: is Langston Hughes going to be okay with us eating in his car? Southern Baptist ministers in the run up to and in the Civil Rights era—it's musical, it's rhythmic, it's socially conscious . . . is it the precursor to rap?

I'm inclined to say that the DNA of all of this rich, ancient, and global tradition arcs toward rap, but not as directly nor as consciously as direct precursors like poets of the Black Arts Movement of the 1960s and 1970s: Amiri Baraka, Nikki Giovanni (some of her work was set to music like "Ego Tripping" from 1971's "Truth Is on Its Way" for some feminist, Black is Beautiful boasting that feels as welcome and as proud as Lizzo or Nicki

Minaj on a good day). You read "We Real Cool" by my beloved Chicago homegirl Gwendolyn Brooks when you were in school, right? Check out her flow: "We real cool. We / Left school. We / Lurk late. We." Note that each occurrence of "We" is "front phrased" before the "bar line" of the return. Call it jazz, call it staying in the pocket, but she's avoiding bringing the one down a line in a rather sophisticated way . . . and giving voice to teenage pool players on the South Side of Chicago. A classroom might call me corny for drawing a line on the board from Brooks to Chief Keef's "I Don't Like" (and I don't think Ms. Brooks would like it either) . . . but it really isn't that crazy.

There's the Black nationalist The Last Poets, who came out of the Black Arts Movement and not only laid the groundwork for hip-hop but decades later saw members collaborate with rappers like Common and members of Wu-Tang. Chicago saw Al Simmon's poetry bouts and Marc Smith's poetry slams. The Nuyorican Poets Cafe saw slams in New York's East Village beginning in 1973 Gil Scott-Heron's (frequently miscategorized as a member of The Last Poets but rather a legend in his own right). "The Revolution Will Not Be Televised" brought performance poetry out of the cafes and onto the turntables of America when it peaked at number twenty-one on the Billboard jazz chart in 1974, and now lives on *Rolling Stone*'s list of the top songs of all time. Even a quick listen will reveal the similarity to hip-hop.

From African poems and beats, across the middle passage to spirituals both vulnerable and profound, to the sacred Black music and sermons of church life, to the more earth-bound sounds of blues, jazz, and R&B performance poetry, The Dozens, and Jamaican toasting, Black music and the impassioned ideas of Black thought pushed ever forward toward hip-hop. Black culture, and Black music with it, has had to invent itself again and again to construct life in the face of a world that would try to snuff out that life.

Hip-hop was born in fire. Fires of rage at institutionally backed injustice and fires of destructive greed by the ruling class. Fires that burned enormous edifices of failed civic planning and greed devouring capitalism. But fire isn't just bringing destruction; it's also a force for renewal. Fire burns away what's dead and what throws shadow on the possibility of new growth.

Hip-hop was also born in joy. Born in parties and dancing and poetry and creation taking place in ash and concrete at the edge of civilization. Black joy is so often overlooked in a society with a pornographic obsession for Black pain. Hip-hop is the product of Black Americans doing what Black Americans have always done: curate fashion feasts from scraps, make beautiful music against the rhythm of a whip, and build and rebuild a splendid culture within a culture bent on their suppression and destruction.

Hip-hop.

The music born in a party at the end of the word would quickly take over the world.

Notes

1. *Los Angeles Times*. (n.d.). Hip-Hop and Rap Have Influenced Pop Music More Than the Beatles Over the Last 50 Years a British Study Says *Los Angeles Times*. Retrieved August 18, 2022, from https://graphics.latimes.com/music-evolution-hip-hop-rap/

2. Caramanica, Jon. (2018, December 20). How a New Kind of Pop Star Stormed 2018. *The New York Times*. https://www.nytimes.com/interactive/2018/12/20/arts/music/new-pop-music.html

3. Shah, Neil. (2018, January 16). Hip-Hop's Generation Gap: "Emo" vs. "Dad" Rap. *The Wall Street Journal*. https://www.wsj.com/articles/hip-hops-generation-gap-emo-vs-dad-rap-1516118193

4. lbennett. (2019, November 10). The Cross Bronx Expressway and the Ruination of the Bronx *Real Archaeology*. https://pages.vassar.edu/realarchaeology/2019/11/10/the-cross-bronx-expressway-and-the-ruination-of-the-bronx/

5. Legal Information Institute. Redlining. https://www.law.cornell.edu/wex/redlining

6. McLaughlin, Carolyn. (2019). *South Bronx Battles: Stories of Resistance, Resilience, and Renewal*. Oakland, CA: University of California Press.

7. "The Bronx County Historical Society." Retrieved August 20, 2022, from http://bronxhistoricalsociety.org/wp-content/uploads/2018/07/M.Roby_.pdf

8. Robin, Helenan S., and Stanley S. Robin. "The Resurrection of the South Bronx: An Event of Fin de Siecle." *Sociological Focus* 31, no. 1 (1998): 10. http://www.jstor.org/stable/20831971

9. Robin, Helenan S., and Stanley S. Robin. "The Resurrection of the South Bronx: An Event of Fin de Siecle." *Sociological Focus* 31, no. 1 (1998): 10. http://www.jstor.org/stable/20831971

10. "The Five Pillars of Hip Hop." n.d. Harlem Gallery of Science. https://hgs-ny.org/five-pillar-of-hip-hop.

11. Laurence, Rebecca. (2014, October 21). 40 Years on from the Party Where Hip Hop Was Born. *BBC Culture*. https://www.bbc.com/culture/article/20130809-the-party-where-hip-hop-was-born

12. Laurence, Rebecca. (2014, October 21). 40 Years on from the Party Where Hip Hop Was Born. *BBC Culture*. https://www.bbc.com/culture/article/20130809-the-party-where-hip-hop-was-born

13. Barton, Gina. (2017, June 20). How the Bronx Brought Breaking to the World. *Vox*. https://www.vox.com/videos/2017/6/20/15836346/how-bronx-created-breaking-breakdancing

14. Latour, Francie. (2012, August 5). The Dozens as American as *Your* Mama! *Boston Globe*. https://www.bostonglobe.com/ideas/2012/08/04/the-dozens-american-art-form-yourmama/7l3M0YAmr3kPJexgMllIvL/story.html

15. Augustyn, Heather. (2015). Spinning Wheels: The Circular Evolution of Jive, Toasting, and Rap. *Caribbean Quarterly*, 61 (1): 60–74.

16. Parmar, Priya, and Bryonn Bain. (2007). Spoken Word and Hip Hop: The Power of Urban Art and Culture. *Counterpoints*, 306: 131–56.

17. Benard, Blake. (2016, February 25). Hip-Hop Rooted in African Culture. *Cronkite News*. https://cronkitenews.azpbs.org/2016/02/25/hip-hop-rooted-in-african-culture/

18. Edwards, Matthew. (2014). *So You Want to Sing Rock 'n' Roll: A Guide for Professionals*. Lanham, MD: Rowman & Littlefield, 2.

19. Frances, Sherese. (2012). African Vibrations: The Percussive Approach in Hip-Hop Music. Undergraduate thesis, University of New York. https://www.academia.edu/7089534/African_Vibrations_The_Percussive_Approach_in_Hip_Hop_Music

20. Cochrane, N. (2020, August 28). The History of Hip-Hop Going Gospel, from MC Hammer to Sunday Service. *Billboard*. Retrieved October 31, 2022, from https://www.billboard.com/music/rb-hip-hop/hip-hop-gospel-kanye-west-jesus-is-coming-8531931/

21. Cochrane, N. (2020, August 28). The History of Hip-Hop Going Gospel, from MC Hammer to Sunday Service. *Billboard*. Retrieved October 31, 2022, from https://www.billboard.com/music/rb-hip-hop/hip-hop-gospel-kanye-west-jesus-is-coming-8531931/

22. Younger, B. (2018, August 31). How Gospel and Rap Finally Found Each Other and Created a New Batch of Hits. *The Washington Post*. Retrieved October 31, 2022, from https://www.washingtonpost.com/lifestyle/the-moment-for-gospel-and-rap-crossovers-has-arrived/2018/08/30/066653d2-ab00-11e8-a8d7-0f63ab8b1370_story.html

23. Winters, Joseph. (2013). Contemporary Sorrow Songs: Traces of Mourning, Lament, and Vulnerability in Hip Hop. *African American Review*, 46 (1): 9–20.

24. Maultsby, Portia K., and Zanfagna, Christina. (2021). Holy Hip-Hop/Christian Rap. A History of African American Music. *Carnegie Hall*. Retrieved March 27, 2023, from https://timeline.carnegiehall.org/genres/holy-hip-hop-christian-rap

25. Nero, Mark Edward. (2018, September 27). The American Musical Art Form of Rhythm and Blues. *LiveAbout*. https://www.liveabout.com/what-is-randb-music-2851217

26. WhoSampled. (n.d.). Most Sampled Tracks. Retrieved August 21, 2022, from https://www.whosampled.com/most-sampled-tracks/

27. Vincent, Rickey. (1996). *Funk: The Music, The People, and The Rhythm of The One*. New York: St. Martin's Griffin.

28. Ewoodzie Jr., Joseph C. (2017). *Break Beats in the Bronx: Rediscovering Hip-Hop's Early Years*. Durham: The University of North Carolina Press.

29. Malloy, Emmett (director). (2021). *Biggie, I Got a Story to Tell*. Netflix. https://www.imdb.com/title/tt14058484/

30. Williams, Justin A. (ed.). (2015). *The Cambridge Companion to Hip-Hop*. Cambridge: Cambridge University Press.

Two

Back 'n the Day (Dr. Dre)
A History of Hip-Hop as a Culture, 1973–1999

Like ragtime, blues, jazz, and rock and roll, once hip-hop had been released into the cultural conversation, there was no stopping it. To paint a bit of a picture for you: it was post-Vietnam and the assassinations of the 1960s (John F. Kennedy, Robert F. Kennedy, Malcolm X, and Martin Luther King Jr.), and just after the fallout and reactions to the Civil Rights era. It was a complicated world, and rap spoke the—often deeply uncomfortable—truths of this world: "The poet Rainer Maria Rilke wrote that 'a work of art is good if it has sprung from necessity.' Rap is the music of necessity, of finding poetry in the colloquial, beauty in anger, and lyricism even in violence."[1]

Hip-hop could have ended as it began, as a momentary distraction from troubled times in a rec room on Sedgwick Avenue. Instead, it revolutionized American cultural aesthetics and by extension a worldwide movement.

> "It's always it's always been underground since the beginning."
>
> —AC Tatum

The OGs

Musically, the innovation continued: a new set of pioneers picked up Herc's break methods. South Bronx DJ Afrika Bambaataa created his breaks from obscure records[2] that had eluded the notice of other DJs and represented and inspired a new search and a new page in Black and youth identity. In his book *Bomb the Suburbs*, William Upski Wimsett[3] wrote:

Bambaataa already got us searching "for the perfect beat." Why shouldn't we be searching for the perfect self, the perfect religion, the perfect economics, the perfect politics and law, the perfect science, the perfect society? Why shouldn't we be every bit as versatile with dusty ideas in those areas as Bambaataa is with dusty records—and every bit as selective.

Grandmaster Flash, "The Toscanini of Turntables," experimented with how the use of his equipment could be expanded by marking up records with a crayon, feeling the revolutions with his fingertips, and developing methods such as "scratching," which would ultimately be heard not just on rap, but pop hits across the 1980s and beyond.

Graffiti

Even though this chapter is, of course, about music, it's crucial to mention the visual art component of hip-hop. Rarely does a musical movement come without its graphic component, its fashion, and other elements to bring appeal in the new mode to mass audiences. The Beatles had Peter Max and the Carnaby Street look. Grunge had David Carson and mountains of flannel. Hip-hop kicked off with track suits and its elevated take on graffiti. It wasn't just tagging or defacing. Graffiti was both a political act and the look of the hip-hop movement, with color schemes, "fonts," and iconic imagery. Why did it come about? Well, the protagonists of our story (the hip-hop generation) who struggled to survive amid Robert Moses's bulldozers, the landlords' fires, and zoning's redlines responded not just through their music but visually as well. It was "a socio-political counterpoint to the failed architecture and displacement ... within graffiti, the synergy between the making of art and the political act of free art and territorial ownership was paramount to its success."[4] Graffiti was territorial and implied a level of ownership. Like the music of hip-hop, it expressed the spirit of a people under attack, saying "this is our home, and we're still here."

The "kings" or graffiti writing crews developed their signature look. Their canvases could be as large as a series of subway cars or walls connected to more walls until a mural became a landscape: "That arrow, that #1 with the curly flourish that makes the digit look like a capital 'L' in script, that smooth halo that lives above a signature and protects it, that drippy star that resides to the left and right of a signature: these are accouterments that scream, 'I am here. You can't ignore me. I am different. I stand out. I am the best. Battle me and you will be defeated. Test me at your own risk.'"[5]

The process linked form to vision—the greater the risk in creating the work (the higher from the ground, the more publicly exposed), the greater the artistic and cultural reward. The artists had to be nearly as good at a quick escape as they were at the craft of painting, and as good at acquiring or creating the tools of their trade as they were at implementing them. To create a surreal and beautiful landscape that spoke poetically about life in a typically harsh concrete environment, a graffito had to go all in. Lady Pink, a rare female graffiti artist who came on the scene in the late 1970s and became a celebrity in the "legitimate" art world, rubbing elbows with Warhol, Basquiat, and still exhibited in galleries around the world, spoke of just how harrowing it could get:

> there were crazy missions. I lost my friends in the train yard, I'd hear screams. Your friend falls through the elevated train tracks, down into the street below, breaks a leg. One night we thought we found a dead body. It was just a piece of machinery, but we thought it was a dead body lying under a tarp on the train. There were some scary incidents, chased by the police and you barely get out alive and go home battered and bleeding. All kinds of adventures like that.[6]

When MTV launched in 1981, they were *all* about rock and were famously dismissive of black music, not airing a single video by a black artist until Michael Jackson's "Billie Jean" in March of 1983. "Yo! MTV Raps" didn't air in the United States until August 1988. But, MTV's logo? A block letter M with a spray painted "TV." They tried, but they couldn't represent youth culture without a reference to graffiti.

Fashion

Another visual component to hip-hop is its fashion, and the fashions trends (many, over the years) developed by hip-hop have taken the world by storm. In case you're thinking, "wait wait wait I just want to read about rap," don't worry, you are. Many of the essential vibes of hip-hop carry over into its dress. The competitive nature of hip-hop as embodied by rap battles, b-boy dance offs, and beefs that range from the ridiculous to the deadly (R.I.P. Biggie) carry over into fashion: who has the newest, most expensive sneakers, or the flashiest jewelry, the freshest fit or drip or [insert your decade's slang for a sharp look here]. Likewise, hip-hop's often brutal honesty about society, lifestyle, and relationships has given much of hip-hop fashion a grounded look, as evidenced by the athleisure wear or variations on a t-shirt and jeans often at the heart of the silhouette of the moment. Hip-hop's concern with material and capital (the acquisition of it, the lack of it, the presence of it) explains its love of conspicuous jewelry and the aforementioned prestige kicks.

In the early days, hip-hop looks tended to move in opposing directions, embracing either the glamor of its disco and funk roots, or the streetwear and sportswear genuinely worn by its fans and creators. Grandmaster Flash and the Furious Five's wardrobes leaned into the excesses of disco and funk: leather pants and studded belts (leather and studded everything sometimes), tall suede boots, headbands, vests, gold lamé, headbands, and caps from fedoras to motorcycle caps, their appearance closer to Parliament-Funkadelic or Earth, Wind, and Fire than what people traditionally think of as hip-hop fashion. Afrika Bambaataa and the Soul Sonic Force leaned into afro-futurism, eventually appearing in full Native/Samurai/Viking/Spaceman gear, basically looking like KISS or the Village People somehow got soul. In the other direction were acts like Run DMC, who appeared in bucket hats, tracksuits, bomber jackets, and shell toe sneakers, pretty much a slightly elevated version of what they already wore. They wore brands they and their fans loved, like Adidas. Indeed, their 1986 song "My Adidas" led to hip-hop's first endorsement deal (but certainly not its last). When Kurtis Blow's first album (containing the first gold certified rap song "The Breaks") dropped, it pictured him with a lot of gold around his neck. Fat gold chains would be ubiquitous in hip-hop ever after, and the Run DMCs and LL Cool Js accessorized their honest tracksuits with all manner of fat gold chains.

Each of the pillars of Hip-hop required different attire thanks to the demands of their trade:

> B-Boys were known to wear T-shirts, sneakers, and sweatsuits in cool colors because they had to move and bounce. The MC was the flashiest out of the bunch. He wore T-shirts and sneakers at first and later gravitated to Timbs and baggy jeans, but the MC always rocked a customized item whether a cross, a name plate, four-finger ring, or brass buckle belt with his name on it. Graffiti artists, like b-boys, had to wear clothes that were flexible. Due largely to their art, graffiti artists had to climb fences, walls, trains, and fire escapes. The best way to do that was not to sacrifice comfort. But make no mistake, that was accomplished without sacrificing style.[7]

One Foot in the Mainstream

How did hip-hop take the first steps from homegrown phenomenon in the outer boroughs to (inter)national phenomenon? It traveled on vinyl. "Rapper's Delight" by the Sugar Hill Gang was a top forty hit in 1979, but it was largely considered a novelty hit lacking support from hip-hop hardcores and backing from a major label.[8] When Kurtis Blow released "The Breaks" in 1980 on Mercury Records on his self-titled album, hip-hop got its first gold record and its first big star. The airplay and distribution for that record, and those that followed, brought hip-hop to a considerably wider audience and influenced scores of artists who would become the next generation of rappers and DJs. By January 1981, the punk/disco/new wave act Blondie had released "Rapture"—a hit single that contained an entire verse of Blondie rapping. The video for that song (the first rap video to be shown on MTV, which is interesting, to say the least, since it's performed by a white woman) featured cameos from legendary graffiti artists Fab Five Freddy, Lee Quiñones, and Jean-Michel Basquiat.

The mainstreaming of hip-hop led to a mainstreaming of the attitudes of a new emergent Black youth culture. This culture expressed itself through a variety of media including new hip-hop fueled "hood" films—from 1975's *Cooley High* (referred to by the *New York Times* as a "Black *American Graffiti*") through an explosion of work in the 1990s by such now-giants as Spike Lee and John Singleton, and magazines like *The Source*.[9]

> You see it in the defiant attitude and disposition of our generation's professional athletes and entertainers like Allen Iverson, Ray Lewis, Mike Tyson, Randy Moss, and Albert Bell. You see it in the activism of the younger generation, which not only fights the power coming from mainstream politics but is often at odds with older-generation activists like Jesse Jackson, Kweisi Mfume, and Al Sharpton. You see it coming from happy-to-be-middle-class-themed magazines like Honey and Savoy as well as like-minded, youth-oriented television programming such as MTV and on-line publications like BET.com.[10]

Old School

Keeping It Real

The first few years of the 1980s represent the culmination of all the cool things that started brewing in the 1970s, and a move into the phase known as "Old School." The music slowly shifts from the funk- and disco-fueled samples of the 1970s and gradually moved away from the overly simplistic rhyming about clapping one's hands or putting them in the air, in favor of a more stripped down and forceful style that would eventually become the "Boom Bap" of the late 1980s and 1990s. (Boom Bap is important, so we'll unpack it in a bit.)

Social consciousness, unvarnished truths about urban life, and discussions of injustice were gaining traction in hip-hop. 1980 brought Kurtis

Blow's "Hard Times" about financial struggle, and Brother D and Collective Effort's "How We Gonna Make the Black Nation Rise" with lyrics that straight up call out the vapid content of Disco and early rap:

> The Ku Klux Klan is on the loose
> Training their kids in machine gun use

Next, along comes a song that, in my opinion, changes everything. "The Message" by Melle Mel and Duke Bootee, credited to Grandmaster Flash and the Furious Five, was written in the wake of a transit strike. It describes the challenges of growing up in urban poverty, and of trying to survive in your neighborhood when a life of crime seems like the only option. The end of the songs features a vignette in which the performers are arrested by the police for no evident reason. Hip-hop stayed neighborhood oriented and proud, but likewise cynical about the state of things. As Marcyliena Morgan, founding executive director of the Hiphop Archive and Research Institute at the Hutchins Center for African and African American Research, Harvard University (yes, that's a real thing), told the *Harvard Gazette*:

> You work within a contradiction at the very beginning of hip-hop where, for example, "New York is horrible! I love New York!" And once it's clear that hip-hop resists simplicity when discussing injustice, [meaning] that there's never this moment when things will always be good or the idea that there's going to be a consistent idyllic setting, you are ready for hip-hop. But [even then] there is still the dream of an amazing and just future. So, you get this contrast where hip-hop heads are basically saying: "Look, we are the children of the Black Panther Party. We were taught to thrive in the midst of all of this knowledge and keep moving forward. We are hip-hop."[11]

As hip-hop told the often-hidden tale of life in the dreaded "inner city," it reported (and continues to report) on marginalized culture, even if that marginalized culture takes up maximal space on the current pop landscape.

The fallout from the war on drugs, increased income inequalities, problematic policing techniques (this is the understatement of the century, but I digress)—the issues which could have been kept from mainstream—were suddenly on the lips and in the minds of those attracted to hip-hop's tunes, dances, looks, or aesthetic appeal. Public Enemy's Chuck D famously described rap as "Black people's CNN." Author Tricia Rose describes rap as a "hidden transcript" challenging power inequality. Specifically, she notes, "not all rap transcripts directly critique all forms of domination; nonetheless, a large and significant element in rap's discursive territory is engaged in symbolic and ideological warfare with institutions and groups that symbolically, ideologically, and materially oppress African Americans."[12]

The Rap Battle

While bragging, belittling, and a sense of competition with a winner and a loser has been a part of hip-hop since early MCs took the mics and parties and b-boys traded off dance challenges on the breaks, the "rap battle" (or "battle rapping") took formal shape in the 1980s when MCs would sign up to go toe to toe, or rather rhyme for rhyme, against one another.

Long before the movie *8 Mile*, an infamous rap battle took place at the Harlem World club on 116th and Lenox in December 1981 between Busy Bee Starski and Kool Moe Dee. "At the time, Busy Bee was known as a 'party MC' because of his style of rapping and ability to hype crowds. He was also a very funny person, oftentimes comparing himself to Muhammad Ali, calling people 'bums' and taking photos with the trophies he was sure to take home that night."[13]

Evidently, Busy Bee made a mistake in slighting Kool Moe Dee, who was in the crowd. Kool Moe Dee, the MC of the Harlem-based hip-hop group the "Treacherous Three," added his name to the battle list for the evening, and soon spit numerous battle verses, including the following:

> Hold on, Busy Bee, I don't mean to be bold
> But put that "ba-ditty-ba" bullshit on hold
> We gonna get right down to the nitty-grit

> Gonna tell you little somethin' why you ain't shit
> It ain't a emcee's jock that you don't hug
> You even your name from the "Lovebug"[14]
> And now to bite a n***a's name, that's some low-down shit
> If you was money, man, you'd be counterfeit

Kool Moe Dee came out the victor. Tapes of the event began being distributed, and suddenly hip-hop became more lyric focused (and with higher expectations of lyrical virtuosity) than it had been, and anyone bragging about being the greatest MC would have to put their skills where their mouth was.

New School

The OGs invented hip-hop. The Old School put it on records and introduced it to the world at large. With the New School, hip-hop truly arrived at the mainstream party. That's how I break down the progression, anyhow. As with the timelines of most artistic movements, your mileage may vary.

Enter Run DMC, a trio from Hollis, Queens: (the late) Jam Master Jay, (the now Rev.) Run, and D.M.C. Their signature look of Adidas tracksuits and sneakers (sans laces, allegedly to echo the lack of laces worn by the incarcerated), Cazal glasses, and bucket hats became the costume of the era. Their sound used hard-hitting drum machines as well as rock elements (one of their biggest hits would be a full-on collaboration with Aerosmith, a rap-infused cover of "Walk This Way"). Okay, while it's perhaps a little corny to the modern eye (although isn't everything?), this style was tougher and less goofball than the disco infused semi-novelty of Old School hits, and the songs were much shorter, making them "radio play length." These changes resulted in their first three albums going gold, platinum, and triple platinum, respectively.

> "I think hip hop in general takes from jazz, funk, has pop elements as well as rock and roll elements."
>
> —Nezi Momodu

The New School also brings about a new era of commercialization. As I touched on earlier, Run DMC struck a million-dollar endorsement deal with Adidas related to their song "My Adidas" from their 1986 album, *Raising Hell*. They were already wearing Adidas and had already released a song about them, but now they were getting paid and getting an exclusive shoe line, thirty years before YEEZYs. DMC told *GQ* that at their 1986 Madison Square Garden show promoting the album, when he held his shoe up and rapped, "Take your trainer off and hold it up," the entirety of the Garden followed suit. In the interview with Adidas Group "Insights from Run DMC," DMC said:

> I think the relationship with Adidas legitimized our culture, because before it happened, people said it's just a fad, rap music is just a fad, it's negative, it's not good, nobody will ever like it. So, our relationship with Adidas legitimized us, because it was a whole other world, that was very well respected, that was very household, families; so, people said if rap is so bad, how come Adidas is messing with these rappers right here? So, it gave us some legitimacy, for sure. And it took us from the streets to mainstream white America.[15]

The Big New School Names

Another titan of this era was LL Cool J. "Cool James" would become the first hip-hop act on the music-performance and dance television program *American Bandstand*, beginning his career with the twelve-inch single "I Need a Beat," and eventually ending up a popular film and television actor. By 2017, he was the first hip-hop recipient of the Kennedy Center Honors for lifetime contribution to American culture. LL Cool J's success was facilitated by Def Jam Recordings, a label founded in a New York University dorm room by then-student Rick Ruben, who would soon add partner Russel Simmons (brother of Run DMC's DJ Run and eventual mega-entrepreneur and founder of the Phat Farm clothing line). From those beginnings, Simmons gradually became one of *Time*'s Most Influential People in the world.

Def Jam signed the Beastie Boys, a trio of hardcore punks turned rappers. Their background was considerably different than most of their counterparts, with Mike D, Ad-Rock, and MCA being three Jewish kids from the Upper West Side, Park Avenue, and Brooklyn Heights, respectively. They began rapping with a comedy single called "Cookie Puss," based on a prank call to the Carvel ice cream company (Cookie Puss was an ice cream cake popular at New York kiddie birthdays), and by 1985 they were a rap act opening for Madonna on the Virgin tour. Their 1986 album *License to Ill* became the first hip-hop album to top the Billboard charts and would have every white kid in suburbia singing "Fight for Your Right" and "No Sleep Till Brooklyn." For all our talk about hip-hop being a chronicle of Black life in post–Civil Rights America and the war on drugs, the first rap video was Blondie, and the first number one album was the Beastie Boys. Do we attribute that to a numbers game, or to bias by consumers and institutional racism on the part of the media and distributors? I'll leave that decision up to you. (It's the second one, though.)

> **"I think what we what happened is like you had the late 80s, early 90s, where social justice was a focal point of rap music, or at least a very controlling part of it. You had a lot more conscious rappers. We had conscious labels, you know, like raucous records, you had people that were that were specifically pushing conscious rap music. And then that kind of got weeded out in the big money era of music."**
>
> **—AC Tatum**

Eric B. and Rakim entered the scene in 1986. Eric B., the DJ, instituted a fascinating mix of classic and forward-thinking techniques—he used heavy sampling and raised the bar on depth and breadth of samples. He also brought back live turntable mixing which had fallen by the wayside, and sampled classic soul material (i.e., James Brown's "Get Up, Get Into It, Get Involved" and "Funky President" in their bop "Eric B. Is President").

Rakim, a man on every list of the greatest MCs of all time, quickly became known as a lyricist's lyricist, rapping through bar lines with jazz-like phrasing, an aloof delivery, and a genius use of techniques like internal rhyme and "multis" (rhymes using words of two more syllables, i.e., multisyllabic rhymes). His content ranged from the ridiculous to the sublime, with elevated versions of typical hip-hop bravado, bluntly raw coverage of life on the streets, and mystical Afrocentric beliefs descended from his membership in the Five-Percent Nation, an offshoot of the political/religious movement the Nation of Islam, which also had Big Daddy Kane, the members of Brand Nubian, members of Wu-Tang Clan, and Busta Rhymes as members.

The Bronx continued to be a fountainhead of hip-hop realness, and the group Boogie Down Productions became a banner holder for the South Bronx (also known as the "Boogie Down"). Boogie Down Productions fused Jamaican dancehall rhythms into their work, further connecting hip-hop and the West Indies beyond the early influence of toasting. Membership changed over the years, but the mainstay was rapper KRS-One, who brought info-packed lyrics to the stage. The group's DJ, Scott La Rock, a social worker who met KRS-One when the MC was living in a men's shelter, was shot and killed in 1987 at age twenty-five in what would be the first, and sadly not the last, murder of a hip-hop star. Following La Rock's death and the death of a young fan following a scuffle over a gold chain at a concert at Nassau Coliseum, KRS-One became an activist both in his lyrics and actions. He started the Stop the Violence Movement with some of rap's biggest stars, including, but not limited to Kool Moe Dee, Heavy D, and MC Lyte, in an effort to bring a message of anti-violence to the community. That group created "Self-Destruction," a track and video honoring La Rock and promoting anti-violence. It went to number one on the rap charts, with all proceeds going to the National Urban League, an organization "that advocates on behalf of economic and social justice for African Americans and against racial discrimination in the United States."[16] I wish I could say this began a sea change in violence in the community and in the hip-hop world, but if you've heard of Tupac or Biggie, you know I'd be lying.

The Golden Age

You might want to fight me on this one, but I'm going to say that the late 1980s to the mid-1990s are rap's "Golden Age." Numerous scholars and sources agree, but some call some of these years more of the New School, some call it the Middle School. Honestly, it's messy so go with me on this. Things are about to get a lot more politically and musically complicated as well as a lot more serious. Additionally, there is a lot more regional flavor than just the various boroughs of New York. Be warned: these next few pages contain a lot of info, but it's all absolutely essential to your understanding of rap, so get a soda and a snack and settle in.

Advancements

Each new era in rap brings along with its technology advancements, and typically, a leveling up of artistry. The Golden Age is bursting with advancements:

- More and more complex electronic sampling, growing from literally spinning a portion of an old record to incorporating numerous samples from numerous songs at varying lengths (samples could be a few notes or full choruses into a song)
- Innovation and diversity of sounds used for tracks
- The skill level of the artists along with an unprecedented complexity of flows
- Gimmicks were everywhere, which makes rap all the more popular to the mainstream

Many disparate styles of hip-hop existed for many different tastes (or lack thereof . . . I'm looking at you, Vanilla Ice). If it seems like with each subsequent era, I'm saying that "hip-hop reached new degrees of commercial success," it's probably because with each subsequent era, hip-hop reached new degrees of commercial success.

Boom Bap

Quick: do an impression of the kick drum and snare most rap songs from the mid-1980s well into the 1990s rap song: "Boom BAP—Boom Boom BAP—Ba Boom BAP—Ba Boom Boom BAP." There's actually a subgenre, or perhaps a particular technique, of hip-hop named after that; it contains a ton of music, and it's glorious. If that sounds rhythmically limiting, you can actually play around quite a bit with the percussion within that larger pattern. Lyrically? You can have all manner of flows over the top of it. MCs had the freedom to really play with flow and create the most legendary bars of all time. Go listen to "Scenario" by Tribe. Go listen to "C.R.E.A.M." by Wu-Tang. In the words of KRS-One, "Boom Bap/Original Rap/See how it sounds!"

New Jack Swing

At the start of this book, I said that all pop is now hip-hop. Well, most pop from the mid-1980s to the end of the century was a kind of hip-hop called new jack swing. The term is not thrown around as much as you might think when you consider how many top forty hits were part of this genre—this music really was *everywhere*—so maybe it didn't need a label . . . it's just what pop and dance and R&B music was. Janet Jackson, her brother, Paula Abdul, Blackstreet, C&C Music Factory, Salt-N-Pepa, and let's not leave out *all* those boy bands: Boyz II Men, Backstreet Boys, New Edition, New Kids on the Block, Bell Biv Devoe, NSYNC, Color Me Badd. New jack swing was 4/4 (or 12/8) beats on the 808 drum machine, funk-inspired heavy bass line, classic samples, melodic synth lines, dope vocals, and rapped verses.

The term was coined in the *Village Voice* by writer Barry Michael Cooper, who was discussing something special happening in the (at-that-time) flailing Harlem neighborhood thanks to Uptown Records producer Teddy Riley working with artists like Al B. Sure!, Keith Sweat, and Bobby Brown: "what Teddy was doing was brand new. That's why I named it 'New Jack Swing.' Teddy's music was the soundtrack to a new version of the Harlem Renaissance, and I wanted my reporting and writing to reflect that, too:

a sense of historical relevance, social and political accuracy, and spiritual uplift to make it memorable."[17] He picked up the beat from earlier music, swung it, and made it busier. Los Angeles producers like Jimmy Jam and Terry Lewis, LA Reid, and Babyface picked up on that sound. MTV picked up that sound. It became *the* defining sound of an era. That empirical period of movies for Spike Lee and John Singleton? The popularity of Black television comedies like *A Different World, In Living Color, All That, The Fresh Prince of Bel-Air*, and, yes, even *Homeboys in Outer Space* and the creation of networks like the WB and UPN to show them? The Kid and Play 1-900 hotline number you got in trouble for calling at two dollars for the first minute and thirty-five cents each additional minute? Cross Colors and Tommy Hilfiger, and FUBU clothes? Your sweet fade? All that was the new jack swing era. I love this music so much, I could go on and on, but for now, you get the gist.

Conscious Rap

Conscious rap is a movement, or perhaps a phenomenon, that defies a timeline, as socially conscious messages can and are included in rap of every decade. Sometimes it is instead called political rap, sometimes that hair is split: here I choose to call these the same thing. The argument can of course be made that all rap has plenty to say about society, but in conscious Rap the message is intentional. It is traditionally constructive and socially positive. No matter how sober the tone or thorny the delivery may be, conscious rap is a tug of war between prevailing power structures and the worldview of the MC. The flipside of the coin that is conscious rap (by my categorization) would be something like gangsta rap (to be discussed shortly), which discusses get-money empowerment or the message that crime is the tough but necessary way to survive or escape "hood" life. That is certainly a message and perhaps you believe the message, or perhaps you think that the existence and perhaps necessity of that thought process speaks volume about socio-economic reality. I'm not saying one is superior; I'm merely using the opposition of these subgenres to further classify both the message and method of conscious rap.

Consciousness was there from the beginning—listen to Gil Scott Heron's "The Revolution Will Not Be Televised," Brother D's "How We Gonna Make the Black Nation Rise," or the aforementioned Grandmaster Flash's "The Message," all of which are songs about casting off oppression, about perseverance in the face of injustice, and typically about the elevation of Black people and culture.

Some conscious rap comes from artists rooted in offshoots of the Nation of Islam like the Five Percenters, and this includes the New Rochelle hip-hop group Brand Nubian. Peep the lyrics on their 1990 song "Drop the Bomb" and notice the religious, economic, and political ideas on display:

> On equal planes we can bring forth gain
> Rise the dead, from the graves of the slaves

Themes are often Afrocentric or Afrofuturist, and the artists sometimes worked as collectives, as in Afrika Bambaataa's Universal Zulu Nation (remember, he's an OG). There were The Native Tongues, another New York–based collective including the Jungle Brothers, De La Soul, A Tribe Called Quest, and Queen Latifah. Their music was often extremely fun, jazzy, and occasionally, though far from always, comical. The music frequently criticized capitalism, though sometimes it promoted economic independence and prosperity. Lyrics attack law enforcement and racist judicial- and prison-related policies. Do you think that was well received by the politicians? Take a wild guess. No? Ding ding ding—you get a gold star. For instance, then-presidential-candidate Bill Clinton called out rapper Sister Souljah in 1992 as a way to distance himself from hip-hop's more confrontational rhetoric to align himself with "Reagan Democrats." I'll stop myself from ranting, but take a minute to reflect on why that might be problematic.

Jumping forward in time for a second to help connect the dots, the artist most closely associated with conscious rap is Chicago's Common. If you haven't heard his flow over the past three-plus decades and fourteen studio albums, you've seen him in dozens of television shows and films from *Suicide Squad* to *Selma* (for which he and co-writer John Legend won the

Academy Award for Best Song) and a Pulitzer-winning Broadway play (*Between Riverside and Crazy*). He's also recorded with a number of other artists also known for conscious work, including Lauryn Hill, De La Soul, Erykah Badu, and more. In these lyrics from his 2005 song "The Corner," featuring The Last Poets and fellow Chicagoan Kanye, Common paints a picture of life on the streets in Chicago, and the hopes of potential rapper currently stuck hustling:

> These are the stories told by Stony and Cottage Grove
> The world is cold, the block is hot as a stove

Gangsta Rap

What term made politicians and suburban parents more uptight in the 1990s than "gangsta rap"? Images of shirtless Black men in grills and durags holding Uzis and fans of money—the perfect boogiemen for cul-de-sacs full of Karens and governments full of Newts and Tippers. The music industry was happy to supply plenty of fuel for the outrage machine, because there's money in all that outrage.

What was gangsta rap? Well, it was rap about life on the street and as a street gang member. It started in Los Angeles. Some of it comes out or speaks to authentic experience and some of it was a cash in to get money from suburban white teenage boys.

In these years starting in the mid-to-late 1980s and continuing into the 1990s, gang life reached new numbers of involvement and new levels of violence. Hip-hop both commented on and was driven by this rise. The level of violence and hopelessness in the inner cities of the late 1980s and 1990s made novelty rhyming and trying to dance off the poverty and the crushing societal pressures seem both naive and vapid. The Civil Rights era was ancient history, "Black is Beautiful" and "Black Power" long in the rearview mirror. Social mobility? Nope. So, a siege mentality (and a sales market) built up around neighborhoods, around blocks, around buildings: "A common denominator of gang growth in New York City, Chicago, and Los Angeles is the policy of concentrating poverty in the high-rise public housing units—a remarkable urban planning blunder. In major cities, high-rise public housing settings provided gangs with cohesion because it was a clearly identified and secure home base."[18]

NWA

Ice Cube of the iconic hip-hop group NWA knew that if he wanted to speak the truth, his message wouldn't be heard if it was sanitized, sugar-coated, or spoken in the language of the televangelists and Washington wives trying to ban the music of The Real:

> I know we're all addicted to sex and violence. We all grew up on it. We can't help it. If there's a fight after school, everybody wants to see it and whoever says they don't is a liar. . . . Since we're addicted to sex and violence, that's how I get your ears. I put it in the music. But I also put some knowledge on top of that, so you can get the medicine you need to fight this beast we've got to fight.[19]

The music was shocking, and the words hit hard, but the truth hurts, doesn't it? Who was offering a truer message or a better deal?

> Reaganism had eliminated youth programs while bombarding youths with messages to desist and abstain; it was all about tough love and denial and getting used to nothing. Even the East Coast Utopians like Rakim and Chuck talked control and discipline. By contrast, excess was the essence of NWA's appeal. These poems celebrated pushers, played bitches, killed enemies, and assassinated police. Fuck delayed gratification, they said, take it all now.[20]

The rappers themselves became icons of "The Real"—heavily muscled and heavily armed—hypermasculinity as a reflection of the environment, but also hypermasculinity as a necessary tool of survival in the cold and violent world of "thug life." This masculinity was not presented via a socio-economic utilitarian like Booker T. Washington nor via a peaceful orator like Martin Luther King. Why? Because the Los Angelino was experiencing "realness," and this kind of manliness was ineffective and accepted continued white dominance. Gangsta projected the urban Black man as an unyielding and violent force that would receive the winnings he deserved or die trying.

NWA shed light on dark times on the west coast and the nightmare tactics of the Los Angeles Police Department but did so while creating reams of deeply misogynistic rhymes and shockingly violent sentiments. Dr. Dre himself was confronted with his own history of abuse of women which he was forced to address when the hit 2015 NWA biopic *Straight Outta Compton* dragged it into the public sphere. History, and your own capacity for this sort of thing, will determine whether the net influence of this music is positive or negative. Perhaps positivity and negativity are useless when dealing with "The Real": "As unapologetically violent, misogynist, and problematic as their lyrics often were, the group's harrowing depictions of urban nightmares provided a vital response to the growing disenfranchisement from the Reagan-era politics that had transformed the nation and created an economic catastrophe for metropolitan Los Angeles. N.W.A introduced an antihero."[21]

Those who came next took this ironclad realness to the next level. Originally a roadie, dancer, and guest rapper with Digital Underground (this fact still shocks me ... and if you don't know why, listen to Digital Underground's "The Humpty Dance" and then think about Tupac and you'll understand why), Tupac Shakur embodied, "the political and social threat facilitated by the violent and sexual attributes of an urban, black hypermasculinity. ... Rapping about brutal acts of violence Tupac is injecting ... an oppositional comprehension of masculinity into the existing cultural understandings."[22] Tupac provided the perfect icon of the gangsta aesthetic: tough, rich, violent, womanizing, heartbroken (listen to his raw and tender ballad, "Dear Mama"), and devastatingly dead. Murdered by gun violence providing the expected poetic end to a "Real" man.

Tupac may have loved his mother,[23] but the classic Madonna/whore binary of womanhood could be found everywhere in gangsta rap (and all too commonly in hip-hop at large):

> The most visible representations of black women in hip hop reflect the hallmarks of mainstream masculinity: They regularly use women as props that boost male egos, treat women's bodies as sexual objects, divide women into groups that are worthy of protection and respect and those that are not. Thus, hip-hop does not break from the fundamental logic of mainstream masculinity so much as convey it with excess, bravado, and extra insult.[24]

PSA: I need to take a quick pause. Look, there could be an entire book about gangsta rap, but this book is not that book. It's so incredibly complicated, and it's far too easy to stand in judgment, frown, and blame gangsta rap when your ice cream cone drops on the floor or you get a paper cut. Instead, I encourage you to read on with curiosity and remember the time machine you traveled in not too long ago in chapter 1. Remember not just the what, but also the how and why.

Speaking of why: *Why* did this harder rap come out of Los Angeles and not the famously hard New York City, which, broadly speaking, is more known for conscious rap? Los Angeles had developed a large African American population in the Second Great Migration in the 1940s, but restrictive housing practices and one of the country's first militarized (but certainly not the last) police forces lead to an oppressed and frustrated community, and massive riots in 1965 (Watts) and 1992 (Rodney King): "What L.A. rappers did that was revolutionary was to make music for themselves. L.A. rappers made music that was sometimes violent, sometimes vulgar and always unapologetically black and militaristic in terms of its references to policing and institutions of white power. That sold."[25]

G-Funk

"Urban" music has always been pretty bass heavy. Hip-hop, yes, funk for sure, but there is major bass all the way back to jive. Is it because of the cities' constant hum of low frequencies: car engines, subway and elevated train rumbles, airplanes, construction equipment? Or is it because of the people in those cities—perhaps we go one step further and say that bass-heavy music exists throughout the African diaspora:

> the timbral world the subwoofer has made, a virtual archipelago of thumping music situated along the old trade routes of the African diaspora—from Jamaican reggae, dub, and dance hall through the "Dirty South" hip-hop, Miami bass, and other Latin American derivatives, (cumbia reggaeton), and then back across the Atlantic in a dizzying explosion of UK dance styles ... they all come together a culture of musical resistance predicated on the ability to dominate collective spaces with large quantities of low-frequency sound.[26]

There's a subgenre of gangsta rap, also born on the West Coast, and pioneered by producer/rapper Dr. Dre and lesser-known figure Gregory "Big Hutch" Hutchinson. It samples P-Funk (the music of the 1970s outfit Parliament-Funkadelic) extensively:

> The sound of West Coast rap was rooted in the music of Ohio Players, George Clinton and Parliament Funkadelic, Isaac Hayes, Gap Band, Marvin Gaye, Curtis Mayfield, and Sly Stone, as well as New York hip-hop favorite James Brown. The combination of the funk rhymes and rhythms with the poignant soul licks gave rise to the development of a slower, bass-driven meter and the minor-keyed, catchy loops, which cohered with LA cruising culture and became the classic gangsta groove.[27]

G-funk has deep, groovy Moog bass, heavy snare, and a high sliding synth over the top. The songs are laid back (with their mind on their money and their money on their mind) and intended to be listened to in booming bass-heavy automotive car stereo, because Los Angeles is a driving city. "An example typical of Dr. Dre's early-1990s production that demonstrates this hybridity of material and suitability for automotive listening is the Dr. Dre produced single 'Who am I? (What's my Name?),' the debut single from Snoop Doggy Dogg's *Doggystyle* (1993)—it is likely that heavy dynamic compression was used in production to elevate the volume over the road and engine noise of a car."[28]

If you are sitting here saying, what the heck is G-funk? Go listen to these classics: "Regulate" (Warren G featuring Nate Dogg), "Nuthin' But a G Thang" (Dr. Dre featuring Snoop), and "Gin and Juice" (Snoop Doggy Dogg).

East Coast

As for New York, it has its own subdivisions and cultures and sounds. We talk a lot about the Bronx, of course, since Herc was there by way of Jamaica, and Grandmaster Flash by way of Barbados, and KRS-One, and the Puerto-Rican/Cuban American rapper Fat Joe, and his remarkable Nuyorican collaborator Big Pun, and many more.

Brooklyn

Brooklyn produced so many great rappers that listing them will probably only draw attention to those I leave out, but Big Daddy Kane, Mos Def, much of the Wu-Tang Clan (though they formed in Staten Island), and Busta Rhymes. Not to jump ahead, but it's worth mentioning that it continues to produce: Lil Kim, a certain member of American royalty you may have heard of by the name of Jay Z, Nas, Pop Smoke, and many more yet to come. Saving the best name for last, Brooklyn also gave us one of the greatest emcees of all time (if not the greatest): Biggie Smalls aka The Notorious B.I.G. If you don't know Biggie's work, please put down this book and the snack you're eating and listen to "Big Poppa," "Hypnotize," "Juicy," and my personal favorite, "Mo Money, Mo Problems" (which features Mase and Diddy, as well as a spectacular Diana Ross sample). Why is Biggie so special? His tone quality is really distinctive. His subject matter was inventive, versatile, and often strayed away from the typical gangsta rap subject matter, both giving voices to new thoughts and subject matter—he was both prolific and a party. Most importantly, however, is his legendary flow. When he was young, Biggie was taken under the wing of a jazz saxophonist in his neighborhood, Donald Harrison, and this training was instrumental in Biggie's rhythmic prowess. Harrison wanted to make his neighbor a jazz musician. He gave him homework, made him learn how to scat a Cannonball Adderley solo, and made him listen to Charlie Parker and Ella Fitzgerald. "We worked on various tonguing and speed and agility," Harrison says. "You have to slow things down really slow and take the time to phrase each note."[29] This blossomed into phrasing that would become Biggie's signature—phrases that would cross bar lines; meaning he'd end his phrase on the one of the following measure, and perhaps start the next phrase on beat three of that measure. That, paired with intricate and clever internal rhyme schemes, forever changed rap.

Philly

While it isn't New York, Philadelphia, Pennsylvania, is certainly the East Coast. Known for its smooth soul sounds in the 1960s and 1970s, Philly would start a neo-soul trend in the 1980s and 1990s that birthed the multitalented and hard-to-label band The Roots (featuring band leader Questlove and MC Black Thought). You might not know it watching them back up the giggling Jimmy Fallon (I'm not imagining it, he's always giggling, right?) for middle-class American grandparents every night on NBC, but they're as talented as anyone who was ever in the game, as well as DJ Jazzy Jeff and his MC The Fresh Prince, who would go on to do some things besides rap, Eve, Schooly D, Meek Mill, Lil Uzi Vert, and so many more.

East Coast Versus West Coast

Rap in the early 1990s was known for a coastal war that spurred conversation and sales, but which ended in the deaths of two of hip-hop's greatest artists: Biggie Smalls and Tupac Shakur. Central to the feud were their labels, Bad Boy records on the East Coast—with executive, producer, rapper, and fashion mogul Sean "Puffy"/"Puff Daddy" Combs at the helm (musical home of Biggie)—and Death Row Records on the West, home of producer Dr. Dre, run by executive Marion "Suge" Knight (and the eventual musical home of Tupac).

As evidenced in our discussion of rap battles, confrontation, competition, diss tracks (raps disrespecting other rappers), and other forms of "beef" (conflict) have always been a part of hip-hop, and hip-hop's close association with gang culture and gang life has at times made that beef more dangerous than just some verbal sparring.

The rivalry heated up after Tupac was shot in an evident robbery while recording a track at Manhattan's Quad studio in 1994. Tupac was subsequently jailed on unrelated charges, and while Puff Daddy told Tupac that the shooting was not condoned by Bad Boy Records, rhetoric on several rap tracks (including a track by Biggie entitled "Who Shot Ya?"), discussion in the press, and smack talk by Knight at the 1995 Source Awards kept elevating the conflict. Knight bailed out Tupac, who then dove *hard* into a rivalry with Biggie. Bullets continued to fly, with another fatality (a member of Knight's crew) at a party in Atlanta attended by both Knight and Puffy. No one was convicted and Combs once again denied involvement, but the conflict kept escalating. In 1995, shots were fired at Snoop Dogg and his group The Dogg Pound as they recorded in Brooklyn, not long after Biggie called attention to their presence in the borough on a radio show, and in September 1996, Tupac was shot and killed at an intersection in Las Vegas. Claims that he was likely killed by a member of a Los Angeles gang following a fight with other members of that gang were pretty much ignored by the press and a number of players in the conflict. In March 1997, about six months after the death of Tupac, Biggie was shot to death in a vehicle after leaving the Soul Train awards in Los Angeles. No one ever did time for either murder, or the men most frequently cited as the trigger men died in unrelated shootings. Death Row Records went bankrupt in 2006. Suge Knight had many years of subsequent violent run-ins and legal problems and is currently serving a twenty-two-year sentence for running over a guy after an argument on the set of the NWA biopic *Straight Outta Compton*. In recent years, Sean "Puffy" Combs received a BET Lifetime Achievement

Awards and gave millions to some Historically Black Colleges and Universities, but he also shared anti-Semitic videos from Louis Farrakhan. Oh, and in 1998 he made that terrible Godzilla song with Jimmy Page. History is complicated.

Hip-Hop from Flyover Country

I've now written extensively on hip-hop being born in, and coming of age in, New York City. When the West Coast came online hard in the 1990s, it changed the game and created dangerous rivalries, but hold up a sec... the coasts aren't the only place anyone ever lay down a track or spit a rhyme. We should make some space for other regions in the narrative. At the risk of being even more exclusive by expanding the map (as soon as I mention Atlanta and Detroit, a rapper from Boise is going to angrily point out that I omitted their scene), let's take a look at some other regions.

The Dirty South

As a Chicagoan, I'm both a child of the Great Migration of Black folks from the South (Georgia *REPRESENT*) and a Northerner utterly baffled by the South. It's a land with dense populations of Black people in the cities and the countries, but also a block of the country in the grip of some of the most malignant forces of the white supremist beliefs. To be a rapper in, say, Atlanta (or Houston, New Orleans, Memphis, or Miami—the Southern cities typically considered to be under the umbrella of the hip-hop designation "The Dirty South"), you're dealing with not only the classic themes of urban Black marginalization, but doing so in a larger realm of Black marginalization, and trying to give local flavor to a classically northern coastal art form.

Atlanta

OutKast: The Atlanta hip-hop duo OutKast, who found superstardom in the early 2000s, put the frustration of these paradoxes to use:

OutKast displayed an intense disdain for whitewashed versions of southern history and an especially acute hatred for Atlanta's white elite, calling them "p***y motherfuckas" who wanted to "put that [confederate] flag up" but should "work a little bit faster / Because of the shit that I done been through / I shall never call you master / You D-E-V-I-L." By highlighting local problems and bragging about how their experience as marginalized black southerners actually reinforced their superiority over the status quo, OutKast set up a nuanced definition of regional blackness.[30]

Goodie Mob: Atlanta's Goodie Mob came up in the mid-1990s with socially incisive lyrics and a gradual increase in use of the unique tone quality of CeeLo Green: "Goodie Mob spoke for the Black residents who were surviving off the scrap's leftover by the white and Black elite. The rappers weren't afraid to call out the violence of former Atlanta drug unit the Red Dogs or former President Bill Clinton (referring to him as Bill Clampett, a reference to the Beverly Hillbillies character Jed Clampett)."[31]

The Dirty South in the Big Apple

It was in New York City that OutKast stuck the South's flag into the soil of hip-hop at the 1995 Source Awards where they won for Best New Artist, and André 3000 famously declared that "The South has something to say." And say it they would. By the early 2000s, Southern hip-hop roundly dominated the charts, with OutKast, Ludacris, Beyonce, and many more taking the lion's share of Billboard slots and radio airplay. The coasts, of course, flipped out about it, and labeled this era of rap "The Ringtone Era" to diminish the success of Southern artists by labeling it flashy, fleeting, and of little substance. Jealous much?

Today's charts are inundated with Atlanta hip-hop stars with a variety of sounds, including 2 Chainz, Jermaine Dupri, Donald Glover, Killer Mike, Young Thug, Ludacris, Lil Baby, Lil Jon, Lil Yachty, Playboi Carti, Soulja Boy, Young Thug, and Waka Flocka Flame.

Elsewhere in this book I cover "trap," which has largely taken over all of hip-hop, but it began as an Atlanta phenomenon and is generally attributed as originating with Atlanta rappers T.I., Gucci Mane, and Young Jeezy. If Atlanta didn't have enough bona fides prior to that phenomenon, it could be argued it's as influential a place as has existed for rap since Los Angeles in the 1990s or New York City at the start of it all. Perhaps its legacy will be that of the city that ruined hip-hop by introducing trap into the bloodstream, but that's an impressive legacy. (I know, you want to fight me now, but please keep reading.)

Houston

Houston led the charge for Texas rap with Geto Boys beginning in the late 1980s, who wrote "Damn It Feels Good to Be a Gangster," which would propel them back into the public consciousness in 1999 when it was used in the comedy *Office Space*. Houston also gave us DJ Screw, who is responsible for chopped and screwed recording style. In chopped and screwed music, DJ Screw would slow down the tempo of rap music. This purposefully slowed down tempo is said to have mirrored the city of Houston itself, with its nine-month summers and laid back energy. Julie Grob, coordinator for digital projects and instruction, special collections for the University of Houston Libraries, explains the chopped and screwed sound: "DJ Screw would slow down all of the music and he would repeat certain beats and words and phrases . . . The style became known as 'chopped and screwed.' Other Houston artists began using that style. People started releasing one album that was regular, and one that was a 'chopped and screwed' production."[32] Also from Houston is Travis Scott, who was nurtured by Chicago's Kanye West and would go on to become immensely popular of late.

Memphis

Memphis—what a music city—just . . . wow. As a link from South to the North during the Great Migration, it became an incubator for the blues, and as the home of Stax Records it was a deeply important home for R&B

and soul, not to mention its legacy of gospel, jazz, and early rock 'n' roll. The hip-hop scene had an essential existence in a city wrecked by racist housing and zoning policies, nuked by "urban renewal," and flooded with drugs and crime. Memphis hip-hop back then was intensely lo-fi indie work, coming out of bedroom studios, then handed out on mixtapes from the trunks of cars and in the parking lots of skating rinks turned clubs. The samples could be unique, taken from the Stax catalog and/or other local artists, the beats were lower, and the content was often very dark—reflecting the nature of the city in the 1990s.

"Memphis horrorcore" was also born, piling onto the already dark music with horror themes, samples from horror movies, and references to the occult. There's an urban legend[33] connected to this subgenre: the "Memphis Rap Sigils." As the story goes, there are eight specific 1990s Memphis rap tapes which have energy from the souls of murdered people baked right into the music. The rappers ritually murdered people, you see, and sampled their screams—they definitely did *not* get the screams from sound effects tapes and VHS horror. The energy was made into symbols which give the makers power and grants their wishes when the tapes are heard by the public . . . I guess. Again, this is just an urban legend, but if you happen to own a cassette player and find the tapes on eBay—proceed at your own risk.

The Southern hip-hop subgenre known as "crunk" also has roots in Memphis—a stripped down, aggressive, party/dance sound that focuses on beats and call-and-response more than on complicated lyrics. There are no Satanic rituals attached to that one.

In 2005, the movie *Hustle and Flow* showed a light on the Memphis hip-hop scene that had struggled in the shade of the coastal royalty, far from the attention of labels, for so long, and Memphis's Three 6 Mafia won the Academy Award that year for "It's Hard Out Here for a Pimp."

Miami

Miami put its own stamp on hip-hop with Miami bass, a sound using heavy kick and bass and first brought to national attention by the shock-rappers 2

Live Crew, whose sexually explicit 1989 album *As Nasty as They Wanna Be* (featuring the hit single "Me So Horny") led to a clutching of *all* the pearls at the country club bridge tournaments. The governor of Florida ordered an investigation into whether the album, and even the selling of the album, broke obscenity laws, leading the Broward County sheriff to arrest members of the band and some retailers who sold the album. The arrests were overturned, but Florida remains Florida.

South Florida, with its mix of cultures and sounds, and Miami specifically, have produced a lot of big rappers, including Denzel Curry, Pitbull, Flo Rida, Trick Daddy, DJ Khaled, Lil Pump, $not, and more.

New Orleans

New Orleans loves its jazz, but it's no stranger to hip-hop either, and it gave the world "bounce," another dance friendly, beat-heavy, call-and-response style that would influence crunk and other Dirty Southern forms. Master P is from New Orleans, as is Lil Wayne, and plenty of artists have incorporated the bounce sound, including Beyonce ("Break My Soul"), who featured bounce icon and gender non-conforming artist Big Freedia on "Formation." Oh, and you know "twerking"? That started with bounce (not with Miley Cyrus).

North Carolina

North Carolina is a musical state with an impressive history of Black culture including eleven Historically Black Colleges and Universities. Fayetteville's Dreamville Records[34] gave us J. Cole, and other rappers are popping up from the state, including DaBaby, hailing from Charlotte.

Detroit

Any discussion of American popular music has to mention Detroit, but Berry Gordy and the Motown sound weren't the only forces out of the Motor City to revolutionize music. By 1982, Detroit had its own locally popular rap duo, Felix and Jarvis, and a daily dance party television show called *The Scene*. The local electronic music scene always had some juice, from "electro" music around 1980 to Detroit's own "hip-house" scene in the late 1980s. By then the streets of Detroit, as in so many other cities, had grown hard from the crack epidemic and the war on drugs, and suffered a long-term collapse of infrastructure and services. Hard musical acts spread from this unfriendly ground, including Detroit's metal-fusion "acid" rappers Natas and Flint's MC Breed.

What truly popped outside of Michigan? If I'm mentioning fusion, I have to mention country-rock-rapper Kid Rock. Kid Rock was born in the suburbs and his parents owned a whole bunch of car dealerships and an enormous house. Today, he is emblematic of working-class country living and an urban sound and has the notable distinction of making Lynyrd Skynyrd sound less racist and Ted Nugent seem less greasy by comparison.

Other notable Detroit hip-hop figures are the rapper Big Sean (whose 2012 mixtape was titled *Detroit*, with a studio album in 2020 called *Detroit 2*) and the eccentric wordsmith Danny Brown. The producer, MC, and drummer J Dilla is a notable Detroiter with much respected work on recordings by Common, Tribe, De La Soul, Janet Jackson, and Erykah Badu as well as his own solo career. He had a lasting influence on drum programming, looping, and sampling, despite his untimely death from lupus at age thirty-two.

Someone has to end this novella of a chapter, so let's make it someone good, shall we? Enter Shady. A robust hip-hop scene emerged in Detroit in the 1990s, with vicious rap battles taking place on open mic night at a clothing store called the Hip Hop Shop. Notable performers of those nights were notable (notably white) rapper Eminem and his DJ, Proof. (Proof would be gunned down near Eight Mile Road in 2006). Born Marshall Mathers, Eminem's struggles with poverty, unstable family life, and drug addiction have been well published, but when Mathers attended the 1997 LA Rap Olympic (he came in second), his demo "Slim Shady EP" (Slim Shady being his harsher alter ego, like a horrorcore Hannah Montana) found its way to the hands of legendary rapper and producer Dr. Dre. Over the course of the next couple of decades, Eminem would become one of the top-selling popular artists of any genre of all time . . . and if rap wasn't solidly part of young white America's listening habits before Eminem, it was right in the center of it afterwards. He's also the first rapper to win an Oscar for Best Original Song ("Lose Yourself" from the semi-autobiographical film *8 Mile*). In addition to being history's top-selling rapper, he's generally considered to be a major contender for "Greatest of All Time."

> **"As a kid there was a lot of rap that I really couldn't, like it really didn't do anything for me, it didn't register. He talked about love and dealing drugs or hardships you're going through. I didn't understand at the time, like, I'm, you know, however, old I am, I'm a kid. But Eminem felt like watching a movie, or a TV show or something. Like all my friends would come over and just listen. And we'd be like, 'What in the world? What is this?' You know, it's like a episode of South Park or, you know, a crazy movie."**
>
> **—Joseph Chilliams**

Notes

1. Riesch, R J. (2005). Hip Hop Culture: History and Trajectory. Research Papers. Paper 32. Southern Illinois University. http://opensiuc.lib.siu.edu/gs_rp/32

2. Ettelson, R. (2017, October 2). Ultimate Breaks & Beats: An Oral History. *Medium*. Retrieved November 8, 2022, from https://medium.com/cuepoint/ultimate-breaks-beats-an-oral-history-74937f932026

3. Wimsatt, W. U. (2008). *Bomb the Suburbs*. New York: Soft Skull Press.

4. De Paor-Evans, A. (2018, November 16). The Intertextuality and Translations of Fine Art and Class in Hip-Hop Culture. *Arts*, 7 (4): 80.

5. Chalfant, H., and S. Jenkins. (2014). *Training Days: The Subway Artists Then and Now*. London: Thames & Hudson Ltd.

6. Cascone, S. (2020, September 29). "I Was a Feminist, and I Didn't Know It": How Lady Pink Made a Space for Herself in the Boys Club of New York's Graffiti Scene. *Artnet News*. Retrieved November 10, 2022, from https://news.artnet.com/art-world/lady-pink-interview-1602208

7. Romero, E., and D. John. (2012). *Free Stylin': How Hip Hop Changed the Fashion Industry*. Santa Barbara, CA: ABC-CLIO.

8. Inc, P. F. (2022, November 19). And You Don't Stop: 30 Years of Hip Hop—Episode 1 library # 9051. *Vimeo*. Retrieved November 19, 2022, from https://vimeo.com/376910942

9. Kitwana, B. (2008). *The Hip Hop Generation: Young Blacks and the Crisis in African American Culture*. Jackson, MS: Civitas Books.

10. Kitwana, Bakari. (2005). *The Hip Hop Generation: Young Blacks and the Crisis in African American Culture*. New York: Basic Civitas Books, 2005.

11. Siliezar, J. (2020, October 21). Hiphop's Long History of Exposing Police Brutality. *Harvard Gazette*. Retrieved November 23, 2022, from https://news.harvard.edu/gazette/story/2020/07/hiphops-long-history-of-exposing-police-brutality/

12. Rose, Tricia. (1991). "Fear of a Black Planet": Rap Music and Black Cultural Politics in the 1990s. *The Journal of Negro Education*, 60 (3): 276–90.

13. Wynona, J. (2020, April 3). "A Brief History of Hip Hop Rivalries and Why They're No Longer Relevant—Office Hrs." https://medium.com/@writeronthe radio/a-brief-history-of-hip-hop-rivalries-and-why-theyre-no-longer-relevant -office-hrs-e0a798ca60c8

14. "Lovebug Starski" was a Bronx-based rapper at the time. Adding "ski" (or "snow") to one's rap moniker implied resonance with the now burgeoning cocaine trade. Lovebug is sometimes attributed with having coined the phrase "hip-hop."

15. WordWeaver, MC. "Run–D.M.C. Signed Hip Hop's First Endorsement Deal with Adidas." *Beats, Rhymes & Lists*, July 11, 2021. https://beats-rhymes-lists .com/facts/run-dmc-signed-hip-hop-first-endorsement-deal-adidas/

16. National Urban League. (n.d.). About. Retrieved November 25, 2022, from https://nul.org/about

17. Williams, C. L. (2020, June 24). How the New Jack Swing Movement Redefined an Era. *Pop Matters*. Retrieved December 19, 2022, from https://www.popmatters.com/new-jack-swing-1991-2495947856.html

18. Howell, James C., and Elizabeth A. Griffiths. (2018). *Gangs in America's Communities*. Newbury Park, CA: SAGE Publications Inc.

19. Brown, M. (2021, September 29). Ice Cube's Message is Starting to be Heard Over the Shocking Words. *Baltimore Sun*. Retrieved December 18, 2022, from https://www.baltimoresun.com/news/bs-xpm-1993-12-24-1993358062-story.html

20. Chang, Jeff. (2006). *Can't Stop Won't Stop: A History of the Hip-Hop Generation*. New York: Picador USA.

21. Kennedy, G. (2018, January 13). The Moment N.W.A. Changed the Music World. *Los Angeles Times*. Retrieved November 23, 2022, from https://www.latimes.com/entertainment/music/la-et-ms-nwa-parental-discretion-20171205-htmlstory.html

22. Morris, M. (2014). Authentic Ideals of Masculinity in Hip-Hop Culture: A Contemporary Extension of the Masculine Rhetoric of the Civil Rights and Black Power Movements. *Sydney Undergraduate Journal of Musicology*, 4: 26–40.

23. To be fair to Tupac, he also wrote 1993's "Keep Ya Head Up":

> since we all came from a woman
> Got our name from a woman and our game from a woman (yeah, yeah)
> I wonder why we take from our women
> Why we rape our women, do we hate our women? (Why? Why?)
> I think it's time to kill for our women (why? Why? Why? Why?)
> Time to heal our women, be real to our women
> And if we don't, we'll have a race of babies
> That will hate the ladies, that make the babies (oh, yeah, baby)
> And since a man can't make one
> He has no right to tell a woman when and where to create one
> So will the real men get up
> I know you're fed-up ladies, but keep your head up

Perhaps proof that as much a gangsta rap touted "The Real," it also contained a whole lot of posturing it could turn right around and contradict!

24. Rose, T. (2008). *The Hip Hop Wars: What We Talk about When We Talk about Hip Hop*. New York: Basic Civitas.

25. Oppenheim, Jamie. (2020, February 28). Historian Explores "Gangsta" Rap Origins in New Book. *SF State News*. Retrieved December 15, 2022, from https://news.sfsu.edu/archive/news-story/historian-explores-gangsta-rap-origins-new-book.html

26. Wallmark, Zachary, and Melinda Latour. (2018). *The Relentless Pursuit of Tone*. Oxford: Oxford University Press.

27. Quinn, E. (2005). *Nuthin' but a "G" Thang: The Culture and Commerce of Gangsta Rap*. New York: Columbia University Press.

28. Williams, Justin A. (2013). *Rhymin' and Stealin': Musical Borrowing in Hip-Hop*. University of Michigan Press, 2013. https://doi.org/10.3998/mpub.3480627.

29. Kelley, F. (2010, August 2). Biggie Smalls: The Voice That Influenced a Generation. *NPR*. Retrieved March 8, 2023, from https://www.npr.org/2010/08/02/128916682/biggie-smalls-the-voice-that-influenced-a-generation

30. Grem, Darren E. (2006). "The South Got Something to Say": Atlanta's Dirty South and the Southernization of Hip-Hop America. *Southern Cultures*, 12 (4): 55–73.

31. NPR. (2020, August 3). The South Got Something to Say: A Celebration of Southern Rap (1995–1999). Retrieved November 26, 2022, from https://www.npr.org/2020/08/03/896254950/the-south-got-something-to-say-a-celebration-of-southern-rap-1995-1999

32. Lindsey, Shawn. (2012, August 29). Houston PBS UH Moment: The "Chopped and Screwed" History of Houston Hip-Hop. *University of Houston*. https://www.uh.edu/news-events/stories/2012/august/08282012UHMDJScrew.php

33. Terich, J. (2021, October 15). How '90s Memphis Rap Tapes Gave Rise to a Chilling Legend. *Treble*. Retrieved December 19, 2022, from https://www.treblezine.com/memphis-rap-tapes-90s-chilling-legend/

34. Payne, O. (2016, July 16). How Dreamville Records Is Altering the Major Label Business Model. *Forbes*. Retrieved December 19, 2022, from https://www.forbes.com/sites/ogdenpayne/2016/04/22/how-dreamville-records-is-altering-the-major-label-business-model/?sh=70bede6b6e39

Three

"Harder, Better, Faster, Stronger" (Daft Punk, The Neptunes)
An Examination of the Master Producers

If you're a fan of hip-hop, then you've heard of "producers" being spoken of in reverent tones. All commercial music involves "producers," but hip-hop producers tend to be more publicly known and discussed than in other forms of popular music. We're going to take this chapter to describe the role of the producer in hip-hop. We'll also discuss notable producers and notable work by producers in hip-hop history.

A Producer's Role

So, what is the producer's job? Well, that's a slightly more complicated answer than I wish it were (and part of why it gets a whole chapter), but a producer is, essentially, the creative director of the music. In film and theatre, the producer often assembles the financing of a work and the team which creates it. This is more often the role of a label or executive producer in music but can be the role of the producer. More likely the label hires the producer to work with the recording artist, and if it's a famous producer, they might end up making more money than the recording artist. (The same happens in movies—sometimes, a famous film director might make more than a lead actor.) Like the director of a film or play, the producer of hip-hop music makes artistic choices regarding composition, sound, technical matters, collaborative affairs, and even content, ideally collaborating generously with the recording artist themselves.

The producer is typically doing the "arranging," deciding what instruments, sounds, and artists fill out the melodies and give shape to the ideas of the original artist, and what notes those instruments will play. The music producer often employs "engineers" to work the actual boops and beeps in the studio (more about that in chapter 18), which determine a record's sounds, but the producer often has a big hand in those engineering matters, too. The producer typically "mixes" the album after the recording session as well, determining what sounds are brought to the forefront and potentially adding even more layers after the fact.

Are the producers composing and writing? Sometimes. *Sometimes* a lot and *sometimes* a little. They are sometimes "beat makers" who come up with the underlying tracks you might consider the most recognizable part of a song. This can also mean finding signature samples or adding live musicians, but the value of the beat can't be undersold. You've heard Nas's "NY State of Mind"? (1994). If you haven't, younghead, give a listen. The beat is pretty simple, including a drum, double bass, and a high piano plink that together became boom bap's boomiest bap, and it was most likely created by producer DJ Premier. Without that beat, that song isn't that song.

> "The beat inspires a storyline. Pretty much the moment you start vibing out the melody on the mic, I can start to hear where I want to take this song. Is this a moody song? Is this an upbeat song? So then I'll write lyrics that relate to that."
>
> —Raeshaun

Are producers engineering? Are they literally choosing equipment and setting up the studio and putting their hands on the knobs and sliders and keyboard and touchscreens? Sometimes. Sometimes a lot and sometimes a little. Do they have a hand in the dressing up and marketing of the work? Ditto. They can be paid on the front end (before the recording begins and for a set fee) or on the back end (with a cut of the proceeds). They often determine what songs end up on an album (insofar as albums still exist).

From project to project and producer to producer, the parameters of the role can fluctuate, but the fingerprint of the producer on the final work is more often than not quite apparent. Once you know that particular sound and style of a producer, it's likely you'll identify that fingerprint across their body of work regardless of the artist. If they're good, and if everyone in the collaboration is lucky, then thanks to the producer, the final work is greater than it might be otherwise.

Now that you know what a producer does, let's take a look at a handful of hip-hop's greatest producers—the beatmakers, hitmakers, and game changers that advanced the sound of the genre over the decades.

DJ Premier

I already mentioned DJ Premier, so let's start with him. DJ Premier was born in Houston and rose to fame in Brooklyn in the 1990s as part of the hardcore hip-hop duo Gang Starr. His discography as a producer includes collaboration with monster artists across decades and musical lines, working with or remixing work from everybody from Ice-T to Neneh Cherry to KRS-One to Nas to Janet Jackson to Branford Marsalis to Biggie to Jay-Z to J. Cole.

Notable evolution in hip-hop often comes when an innovator reaches a little further to find sounds or samples or to make a beat with a new (or interestingly retro) flavor. Known for his encyclopedic knowledge of music hip-hop and otherwise, DJ Premier can build a chorus of artists from jazz to soul to rap all in the same phrase. It's been said that "he would also sample Beatles covers, KRS-One's impression of an Emergency Broadcast tone, and the sound of analog dirt on vinyl. The grit was real."[1]

His work utilizing jazz earned him respect, including the respect of film director Spike Lee, who heard Gang Starr's "Manifest," which sampled Charlie Parker and Miles Davis's "A Night in Tunisia." Lee enlisted Premier as a producer on the soundtrack to Lee's 1990 film *Mo' Better Blues*, a musical comedy about a jazz trumpeter. The soundtrack was composed by Branford Marsalis, Terence Blanchard, and featured numbers by Gang Starr. Premier has made a career drawing connection between genres and likewise erasing the barriers. "Jazz came from the streets, hip-hop came from the streets," he says. "It's just a different language. It's all borne out of hard times, struggle, and the fight to have equality and things be better. To talk about the fucked-up things that go on in our community, when it comes to us being minorities. We've contributed so much to this planet to make it dope."[2]

Rick Rubin

Perhaps it's a controversial choice to include a man who is allegedly not a musician. In excerpts from a *60 Minutes* interview that perpetually seems to populate my social media feed, Rubin says he has "no technical ability. I know nothing about music. . . . I know what I like and what I don't like. And I'm decisive about what I like and what I don't like. . . . The confidence I have in my taste and my ability to express what I feel has proven helpful for artists."[3] Helpful indeed, if "helpful" is the right term for making a lot of people rich and famous on his Def Jam label and beyond. His legend and his eight Grammy awards aren't only for hip-hop; he's had a hand in the work of dozens of artists from the Chicks (Album of the Year 2007) to Adele (Album of the Year 2012) to Slayer to the Red Hot Chili Peppers to Imagine Dragons to Neil Young.

He began Def Jam as a teen, with a DIY aesthetic, creating recordings for his punk band Hose. However, he quickly made scene-y connections. In 1984, he officially launched Def Jam with then promoter Russel Simmons out of his New York University dorm room with a recording of LL Cool J's "I Need a Beat." Soon after, he convinced a punk band that had created some novelty rap work into becoming a rap act . . . and the Beastie Boys were born! He signed Public Enemy. He produced LL's "Radio." He signed the Geto Boys. During the Def Jam era, Rubin also oversaw Run DMC's collaboration with Aerosmith on "Walk This Way," which became one of the biggest mainstreaming (i.e., selling it to white people) moments of hip-hop history.

His approach is famously, if not infamously, hands off. His mixes are compressed and loud (this is a guy who produces the heavy metal bands

Slayer and Black Sabbath, after all) but his "sound" is virtually impossible to pin down or doesn't exist at all. The man has launched a lot of careers, sold a lot of records, erased a lot of genre lines (from the aforementioned Run DMC project to a latter-day reinvention of country legend Johnny Cash via Cash's cover of Nine Inch Nails "Hurt"), spurred a great deal of creativity, and even produced the producers, producing Jay-Z's "99 Problems."

Timbaland

Next up: multihyphenate artist best known as a writer-producer Timbaland. His (oodles of) multiplatinum albums have earned him a slew of awards for his work with various top pop artists in the world since coming on the scene in the 1990s. The Virginia-born Timothy Zachery Mosley's sound is unmistakable and had immediate resonance with listeners: "In August 1996, Timbaland shocked the world with [the single "Pony"] from Ginuwine's debut album, The Bachelor, marking the producer's continued success within the realm of R&B. Using a mix of quirky sound effects and pairing them with kicks, snares and synths, Timbo crafted a sound bed unlike anything R&B fans had heard to that point, helping jumpstart Ginuwine's career, as well as his own."[4]

It's those unique rhythmic patterns and dizzying display of sound effects, found sounds, and exotic instruments that make a Timbaland project interesting whether he's working with a hip-hop icon like Jay-Z or an alt-rock refugee like Chris Cornell. The man is going to get creative with the beat:

> What had swung before began to stutter and syncopate in ways that felt both ancient and completely new. Listen to the hi-hat in a song like Aaliyah's "One in a Million"—the patterns pause, and come back doubled and tripled, closer to tap dancing than to any dull timekeeping. Then the innovations began to bloom in size and style. Aaliyah's "Are You That Somebody?" is among the most significant singles of the nineties: the beat refuses to fully engage, using more dead space than you would have

thought possible in a hit. And it wasn't just because Timbaland performed a cross-rhythm of mouth noises—pops and clicks. (Oh, and there's a baby gurgling.) He was obviously heading somewhere else.[5]

Many of his collaborators, like former Mouseketeer and Ramen-haired boy bander Justin Timberlake, owe any hip-hop respectability they may have to Timbaland's magic in the studio. He's also the songwriting and producing partner of one of hip-hop's greatest female artists, Missy Elliot, and together the pair created the late Aaliyah's double-platinum "One in a Million," as well as Elliot's own career-establishing "Supa Dupa Fly." From Rihanna to Jessica Simpson to Ludacris, to Flo Rida to Sam Smith to Beyonce, Timbaland applied his signature sound of stuttering kick-drums and fascinating sonic finds to the work of, well, *a lot* of artists.

Dr. Dre

No one has defined the sound of California in the popular landscape more than André Romelle Young, aka Dr. Dre. (Now someone is out there saying—what about the Beach Boys? Yes, the Beach Boys can definitely claim the beaches, but Dr. Dre can claim the cities.) Dre started out as club DJ and a member of the Los Angeles electro group World Class Wreckin' Cru, then went on (along with fellow Wreckin' Cru member) DJ Yella to link up with Ice Cube, Eazy-E, MC Ren, and Arabian Prince to form N.W.A., popularizing gangsta rap in the process. After Dre's acrimonious split from NWA and Reckless Records, he moved on to Death Row Records. For a time, Dre was co-owner of Death Row with the infamous Marion "Suge" Knight, where the release of his album *The Chronic* in 1993 made him a top-selling solo artist (he'd later have an even more acrimonious split from the dangerous Knight and would start his own label, Aftermath Entertainment). Clearly a man with an ear for talent, Dre introduced a number of major rappers to the mainstream, including Snoop Dogg, Eminem, and 50 Cent. He's a headphone mogul and elder statesman now, but in his golden age he perfected and popularized the sound known as G-gunk and put the West Coast on the hip-hop map.

So, what is G-funk? Well, the G is for "gangsta," and it's part of that scene, with violent lyrics about the life—and it samples and leans heavily (often favoring live instruments to samples) on "P-Funk," George Clinton's flamboyant musical collective Parliament-Funkadelic and other funk music of its era. While the East Coast had sampled heavily over the years from soul and disco, the eccentric sounds of G-funk gave a magical ironic twist to the tough themes of gangsta rap. G-funk is all about "slow hypnotic grooves, heavy bass, melodic synths and female backing vox. It's a sound that would come to dominate early to mid-'90s Hip Hop. Kanye West wrote of [Dre's solo debut], 'The Chronic is still the hip-hop equivalent to Stevie Wonder's Songs in the Key to Life. It's the benchmark you measure your album against if you're serious.'"[6] The Grammy-winning album spent eight months in the Billboard Top 10, peaking at number three and producing three top-forty singles. Snoop would appear on eleven of the album's sixteen tracks and in doing so, established himself as the "laid-back" icon of West Coast rap sound and culture: "Whilst it was late-'80s gangsta rap that launched the West Coast to national prominence, it was G-Funk that threatened to upend the NY-centric view of hip hop. The sun-soaked, synth-laden subgenre was tailor-made for drop tops and palm trees, a stylistic signature to the West as boom-bap was to the East."[7]

Pharrell Williams

A great performer and an ingenious producer, Pharrell wears a lot of hats, including a big one that looks like the Arby's sign. Pharrell is a juggernaut of twenty-first-century pop. If you are old enough, think back to 2013, which was the summer of the summer jam. If you aren't old enough—go, ask your mom about it. Remember that you couldn't get away from three bops; "Get Lucky," "Blurred Lines," and "Happy"? *All three of them* are Pharrell (he's also nearly fifty years old and looks fourteen . . . it does not crack, people. It does not crack).

When you think of Pharrell, you might think of Louis Vuitton, since he has recently become the men's creative director for the posh fashion brand. But as mentioned, his career began decades before. He first formed The Neptunes with partner Chad Hugo and they became a pop act in their own right (many years later they would add a third and become the band N*E*R*D). Interestingly, they released their debut album in two versions, one very electronic, one very rap-rock. Creativity was never in short supply. The Neptunes were discovered in Virginia Beach by the new jack swing era's producing genius Teddy Riley:

> Riley took the duo under his wing, and they became acolytes of the Teddy Riley school of production. Pharrell earned one of his earliest production credits for Wreckx-N-Effect's 1992 hit "Rump Shaker," writing Riley's verse and helping out with production. From then on out, Pharrell would have a hand in many of Riley's biggest productions, including SWV's "Right Here" (those are his backing vocals on the Human Nature Radio Mix) and Blackstreet's "Tonight's The Night."[8]

But when the Neptunes (Pharrell and Hugo) produced Britney Spears's 2001 single "Slave 4U," their career as major hit makers was officially off to the races. They produced "Hot in Here" (Nelly), Justin Timberlake's "Rock Your Body," and honestly, much of the iconic music of the day. "In fact, by 2003 The Neptunes had produced 43% of songs played on US radio. They had also produced approximately 20% of British songs played on British radio in 2003. Songs with Pharrell's name on them in 2003 included Timberlake's 'I'm Lovin It,' Kelis' 'Milkshake' and Snoop Dogg's 'Beautiful.'"[9] He even produced Jay-Z's famous "Change Clothes" on *The Black Album*, Jigga's farewell album that wasn't.

"The sound of a Pharrell production is unmistakable. A deceptively simple blend of hip-hop, funk and pop, he is primarily influenced by A Tribe Called Quest, Stevie Wonder, and his mixed Virginia background. His firm grasp of all of those genres means he can easily mix the three in a multitude of different combinations like a culinary chef."[10]

I'll point out that Pharrell has a well-known musical tic—he begins a huge portion of his songs the same way, looping the first beat of the first bar four times and then heading into the song. It seems to be his equivalent of a count-in or clacking drumsticks together. It certainly makes for a radio-friendly beginning, and seven of ten songs on his solo album *Girl* begin this way.[11] Honestly though, it doesn't diminish his genius. Once you're past his formulaic opening, he opens a beautifully harmonic world of neo-soul married to rich beats.

Kanye West

Performer, producer, writer, provocateur—Kanye West is a challenging artist to discuss. At the time of this writing, he's better known for puzzling political stunts and upsetting anti-Semitic social media remarks than for music making, but over the past twenty-five years he went a long way to taking hip-hop out of a cynical late gangsta rap swamp into a more sophisticated sound with more sophisticated subject matter in the twenty-first century. Kanye is known for incorporating orchestras, and vocal melody (often heavily autotuned ... in fact, pause your reading, turn on his album *808s & Heartbreak*, and then come back to finish this chapter). In his later work, Yeezy (Kanye has *a lot* of nicknames) incorporates a great deal of gospel music in his beats.

Ye appeared on Roc-A-Fella Records (Jay-Z's label) and established the sound of post Bad Boy era (Diddy's label, with Biggie as his biggest artist) New York hip-hop. Along with producers Just Blaze and Heatmakerz, he created a new sound now known as "chipmunk soul," using pitched-up soul samples (and later pitched-up samples from all manner of sources). It's a goofy sound, and Chaka Khan did *not* like that West chipmunked a sample of her song "Through the Fire" on his broken-jaw opus "Through the Wire"—but the sound was everywhere at the time and twenty years later still appears in hip-hop songs.

Yeezus's (yet *another* nickname) "college trilogy" of studio albums, 2004's *The College Dropout*, 2005's *Late Registration*, and 2007's *Graduation*, would form both a sonically and thematically important cultural trifecta:

West filled an as-yet-unnoticed void in rap music and hip-hop culture. The hip-hop audience, apparently tiring of an endless string of interchangeable gangster rappers, found Kanye West's college boy image and intellectual musical narrative a refreshing change. [Fellow Chicago rapper] Rhymefest was not surprised at this as he cites Kanye's mom [the late Donda West] as heavily influencing the rapper's voice. So what she did was say, "Hey, you know, I think it would sound better if you kind of moved into the realm of . . . talking about . . . what means something to you and, your family life, and not just . . . money and just this and that," and what's interesting is when she would talk like that, Kanye would stop everything and look at her like God was speaking.[12]

Donda West's maternal guidance as well as her untimely death would heavily affect Kanye's musical choices.

While hip-hop has always used melody, earlier hip-hop melodies primarily came from samples employed choruses sung by collaborative artists. Kanye changed the game when he began to incorporate auto-tune. "He had a formula, and it was working, but then he pivoted into a completely new direction. Kanye's auto-tune era, signaled by *808s & Heartbreak*, changed the game forever, inspiring a generation of artists making introspective, melodic rap music."[13]

Playing with vocals, heavily auto-tuned melody (particularly on his 2008 *808s & Heartbreak*), synth that evoked human voice, the human voice manipulated into synth-like sounds, and the use of a choir or choirs are hallmarks of West's work. This includes his Sunday Service Choir, used heavily in 2019's *Jesus is King*—a controversial album focused on Christian themes. By 2019, Ye was a controversial being, having declared that he would no longer take medication for his bipolar disorder, and for his dive into the culture of far-right wing media and politics.

His producorial prowess hasn't been limited to his own studio work, of course. Ye has produced the best of the best, from Beyonce and Mr.

Beyonce ("03 Bonnie and Clyde") to some of the best work by Drake ("Feel No Way"), Alicia Keys ("You Don't Know My Name"), Common ("Go!"), and Rihanna and Paul McCartney ("FourFiveSeconds").

It seems unlikely that a return to form is in the cards for West, but as trap-based hip-hop reaches a similar place to the one gangsta rap inhabited in the early 2000s, the musical landscape is set for another such innovator to appear. There are certainly some folx at the top of their game right now, such as Beat Butcha (producing for Chance the Rapper and Benny the Butcher), Tay Keith (producing for Lil Durk and Cardi B), Jahaan Sweet (producing for Kendrick Lamar and Beyonce), Jasper Harris (producing for Future and Post Malone), Metro Boomin (producing for Migos, Future, and Drake), and Take A Day Trip (producing for Kid Cudi, Lil Nas X, and Youngboy), just to name a few. What's for certain is that creativity and innovation in hip-hop continues to flow. Who will be next? Only time will tell.

Notes

1. Tompkins, D. (2017, December 20). Where We Dwell: How DJ Premier Changed the Sound of Hip-Hop in New York. *Vulture*. Retrieved January 28, 2023, from https://www.vulture.com/2017/12/how-dj-premier-changed-hip-hop.html

2. Weiner, Natalie. (2015, December 9). DJ Premier Discusses the Seven Jazz Albums Every Hip-Hop Head Needs to Know. *VICE*. Retrieved January 28, 2023, from https://www.vice.com/en/article/6azykz/dj-premier-favorite-jazz-records-joey-badass-golden-era-premiere

3. CBS News. (2023, January 17). 1/15/2023: Star Power, Hide and Seek, the Guru. *CBS News*. Retrieved January 29, 2023, from https://www.cbsnews.com/video/60minutes-2023-01-15/

4. Brown, Preezy. (2018, November 21). The Produce Section: 13 of Timbaland's Most Iconic Beats. *REVOLT*. Retrieved February 20, 2023, from https://www.revolt.tv/article/2018-11-21/95745/the-produce-section-13-of-timbalands-most-iconic-beats/

5. Frere-Jones, S. (2008, September 29). The Timbaland Era. *The New Yorker*. Retrieved February 20, 2023, from https://www.newyorker.com/magazine/2008/10/06/the-timbaland-era

6. *Rolling Stone*. (n.d.). 500 Greatest Albums of All Time. https://www.rs500albums.com/50-1/37

7. Herbert, C. (2019, June 17). Anatomy of the Funk: G-Funk Deconstructed. *CentralSauce Collective*. Retrieved February 19, 2023, from https://centralsauce.com/g-funk-producers-samples

8. Bierut, P. (2022, April 5). Pharrell Williams: From Music N*E*R*D to Pop's Top Producer. *uDiscover Music*. Retrieved March 8, 2023, from https://www.udiscovermusic.com/stories/pharrell-williams-best-producer/

9. Walters, M. (2014, July 16). When He Was 12 Pharrell Went to Band Camp and Met Someone That Would Hugely Impact His Future. *Capital XTRA*. Retrieved January 29, 2023, from https://www.capitalxtra.com/artists/pharrell-williams/lists/the-most-influential-man-in-music/band-camp/

10. Evans, N. (2021, January 19). Why Pharrell Is the Greatest Producer of All Time. *KEYMAG*. Retrieved January 29, 2023, from https://www.keymag.co.uk/features/modernmavens/pharrell-williams

11. Mrdiscopop. (2020, December 29). Is Pharrell Williams Incapable of Writing Intros? Retrieved January 29, 2023, from https://blog.discopop.co.uk/2014/05/is-pharrell-williams-incapable-of.html

12. Bailey, J. (2015). *The Cultural Impact of Kanye West*. London: Palgrave Macmillan.

13. Hrose, Jordan, Jessica McKinney, Andre Gee, and Eric Skelton. (n.d.). How Ye Changed Music. *Complex*. Retrieved January 28, 2023, from https://www.complex.com/music/kanye-west-changed-music

Four

"Top Notch" (City Girls Featuring Fivio Foreign)

Hip-Hop's Rise to the Top, 2000–Present

The most recent twenty-plus years of music history account for the time in which hip-hop took its seat on the throne of popular music. To observe hip-hop's rise to "royalty," let's play a little game called "drop the needle" (a reference to the needle dropping on a record, which seems appropriate with the comeback of vinyl). We'll go into the middle of a few decades to look at what sounds, styles, and artists dominated the music sales charts.

Before we drop that needle though, it's worth noting that the relationship between hip-hop and the charts raises some challenging issues. When we talk about "the charts," we're generally talking about *Billboard*, a weekly magazine featuring, among other things, charts related to the industry performance of music. *Billboard* got its start in 1894 as a trade magazine for bill posters (literally the folks sticking up ads for, like, the circus). When you track entertainment through America's intricate and troubled history, from circus posters to sheet music to juke boxes and radio to MTV and streaming, it gets very, very complicated. It makes sense, then, for those challenges to carry over to American popular music, which has a multicentury history of being invented by Black people, stolen, and monetized by white people.

"Black music, more specifically Hip Hop, has been underrepresented on Billboard's charts. Black music has gone through a variation of names; . . . artists like LL Cool J, Salt-N-Pepa, DMX, and Wu-Tang Clan were considered R&B acts by Billboard's standards. As Hip-hop grew in popularity, it lapped other genres like rock and pop, but just wouldn't be recognized by any of the major platforms."[1] You don't have any charts for Black music until *Billboard*'s "Harlem Hit Parade" started in 1942. "Harlem's Hit Parade" was a chart that tracked sales in record stores in the Harlem neighborhood of New York. Just as the Beastie Boys topped rap sales in the 1980s, your first top dog on the Harlem Hit Parade was Bing Crosby singing "White Christmas." Much of the rest of the chart was Black folks, though. The name of this chart changed many times since then, from the oh so charming "Race Records" (1945–1949), to various titles using the term "Rhythm & Blues" (1949–1969), switching to "Soul" (1969–1982), to the telling "Hot Black Singles" (1982–1990), then back to playing with the term "R&B" (1990–1999), to "Hot R&B/Hip-Hop" singles and tracks (1999–2005), and as of 2023, "Hot R&B/Hip-Hop Songs."

The segregation of the charts represents the segregation of how music was marketed and sold. Music by Black artists was only promoted via Black channels, and if it *really* hit, it was marketed to the "mainstream." The handling of megastar Michael Jackson changed all that to some degree, when *Off the Wall* (1979) was promoted everywhere: to pop radio and R&B radio, and to white and Black magazines,[2] and it ended up topping the Hot Soul Singles charts and nearly conquering the Billboard Hot 100. *Off the Wall* set a record for an album by a solo artist with *four* top ten (Hot 100) singles: "Don't Stop Til You Get Enough," "Off the Wall," "Rock with You," and "She's Out of My Life."[3] However, not all artists are going to get the "King of Pop" treatment.

"Don't Stop 'Til You Get Enough" and "Rock with You," followed by "Off The Wall"

Segregation always means separate and never means equal. To have a Black department and a pop department is never going to work out in the marginalized music's favor. The effort, the budget, the manpower, will never be the same across those departments. So, do you get rid of the Black categories? Do you get rid of the pop categories? The best answer is both: "To get rid of the 'urban' category while not wiping out 'pop' simultaneously amounts to a new frosting on the same old cake—preserving a system in which Adele and Jazmine Sullivan could sing the exact same song with identical power and grace, but Adele's version will go straight into every supermarket across the country, while Sullivan's will be pushed only to black listeners in select cities."[4]

1975

The charts, even in their historical problematic form, still have something to say. So, let's take a deeper look. Rap in the 1970s wasn't yet a national enough phenomenon for the radio, the charts, nor the suburbs to take much notice, but the 1980s are a different story. Some of the very classic OG rap songs we've already mentioned did well on the Hot Soul/R&B/Hot Black charts, but even "Rapper's Delight" (Sugar Hill Gang), "The Breaks" (Kurtis Blow), "The Message" (Grandmaster Flash & the Furious Five), and "Planet Rock" (Afrika Bambaataa @ the Soulsonic Force), only rose to number four (and peaked much lower on the Hot 100). The only rap number ones in the 1980s were "I Need Love" (LL Cool J) and "My, Myself, & I" (De La Soul) in the late 1980s, and then still only on the Hot Black chart.

1985

Let's get to the drop the needle game and go to the middle of the decade, where the top selling sounds of 1985 according to the Billboard Year-End Hot 100 Singles were very light rock, or grocery-store-playlist-friendly R&B. If you want to get an idea of this sound, listen to Foreigner's "I Want to Know What Love Is," Wham!'s "Careless Whisper," or if you truly want a time capsule piece, listen to USA for Africa's "We Are the World." There are also some new wavey bops like a-ha's "Take on Me" and some then scandalous hits with Madonna's "Like a Virgin." Yes, there were some Black folks on there, but Whitney's "Saving All My Love For You" and Lionel Richie's "Say You, Say Me" (and don't get me wrong, I love me some Whitney), weren't out to revolutionize any sounds or categorization systems. As you can see, there's no rap. Twenty-six out of the one hundred songs are by Black artists (Tina Turner, DeBarge, and Kool and the Gang are on their more than once) and including USA for Africa since Michael and Lionel put that one together.

1995

Now let's jump to 1995 . . . what a difference a decade makes. Nielsen's SoundScan was introduced in 1991, making retail music sales tracking more accurate, and that accuracy bumped rap up both the R&B charts and the Hot 100. The number one song from 1995 was Coolio's "Gangsta's Paradise." Biggie appears in four different Top 100 songs (on two of his own tracks and in appearances with Junior M.A.F.I.A. and Total). Dre appears. Obviously so does Tupac. So does Method Man. Luniz with "I Got 5 On It." Bone Thugs. Chicago's Da Brat (who had three major singles on her album *Funkdafied* and was the first female rapper with a platinum album). AZ. 20 Fingers featuring Gillette. Naughty by Nature. 69 Boyz with "Tootsee Roll." Skee-Lo with "I Wish." Shaggy. Eighteen songs one would definitively call rap songs, and R&B is everywhere (Brandy is huge). New jack swing is all over the list, with Boyz II Men appearing four times and TLC appearing three times.

2005

Fast forward another decade to 2005 and drop the needle again. Now fifty-three of the songs, more than half, are rap songs or R&B songs featuring rap or a rapper. Sixty-one songs are by Black artists (down from the 1990s glory days of new jack swing, R&B, and the East Coast/West Coast flap), and a number of songs by non-Black artists are rap songs (Eminem) or definitely hip-hop oriented (like Gwen Stefani's "Hollaback Girl").

Drop the needle in the mid-2000s, well, actually . . . you wouldn't drop the needle, because digital music quickly became the preferred method of music purchasing and radio play and physical media went into freefall. *Billboard*, however, factored in digital sales for the Hot 100, but *not* for the R&B/Hip-Hop chart until 2012, leaving the numbers prior to that change very suspect.

2015

Now, here's where categorization becomes tougher . . . almost all sung songs have hip-hop beats and production. All the hip-hop seeming songs are very sung. How to label The Weeknd? Drake? Sure, Ed Sheeran is definitely white, but a lot of the Top 100 artists have 23 and Me's as beautifully complex as their soundscapes. In 2015, I'd still call about half the songs mostly hip-hop, even with country music all over the chart (is this cultural pushback? I'm not sure). But the takeaway is that hip-hop isn't the exception, and it isn't an invader from another chart. Folx, we're looking at over twenty years of hip-hop songs being most of the chart. In 2017, Nielsen Soundscan, the system used to determine Billboard's chart, officially declared that hip-hop was the top selling genre in the United States.[5] Toto, we aren't in 1985 anymore.

So, why was hip-hop able to make this breakthrough? How did pop and hip-hop become synonymous? First, on a nuts-and-bolts level, music consumption was being tracked differently (i.e., more accurately), and in a way that allowed hip-hop to rightfully shine. In 2014, Billboard switched to a system that looked at a lot more than just record sales, factoring in the streaming mechanisms like iTunes. These streaming services were favored by youth and was where much of hip-hop was being found and listened to.[6] It's now hard to imagine claiming that you're ranking the popularity of music when you're only taking into account people walking into a Barnes & Noble and buying physical media. *The Vancouver Sun* asked *Billboard* for specifics: "Using [Ariana] Grande as an example. For the Billboard 200 chart ending on Nov. 9, her latest album My Everything sat at No. 36. Under the new methodology, it would have landed at No. 9 . . . among the losers in the revamped system would have been Barbra Streisand, who would have fallen out of the Top 10: Apparently her fans don't listen to as much streaming music."[7]

By 2017, when hip-hop was officially recognized as the most profitable and the most listened to form of popular music, Cardi B was beating out Taylor Swift. "It was kind of a 'Well, duh,' moment," says Ross Scarano, *Billboard* vice president of content. "Rap has been the most dominant force in American culture for years."[8] The new tracking system better reflected what music was being consumed. "We didn't change anything," notes Kevin "Coach K" Lee, one of the founders of revered Atlanta label Quality Control, about why rap is hitting its stride now. "We just kept it real. It just started connecting. Now it's going to start expanding."[9]

Pop Culture Dominance

Tastes have changed, music has changed, the charts have changed. And what's gone down on the hip-hop side? A whole lot, especially when we remember that almost everything is hip-hop, or hip-hop adjacent. It's very hard not to call most R&B singers and most boy and girl bands hip-hop (or at least hip-hop-ish). Think about this when you listen to their beats, production, and vocabulary, and when you look at the dance style and wardrobe. This is true even if they're not rapping, and regardless of their heritage.

The early 2000s are sometimes referred to as the "Bling Era," mostly after a phrase popularized by rapper Lil Wayne's verse in rapper B.G.'s 1999 song "Bling Bling." This term seems like an appropriate name given the amount of treasure flowing through the hip-hop world.

If you aren't convinced that hip-hop sits on the iron throne, then think about pop culture beyond music, and you will immediately see hip-hop's influence. Eminem from Detroit drops *The Slim Shady LP* in 1999 and *The Marshall Mathers LP* in 2000, and he has an Oscar by 2002. Dr. Dre produced this album, but by this time he's no longer releasing his own albums and as the decade goes on, he becomes . . . a headphone mogul with his Beats brand.

50 Cent from Queens released a mixtape on Eminem's Shady Records, then released the nine-time platinum *Get Rich or Die Tryin'* in 2003 and

became a new major player. These days he's still recording, and he's starred and executive produced his own long-running television show, "Power."

Brooklyn's Jay-Z, a rapper and producer and mega-entrepreneur, would become a pillar of pop culture over the next two decades, and by 2019, *Forbes* was calling him the first hip-hop billionaire. Yes, I said billionaire with a "b." Jay-Z (born Shawn Carter) began releasing albums on his own label in 1996, and now runs his own clothing retailer, entertainment company, sports bar enterprise, liquor brand(s), cannabis product line, the Tidal streaming service, and much, much more. In 2008, he became the first hip-hop headliner of the Glastonbury festival *and* married Beyoncé, the queen of twenty-first-century American music. He's won dozens of Grammys, made the most Billboard number one albums by any solo artist (sorry, Elvis), and was a frequent guest of the Obama White House.

Meanwhile, Back at the Ranch

What else was happening? More importantly, *who* else was happening? Well, as mentioned in our discussion of regions, the Dirty South rises to compete with or even eclipse the East and West coast sounds, including College Park Atlanta's OutKast and Memphis's Three 6 Mafia (all this prior to the rise of trap).

In 2004, Chicago's Kanye West released *The College Dropout*, which did a lot to push hip-hop into a more musically adventurous style. Kanye, who had already been producing for major figures such as Jay-Z, sampled and fused a great deal of gospel, electronic, classical, and rock into his music, rapped in a variety of styles and tempi, and added a lot of singing to his tracks, such as it was.

The late 2000s are sometimes called the "ringtone era," when some rap one-hit wonders like D4L or Huey rose to fame from one-off sales of tunes for cell phone ringtones. The ringtone era overlaps with the "blog era" in which underground and alternative rap found its audience through new channels via the internet. Rappers could gain popularity and prove they had a fanbase through their mentions on fan-based sites like WorldStarHipHop, 2DopeBoyz, or YouHeardThatNew, and leverage that into deals with labels.

New superstars like J Cole, Wiz Khalifa, Soldier Boy, or Chicago's Chance the Rapper (with his digital mixtape *Acid Rap*) came up this way.

Canadian rapper Drake, formerly a teen television actor, released his first mixtape in 2006, and now he's a genre unto himself and a global draw with a record thirty-four Billboard Music Awards. He was even personally responsible for 5 percent of the City of Toronto's tourism revenue in 2018.[10]

Caught in the Trap

And trap? That's a form of hip-hop that's come to dominate the sound in the 2010s and 2020s. It got its start in Atlanta, and the term seems to have several origins, but likely refers to Southern slang for a house where drugs are purchased. The subject of the songs during this era of trap tend to revolve around drug sales and the grim side of life in the hood. Musically, it's a fairly paired down form with emphasis on snare and an ever-present hi-hat cymbal. T.I. popularized the term, and notable trap artists include Gucci Mane, Playboy Carti, Young Thug, and Young Jeezy. A number of number one hits have been influenced by trap's sound, including hits by artists you wouldn't call trap rappers like pop performer Ariana Grande ("7 Rings") and Beyoncé ("Bow Down"), as well as country crossover work like Billy Ray Cyrus and Lil Nas X's once-inescapable "Old Town Road."

The Queens of Rap

The last ten-plus years of hip-hop rap have been the best decade ever for female artists. Nicki Minaj's *Pink Friday* dropped in 2010 and opened up new space for women to better represent themselves however they'd like and discuss whatever they'd like. Her lyrical prowess and razor-sharp flow are undeniable. She vacillates seamlessly between rap and singing (which is a nod to her training at New York City's LaGuardia High School of Music and Art and Performing Arts) and is as comfortable exchanging bars with Ariana Grande or Beyoncé as she is going head-to-head with Drake and Lil Wayne. Women in hip-hop have historically been expected to look (and act) within certain parameters, like "one of the guys" (e.g., MC Lyte, Missy

Elliott) or the hypersexualized kitten (e.g., Lil Kim, Trina). But, following in the vein of Lauryn Hill and Eve, Minaj breaks from tradition.[11]

In the years since, the field has blossomed with major female acts, from Cardi B to Megan Thee Stallion to Saweetie to Doja Cat. In 2020, rapper, singer, and flutist Lizzo was loaned a crystal flute by the Library of Congress which she played on stage. The flute was crafted in 1813 for President James Madison in honor of his second inauguration, and Lizzo became one of very few people to ever have played it. A Black female hip-hop icon in a sparkling bodysuit playing a priceless flute made for a president who at one time owned more than a hundred slaves? That's legendary.

As a final jewel on the crown, I'll mention that 2017's *DAMN* by Compton's Kendrick Lamar became the first hip-hop album, in fact the first album that wasn't classical or jazz, to win the Pulitzer Prize for Music, administered by Columbia University. Yup, the Pulitzer freaking Prize.

It's hip-hop's world and the rest of music is just living in it.

Notes

1. Staff, D. X. (2021, February 19). The Complicated Black History of Billboard's Hip Hop & R&B Charts. *HipHopDX*. Retrieved December 28, 2022, from https://hiphopdx.com/news/id.60686/title.the-complicated-black-history-of-billboards-hip-hop-rb-charts

2. Mitchell, G., and M. Newman. (2009, July 6). How Michael Jackson's "Thriller" Changed Music Business. *Reuters*. Retrieved December 28, 2022, from https://www.reuters.com/article/us-jackson-thriller/how-michael-jacksons-thriller-changed-music-business-idUSTRE56300320090706

3. Simmons, Ken. (2017, March 18). "Nine Reasons Why Michael Jackson's 'off the Wall' Album Was Epic." LiveAbout. https://www.liveabout.com/michael-jacksons-off-the-wall-album-2851669#:~:text=Produced%20by%20Quincy%20Jones%2C%20with,Enough%22%20and%20%22Rock%20with%20You

4. Leight, E. (2020, June 17). "Separate and Unequal": How "Pop" Music Holds Black Artists Back. *Rolling Stone*. Retrieved December 28, 2022, from https://www.rollingstone.com/music/music-features/the-problem-with-pop-1013534/

5. Reuters Staff. (2018, January 4). Hip Hop and R&B Surpass Rock as Biggest U.S. Music Genre. *Reuters*. Retrieved December 28, 2022, from https://www.reuters.com/article/us-music-2017/hip-hop-and-rb-surpass-rock-as-biggest-u-s-music-genre-idUSKBN1ET258

6. Billboard Staff. (2014, November 20). Billboard 200 Makeover: Album Chart to Incorporate Streams & Track Sales. *Billboard*. Retrieved January 2, 2023, from https://www.billboard.com/pro/billboard-200-makeover-streams-digital-tracks/

7. Yahr, Emily. (2014, November 24). Billboard Overhauls Metrics for Musical Success. *Vancouver Sun*. Retrieved January 2, 2023, from https://vancouversun.com/entertainment/music/billboard-overhauls-metrics-for-musical-success/wcm/b4fcba84-5cd4-440e-998e-b9917264a4dc/

8. Bruner, R. (2018, January 25). Kendrick Lamar to Migos: How Rap Became Sound of Mainstream. *Time*. Retrieved January 2, 2023, from https://time.com/5118041/rap-music-mainstream/

9. Bruner, R. (2018, January 25). Kendrick Lamar to Migos: How Rap Became Sound of Mainstream. *Time*. Retrieved January 2, 2023, from https://time.com/5118041/rap-music-mainstream/

10. Stutz, C. (2018, July 6). Drake is Responsible for 5% of Toronto's Tourism Economy, Expert Finds. *Billboard*. Retrieved January 1, 2023, from https://www.billboard.com/music/rb-hip-hop/drake-5-percent-toronto-tourism-economy-expert-8464298/

11. Krishnamurthy, S. (2018, October 3). Nicki Minaj is the 21st Century's Insatiable Hip-Hop Monarch. *NPR*. Retrieved January 1, 2023, from https://www.npr.org/2018/10/03/651761719/nicki-minaj-is-the-21st-centurys-insatiable-hip-hop-monarch

Five

The Big Bang (Busta Rhymes)
A Roadmap to Rap Styles

"A song that's 'Important' is a song that changes the route of the music or introduces a new element to the music.... Important songs birth new things: new rappers, new groups, eventually new movements altogether.... Picture it like branches on a tree. Rap started out in this straight line going up like a tree and then spread out into all these different things. The songs that caused those changes, they're important."[1]

When trying to think of styles, eras, and subgenres of rap, it's almost impossible to determine a concrete, irrefutable definition. For example, one could look at the evolution of rap chronologically. One could also think of it geographically (both dividing up the United States, as well as the world of rap). It could be grouped and subjectively put into major categories, arguing similarities and/or ties in the musical elements. You could even tie things together under the umbrella of lyrical content (then, would Roddy Ricch's "XXXX," Ice T's "6 in the Mornin'," and Schoolly D's "P.S.K. What Does it Mean?" be in the same category?). As you can see, things can become complicated quickly. A person could debate many given angles and be totally justified in their argument.

For the sake of keeping consistent with the majority of other sources, this will (mostly) be organized chronologically. I chose to write chronologically because I think it's fascinating to witness the overlap of new ideas throughout their evolution. It's incredibly innovative, shockingly creative, and somehow makes perfect sense. In other words, it seems destined.

At this point, it's important to note that there are so many subgenres of rap that discussing all of them in detail could (and should) be its own book. It's also important to note that genre, subgenre, era, types, and categories are not always defined by the same variables. Common variables include:

- Artist geographical location/affiliation
- Harmonic information
- Percussive patterns
- Groove
- Flow patterns
- Lyrical content
- Production quality

> **"Social media in my mind as it pertains to rap, like, killed the regional effect of rap. It's harder and harder and harder to know what a region sounds like, because everybody knows what's hot on social media. Like, if ATL music is hot on social media, there's going to be a bunch of people trying to make something that sounds like that."**
>
> —Noah

So please note this disclaimer here and now: this is by no means intended to be an all-inclusive list of subgenres. Hopefully the biggies are here (no pun intended), but please continue to listen and make your own decisions. Ultimately, this framework should help you understand how to listen for specific elements in rap, which will then hopefully make it easier to do yourself. Listening to the genres and seeing how they fit into the larger puzzle will also assist you in finding your own story and relationship to songs. The more you understand the chronological timeline of music and how things are related, the easier it will be to find yourself in the material.

So, without further ado, let's kick it, and kick it off with . . .

Old School

Old School rap is the OG—its artists are the reason you're even reading this book in the first place. Old School artists are the pioneers of rap, the ones who deserve to be mentioned when grandma makes us list the things we are grateful for at Thanksgiving dinner. Taking place from roughly 1979 to the mid-1980s, this period was the death of disco and the birth of hip-hop. In the mid-1970s disco was everywhere. While a lot of successful disco acts were comprised of African American performers, the fun, frothy, life-is-a-never-ending-party music didn't reflect the dark reality of Black life in America. Black pain was prominent, and racism and poverty were far too common (sound familiar? Sigh). The post-industrial decline, the political scene, and an extremely tough economy were unkind to everyone, but for marginalized communities who had less to begin with, well, the suffering was palpable. However, the disco craze hit a peak and jumped the shark, so to speak. This created an opening for hip-hop, which had already become a crucial means of expression, entertainment, identity, and survival for people since the moments surrounding DJ Kool Herc's party in 1973. The subject matter is generally lighter and more party focused both because rap originated from the hype man/MC-ing at parties, and because people's ears had been flooded with the party life lyrics of disco for a decade. The glam and outrageous fashion of disco carried over, as did the instrumentation that used disco and funk sampling. However, conscious rap was born here too, with Afrika Bambaataa, "When hip-hop lost its way, he added a fifth element = 'knowledge.'" Zulus, he explains, are about having "right knowledge, right wisdom, right 'overstanding' and right sound reasoning, meaning that we want our people to deal with factuality versus beliefs, factology versus beliefs." But some facts about his own life are slippery like quicksilver.[2] While the infamous crew Grandmaster Flash and the Furious Five lives here, it's important to know that they released a game-changing song which some think was the bridge into a new era for rap. Released in 1982, "The Message" openly discusses the challenging circumstances of the community. "The Message" is also formally ambitious, its verses gradually increasing in length and sonic intensity as the song progresses. The first verse lasts eight measures, the second eleven, the third thirteen, the fourth sixteen, and its final verse lasts a breathless twenty-eight measures. Mel's delivery is suddenly aggressive in this climactic verse as he opens with the couplet "A child is born with no state of mind / Blind to the ways of mankind." He then relates the harrowing story of a child who grows up without positive role models and dies in prison, a reflection of the isolating, nihilistic experience of growing up poor and black in the ghetto."[3] You might be familiar with its famous hook:

> It's like a jungle sometimes
> It makes me wonder how I keep from goin' under

Sound-wise, the rapping in Old School is generally simpler in structure and rhyme scheme. Words per bar are far fewer than more contemporary rap, sampling was common, and most cadence was in duple meter. Duple meter is when a measure of music has two beats per measure. For example, listen to the duple meter carried out in "The Message" by Grandmaster Flash and the Furious Five. As we are still very close, chronologically speaking, to both disco and funk, "Early 1980s dance-hall rap is generally rhythmically simplistic, with steady eighth notes forming predictable patterns and rhyme schemes."[4] The rap battle you read about in chapter 2 was also loud and proud during the Old School era—these didn't *only* happen in this era, but it's important to note that they were a prominent part of the Old School mechanism.

Artists to listen to in the Old School era:

- Kurtis Blow
- Afrika Bambaataa
- Grandmaster Flash and the Furious Five
- Funky 4+1
- Futura 2000
- Cold Crush Brothers
- Busy Bee
- Fatback Band

- Slick Rick
- Whodini

At this point, opinions start to differ regarding categorization and genre. It could be safe to label what comes next for rap as boom bap, or the Golden Age, but for purposes of doing a deeper dive, this chapter will break things down a bit further. With that line of reasoning, we'll be kickin' it to . . .

New School

In 1984, Shea Serrano, author of *The RAP Yearbook* coined Run DMC's "Sucker M.C.'s" to be the most important song of the year. In his explanation of why it's important, he says that "Sucker M.C.'s marks dual points in rap's evolution. . . . It's when rap parted itself between old and new (or uncool and cool, really), for the first time, and it's also the first time a [recorded] rap song could be described as a 'battle rap' song."[5] This was the jumping off point for rap to change it up musically. For example, drum machines became *the* thing (especially the 808 drum machine, which will be discussed shortly during the examination of boom bap), eliminating the need for live bands in the studio. It became about stripping down the flash. Rappers began dressing like their fans. They were wearing everyday, walking-down-the-street clothes, like the famous Run DMC jogging suits and Adidas sneakers. The songs themselves changed dramatically too. In addition to the use of the drum machine (sometimes it was *just* the drumbeat and the rap), this minimalist approach encompassed the lyrical subject matter as well. Life was most definitely not always a party for the Black American, and rap lyrics regularly became about real life. This could include the harsh realities of street life, but also racial and social injustice. A&R producer Dante Ross discusses the differences of this new era, "Musically, it had the had the aesthetic of Black punk rock, do-it-yourself music. I think a culmination of that was Run-DMC. They're yelling at you, and there's no music, just drums, a stab, and yelling Rapping super aggressive. It was so punk rock to me. It was the record that made me go, 'Punk rock's over. This is so much more punk than punk.'"[6]

Structure-wise, the songs were shorter to appeal to the inevitable success of rap on the radio. In general, the sound, the lyrics, the image, and the rappers had an edge that was anything but the past chic of disco. This edge was described as harsher and grittier, painting a more realistic view. Russell Simmons said, "I like real sounding music, real sounding instruments-even our drum machines sound hard. And I like loud music,"[7] and he also said "I want to make successful black heroes, like what I've tried to do with Run-D.M.C. and Kurtis. I didn't say 'positive' because that's a trap. It's got to be real."[8]

Artists to listen to in the New School era:

- Run DMC
- LL Cool J
- The Beastie Boys
- Salt-N-Pepa
- KRS-One

Boom Bap

More than an era, boom bap is a sound that spans several subgenres. It is arguably one of the most influential elements in rap history. It's common for people to think that boom bap is synonymous with rap. But if you said to a hip-hop fan, "I listen to boom bap," that fan would most likely not solely think of rap. Technically, boom bap is an element within the rap sound; it's an onomatopoeia, where a word sounds like its definition. Boom bap is a raw, beat-driven sound, specifically a kick and snare drum pattern. For sound to qualify as boom bap, the beats and lyrics are paramount: sampling can be present, but it is secondary to the kick and snare beats as well as the lyrics. It's hard not to nod your head to the beat when listening to boom bap (although I challenge you to try it). The Daydream Sound describes some 1990s boom bap as "Jeep music" saying:

> hip-hop was in the clubs but the music was more made for the cars. I mean, if you're from that era I'm sure you have vivid

memories of just hangin' out, on the block, and you would hear cars coming from a block away. You would hear bass, like, *ground shaking bass* from blocks away and as it came to you, you would recognize the song that the person was playing but if you're from that era you just know, it was an amazing time.

The roots of this term comes from a song called "It's yours" by T La Rock, one of Def Jam's 1st releases. . . . The MC literally says it to a pattern of the drums in the song, leaving the listener in no doubt. One of the next times it surfaced as part of a lyric in a hip-hop song was on A Tribe Called Quest's 1st album (Push it along), where Q Tip varies the "bap" for "Bip." The year the phrase really took root was 1993. As a guest on Tim Dog's "I get wrecked" Blastmaster KRS ONE mentions it. The next time the phrase emerges is arguably the solidification moment of the term in hip-hop. It may have been said in conversation, but not popularly so in print until the release of KRS one's album, "The Return of the Boom Bap" on Jive Records. There is little doubt that this album title gave unquestionable identity to the orientation and constituency of the sound which many longtime hip-hoppers have related to, before its recent recognition and categorisation in the mainstream. It is essentially the basis of hip-hop music and all its subsequent subgenres, truth be told. Trap and other offshoots are children of Boom Bap, which itself is a child of most musical genres that came previous which had pronounced drums AND it also came from the era of drum machines.[9]

Listen to these artists to hear boom bap:

- Mobb Deep
- Audio Two
- Run DMC
- KRS-One
- SaRoc
- T-La Rock

- Crystal Casino
- Wu-Tang Clan
- Das EFX
- A Tribe Called Quest
- Nas
- Gang Starr

The Golden Age

When this era begins is a frequently debated topic. Some would say the New School category is unnecessary, as it could fall under the umbrella of the golden age. The appearance of hooks, the commercialization, and the enormous mainstream popularity makes it easy to group them together. But once again, this is *such* an enormous umbrella—it's difficult to unequivocally determine what should be included beyond labeling the Golden Age as a timespan from the mid-to-late 1980s to mid-to-late 1990s. This book is going to claim the years 1984/1986 to 1997. What might be helpful is to discuss some different subgenres of rap that can be labeled "golden age."

"The Nineties, to me, is the golden era of hip-hop—it's when I fell in love with it," Fabolous says. "There was everything from gangster rap, to backpack rap, to flashy, flossy rap, to dance rap, to pop rap, to female MC rap. There were so many lanes and styles, and that's one of the things that helped it flourish."[10]

The fact that there were so many different styles and sounds all happening at once, and all happening prolifically, is precisely *why* it is the Golden Age of rap. You have different sounds coming out of different regions of the country (not to mention world), and those sounds are influenced by life experience and rich culture. In the South, you have TLC, OutKast, and Kris Kross. Detroit brings you Eminem. Philly births The Roots and DJ Jazzy Jeff & the Fresh Prince. New York brings you, well, everyone, but specifically, I'll say, Biggie, Wu-Tang, and De La Soul. But most certainly not least, we've got California which brings everyone else, but let's leave it with Dre and Death Row Records.

When I think about a summary of this age, I can sum it up with this list:

1. Eclecticism
2. Virtuosity
3. Decisively distinctive sound

> **"My introduction to rap was in the early 90s, mid-90s, but also when I discovered rap music, it was big to go back and do the research on artists that came before . . . I went back and listened to them because I started to figure out okay, in order to understand what rap is now I'll kind of want to understand the evolution of it."**
>
> **—AC Tatum**

Gangsta Rap

Within the category of gangsta rap, it's important to recognize the differences between East Coast and West Coast/G-funk. Gangsta rap falls under the boom bap era, apparent by its heavy beats. While the coasts have differences—for example, the lyrical content differs on the opposing coasts—it's important to note the overlap of the era: both have the kick and snare boom bap emphasis, and they rely on looping orchestrated samples.

As a gross generalization, the East Coast focused on poverty and crime. There is an urgency prevalent, which affects use of consonants, and flow. East Coast gangsta rap is known for its intricate rhyme schemes and its multisyllabic words wrapped prolifically into long phrases. Wordplay, use of metaphors, inside baseball terminology, and drop-the-mic punch lines are a classic part of the East Coast feel as well. It's gritty and retains some of the hard-hitting rawness of the late 1980s New School. I think a lot of the true GOATs come from the East Coast gangsta scene.

The West Coast lyrics lead with gang life and police brutality. Gangsta funk is iconically West Coast. Lush and layered, G-funk has a synth sound that prioritizes a laid-back tempo and 1970s funk (especially George

Clinton's Parliament-Funkadelic collective) sounds. There is lots of high keyboard lead as well as a funk bass, as is found in "Nuthin' but a 'G' Thang" by Dr. Dre and Snoop Dogg. This song itself is so important it could receive its own chapter, but we can get to that another time. In short, it ushered in a side to gangsta that discussed different elements of the "gangsta" lifestyle. There is an unflappable confidence with a slower flow and a relaxed articulation style. The slower, laid-back flow does not mean that it is less prolific in lyrical quality; in fact, it is quite the opposite. It is a sneaky genre like that, where tongue twisters and difficult rhythms abound. G-funk is the escape side of gangsta rap: beach and pool party music, with a top down, rolling with the crew, smoking weed kind of vibe: "Dre's songcraft, rather than his sociology, was now the focus. He was hailed as Spectorian in his pop majesty, and 'G-Thang' and 'Let Me Ride' were celebrated as All American Music, compared to the endless summer vibes of the Beach Boys and the Mamas and the Papas."[11]

Diction and pitch are different in these two coasts—keep that in your head until you get to the second half of this book.

Listen to these artists to hear East Coast gangsta:

- The Notorious B.I.G.
- Wu-Tang Clan
- Nas
- Mobb Deep
- Rakim
- Big Daddy Kane

Listen to these artists to hear G-funk:

- Snoop Dogg
- Dr. Dre
- Tupac
- The Game
- Cypress Hill

- The D.O.C.
- Ice Cube
- Mack 10

The Native Tongues

Often labeled under conscious, progressive, and sometimes jazz rap, the Native Tongues are a family of groups that preach unity, Afrocentric pride, political theory, and lighthearted fun. "Their influence helped hip-hop evolve into something more expansive. Pharrell Williams and Kanye West, two of the most successful and influential figures in music over the past two decades, are Native Tongues disciples."[12] Musically, listen for the boom bap beats, jazz samples, and sometimes, a swung drum beat (thanks, J Dilla). This combination gave the Native Tongues a danceable nature, making some of their tunes prime party music, with deep underlying meanings.

Though not officially part of the Native Tongues, The Roots and Arrested Development should get a shout out. They aren't from New York and thus aren't officially part of this family, but if you like the Native Tongues, then you'll probably like The Roots (Philadelphia) and Arrested Development (Atlanta). As mentioned, the Native Tongues are often categorized as conscious rap which also includes later artists like Common, Talib Kweli, and Kendrik Lamar.

The Native Tongue family includes:

- Queen Latifah
- Jungle Brothers
- De La Soul
- Black Sheep
- Monie Love
- Brand Nubian
- A Tribe Called Quest

"Once upon a time, Q-Tip took the rhyme further than sensible, dropping great aphorisms, parables, and novellas on our heads. Once upon a time A Tribe Called Quest, De La Soul, and Brand Nubian defined the term Progressive hip-hop, setting the standards for thematic genius in the idiom."[13]

Party Rap

Though not officially labeled, it is sometimes tempting to call this subgenre "silly rap." Big radio hits, very user friendly, but along the lines of weight, think of this as a feather. Sometimes it is nice to have something light to listen to, but in terms of prolific genius, this subgenre often misses the mark. It really depends on the artist and how much they strayed from hip-hop values. A great rapping practice tool that this era gives us is the extensive play with vocal tones and colors, which can be useful in this as well as other genres of rap.

Listen to these artists to hear Golden Age party rap:

- Kid 'n Play
- Kris Kross
- MC Hammer
- DJ Jazzy Jeff and the Fresh Prince
- Wreckx-N-Effect

Crunk

Since we're discussing party music, it seems appropriate to give a brief mention to crunk. Originating in the South, this "turnt up" hype music has heavy beats, throbbing bass lines, and danceable up-tempo melodies. It's important to note that one of the defining features of this genre is the scream nature of the vocals.

Listen to these artists to hear crunk:

- Three 6 Mafia
- Lil Jon and the East Side Boyz
- Crime Mob
- Lil Scrappy
- Juicy J

Music mixes with memory. As we think back over the twentieth century, every decade has a melody, a rhythm, a soundtrack:

> And how will we remember the last days of the '90s? Most likely, to the rough-hewn beat of rap. Just as F. Scott Fitzgerald lived in the jazz age, just as Dylan and Jimi Hendrix were among the rulers of the age of rock, it could be argued that we are living in the age of hip-hop. "Rock is old," says Russell Simmons, head of the hip-hop label Def Jam, which took in nearly two hundred million dollars in 1998. "It's old people's s____. The creative people who are great, who are talking about youth culture in a way that makes sense, happen to be rappers.
>
> Consider the numbers. In 1998, for the first time ever, rap outsold what previously had been America's top-selling format: country music. Rap sold more than 81 million CDs, tapes and albums last year, compared with 72 million for the country. Rap sales increased a stunning 31% from 1997 to 1998, in contrast to 2% gains for country, 6% for rock and 9% for the music industry overall. Boasts rapper Jay-Z, whose current album, Vol. 2 . . . Hard Knock Life (Def Jam), has sold more than 3 million copies: "Hip-hop is the rebellious voice of the youth. It's what people want to hear."[14]

If you're reading this book, you know how badly the deaths of Biggie and Tupac shook the community. Until now, G-funk was king of the castle. This isn't a statement to its superiority, but rather to its commercial success. It seemed that the West Coast was winning the battle, but after these tragedies, things shifted. Since this chapter is loosely organized chronologically this needs to be mentioned, but this section is more of an era than a specific sound. The specifics of sound could include "talk rap," with defining qualities being that the pitch is where you'd naturally talk and it isn't heightened with diction but isn't quite as slurred as G-funk (listen to Diddy and Missy Elliot to really hear examples of this). Lyrical content and music videos would better define this era:

> Among the most visually potent images to come out of popular culture in recent years is a scene from the video for "Mo Money Mo Problems" a Notorious B.I.G. single featuring Puffy and Mase. As the song begins, Puffy and his posse are shown emerging from a car, an imposing group of young men, advancing in ominous slo-mo . . . except the car is a Bentley, the men are wearing beautiful linens and sweater-vests, and they're off to storm the links,-to play golf, the most racially exclusionary of sports. "The message" says Puffy of the video, "is that we have arrived."[15]

We've left the dominance of boom bap; we've got drum machines but the variance is marked. There is some holdover of G-funk tempo, use of samples, sound effects, and conversational pitch. There are sometimes sung choruses, sometimes by the artist and often by guest R&B celebrities.

Artists to listen to for this (enormous) era:

- Missy Elliott
- Puffy
- OutKast
- Laryn Hill
- Jay-Z
- Eminem
- Nas
- Eve
- Lil' Kim
- Kanye West
- Lil Wayne

Trap

I won't try to deny it: this term is problematic. It means different things to different people, and there are so many subgenres of trap that it would take an entire book to discuss them. The meaning of this term has also changed dramatically and now a lot of folks say that "all rap is trap" or that "Drake is trap." But that's a big debate that is not the point of this section dedicated to this subgenre. Most importantly, if you don't already know, you'll need to learn what a triplet is, and how to sing on the same pitch for long phrases—yes . . . sing! "The term 'trap' was literally used to refer to the place where drugs are hidden in a car, where deals are made and how it is difficult to escape the lifestyle."[16]

Remember the "kick" part of the kick and snare of boom bap? Well, that low, booming kick drum from the 808 is back to add an almost ominous bass. You'll also hear the triangle and a healthy amount of synthesizer, which of course you've heard in other genres. Only this time it's used with what seems like a never-ending loop of the hi-hat—like, wow, trap loves the hi-hat.

Listen to these artists to hear trap:

- Rick Ross
- Future
- T.I.
- Young Thug
- Playboi Carti
- Gucci Mane
- Three 6 Mafia
- Waka Flocka Flame
- Lil Yachty
- 2 Chainz
- Migos
- 21 Savage

Holy Hip-Hop

Christian/gospel rap started way back in the 1980s, but it is alive and well today, and like most rap, becomes more complex regarding production quality and flow patterns. As you can probably guess, the defining characteristic of this genre are the lyrical themes that are anchored in the Christian faith. "Historically, holy hip-hop artists have been Christians who use rap as a means to evangelize, teach, or encourage others. The emphasis on personal character and practicing Christian morals is of paramount importance within the holy hip-hop movement."[17] Artists that live in this genre include:

- Michael Peace
- LeCrae
- Trip Lee
- D.O.C.
- Andy Mineo
- Dc Talk
- 116 Clique
- Tobymac

Today's Storytellers

Today's rappers are each so uniquely innovative that it's difficult to group them. They are sometimes called alternative rap, and sometimes simply contemporary rap. What do all of these rappers have in common? They are all lyrical rappers (meaning they are lyric driven, and still predominantly use speech instead of autotuned singing to deliver their words). Their songs are loaded with clever puns, a tendency to rap across the downbeat, insanely challenging flows, and the retention of the drop-the-mic punchlines. They are standing on the shoulders of all the greats that came before them, and they have put these influences to good use. I've named them today's storytellers because their songs are often story driven in nature. As mentioned, these artists are lyrics (versus melodic) much like their predecessors, but this time their music utilizes innovative digital samples, self-sung hooks, and the integration of musical genres like neo soul, R&B, and pop. Artists that nestle into this category include:

- Janelle Monae
- Tyler the Creator
- Chance the Rapper
- Nicki Minaj
- J. Cole
- Kenrick Lamar
- Childish Gambino
- A$AP Rocky

Melodic

Melodic rap and pop rap are oftentimes used as interchangeable terms. It would be safer to think of pop rap as the larger umbrella, with melodic rap being a subgenre inside of pop rap, because there would certainly be plenty of exceptions found that were/are topping the charts and aren't melodic in nature. Think of Flo Rida's portion of "Wild Ones" (his duet with Sia), Nicki Minaj's "Super Bass," or Damien's "Catch Me." There are melodies, sure, but not in the rap portions. Melodic rap began earlier, *much* earlier.

World-renowned voice expert Ingo R. Titze attempts

> to make the distinction between speaking and singing at an acoustic level. [He] came up with the following contrasts: 1. In speech, articulation (word intelligibility) dominates, whereas in singing word intelligibility is sometimes compromised for aesthetic reasons. 2. In speaking, pitch, duration, and intensity vary according to the speaker's wishes to express the content of the verbal message, whereas in singing, pitch, duration, and intensity are prescribed by the composer via his/her interpretation of the musical message. 3. In speech, accents are for semantic clarity, whereas in singing accents are dominated by rhythm

and meter. 4. In general, speech occurs at lower overall intensity levels than singing and within a narrower range of intensities. Singing has a higher average intensity level than speech and features a wider variation in intensities than speech. 5. In general, speech occurs at lower average than singing and within a narrower range of fundamental frequencies. 6. In general, speaking uses only a small percentage of the vital capacity of the lungs (lower tidal volume with each spoken phrase). Singing uses more of the vital capacity (larger tidal volume with each sung phrase). 7. In singing, vowels make up a much greater percentage of the total phonation time relative to speech.[18]

On a basic level, melodic rap is rap that is sung. There is the potential for such a range in how much of a song is melody versus rap ratio nowadays, and it's still falling under the melodic rap umbrella. Plus, we need to be able to drop the mic if we enter a debate with Ben Shapiro (who claimed that "rap isn't music" in a 2019 interview . . . Twitter had a field day with that one). Many credit Drake as being the reason for the season when it comes to melodic rap becoming the dominating popular rap form (and pop form, for that matter):

> Drake's *So Far Gone* mixtape—released in February 2009—marked the arrival of a new path: singing as rapping, rapping as singing, singing and rapping all woven together into one holistic soup. Drake exploded the notion that those components had to be delivered by two different people, and also deconstructed what was expected from each of them. His hip-hop was fluid, not dogmatic. And in so remaking it, he set the template for what would eventually become the global pop norm.[19]

It is most definitely true that many people link Drake with the weaving together of what used to be two very different (almost opposing) forms. It used to be that singing, or even coming close to singing, could lose a rapper major street cred. "This brings up a sociocultural subtext underlying the question of melody in rap. The need for rappers to maintain 'hardness,' and hence, a certain machismo."[20] These rappers stayed staunchly in the lyrical rap camp, as far away as possible from anything Pop or R&B crossover: "Lyricism in hip-hop meant rappers not only dropped kyller rhymes, but maintained a wall between rap, and musical cadence."[21] It could be argued, however, that melodic rap was around long before Drake ("Just A Friend" by Biz Markie, "Friends" by Whodini, "U.N.I.T.Y" by Queen Latifah, "No Scrubs" by TLC, and most of Bone Thugs-N-Harmony's cannon). Summertime by DJ Jazzy Jeff and the Fresh Prince has one of the most memorable sung hooks (albeit not sung by them, but it does raise an interesting argument as to how far the tentacle of what counts as melodic rap can reach).

This is a good segue into the difference and similarities of melodic rap and mumble rap. This can get confusing. Let's talk about what some would consider the granddaddies of melodic rap: a quintet birthed in the early 1990s called Bone Thugs-N-Harmony. MTV named Bone Thugs-N-Harmony the "most melodic hip-hop group of all time." Lightning fast flow combined with melodic patterns made them like no others out there. (Listen to their chart-topping hit "The Crossroads."[22])

Now, some people think of Bone Thugs as mumble rap. This is a gross misconception. In an interview on VLAD TV, Krayzie and Bizzy Bone dig into their thoughts on mumble rap:

> it's like one of those kinda vibes, ya know that. . . . That people, they bounce. You don't have to be a super great rapper to make it. . . . It ain't like they could do a song with Rakim, where they'd get respect, but they have a lot of fans, and a lot of kids. You know, you don't gotta train your mind to listen to something that you don't understand anyway when the beat is already slammin. But with us . . . we was raised on East Coast Rules . . . you gotta have lyrics, you gotta have content, like nobody's supposed to steal your stuff, you know, just a firm, solid [book] of East coast rules.[23]

If we were in school, and the project was to make one of those timelines on butcher paper, this timeline could take up the entire bulletin board (you know the one—it goes between two classroom doors in the elementary school hallway, that usually says "Eagles Soar with Perfect Attendance" or something similar). It would start long before Drake with songs that pull from reggae, dance hall, toasting, disco, and more. But with Drake's "Take Care," the separation was obliterated. By 2011, journalist Miles Raymer stated, "many successful pop artists have acknowledged rap in their music, but Drake goes further—he seems to be working under the assumption that hip-hop is now the lingua franca of all forms of popular music, making the distinction between rap and pop outdated."[24] And look where we are a decade later.

So, let's say that Drake was a turning point that changed the landscape and created a street that many drove down toward the intersection of Melodic Rap Road and Pop Pathway. This is actually one of those big, six-way intersections, and some turned down Melodic Rap Road initially but then veered to Mumble Avenue, and others are standing in the median in the very middle of the six-way intersection.

About now, there would usually be a list of artists to listen to in order to hear melodic rap. But we've acknowledged that things are a bit more complicated than that because of the combination of styles. Before that happens, it's important to acknowledge that by 2017, things are significantly overlapping. This is actually a great thing, since it not only gives props to the *massive* influence that hip-hop has on *everything*, but also is such a wonderful thing in some ways, because it just wasn't all that long ago that African American popular music was labeled as "race music" and had separate radio stations. The blending and overlapping, as long as it isn't due to appropriation and silencing, but instead honoring and appreciation, well... it means that things are moving in the right direction, with music leading the way.

Pop rap, melodic rap, mumble rap—ack—are these all the same thing? Yes. And no. And yes. And most definitely no.

To put it simply, some artists can claim two of these three labels. For example, Drake can claim pop and melodic. Roddy Rich can claim mumble and melodic. But Lanze seems strictly mumble. Kodak Black? Mumble and melodic. Young Thug can claim all three but leans toward mumble/melodic (if the categorization of "pop" means Juice WRLD .... well, ok maybe Juice WRLD can claim all three). So, this is an attempt, but it's probably just safe to say that there can be an exception and argument against every categorization made in the following. Let it also be mentioned that hype rap could/should probably be discussed within this category, but this chapter is just getting too darn long.

Pop rap artists (catchy, repetitive hooks, instrumentation and orchestration found in other pop subgenres):

- Juice WRLD
- 24KGoldn
- Justin Bieber
- Iaan Dior
- Nav
- Macklemore
- Chris Brown
- Jack Harlow
- Megan Thee Stallion
- Megan Trainor

Melodic artists:

- Travis Scott
- HangtimeKyul
- Roy Woods
- Post Malone
- Polo G
- Lil Mosey
- Saba
- Don Toliver

Mumble:

- Young Thug
- Rich The Kid
- XXXTentation
- Lil Keed
- Lil Uzi Vert
- Future
- Lil Pump
- Gunna
- Young Thug

Cloud Rap

Often described as ethereal, spacy, hazy, and dreamlike, this subgenre offers a chill, loopy, layered soundscape. "The slow, viscous flows are underpinned with the double-time snares and booming kicks of trap. The beats are then layered with collages of hazy, psychedelic samples. It was more like being haunted by a rap song than listening to one."[25] This genre is truly a stew, taking inspiration from trap, chillwave, chopped and screwed, and lo-fi. Is it called "cloud rap" because it sounds like you are floating on a cloud? Or because it grew in its creation and popularity in the cloud (meaning both the internet and also specifically SoundCloud)? It depends on who you ask, but both contain truth. Clams Casino is indisputably the godfather of the beats, and thanks to him, you can expect to hear everything from videogame to found sounds, along with layered, wordless harmonies in this lush genre. If you listen to a lot of lo-fi today, you can thank cloud rap for giving your favorite artists some great ideas. Artists to listen to when you'd like some cloud rap in your life:

> **"Nobody listens to that type of grungy, hard rap no more. People don't relate to the content behind the rap anymore. They relate a lot more to your Juice WRLDs."**
>
> —gobylc

- A$AP Rocky
- Yung Lean
- Lil B
- Space Ghost Puurp
- Bladee
- Ecco2k

Drill

"With rare exception this music is unmediated and raw and without bright spots, focused on anger and violence. The instinct is to call this tough, unforgiving and concrete-hard music joyless, but in truth it's exuberant in its darkness."[26]

Drill originated in my lovely city of Chicago (can we all scream *South Siiiiiiide*) in the early 2010s, with the huge breakout being Chief Keef's song "I Don't Like," and in more recent years, expanded to booming scenes in both the United Kingdom and, most recently, New York. Drill was heavily inspired by Atlanta's trap sound, and "stylistically, the two sounds are clearly linked: typically . . . [utilizing] a woozy halftime feel, drill beats adopt much of the 808 instrumentation of the typical trap sound, but mix things up with more wonky snare and clap patterns, sparser hi-hats and often a distinctive sliding [heavy, sinister] 808 bassline."[27] The lyrical content and subject matter differs from Atlanta trap, instead focusing on violence, drugs, revenge, and gang affiliation. Instead of intricate metaphors and complex flows, the words are straightforward and delivered in slower-paced monotone voices. Drill is reminiscent of gangsta rap in that the subject matter is upsetting to some; in 2022, the mayor of New York called for the ban of playing drill music on social media after the two drill rappers were killed. It's controversial, with the other side arguing that these rappers are expressing the very real day to day of their lives. Major drill artists include:

- Chief Keef
- Fivio Foreign
- Pop Smoke
- Lil Durk
- Lil Bibby
- Cheff G
- Sasha Go Hard
- Polo G
- CJ
- Kay Flock

There are other genres: nerdcore, grime, rage, horrorcore, industrial rap, meme rap, and many more. Hopefully, after reading these first five chapters, you have a better grasp of the enormity of the more than fifty years that is hip-hop, both historically and musically speaking. If you purchased this book for the practical tips and lessons regarding the how-tos of rap, it might have been extremely tempting to skip chapters 1 to 4, and start here, figuring that this gives you a good thumbnail into rap. But if this is you, please stop now, go back, and read chapters 4 to 4. They're crucial to your ability to be not only respectful to the artform, but also a necessary part of the journey of bringing your authentic self to the table. It's not impossible that you could start here and proficiently learn to rap, but without understanding the origins and the reasons *why* hip-hop talks about what it does, and sounds the way it does, you'd kind of be, well, a scumbag. You'd be good at rapping, but you'd still be a scumbag.

Notes

1. Serrano, Shea, Arturo Torres, and Ice-T. (2015). *The Rap Year Book: The Most Important Rap Song from Every Year Since 1979, Discussed, Debated, and Deconstructed*. New York: Abrams Image, 5.

2. Chang, Jeff. (2005). *Can't Stop, Won't Stop: A History of the Hip-Hop Generation*. New York: St. Martin's Press, 90.

3. Bunnell, Rich. (n.d.). The Message—Grandmaster Flash and the Furious Five (1988). Retrieved March 22, 2023, from https://www.loc.gov/static/programs/national-recording-preservation-board/documents/TheMessage.pdf

4. Komaniecki, Robert. (2019). Analyzing the Parameters of Flow in Rap Music. PhD dissertation, Indiana University, August, 22.

5. Serrano, Shea, Arturo Torres, and Ice-T. *The Rap Year Book: The Most Important Rap Song from Every Year Since 1979, Discussed, Debated, and Deconstructed*. New York, NY: Abrams Image, 2015, 35.

6. Abrams, Jonathan. (2022). *The Come Up: An Oral History of the Rise of Hip-Hop*. New York: Penguin Random House, 82.

7. George, Nelson. (2020, October 19). Rappin' with Russell Simmons. *The Village Voice*. https://www.villagevoice.com/2020/01/21/rappin-with-russell-simmons/

8. Cepeda, Raquel. (2004). *"And It Don't Stop!": The Best American Hip-Hop Journalism of the Last 25 Years*. New York: Faber and Faber, 50.

9. Cepeda, Raquel. (2004). *"And It Don't Stop!": The Best American Hip-Hop Journalism of the Last 25 Years*. New York: Faber and Faber, 50.

10. Vozick-Levinson, Simon. (2018, June 25). Fabolous on How "the Golden Era of Hip-Hop" Inspired His New Christmas LP. *Rolling Stone*. https://www.rollingstone.com/music/music-features/fabolous-on-how-the-golden-era-of-hip-hop-inspired-his-new-christmas-lp-185819/

11. Chang, Jeff. (2005). *Can't Stop, Won't Stop: A History of the Hip-Hop Generation*. New York: St. Martin's Press, 420.

12. Kimble, Julian. (2019, July 19). Native Tongue Festival Brings Together Hip-Hop's Past and Present. *The Washington Post*. https://www.washingtonpost.com/lifestyle/native-tongue-festival-brings-together-hip-hops-past-and-present/2019/07/19/a517b27e-aa54-11e9-9214-246e594de5d5_story.html

13. Tate, Greg. (2004). *"And It Don't Stop!": The Best American Hip-Hop Journalism of the Last 25 Years*. New York: Faber and Faber, 155.

14. Farley, Christopher John. (1999, February 8). Hip-Hop Nation. *Time*. http://content.time.com/time/magazine/article/0,9171,19134,00.html

15. Kemp, David. (1999). Don't Hate Me Because I'm Ghetto Fabulous. *GQ*.

16. The Music Origins Project. (n.d.). What Is Trap Music and Where Did It Come From? Retrieved July 12, 2022, from https://www.musicorigins.org/item/trap-music/#:~:text=Trap%20music%20is%20a%20music,in%20the%20

Southern%20United%20States.&text=The%20term%20originated%20in%20 Atlanta,the%20term%20in%20their%20music

17. Gustafson, Kyle. (n.d.). Holy Hip-Hop/Christian Rap. Timeline of African American Music, *Carnegie Hall*. Retrieved March 23, 2023, from https://timeline.carnegiehall.org/genres/holy-hip-hop-christian-rap

18. Titze, Ingo R. (2021). Is Rap Music or Speech? *Journal of Singing* 77 (4): 519.

19. Caramanica, Jon. (2019, November 25). Rappers Are Singers Now. Thank Drake. *The New York Times*. https://www.nytimes.com/2019/11/24/arts/music/drake-rap-influence.html

20. Caramanica, Jon. (2019, November 25). Rappers Are Singers Now. Thank Drake. *The New York Times*. https://www.nytimes.com/2019/11/24/arts/music/drake-rap-influence.html

21. *Slate Magazine*. (2022, July 17). Say My Name, Say My Name Edition. https://slate.com/transcripts/bGU3eEtaRm40ZlpBd2FtRWl6NnhWZ0F4Ry94ZHNBaE9vZVlKSk42dGFqOD0=

22. *Slate Magazine*. (2022, July 17). Say My Name, Say My Name Edition. https://slate.com/transcripts/bGU3eEtaRm40ZlpBd2FtRWl6NnhWZ0F4Ry94ZHNBaE9vZVlKSk42dGFqOD0=

23. VLAD TV. (2017, April 27). Krayzie & Bizzy Bone React to Mumble Rap, People Not Understanding Their Lyrics. *YouTube*. https://www.youtube.com/watch?v=cn5uB3_nHfY&ab_channel=djvlad

24. Raymer, Miles. (2021, August 19). Drake Charts a New Course for Pop. *The Chicago Reader*. https://chicagoreader.com/music/drake-charts-a-course-for-pop/

25. Lawrence, Eddy. (2018, April 5). Whatever Happened to Hip Hop Sub-Genre Cloud Rap. *RedBull*. https://www.redbull.com/us-en/whatever-happened-to-hip-hop-sub-genre-cloud-rap

26. Caramanica, Jon. (2012, October 4). Chicago Hip Hops Raw Burst of Change. *The New York Times*. https://www.nytimes.com/2012/10/07/arts/music/chicago-hip-hops-raw-burst-of-change.html

27. Computer Music. (2022, January 17). The Beginners Guide to: Drill. *Music Radar*. Retrieved March 23, 2023, from https://www.musicradar.com/news/the-beginners-guide-to-drill/

Six

Masterpiece Theatre (En Vogue)
Hamilton—Why This, Why Then, and Why Now?

This is a book for people who want to perform hip-hop. You may be looking to be a "traditional" hip-hop MC, spitting bars over your beats in your home studio, or on a concert stage. You may be, or may also be, an actor who has found themselves needing to perform rap, or rap-adjacent rhythmic speech, and are looking to build your understanding of rap's underpinnings and your skill in its delivery. If that is you, we should get some things straight about what you're going to encounter in the Broadway repertoire. Some of this "rap" will definitely not be hip-hop. Some of it is the result of hip-hop lodging itself inextricably in the pop music that forms the background of the twenty-first-century Broadway pop rock sound, and some of it actually deals with, or is itself an artifact of, hip-hop. Whatever category it falls into, your rap will require many of the same techniques that a hip-hop performer should cultivate. The context will be different, many stylistic details will be different, but some fundamentals *will* cross over.

Patter Songs: The "Rap" Songs That Aren't Actually Rap

There is a lot of rhythmic speech on the musical theater stage. "Patter songs," in which a character speaks and rhymes very quickly, usually returning repeatedly to a sung chorus, has long been a way to show that a character is braggadocious, insincere, intelligent, condescending, harried, nervous, or any combination of those traits. "Patter songs"' can be traced all the way back to breakneck comic arias like "Largo al Factotum," the one Figaro, the all-propose "fixer" character sings in Rossini's *The Barber of Seville* (1816). You might be familiar with "I am the very model of the modern major general" from the British operetta duo Gilbert and Sullivan's *The Pirates of Penzance* (1879), in which a know-it-all goes on and on about the subject of his own brilliance. Nearly every Gilbert and Sullivan operetta, from *The Sorcerer* to *Utopia, Ltd*, has such a number. One of these songs, "When You're Lying Awake with a Dismal Headache," aka "The Nightmare Song" from *Iolanthe* (1882), is a lot trickier than the major general's song and might even make Twista break a sweat.

Move across the pond to the United States and you find patter songs *all* over musical theater. Many times, these songs are for characters who are themselves operators, like the slick charmer Harold Hill in Meredith Wilson's *The Music Man* who whips the uptight citizens of River City, Iowa, into a moral frenzy with this song "Ya Got Trouble," or P.T. Barnum in the musical biopic *Barnum* (1980). The con man Freddie in the musical version of the film *Dirty Rotten Scoundrels* (2004) speak-sings the number "Great Big Stuff." Interestingly, this song shares a "get money" aesthetic with rap, but this number feels white-coded, including a didn't-sound-good-then-and-aged-even-worse lyric about "Sittin' pretty in the caddy / With P. Daddy or Puff Diddy / Or whatever! I'll change my name too! I'll get my hatchback all pimped-out." There's even an oily take on William Shakespeare who laments about the difficulties of fame in his number "It's Hard to Be the Bard" from the musical *Something Rotten!* (2015).

Other patter songs live in a self-consciously intellectual place. The king of this, Stephen Sondehim, offers several in this vein, like "Now" by the sexually frustrated lawyer Fredrik in *A Little Night Music* (1973), "Franklin Shepard, Inc." sung by the aggravated playwright Charley in *Merrily We Roll Along* (1981), and "Putting it Together" by the professionally frustrated artist George in *Sunday in the Park with George* (1984). In all of these scenarios, the character's agitation helps drive the manic tempo.

Even when Sondheim's characters aren't cerebral by nature, their anxiety often leaps out in patter, as in "Not Getting Married" from *Company*

(1970), a song performed at breakneck speed by a character contemplating running away on her wedding day. "In this patter song, 68 words are sung in a total of 11 seconds! . . . Notable for being one of the most difficult musical songs with the fastest verse in history, it depends on clear diction, implicit pitch accuracy and breath support, alongside imperative comedic timing."[1] Anxiety drives the patter of characters from other composers and lyricists, too, such as "Sing" from *A Chorus Line* (1975), wherein a bad singer apologizes for her shortcomings at an audition, or "Both Sides of the Coin" from *The Mystery of Edwin Drood* (1985) sung by two possible murder suspects.

There are other drivers behind a character breaking into a patter, such as pure celebration as in "La Vie Boheme" (*Rent*, 1996) or a zany comedy list song "Tchaikovsky" from Weil and Gershwin's *Lady in the Dark* (1941). Regardless of the song's dramaturgical objective, impeccable diction is essential. Detailed communication of information is not a mandatory facet of a pop or hip-hop song. Popular music can be about the groove, or just celebratory, or visceral; it can be about getting up or getting down, hooking up or throwing down . . . it can be "vibes." Musical theatre is character driven and typically involves plot, so there's a lot to share, and it has to be shared in time, so it must be clear, because the audience has to receive and unpack a great deal of information quickly. Sometimes a super-fast rap is also delivered with remarkable clarity, Busta Rhymes on "Gimme Some More" or "60 Second Assassin"—a verse that nearly breaks into hyperspace is remarkably decipherable. But many other rappers send the listener right to the website Genius to figure out what just flew by. If you can't understand the words in musical theatre, then Houston, we have a problem. Much is lost. In a patter song, pure speed is valued less than moderately speedy with clarity. In rap, you get that second, third, twenty-seventh listen to catch what you missed—rap is a gift that keeps on giving.

Now that you understand patter songs and their place in musical theatre, it's important to understand their place within hip-hop. These songs are not hip-hop, full stop, even though they may sound like it at times. They're rhythmic, they rhyme, they're fast, and they're often performed as much straight to the audience as to the characters on stage, but they don't stem from the hip-hop tradition and can't be traced back to the contemporary urban Black experience. Meryl Streep described the difference with regard to the witch's entrance number in Sondheim's *Into the Woods* (1987). Streep played the iconic character in the 2014 film version, and her first musical number, entirely spoken, is frequently referred to as a rap, even casually so by Sondheim himself. Steep discussed preparing for her "big rap scene" at a press conference, but qualified the use of the word, "I don't know. When Stephen wrote that, was he aware that he was . . . ? Did they even call it a rap then? . . . was he influenced by like . . . ? Who were his influences? Ice Cube or where are we?"[2] It's a hell of a patter number, but you wouldn't want it anywhere near a club.

Just as hedgehogs and porcupines are both little animals with spikes but aren't related (hedgehogs are "Eulipotyphla" and porcupines are "Rodentia"), Harold Hill and Humpty Hump are not in the same family tree.

Hip-Hop-Inspired Rap Showtunes

Many modern musicals are now based in a pop music sound, and we've discussed repeatedly that pop music has been colonized by hip-hop (take that, colonizers!) And so, more and more hip-hop (both R&B and rap) is finding itself on the Great White Way. This kind of song is where you, the musical theatre performer, will find your greatest need for rapping skills, and there's a distinct possibility you'll need a number like this in your audition book.

Some examples include "Positive" from *Legally Blonde* (2007), "No More Giving It Up" from *Lysistrata Jones* (2011), "When the Going Gets Tough" from *SpongeBob SquarePants: The Musical* (2016), and "Whose House is This?" from *Mean Girls* (2017). Kicking it quasi-old school is "Fabulous One," a David Byrne–style rap from *Here Lies Love* (2013), "Tyrone's Rap" from the musical version of *Fame* (1988), "One Night in Bangkok" from *Chess* (1986), which was also a new wave/disco/pop hit in the 1980s and sounds related to Blondie's "Rapture" (logical, given that it was written by Benny and Bjorn from ABBA), "Jimmy's Rap" from *Dreamgirls* (1981), which is really a pastiche of James Brown's "Sex Machine" or "Get on the

Good Foot" rhyming, and Rent (1996) has "Today 4 U." It was written years before the 1996 Broadway premiere, which explains its Old School flow.

The 2019 musical (though only making it to Broadway post-pandemic) "& Juliet" uses Swedish producer Max Martin's catalog as its score, as does the Britney Spears jukebox show "Once Upon a One More Time," so both shows are full of very hip-hop-tinted bubblegum music and dance. No doubt many more like these are on their way.

Hip-Hop Musicals

What is the difference between hip-hop-inspired musicals and dedicated hip-hop musicals? "Long-time hip hop theater writer/actor/director Danny Hoch says it this way: 'Hip-hop theatre . . . must be *by*, *about* and *for* the hip-hop generation, participants in hip-hop culture, or both.'"[3] There's been some work on film that has turned hip-hop music into a "book" musical (in which the characters sing and the songs help move the story forward) like 2001's all-star *Carmen, A Hip Hopera* or the OutKast musical movie *Idlewild* (2006). There was the short-lived Broadway run of *Holler If You Hear Me* (2014) which featured the music of Tupac Shakur. There's the Off-Broadway musicals *The Bomb-itty of Errors* (1999) and *Venice* (2013). There's a stellar number called "Get Down" in the Broadway musical *Six* (2020). Let's not dismiss the Disney enterprise and their use of rap in their Zombies movie musical franchise, with songs like "Bamm" in *Zombies 1* (2018), and an all-out rap battle in *Zombies 2* with the song "I'm Winning" (2020). There are almost too many to name in the Disney Descendants trilogy, so I'll choose a few highlights and advise you to listen to "Good to Be Bad," "Be Our Guest," and "It's Goin' Down." We can't leave out Disney's Camp Rock franchise when they feature rap in "It's On" or *High School Musical*'s (2006) ear worm, "Get'cha Head in the Game."

And then there's Lin-Manuel Miranda's work, including *In the Heights* (2008), half of the musical version of *Bring It On* (2012), his bite-sized one-act musical *21 Chump Street* (2014), and that Obama-era cultural phenomenon *Hamilton* (2015). These shows lean hard into hip-hop, and "Hamilton" in particular is neck deep in hip-hop. It plays with hip-hop, pays tribute to hip-hop, and usually sounds like hip-hop; in doing so, made the world go nuts. It also quite possibly changed the direction of future musical theatre composition regarding the presence of hip-hop.

Hamilton

The financial success of the musical *Hamilton: An American Musical* has been staggering. The franchise (Broadway show, Disney+ broadcast, tours, recordings, publishing, merchandise, etc.) surpassed one billion dollars in earnings in 2020,[4] only its fifth year of existence. The show made a record quick climb into exceedingly rare air.

Hamilton's cultural impact has been likewise stunning: eleven Tony Awards (a record-breaking sixteen nominations), a Grammy, the Pulitzer Prize in Drama, and for its creator and star, the then thirty-something Lin-Manuel Miranda, a Kennedy Center Honor, something typically reserved for superstars near the end of their lives, as well as a MacArthur Genius Grant. Standing companies abounded, with productions currently or formerly running in New York, London's West End, Berlin, Los Angeles, Chicago, Puerto Rico, Sydney, Hamburg, and multiple tours taking off across the world.

There were prolific musical recordings stemming from the show. The original cast recording debuted in 2015 at number twelve on the Billboard charts and went to number two, achieving number one on the Billboard Rap chart. That recording was followed in 2016 by *The Hamilton Mixtape*, a series of remixes and covers, often by hip-hop icons like Busta Rhymes, Wiz Khalifa, Chance the Rapper, and many more. That album debuted at number one on the Billboard 200. 2017 saw the release of *The Hamilton Instrumentals*, as well as a number of authorized sing-alongs to the cast recording (in answer to the many *unauthorized* sing-alongs that were popping up). From 2017 to 2018, Miranda released the *Hamildrops*, thirteen Hamilton-related recordings, including trunk songs and covers, released once a month.

In July 2020, during the depths of the COVID-19 pandemic when Broadway houses were still shuttered, as were many movie theaters, a stage-to-film version of *Hamilton* dropped on the Disney+ streaming service to its fifty million subscribers. The streaming rights reportedly cost the House of Mouse seventy-five million dollars to acquire, but in only the first ten days of streaming, it's likely that more people watched Hamilton at home than the 7.8 million who had seen it live in every city combined.[5] At a cost of only $7.99 dollars a month per household, this was a steal . . . far less than ticket prices that *averaged* $381 a pop, but rose as high as $849, not counting third-party sales.[6]

Hamilton is a piece Miranda has repeatedly referred to as a "love letter to hip-hop," and which stands as a rare piece of musical theatre that sounds a little more like what we would listen to in our own earbuds than most other musical soundtracks. *Hamilton* is a sung and rapped-through piece . . . they almost never stop to talk. The flow is complex, accomplished, and bespoke to the character who is singing. With the exception of the "white" characters like King George and Samuel Seaberry, the British monarch and British sympathizer who sing in styles deliberately contrary to the rest of the score, the music has a sound distinctly beholden to hip-hop and R&B. It would be difficult to listen to fully sung numbers like "The Room Where It Happens" or "Burn" and not say that this is musical theatre, but Jefferson's numbers and the cabinet rap battles are requiring such skill that an experienced rapper, Daveed Diggs, was brought in to originate the role.

Broadway orchestrator and music director Alex Lacamoire brought a wealth of hip-hop sounds into the mix and was aided in producing the original cast recording by The Roots' Questlove and Black Thought. These sounds included digital effects on voices, DJ scratching sounds, distorted high hats, and more.[7]

Miranda is famously well-versed and fond of both traditional Broadway fare and the hip-hop music he enjoyed growing up in the Bronx. He frequently speaks of borrowing early 1990s albums from his sister, including A Tribe Called Quest's *The Low-End Theory* and Dr. Dre's *The Chronic*. The show is loaded with references to musical theatre, including *South Pacific*, *The Last Five Years*, and nineteenth-century operetta *The Pirates of Penzance*, as well as rap Easter Eggs from DMX ("Meet Me Inside") to Biggie ("Juicy," "Going Back to Cali," and "The Ten Crack Commandments")

> "Rap in musical theater is a beautiful combination of musical arch, story telling, emphasis on diction, enunciation, and knowledge of the rhyming cadences. On the base level, just like any other song that one might sing, you have to know where the important words are and give them emphasis. The next level to this (and sometimes exception) would be when the rhyme is written in a rhythmically creative pattern. For example, George Washington's first words in Hamilton are 'Moved in with a cousin, the cousin committed suicide. Left him with nothin' but ruined pride, something new inside.' In this example I would emphasize the first 2 'cousin's.' Then the next rhyming pattern is 'suicide,' 'ruined pride,' and 'new inside.' Musically, those words/phrases are nicely pitched one step away from the less important words so that they stand out even more. The combination of all these layers makes the storytelling and flow really interesting and beautiful."
>
> **—Tamar Greene, George Washington, Broadway**

to Mobb Deep ("Shook Ones, Pt. II").[8] This piece lives at the intersection of American musical theatre and hip-hop. As rapper Talib Kweli told *Vulture*, "It's a musical that's greatly influenced by hip-hop, and the hip-hop influence on it is wonderful."[9] Everything in Hamilton is intentional to marry the delivery of story with the authenticity of hip-hop.

As far as subject matter in relation to hip hop, *Hamilton* is about a lot of things. An important element is writing and talking your way out of your socio-economic circumstances. That's where Miranda got his idea of combining hip-hop with a book about the Founding Fathers in the first place. "I mean, hip-hop's the language of revolution and it's our greatest American art form. . . . It was the fact that Hamilton got everywhere on the strength of his writing. That was the whole idea, was, 'Well, that's what my favorite MCs do.'"[10] He saw Alexander Hamilton's difficult upbringing, his flair for language, his capacity for beefs (beefs often ending in violence) and made a connection. Beyond the initial conceit, Miranda went even further

"In the most successful examples of musical theatre, every element of the show is crafted to serve the story being told, and Hamilton is no exception. In Hamilton, rhythm and flow are deployed strategically through Miranda's writing and Lacamoire's music direction to distinguish the identities and attitudes of different characters and track them as they evolve through the show. Imagine speaking on the beat, precise and straightforward; this can convey a neat, orderly, or even commanding tone, well suited to a character like Aaron Burr or George Washington in his role as military commander. On the other hand, a looser approach to rhythm, using syncopation, anticipating, or delaying ('backphrasing') is often used to indicate a character's relaxation or comfort in a given situation, notably in Alexander Hamilton's 'freestyling' or the Marquis de Lafayette's raps in 'Guns and Ships.' Rhythm also aids in maintaining clarity—especially in lyrically dense passages, the rhythmic emphasis of a word or rhyme gives the audience's ear a 'guidepost' to ensure each line is clearly understood. Pitch also plays a key role in conveying the show's text with clarity. In a musical theatre setting where much of the audience may not be accustomed to listening to rap and words are competing with the orchestra, background vocals, sound effects, and more, maintaining consistency of pitch in a range well suited to the actor's voice can be a useful way to help the audience better absorb the text."

—Noah Landis, music associate (Angelica Tour)

in hip-hoppifying the show. He connected different characters to the identity and the flow of various rappers: Hamilton with Eminem and Big Pun, George Washington with Common (and John Legend), Hercules Mulligan with Busta Rhymes, and loaded the show up with many specific references, as when Hamilton sings, "Only 19 but my mind is older," a call to Mobb Deep's "Only 19 but my mind is old."[11]

Vulture discussed the show with MC Talib Kweli and asked him if the show contained technically impressive rap. He answered with an enthusiastic affirmative:

> My heart swelled with pride after I heard the Alexander Hamilton song, because I was like, "This right here is hip-hop." Hip-hop has no boundaries and no limits, and Lin-Manuel and his crew are proving it. All the songs are so well written. . . . When I first heard [Washington on Your Side] I thought, I want to know who wrote these lyrics. The rhyme scheme and what he's saying is very impressive. It's similar to Macklemore in terms of the fact that they're enunciating their words clearly and telling stories . . . they're accentuating their words, but they're doing that because it's a play and people have to hear them . . . you have to take that into account when you're listening to these songs, but as a 20-year veteran of hip-hop, I was highly impressed.[12]

It bent traditions in musicals so it could contain hip-hop, and it bends hip-hop technique, so it'll work as a musical. It's the perfect example of the importance of rap pedagogy for music theatre students. If you want to rap in musicals . . . well it doesn't matter if you want to or not, because it's becoming commonplace in contemporary pop/rock musical theatre. So, I'll rephrase: to best prepare for a future in musical theatre, you'll have to marry your musical theatre technique with your hip-hop technique and vice versa.

So, get to work!

Notes

1. Paskett, Z. (2020, May 22). The Most Difficult Musical Theatre Songs to Sing of All Time. *Evening Standard*. Retrieved March 22, 2023, from https://www.standard.co.uk/evening-standard/culture/theatre/hardest-musical-songs-to-sing-high-note-a4448611.html

2. Butler, Karen. (2014, November 23). Meryl Streep Discusses Her Witch's Rap for "Into the Woods." *UPI*. https://www.upi.com/Entertainment_News/Movies/2014/11/23/Meryl-Streep-discusses-her-witchs-rap-for-Into-the-Woods/1381416787067/

3. The Kennedy Center. Hip-Hop: A Culture of Vision and Voice. March 28, 2023, from https://www.kennedy-center.org/education/resources-for-educators/classroom-resources/media-and-interactives/media/hip-hop/hip-hop-a-culture-of-vision-and-voice/#:~:text=Long%2Dtime%20Hip%20Hop%20theater,Hip%20Hop%20plays%20and%20musicals

4. Chmielewski, Dawn. (2020, June 8). Lin-Manuel Miranda's "Hamilton" Crashes Broadway's Billion-Dollar Club. *Forbes Magazine*. https://www.forbes.com/sites/dawnchmielewski/2020/06/08/lin-manuel-mirandas-hamilton-crashes-broadways-billion-dollar-club/?sh=376d1bd55b3c

5. Tinubu, Aramide. (2020, May 12). It Cost Disney an Insane Amount of Money for "Hamilton" to Stream on Disney+. *Showbiz Cheat Sheet*. https://www.cheatsheet.com/entertainment/it-cost-disney-an-insane-amount-of-money-for-hamilton-to-stream-on-disney-plus.html/

6. Passy, Charles. (2019, June 6). A "Hamilton" Ticket for $849? Experts Call That a Bargain. *The Wall Street Journal*. https://www.wsj.com/articles/a-hamilton-ticket-for-849-experts-call-that-a-bargain-11559860459#:~:text=With%20a%20current%20top%20ticket,Broadway%E2%80%94by%20a%20wide%20margin

7. Evans, Suzy. (2015, November 27). The Man Behind the "Hamilton" Sound: Hidden Beatles References, the "Hip-Hop Horse" Sample and Why If "It's All Computerized, There's No Heart to It." *Salon*. https://www.salon.com/2015/11/27/the_man_behind_the_hamilton_sound_hidden_beatles_references_the_hip_hop_horse_sample_and_why_if_its_all_computerized_theres_no_heart_to_it/

8. Ross, Bella. (2020, August 30). Hamilton: Every Music Easter Egg & Reference. *ScreenRant*. https://screenrant.com/hamilton-musical-songs-references-easter-eggs-rap-broadway/

9. Charlton, Lauretta. (2015, October 20). Is Hamilton Technically Impressive Rap? Talib Kweli Analyzes the Broadway Smash. *Vulture*. https://www.vulture.com/2015/10/talib-kweli-analyzes-hamilton.html

10. Mamo, Heran. (2020, July 7). Lin-Manuel Miranda Explains How "Hamilton" Serves as a "Love Letter to Hip-Hop" That He Grew Up On. *Billboard*. https://www.billboard.com/music/rb-hip-hop/lin-manuel-miranda-apple-music-interview-9414834/

11. Wickman, F. (2015, September 24). All the Hip-Hop References in Hamilton: A Track-by-Track Guide. *Slate Magazine*. Retrieved March 22, 2023, from https://www.slate.com/blogs/browbeat/2015/09/24/hamilton_s_hip_hop_references_all_the_rap_and_r_b_allusions_in_lin_manuel.html

12. Charlton, Lauretta. (2015, October 20). Is Hamilton Technically Impressive Rap? Talib Kweli Analyzes the Broadway Smash. *Vulture*. https://www.vulture.com/2015/10/talib-kweli-analyzes-hamilton.html

Seven

Stakes Is High (De La Soul)
The Need for Authenticity

Hip-hop has the Black American experience baked into nearly every facet of its sound, content, and performance. It's been around for fifty years and has conquered nearly every part of popular culture in the United States, as well as many other parts of the world. It's reasonable to assume then that many different kinds of people like hip-hop, listen to hip-hop, create hip-hop, perform hip-hop, and profit from hip-hop. The intersection of hip-hop's origin story on the margins and its popularity in the mainstream is a dangerous one which directly connects to questions about who gets to enjoy, create, perform, analyze, and profit from hip-hop. There's a possibility that you yourself are reading this book to ask, "Hey, Black Professor Lady, please tell me in clear and uncertain terms who gets to enjoy, create, perform, analyze, and profit from hip-hop. Most importantly, do *I* get to enjoy, create, perform, analyze, and profit from hip-hop?"

If that's the case, dear reader, I've got bad news for you. I don't know. I am not here to tell you who gets to own hip-hop. It's complicated, the jury is out, and if anyone tells you they are the arbiter of who gets to deal in hip-hop (or, more frighteningly, who *doesn't*), I suggest you call BS.

"Okay," you say, "That's all very moderate and magnanimous of you, but *surely* you have an opinion on the matter." Well, everyone has an opinion on the matter, but if there *is* an actual answer to the question, it's complicated and ever evolving. Ultimately, you the artist will have to determine what is authentic and appropriate with regard to your performance, and you the human will have to go to sleep believing that you did or didn't do the right thing. Did you just put on a hip-hop "costume" or persona, or did you speak from the art and present yourself respectfully and authentically as a member of a continuity of poets and musicians? These are questions that only you can answer. But fear not! Help for all of us lies in taking a look at instances of clearly inauthentic behavior, theft, and erasure within popular music. Just as a spelling bee contestant asks the judge to "use the word in a sentence," context will hopefully add clarity.

Categories of Authenticity

Authenticity: it's a hot topic, and something we're constantly told to strive for. But what is it *really*? Authors Hugh Baker and Yuval Taylor help us by subdividing the massive concept of authenticity into subcategories:

> The word seems to be defined in opposition to the "faking it." In a KISS concert, the band wears makeup and plays songs about people they pretend to be, all with the explicit aim of making money rather than telling the truth about themselves or the world they live in. Such a performance can be wildly entertaining, but it's not considered authentic. When people say music is authentic, they might refer to representational authenticity, or music that is exactly what it says it is . . . they might refer to cultural authenticity, or music that reflects a cultural tradition. . . . They might refer to personal authenticity, or music that reflects the person or people who are making it.[1]

When people say music is authentic, they might mean different things. To help you understand these different categories, I'm going to ask you some difficult questions. There is not an answer key at the end of the chapter. These are all for you to ponder, and how you answer might help you decipher your authentic inner rapper. But they're difficult, and I'm pushing your buttons on purpose, so don't say I didn't warn you.

Representational Authenticity

When people say music is authentic, they might be referring to representational authenticity, or music that is exactly what it says it is. So, on the representational side, are rappers really writing their bars and making their beats, or are they merely positioned products who have had their material handed to them? Does the technology involved in making hip-hop in the twenty-first century detract from the value of the work? Underneath all the production and samples, is there a "there" there?

Cultural Authenticity

When someone refers to cultural authenticity, they might mean music that reflects a cultural tradition. So, on the cultural side, can rap only be a representation of Black urban life? If so, has the artist lived a Black urban existence? Does it have to be a specific definition of Black and urban? Could Carlton rap on a very special episode of *The Fresh Prince of Bel Air*? He's Black, and he lives in a city, so does that count? Okay, let's put the urban setting aside for a second, do you have to be Black to rap? What other cultures and lifestyles can be represented?

Personal Authenticity

When someone refers to personal authenticity, they might mean that "you're true to your own personality, values, and spirit, regardless of the pressure that you're under to act otherwise."[2] So, on the personal side, do the adventures contained in a song *always* have to be the lived experience of the rapper? I mean, wow, all those Glocks and Benjamins and hos, and all the popping of caps you're rapping about poolside or on a boat, or poolside while on a boat . . . is this really part of your day to day? If you just made it all up, do these things need to be true? Can you play a character or share info secondhand? When is that okay, and when is that not okay?

> "I'm pretty much who I am in my music. It's pretty much the way I am in real life, but there can be slight artistic exaggerations, times when I'm a bit more aggressive or bit more, you know, like assertive or right in your face with my content. But for the most part, like I always tell my manager, I'm a guy that wears a shirt and pants and I rap."
>
> —Cashus King

Authenticity has long been something many music genres have valued, particularly those rooted in a culture that feels under siege, or existing in opposition to a prevailing power. "Rockism" presents classic rock as the only true music, as well as authenticity and masculinity's savior against pop and glam artifice. Country music lives in an avalanche of symbols and shibboleths involving pick-up trucks, jeans, and flags (and brewskis), back roads and creeks. Punk took "stick it to the establishment" so far it landed on Sid Vicious, a performer who could barely play his instrument or sing and *completely* self-destructed, breaking up his band, getting accused of murdering his girlfriend, and fatally overdosing. That is, well, so *very* punk rock of him. So, what about rap? Rap does the same with the trappings of urban life and sometimes, criminality. But most music is meant to sell, and when it does sell, it becomes "pop." When it's "pop," can it still really rock? Can it be punk? Can it be down-home country drawl genuine? If it's rap, can it be "The Real?" It's awfully hard to be *real* at the half-time show of the Superbowl brought to you by Budweiser, GoDaddy, and Jesus.[3] Perhaps success is, ironically, the philosophical undoing to the music so many strive to have success making.

Authenticity as a Brand

The value of authenticity has never been higher. Everyone and everything from performers to brands leap over one another to sell themselves based on their realness. And marketing, the domain of artifice, is now obsessed with realness. At Northwestern's Kellogg School of Management:

A broad trend [they]'re seeing, particularly in online marketing ... is trying to develop a sense of authenticity as a brand. Pretty much every brand has to stand for something today. One way you can do that is by trying to take an authentic stand on an issue, whether it is fair labor practices or sustainability or in the case of Apple, privacy, in order to make yourself come across as "legit." Pop stars are constantly trying to become brands. That might not be how they want to see it, and they definitely don't want us, their fans, to see it that way. But will.i.am of hip-hop flavored pop confection the Black Eyed Peas proclaimed just that to the *Wall Street Journal* when he declared, "I consider us a brand. A brand always has stylized decks, from colors to fonts. Here's our demographic. Here's the reach. Here's the potential."[4]

Pop stars are becoming brands, brands are selling authenticity, and pop stars are trying to brand their artificial authenticity. Are you dizzy yet? Perhaps this kind of mass-market artificiality isn't so upsetting in bubblegum pop, whose superficiality has always been apparent. But it doesn't seem to be taken as lightly when this artificiality is found in hip-hop. This is because the realness is central to the history of the form and thus to the form itself. From 50 Cent's "9mm stigmata" to Lil Wayne's "8 months on Rykers," some pretty dark stuff has been presented as emblematic of realness. Rappers have been marketed based on what is perceived, rightly or wrongly, as "authenticity."

Authenticity's Value

Why is authenticity so valuable? Well, for one, it doesn't come cheap. It requires lived experience, which is time consuming, often painful, and absolutely impossible to fake. Instead of creating lyrics from cliches, you have to open yourself up and express your personal truths. Instead of imitating the sounds of performers you admire, you have to find your own sound. In an internet-obsessed era in which we portray our best (i.e., filtered and blissful) selves at all times over social media, you have to expose your real life, warts and all. Authenticity requires honesty, vulnerability, specificity, and history, both cultural and personal.

Sometimes performers deliberately eschew the real, instead adopting personas where they can express a particular part of themselves. These personas are usually less socially palatable than their "true self." Take, for example, Beyonce's uninhibited "Sasha Fierce." There's also Nicki Minaj's "Roman Zolanski" and Eminem's "Slim Shady," two violent characters who would make Marvel's The Hulk run for the hills. But those characters are blatant theater—novel experiments with no expectation that the audience think terribly hard about what they believe or why they are who they "are." The trouble comes when these personas are passed off as the presumably true representation of the artist. For example, the 1980s duo Milli Vanilli passed themselves off as singers and had a string of hits before it was discovered that they were actually models lip-syncing to voices not their own. Another example is 1990's rapper Vanilla Ice, who completely invented a narrative of street life but claimed it to be truth. If we jump forward in time, we can look at the Australian Iggy Azalea, whose voice, according to *Complex Magazine*, "consistently strikes a jarringly inauthentic note. She raps with a tightly wound drawl, one that, to American ears, feels tone-deaf not musically, but socially. Her voice, in essence, sounds like a put-on version of a particularly technical rapper from the American South."[5]

You might be thinking, but Black Professor Lady, what's the difference between pop rock playacting and inauthentic presentation in hip-hop? David Johansen is not really the Catskill lounge singer "Buster Poindexter." The members of the 1980s heavy metal band GWAR aren't really elite fighting space scum dogs. Jack and Meg White, the duo in The White Stripes, aren't actually brother and sister. There's theater to music sometimes, and isn't that part of the fun you say? Yes and no, and most definitely yes and most definitely no. There is a difference when it comes to hip-hop. The difference is that there isn't a multicentury history of

> "I think people resonate with authentic music, but people are scared to do that type of music because it just doesn't sell."
>
> —AC Tatum

forcing Catskill lounge singers or elite fighting space scumdogs or rock hipster siblings into literal bondage to pick cotton. No history of segregating them under law. Nor a long history of stealing their music. It's the *Blackness* of hip-hop that makes authenticity such a hot button issue.

A Look Back in History

Minstrelsy

The term "Blackface" is thrown around a lot with regard to appropriation. This is a reference to the historical performance practice of "blacking up," where white performers (and later Black performers) painted their faces black with burnt cork and sang appropriated or wholly invented "Black"-sounding music in comedy and musical revues known as minstrel shows. Minstrelsy was one of America's most popular forms of entertainment in the nineteenth century and remained popular well into the twentieth:

> A blackface minstrel would sing, dance, play music, give speeches and cut up for white audiences, almost exclusively in the North, at least initially. Blackface was used for mock operas and political monologues (they called them stump speeches), skits, gender parodies and dances. Before the minstrel show gave it a reliable home, blackface was the entertainment between acts of conventional plays. Its stars were the Elvis, the Beatles, the NSYNC of the 19th century. The performers were beloved and so, especially, were their songs.[6]

Hearing ragtime music (or ragtime-inspired music) and laughing at grotesque cartoons of Black people was big business. For actual Black performers to get a piece of that action, they had to put the Black makeup over their own brown skin and then tell the same degrading jokes and play the banjos, tambourines, and jawbones that were all a part of the pageant. If only it ended there . . .

Ragtime to Rock and Roll

Ragtime, jazz, blues, do-wop, rhythm and blues, and rock and roll. Disco and hip-hop (and who knows what next) are all Black American musical genres that have been bleached, repackaged, and sold by whites. The twentieth century had an insatiable hunger for Black music, but not as much use for the people who created it:

> By the mid-fifties, most of the rhythm and blues hits written and performed by Black artists were picked up by one or more white artists who sold more. To name just a few examples, "Sh-Boom," written and performed by the doo-wop band The Chords in 1954, was covered by the Canadian band The Crew-Cuts the same year. Their version will remain number one for nine weeks. Faced with such success, the band covered other hits from the rhythm and blues charts such as "Don't Be Angry" (Nappy Brown), "Gum Drop" (The Charms) and "Earth Angel" (The Penguins)." Taking songs originally recorded by black artists, giving them to White artists, and having the "White" versions be more successful both on the charts and as moneymakers was not just a doo-wop thing. Far from it. . . . "Joe Turner's "Shake, Rattle and Roll" is covered . . . by Elvis Presley, who will also cover "Hound Dog" (Big Mama Thornton), "Tutti Frutti," [and] "Long Tall Sally" (both compositions by Little Richard).[7]

White performers became the commercial standard bearer for each new musical form, and Black performers who've wanted a piece of the action on the music they invented have always had to meet certain expectations if they were to appeal to the broader (whiter) market. Louis Armstrong, who dominated the art form of jazz, still had to grin through sidekick roles in Hollywood. Berry Gordy (founder of the Motown label) made sure his Motown artists wore suits and gowns to appear respectable to the white folks. "I wanted songs for the whites, blacks, the Jews, Gentiles . . . I wanted everybody to enjoy my music," Gordy told *The Telegraph* newspaper in

2016. This might have been savvy attitude from a seasoned entrepreneur who fashioned Motown as "the sound of young America."[8] Many later artists, particularly at the height of the gangsta era, went the other direction: exaggerating or inventing a backstory as a hardened criminal to move records to white kids in the burbs who expected their rappers to be shirtless and in knotted durags, waving uzis around. Hip-hop and R&B artist Akon spoke constantly about his three years in prison, fighting to survive after an arrest as the head of a car theft ring when, in fact, he'd only done several months in county for stealing a BMW and was released.[9] But what kind of gangsta bona fide is that? A slap on the wrist for stealing one car? To bring what was expected of him, he had to appear hard. Black music is caught between the rock of appropriation by white artists on one side and the hard place of inauthentic authenticity for Black artists on the other.

More Questions to Ponder

So, if all these forms were born Black and got whiter as they went, does that mean that all music that was born from African American tradition can't be sung by any other race or culture without being labeled "Appropriation" (with a capital A)? It can be upsetting to see latecomers to a genre getting rich while the OGs languish in obscurity, but it also seems segregatory and not in the spirit of the arts to deny music to those who love it and want to make that music. But sometimes a genre's entire downfall can be blamed on appropriation. How did the fabulously Black and queer urban club genre that is disco end up in the hands of Rod Stewart ("Do Ya Think I'm Sexy?") and Rick Dees ("Disco Duck")? Frequently, an artist seems to make appropriation work for them without anyone commenting. I mean, would you deny four working-class lads from Liverpool their twisting and shouting? How about the Stones, who got their start on Willie Dixon tunes?

> To their credit the Rolling Stones did not take their own success as naïve evidence of color blindness among their fans and often expressed frustration that their own performances of R&B were more popular among their countrymen than the original versions

they so revered.... The Rolling Stones did not play Woodstock. The band's own 1969 tour boasted Ike and Tina Turner and B.B. King as opening acts, and the band also frequently played alongside black performers onstage and in the studio, most notably singer Merry Clayton.[10] (If you haven't heard Merry Clayton's naked vocal from "Gimme Shelter" from the documentary *20 feet from Stardom*, it's a life-changing experience).

But sometimes, there *is* a backlash, or at least raised eyebrows, by activists and academics. Let's look at some of the most frequent targets of accusations of appropriation in the hip-hop conversation. Blondie's "Rapture," while probably primitive to the modern ear, was important in its day. Clearly, Blondie's preexisting fan base and her ... blondeness ... gave her power in promoting such a song. She was a known genre experimenter, and her position as a downtown artist made her crossing paths with rap inevitable. She makes no claims to hip-hop authenticity: "I wasn't trying to be black or a Bronx rapper. It was an homage to what I saw and to a form that was exciting for us."[11] So ... Blondie ... pass? Okay, how about the Beastie Boys?

The Beastie Boys are one of the biggest acts in hip-hop history, but with roots as a wildly privileged, white, "nepo baby" punk group. They used Malcolm McLaren's "Buffalo Gals," mixing some beats and scratching with sloppy prank calls to Carvel ice cream stores. The popularity of that song, "Cookie Puss," made them stay in a novelty hip-hop lane and ride their Jerky Boyz meets Run DMC meets rock guitar schtick right into the Rock and Roll Hall of Fame. So, Beastie Boys ... pass?

Some artists make it easy to throw them under the bus of social justice or musical purity tests. Vanilla Ice was caught with an embellished "street" backstory, parties at Mar-a-Lago, and is largely a one-hit wonder. Macklemore? That one is more complicated, because he's publicly trying to work out his place in hip-hop.

> Macklemore, whether intentionally or not, decided to use his privilege to cannibalize whiteness, tearing at his own mythology

in the process. When I saw him last year at a festival, he performed White Privilege II to a captivated white audience. Halfway through the song, he left the stage entirely empty, walking off and making room for two black poets and a black drummer to read poems about police violence and gentrification. It was a stunning image, an artist holding the mouth of his audience open and forcing the slick red spoonful of medicine down their throats.[12]

You may find the public preaching and self-flagellation to be a responsible handling of privilege, or perhaps it comes off as condescending sermonizing, only you know how *you* feel, remember? When dude beat Kendrick for a Grammy (in a much maligned but also typical-for-the-Grammys move) in 2014, he texted Kendrick, "You got robbed. I wanted you to win. You should have. It's weird and it sucks that I robbed you." Should he be constantly wringing his hands about his extremely successful place in the industry? Love it or hate it, he's addressing the elephant in the room.

> **"The biggest thing is always staying authentic. So I try to pull from life experiences that I've had, or anything that I've gone through just because I feel wrong, trying to tell the story of somebody else, or something that didn't happen to me, just doesn't feel right to me."**
>
> **—Eddie Yuma**

And ain't nobody coming for Eminem anymore. As Dr. Dre said, "I don't care if he's purple, as long as he can rap." But why? The Grammys love to pull their regular exalting of a white performer over a Black one and get plenty of ink spilled over it, but when they award Eminem, he gets a pass. How come? Skill, first off. Next, the perception that he's paid his dues in the industry. And third, his seemingly deep and genuine love for the culture surrounding his craft: "the main reason people aren't complaining about Eminem's victory is that, quite simply, he has unequivocally demonstrated his love for hip-hop as a culture and a genre. He long ago recognized his white privilege ('If I was black I would have sold half') and committed himself to the old-fashioned aesthetic of masterful lyricism."[13]

If we're making an "Is this okay?" chart of white rappers, Vanilla Ice and Iggy Azalea tend to fall toward "not okay" without many people speaking up for them. Remember Snow, the reggae rapper from Toronto who "licky boom boom down"-ed on "Informer" in 1992? Most people would say that he goes there, too. Macklemore might not stand the test of time, but he seems okay because he's successful, but he's sad about it. And we've established Eminem. Eminem is almost *always* deemed okay. I know I said I would not answer any questions of what is okay, but I do want to throw in my personal opinion here and scream, "y'all Eminem is all the way in the okay column." But back to the chart: Post Malone distances himself from even being considered hip-hop: "I'm not a rapper. I'm an artist. I don't make rap music. I might rap, but I don't make rap music."[14] Interesting. All right, how about Lil Dicky? The *Harvard Business Review* said in 2014 that:

> In order to differentiate himself from white rappers who play the "cool card," Lil Dicky, an aspiring emcee who gained quite a bit of attention through his creative YouTube videos and impressive first mixtape, incorporates his vulnerabilities, fears, and flaws in order to portray himself—including his middle-class background—genuinely. By accurately depicting his Jewish, middle-class identity, Lil Dicky successfully justifies his position within the genre by claiming a niche.[15]

But, does he? Again, these are things for *you* to ponder and for *you* to decide.

It cannot be said that hip-hop isn't extremely connected to Blackness. It's also very gross to say that you should have to have certain markers on a 23andMe before you can perform a particular kind of music. At the end of the day, you either rap and sing skillfully, or you don't.

Additionally, your content and performance either reflects your lived experience, or it doesn't.

You could lay out virtuosity and authenticity in quadrants:

- Ideally, you would perform skillfully in a way that reflects your lived experience. That's the box you want to be in.
- If you have neither skill nor authenticity, that box is deadly.
- Authenticity poorly performed, well, accusations won't be flung at you regarding keeping it real, but the skillset is an essential component of success, so that's likely not going to get you anywhere either.
- It's that fourth box—performing well but inauthentically—if you're in that box, it's between you and your god if what you can get away with is something you ought to get away with.

As for my belief, and the advice I give my students: hip-hop was created when oppressed people, people whose work is often stolen by their oppressors, told the truth about their circumstances in the face of overwhelming institutional opposition. To deliberately misrepresent yourself or to play with ideas you don't fully understand or appreciate seems disrespectful at best and immoral at worst. If a performer is skilled, honest about their own experience, has a delivery style that seems viable given their backstory (which *will* come out eventually), and carries themselves in an honest way, then . . . hip-hop seems as though it can be, and should be, a space for all who honor it.

> "I definitely had moments where I wanted to conform a little bit more. But like, it's just hard for me to actually make something that I'm proud of when I do that."
>
> —Diz

Notes

1. Barker, H., and Y. Taylor. (2008). *Faking It: The Quest for Authenticity in Popular Music*. London: Faber, 1.

2. Mind Tools. (n.d.). Authenticity. Retrieved March 22, 2023, from https://www.mindtools.com/ay30irc/authenticity

3. Lundstrom, Kathryn. (2023, February 12). "He Gets Us" Is Bringing Jesus to the Super Bowl. *Adweek*. Retrieved March 12, 2023, from https://www.adweek.com/brand-marketing/he-gets-us-is-bringing-jesus-to-the-super-bowl-can-it-convert-viewers-to-followers/

4. Jurgensen, John. (2010, April 16). "Black Eyed Peas: The Most Corporate Band in America." *The Wall Street Journal*. Retrieved February 28, 2023, from www.wsj.com/articles/SB10001424052702303720604575169933636121658.

5. Drake, David. (2014, April 22). Iggy Azalea's "the New Classic" Isn't Really. *COMPLEX*. https://www.complex.com/music/2014/04/iggy-azalea-the-new-classic-review

6. Morris, Wesley. (2019, August 4). Why Is Everyone Always Stealing Black Music? *The New York Times* https://www.nytimes.com/interactive/2019/08/14/magazine/music-black-culture-appropriation.html

7. Djavadzadeh, Keivan. (2013). Blacking Up: Une Histoire du Rock aur prisme du blackface. *Transatlantica: American Studies Journal*, 2. Retrieved March 22, 2023, from https://journals.openedition.org/transatlantica/6553#tocfrom1n3

8. Brown, Mick. (2016, January 23). Barry Gordy: The Man Who Built Mowtown. *The Telegraph*. http://s.telegraph.co.uk/graphics/projects/berry-gordy-motown/index.html

9. *The Smoking Gun*. (2008, April 16). Akon's Con Job. Retrieved March 22, 2023, from https://www.thesmokinggun.com/documents/crime/akons-con-job

10. Hamilton, J. (2016, October 6). How The Rolling Stones, A Band Obsessed with Black Musicians, Helped Make Rock a White Genre. *Slate Magazine*. Retrieved March 11, 2023, from https://slate.com/culture/2016/10/race-rock-and-the-rolling-stones-how-the-rock-and-roll-became-white.html

11. Images, A. T. G. (2019, June 11). The Rap in Blondie's "Rapture." *The Wall Street Journal*. Retrieved March 11, 2023, from https://www.wsj.com/articles/the-rap-in-blondies-rapture-11560178671

12. Abdurraqib, Hanif. (2018, October 8). From Vanilla Ice to Macklemore: Understanding the White Rapper's Burden. *The Guardian*. Retrieved March 11, 2023, from https://www.theguardian.com/music/2018/oct/08/vanilla-ice-eminem-macklemore-understanding-white-rappers-burden

13. Westhoff, Ben. (2015, February 11). Pop Appropriation: Why Hip-Hop Loves Eminem but Loathes Iggy Azalea. *The Guardian*. Retrieved March 12, 2023, from https://www.theguardian.com/music/2015/feb/11/hip-hop-appropriation-eminem-iggy-azalea

14. Caramanica, J. (2016, August 18). White Rappers, Clear of a Black Planet. *The New York Times*. Retrieved March 12, 2023, from https://www.nytimes.com/2016/08/21/arts/music/white-rappers-geazy-mike-stud.html

15. "The Politics of Race in Rap." (2014, June 9). *Harvard Political Review*. https://harvardpolitics.com/politics-race-rap/.

Part II
VOCAL TECHNIQUE

Eight

Strictly Business (EPMD)
The House is Built on This Foundation

If you started at the beginning, you've read about the roots of hip-hop history, explored subgenres of rap, and seen hip-hop's evolution through the eras and into present day. You've read about hip-hop's influence on culture, reaching far beyond influence on other genres of music, into television, sports, fashion, and art. You've seen how hip-hop is a platform for activism and its power regarding the amplification of the Black voice. Having this baseline knowledge will help elevate your own performance by allowing you to find your unique authenticity in the context of the genre as a whole. By now, you've hopefully listened to many of the artists quoted, as well as some of the other greats that were mentioned in chapter 5 and elsewhere. If not, there's a Spotify list with a link in the introduction section of the book, so you can put on some headphones and listen. While it may take time, I promise it will be well worth it and prime you for the work ahead—you cannot expect to be able to perform this type of music without fully engrossing yourself in it. As you enter the following chapters, you'll begin to understand the *how* of rap. The following chapters, including this one, are intended to give you the very first steps to unpacking the how-to-rap toolbox and will also hopefully get you past some stumbling blocks and sharpen your skills along the way. They will discuss breathing, posture, diction, rhythm, flow, tone, expression, vocal health, mic technique, and more. But, before you can dig in, it's probably a good idea to get an overview of the main components of rap. Most of these components will get their starring moment in another chapter, but it's crucial to start here in order to organize your practice. So, let's dive in!

The Building Blocks of Rap

Beat and Rhythm

Imagine yourself spitting bars to a glorious rap. What do you think of first? If you said the cred and the thunderous applause, I commend you for your honesty. But before you get there, you've got to get that speed rap out. Okay—so now you think, the delivery? Yup, that's essential—but the delivery of *what*? Hmm. Okay: lyrics. Lyrics *must* come first. Well, obviously lyrics can make or break a rap. But people love Lil Jon's "Turn Down For What," for example, and that entire rap literally only contains twelve different words. Those same twelve words are repeated over and over and over and over and . . . well you get the point. So, yes, lyrics are essential too—but before that, you need *flow*. Flow is kind of everything. But what is flow when it comes to rap? Simply put, *flow is the rhythmic patterns that the artist uses when saying the lyrics to the song*. To have flow, you have to have rhythmic patterns. To have a series of rhythmic patterns, you'll need to understand the basics of *beat* and *rhythm*.

Beat

Most rappers begin with a beat. What is a beat? Well, in rap, it can mean two things:

- The instrumental track is often referred to as a beat. The producer of a rap song will often create this instrumental accompaniment. This will have percussion, as well as other instruments (bass, synth, keyboard, samples, etc.) layered on top of one another. If you and your friends are listening to the latest Lizzo release, and your friend casually says, "This track has a dope beat," they are probably talking about the instrumental track.
- Beat can also mean a steady pulse. The length of time between beats is both consistent and constant, meaning it repeats over and over at the same rate. To picture what a steady pulse sounds like, think of a heartbeat in your chest. The heart beats repeatedly and the length of

time that there is silence between the beats is the same between each heartbeat. You can also think of the ticking of a clock when trying to think of what a beat is: just like the tick ... tick ... tick ... repeats over and over, so too does the steady beat in your song. You'll probably find yourself bobbing your head along with this steady beat. That repetition is fundamental in forming the groove of the song.

Rhythm

"Rhythm involves time—the duration, or length, of musical sounds."[1]

It's easy to confuse beat and rhythm, but they are not the same thing. "Rhythm (sometimes called cadence) refers to the way syllables are placed on the beat and the different patterns that are created by different numbers of syllables. Rhythm makes the lyrics sound musical and interesting. It's also what makes the lyrics a rap, rather than just words spoken in a random way over a beat."[2] Rhythm is a system of measuring how long or short something is. Just like you'd measure the distance from your house to your school or job in miles, rhythmic notes tell us how long or short a word is. Instead of dealing with distance, in rhythm, you are dealing with time. So, in rhythm, instead of deciding how far something is from one thing to another, you're determining how long something lasts.

Rhythm is a pattern, or group of beats, that have different durations, meaning some are shorter or longer than others. When you put these beats of various lengths together, you'll have a rhythmic pattern that is not consistent, meaning it is *not* the same thing repeated continuously. These rhythmic patterns fit on top of the steady beat. These patterns are the template for your lyrics.

To put this into practice, listen to a rap song that you love. First, identify the instrumental track (sometimes referred to as beats). There will be several musical instruments on this instrumental track. Within that instrumental track, you'll hear the steady beat (which you might think of also as pulse). It is, as discussed, unchanging and constant.

On the instrumental track, the various instruments will also be made up of various rhythmic patterns. These patterns are strung together to create the length of the song. These various instruments are layered upon one another, often with different rhythmic patterns happening simultaneously. Now listen to the next layer: the lyrics. These lyrics will be said in rhythmic patterns, so some of the artists' syllables will have a longer duration than others, meaning they will be held for more time than other syllables. You can think of the rapper's voice as another instrument on that track, and that too, will have different rhythmic patterns, and those patterns don't have to be the same as the rhythmic patterns happening in the other instruments on the track. But to make *any* of this make sense to your ears, you'll need the steady pulse or beat underneath everything, constant and repeating. For a deeper dive into rhythm, check out chapter 12.

> "I have a very rhythmic mind. . . . The way that I listen to music is very different than the way that a lot of other people listen to music. It's not really on purpose. I actually hear things. I hear vocals as melodies, rhythms, articulations, consonants and vowels. I don't really hear the words that are being said."
>
> —daedae

Tempo

What is tempo?

Tempo is *speed*. More specifically, tempo means the speed that a song is played or rapped. There are three basic tempos in rap: fast tempo, mid-tempo, and slow tempo. When discussing tempo, it's important to understand that you are discussing the tempo of the beat/pulse, and thus the tempo of the instrumental track. There might very well be a speed rap over a mid-tempo or even slow tempo beat (instrumental track). For example, listen to 2:21 to 2:31 of "Element" by Kendrick Lamar. That would be considered a slow(ish)-tempo flow, but the tempo of the song is a mid-tempo (ninety-five beats per minute). Taken even farther, check out "Move that Dope" by Future or "Grandmas Make the World" by J-Zone. Both of these have slow tempo instrumental tracks (sixty-five beats per minute), yet the way they say their words are quite the opposite of slow. It is more that the beat/pulse is slow.

Think of your heartbeat when you are sleeping: it is steady and consistent, but it is slow. Now think of your heartbeat when you are jogging. The beat/pulse is still steady and consistent, but the rate of the heartbeat is faster. The heartbeat is still steady, but the number of heartbeats in one minute will be fewer than the number of heartbeats when jogging. If we remember, rhythm and pulse are measurements of time. The length of time between pulses in the steady pulse creates the speed of the song. This speed is tempo.

Why is tempo important?

- **Mood/vibe:** The tempo of a song is one of the tools a rapper has to set their intended mood or vibe for the song. There have even been scientific studies of how tempo affects emotion in listeners. In one study, scientists found that "fast-tempo music evoked the most pleasant emotion, and slow-tempo music received the lowest score in the arousal dimension among the three kinds of music. These findings are consistent with existing research about music tempo and its influence on subjective emotional valence and arousal."[3]

  The tempo (song speeds or the speed of the rap) can dramatically influence the listener's perception of the mood, emotion, or general vibe of the song itself. Listen to "Club Can't Handle Me" by Flo Rida, featuring David Guetta, which has 150 beats per minute. (Note: You've now heard me use this term three times in this chapter. You'll often hear the term BPM in rap music, which stands for beats per minute.) Contrast that with "SMH" by Mavi which has seventy-eight beats per minute. Notice that Mavi's flow is not slow. However, if you listen to the beat/pulse, *that* is slower than the pulse in the iconic Flo Rida song.

- **Flow speed:** The slower the tempo of your track, the faster you'll be able to rap because you can fit more syllables into each beat. The faster the tempo of the song, the slower your flow will need to be. I know this might sound backward but try it out yourself and see if it makes sense. (Note: It might not even sound that way to the listening ear, but it's important to understand how flow and tempo relate to one another so you can best create a flow for your instrumental track.) This has become commonplace throughout pop music today thanks to the city of Atlanta's influence on the hip-hop scene. Different parts of the country have produced numerous acts that share a sound (this sound can be flow, tempo, subject matter, etc.). For example, Atlanta (which is part of what is often referred to as the "Dirty South" in rap) is instrumental in creating music with slower tempos and flows. Part of the slowing is due to the continuing dominance of hip-hop, which now permeates every branch of music, even longtime holdouts like rock and country. "Hip-hop culture is the new pop culture, and our tempo ranges aren't too fast," says Sven Thomas, who helped produce Rihanna's number one smash hit "Work." "Rappers can really swag out on slower beats."[4]
- **Subgenre:** Understanding trends in the region or from the era of the song you are rapping, or the era you are emulating if you are writing or freestyling, might help you master your flow. If you know this, you can listen to the greatest-of-all-times from that era, hearing how they handle and master those tempos. It gives you a reference point and something to study. Hip-hop researchers Ben Duinker and Denis Martin give some great examples of a genre's influence on tempo from raps golden age:

> Hip-hop's crossover with rock, exemplified on albums such as *License to Ill* (Beastie Boys, 1986) and *Raising Hell* (Run DMC, 1986), might account for some of the faster tempi in the early years of the corpus, as do some of the songs that Krims (2000) might classify as "party rap," such as those by

MC Hammer, Sir Mix-a-lot, and Heavy D. and the Boyz. Subsequently, the rise of G-funk-influenced West-coast artists (particularly Dr. Dre, Snoop Dogg, and 2Pac) may speak to the slower tempi of the early nineties.[5]

Cadence

"Cadence is the modulation or inflection of the voice (adjusting the pitch of the vocal), along with variation in speech tempo (changing the speed/flow of the vocal)."[6] You can think of cadence as a small piece of your flow. Put all of your phrases, or cadences together, and you'd get your flow.

Flow

There are entire books on flow, and there is no way to do the term justice within this chapter. There will be more about flow in chapter 12, and as you continue to study, I encourage you to keep reading and listening, as flow is something that can be studied for a lifetime. Listen to your favorite rappers and think about what makes their flow special. Wait . . . hold up—we're getting ahead of ourselves. The question at hand is: what is flow? Here is a basic introduction to the ocean that is flow.

- Flow means different things to different people in rap. For example, music theory Professor Mitchell Ohriner says, "flow encompasses phrasing, rhythm, meter, rhyme, accent, patterning, and groove, not to mention the relations among these parameters. Flow also occurs on different scales. Each decision of an artist contributes to the flow of a verse of rapping, but all the verses of an artist, and the central tendencies that emerge from them, also constitute a flow. And furthermore, all the verses of all the artists contribute to what it means to flow."[7] I love that definition because people use the word "flow" in countless ways, and this definition shows us that perhaps that is okay and necessary in understanding such an important term in the performance world. When we think of flow as being the sum of all parts,

I think it becomes less daunting to understand and becomes easier to do yourself. Another theorist, Kyle Adams, says, "'flow' describes all of the rhythmical and articulative features of a rapper's delivery of the lyrics. Though rappers rarely concern themselves with defining the terms they use, flow has become one of the most important ways that rappers and audiences distinguish among various styles of rapping and make value judgments about other rappers."[8]

- And yet another definition by Kautny, "The rhythmic delivery of MCing is called flow. Flow is all of these things. At the center of flow is indeed rhythm. Rhythmic patterns. But there are nuanced components of flow too—such as syllabic stress, dynamics, word pronunciation choices, Timbre, and choice of consonant stress."[9]

Often a rapper has a distinctive flow. This certainly doesn't mean that all of their songs sound the same—far from it! But each rapper does have a flow style. Twista is known for his incredibly fast flows. Biggie is known for a more relaxed flow with intricate and genius use of carrying cadences over from the end of a bar, spilling the end of the cadence into the next bar and so on. Childish Gambino's ability to seamlessly switch flows never fails to astound. Lauryn Hill's use of a neo-soul groove makes her flow unmistakable. Tyler, the Creator's tricky flows are mind boggling, and there is a reason why people love Roddy Ricch's expertise at evading the trappings of the limitation that the insidious, hi hat beat that trap music provides. Listen to your favorite rappers and see if you can hear their distinctive flow. Ask yourself: why are these folx my favorites? Rap along with them (I'm sure you already do . . . but if you don't, put this book down and start. Right. Now.) You can dig into specifics of flow in chapter 12.

> "I think the flow is something that's super important and needs to have as much attention as lyrics."
>
> —Eddie Yuma

Storytelling/Delivery

You've figured out how to count your rhythms; you've perfected your cadences; you are proud of your flow. You've got your tempo locked in, and you aren't rushing or dragging. Great! You should pat yourself on the back. But you are probably monotone, so no one cares. Sorry, not sorry. Now, you're thinking of monotone rappers people love. You're going to want to play 21 Savage's "Bank Account" and say "SEEEEE?" And sure, if monotone is your thing, then go with it. But, if it's not intentional, then thinking about your delivery so that your story is *felt* is just as important as the lyrics you say.

What does delivery mean? Why is it so crucial to rap?

Delivery is linked to storytelling; it's the way you use your voice to convey your intended emotion when rapping. "A rapper is, in fact, an actor. Not a visual one, but a vocal one. Rappers are voice actors for their music just as much as Seth MacFarlane is for the entire cast of *Family Guy*. Rappers need to convey their story through their voice."[10] For more on emotional delivery, check out chapter 14.

> **"If the word game ain't there and the delivery ain't on point, what are you rapping for?"**
>
> —Kidd Kenn

Diction/Articulation

But but but, hold on a second. Before you turn to chapter 14, or any other chapter for that matter, it's critical to mention that you need to be understood (unless you are a mumble rapper, and, if that's your jam, ignore this paragraph). An essential component of your delivery is the choices you make regarding pronunciation, diction, and articulation. Let's not get too in the weeds on this, but just one example: think about the sounds these letters make: L, Z, R, M, N, V, and a soft TH sound. Say them out loud. These are called liquid consonants because they make a sound on a pitch when you say them. Try it out: say a<u>L</u>ways, or <u>Z</u>ebra, or nu<u>M</u>ber. When you start diving in, there are so many different ways to shape your delivery. Articulation is at the top of the list.

Instrumentation

You'd be cheating yourself out of the roadmap to the treasure of a killer rap if you ignore the instrumentation. Listen to the beat by itself. See what the percussion pattern is doing. When you are first learning to rap, it can even be helpful to lean on this drumbeat to help you create or learn and memorize your flow. But it goes way beyond that. Listen to the instruments, all layering on one another. Think about what instruments are being used. Listen to which one is taking the lead in getting your attention. Listen to the dynamics: when does it get louder, and conversely, when does it get softer? Rishma Dhaliwal, a hip-hop journalist, even claims that drums carry the emotion that could, in some cases, inform the delivery. She notes, "drums can also be used to tell a story. Drums carry and define the emotions of a track. Drums can be harsh or soft. They can be prominent or withdrawn. Regardless of how they are used, drums have the ability to convey the emotions the producer or artist feels as they put down the track. This can be felt in the way drums are used in songs such as 'When I Am Gone' by Eminem."[11]

Anyone that says that rapping is just talking has completely lost their marbles. As you can see, to even begin to think about rapping well, you must consider the beat, the rhythm, the cadence, the flow, the articulation, the delivery, and the instrumentation. Which, yes, I know, *is* a lot! This chapter shouldn't scare you. There is a lot to think about, and a whole lot to learn, but that's why you have ten more chapters to read! So, without further ado, let's get to it.

> **"It's all feeling.
> It's really very free.
> My whole process is
> just very meditative."**
>
> —Keni Can Fly

Notes

1. Kids Brittanica. (n.d.). Rhythm. https://kids.britannica.com/students/article/music/275997#205087-toc

2. Edwards, Paul. (2009). *How to Rap: The Art and Science of the Hip-Hop MC*. Chicago: Chicago Review Press, 111.

3. Liu, Ying. (2018). Effects of Musical Tempo on Musicians' and Non-musicians' Emotional Experience When Listening to Music. *Frontiers in Psychology*, 9: 2118.

4. Leight, Elias. (2017, August 15). Producers, Songwriters on How Pop Songs Got So Slow. *Rolling Stone*.

5. Duinker, Ben. (2017). In Search of the Golden Age Hip-Hop Sound (1986–1996). *Empirical Musicology Review*, 12 (1).

6. Zisook, Brian "Z." (2018, February 12). Kendrick Lamar & The Importance of Cadence in Rap. *Djbooth*. Retrieved March 1, 2023, from https://djbooth.net/features/2017-05-31-kendrick-lamar-cadence-in-rap

7. Ohriner, Mitchell. (2019). *Flow: The Rhythmic Voice in Rap Music*. New York: Oxford University Press.

8. Adams, Kyle. (2009, October). On the Metrical Techniques of Flow in Rap Music. *MTO*, 15 (5). Retrieved March 1, 2023, from https://www.mtosmt.org/issues/mto.09.15.5/mto.09.15.5.adams.html

9. Williams, Justin A. (2015). *Cambridge Companion to Hip-Hop*. Cambridge: Cambridge University Press, 101.

10. Dillin. (2018, July 10). How to Rap: Why Vocal Delivery Is More Important Than Lyrics. *The Culturalist*. https://dillinrandolph.com/2018/07/10/how-to-rap-why-vocal-delivery-is-more-important-than-lyrics/

11. Dhaliwal, Rishma. (2020, January 24). Drumming and Its Importance in Hip-Hop. *I am Hip-Hop Magazine*. Retrieved March 1, 2023, from https://www.iamhiphopmagazine.com/drumming-importance-hip-hop/

Nine

"Let Your Backbone Slide" (Maestro)

Posture and its Relationship to Movement

Merriam Webster dictionary defines posture as "the position or bearing of the body whether characteristic or assumed for a special purpose."[1] Simply put, posture is your body's position when you are standing, sitting, or lying down. Most people describe this whole-body positioning phenomenon as posture, although you might also hear the words stance or alignment thrown around in relation to the way people are standing. There are subtle differences, and we can use those differences to help frame your thinking for practice versus performance. With that in mind, check out the following definitions:

> Stance: "the arrangement of the body and its limbs."[2] We will discuss stance specifically when discussing the way you stand when performing on stage or posing for pictures in photo shoots.
>
> Alignment: "Alignment refers to how the head, shoulders, spine, hips, knees and ankles relate and line up with each other. **Proper alignment of the body puts less stress on the spine and helps you have good posture.**"[3] We can think of alignment as something to think about when striving to obtain relaxed, efficient, and effective posture.

Why Is Posture Important?

The goal in healthy rap technique is efficiency. When practicing, you should always ask yourself, "How can you get the sound that you want in the most efficient manner?" If your alignment is off, it throws everything else out of whack, making rapping more effortful. Think of solid rapping technique as cake with many layers. When baking that cake, you bake each layer in a separate baking pan. You then remove a layer from its baking pan and put it onto a plate. Next you carefully ice the layer. After this, you repeat the process, removing the second cake from its cake pan, but this time you place it directly on top of the first layer. You ice that layer and repeat the process with all the following cakes, stacking the cakes on top of one another. If that very first layer is lumpy and crumbly, the layers you try to stack on top won't have a great foundation to rest upon, and your cake will either fall over, or, at the very least, look like your six-year-old niece made it. Posture is like that first layer of the cake. If it isn't serving you well, it will inhibit the efficiency and effectiveness of the other things you are trying to accomplish in your technique. Okay Melissa, now I'm hungry for cake, and I'm still wondering *how* posture affects these other elements of rap technique. Well gee, I'm *so* glad you asked. Let's examine how posture and alignment play an important role in several aspects of your rap technique.

Breathing Ability

Vocal pedagogy expert Dr. William McKinney states, "It is obvious that the ability to move air in and out of the body freely and to obtain the needed quantity of air can be seriously affected by the posture of the various parts of the breathing mechanism. A sunken chest position will limit the capacity of the lungs, and a tense abdominal wall will inhibit the downward travel of the diaphragm."[4] In other words, the ability to inhale easily and the ability to get enough air for your verse will be compromised if you are slouching. Try this now:

- Roll your shoulders forward so that you are slumped over in your chair (imagine how you sit when you are cramming for a test in the library, and its hour three of studying; my guess is that you're slouching in your seat).

- Try to take a deep breath while in this slumped position.
- Pay attention to your lungs but also your abdomen—does it feel easy to take a deep breath? Do your lungs and abs feel free to expand, or do things feel squished and cramped?
- Try this again, but this time, roll your shoulders back: make three large circles, with your shoulders going in a clockwise motion. After the third rotation, scrunch your shoulders up to your ears, and then slowly roll them backwards and let them rest in a comfortable position.
- Staying in this posture, take some inventory—what feels different? Do you feel taller? Anything else?
- Inhale again. Notice the difference in effort level—was it easier to get a deeper breath?

Chances are, improving your posture with this simple exercise dramatically improved the efficiency and effectiveness of your breathing—and you haven't even read the breath chapter yet!

Projection

If we go back to the Merriam Webster dictionary, it tells us that projection means "the act of throwing or thrusting forward."[5] If you think of how this can be applied to your voice, vocal projection means the method of sending sound from your mouth out into the room. Effective projection occurs when you can easily be heard. Efficient projection occurs when you can easily be heard without undue effort or strain (in other words, you aren't pushing or yelling). Efficient projection occurs because of vocal resonance. You'll read about how to optimize your vocal resonance in a few chapters. But in order for your resonance to be its best little resonance self, *you* must have good posture and alignment. Educator Steve Scott says, "Ideal body alignment creates two distinct physical conditions that help optimize resonance:

1. Longer vocal tract
2. Wider vocal tract."[6]

What Scott means is that good posture opens the vocal tract (imagine a tube inside your throat that houses your vocal folds, and through which sound travels), making it both longer and wider. This sets you up to be able to more efficiently use vocal resonance to project your sound into the room and cut through the noise of the crowd without a ton of effort.

Confidence

Have you seen your favorite rapper perform on stage? How would you describe them? Meek? Nervous? Timid? Do they seem unsure about what they're saying? My guess is the answer is no. Common words to describe rappers are clever, bold, charming, intense, and badass. How are these word groupings different from one another? Which list do you associate with someone who exudes confidence? In all likelihood, you think that the second list is a better fit for someone who is confident.

Close your eyes and picture the timid, meek, nervous rapper in concert. What do they look like on stage? Can you describe how you picture them standing? Are they looking out into the audience, or is their head down? What about their arms? Are they using big hand gestures, or are they slouching, with their elbows glued to their sides? Now imagine the charming, clever, bold, intense, badass rapper. How are they standing? My guess is that their neck is long, and their head is held high. Their shoulders are back, and they aren't afraid to take up space. Sometimes, people can speak without opening their mouth, because body language is a powerful communication tool. Posture is an indicator of your comfort level and your confidence.

Storytelling

Your stance can help inform your audience of your emotions, your reaction to situations or environments, or your persona, especially if it's changing for a particular song in a set and wasn't present in the previous song. For example, acting coach Vanessa Van Edwards discusses something called the "launch stance" as a way to exude power:

the easiest way to project confidence is to claim territory. Own your body and own the space around you by standing or sitting tall. Keep your arms loose by your side or place one or both hands on your hips. Relax your shoulders down your back and open your chest. These expansive postures (what we refer to as a Launch Stance) will show others that you're confident and sure of yourself. Be wary of low power postures (unless the script calls for it!), such as crossing your arms or turtling your shoulders to your ears as this may signal defeat.[7]

Van Edwards gives us a good example of how posture plays a role in the portrayal of status. You might think you are just standing there, but if used purposefully, stance can display what an audience might perceive as character traits.

Elements of Healthy Posture

Posture plays a vital role in both ease of sound production as well as nonverbal communication with your audience. Once you master a healthy posture and gain proper alignment, you will have the power to choose when to adjust for intentional nonverbal communication and storytelling. I mean, think about it—you aren't going to stand still during your performance, odds are, you also aren't going to stand up straight during your concerts. I've got to be honest, if you did, you'd be pretty boring to watch. We'll talk about common rap stances at the end of the chapter, but none of them look like you are a member of the Vienna Boys Choir. The cool thing about posture is that you can still have "good" posture even while standing, sitting, squatting, or kneeling. Remember, your goal is to be in alignment, meaning you don't want parts of your body to be out of whack with other parts, because that results in tension. The easiest way to work on your posture is to focus on the key body parts that have the greatest impact on posture, and make sure that each is aligned and free of tension. Let's work from the ground up, aligning the six body parts that are crucial to efficient and aligned posture.

Feet

When people think of posture, they don't always realize how important the feet are in the equation. But the feet determine whether you feel grounded and will affect everything else. Making sure your weight is balanced on your feet will help you with hip and knee alignment. If you don't feel balanced, you can investigate some common conditions and causes:

- Pronating: lifting the outer edges of your feet while you stand; doing so makes the natural arch of your foot flatten out, making balancing on the balls of your feet difficult.
- Dorsiflexion: standing on your heels.
- Plantarflexion: standing with your weight on your toes/standing on tiptoes.
- Supination (which I am guilty of if I am not careful): standing with too much weight on the outer edges of the feet.

Ideal foot positioning for alignment: Your feet should be facing forward (try not to turn them out (in a V position) or have them turned inward (so the toes are angled inward toward each other). They should be hip width apart, with slightly more weight on the balls of your feet. Then place one foot slightly in front of the other. See how this feels for you.

Knees

Once, during a high school choir concert, a guy in the row behind me was standing with his knees locked for the duration of our performance. In our second to last song, the kid fainted. Ha, that was that funny . . . um, I mean, wow, was that terrible. He fainted because locking your knees hinders the blood flow to your brain, causing a lack of circulation. The lack of blood flow can result in fainting. It would probably kill your mojo to faint in the middle of your set. In addition to fainting, locking your knees messes with your posture by forcing your chest out and causing a lot of stress and strain on your lower back. Go to a mirror. Turn sideways. Stand normally. Now, lock your knees and notice how your back sways slightly and your chest moves. Musician and instructor Stephanie Izzo explains ideal knee position and pitfalls:

> Maintain a nice loose position in your knees. If you lock your knees, you will once again find yourself off-balance with excess tension in the upper body. However, if you bend the knees too much, you will find yourself exerting too much effort in the legs and lower body. This is not the most efficient knee position. You want to stay in a comfortable, loose position, so you can move with ease if needed.[8]

Pelvis

Proper pelvis position in posture is kind of like the porridge that Goldilocks eats in the three bears' house. It shouldn't tuck too far forward or tilt too far backward. You are aiming for a neutral, middle-of-the-road position here so that your spine can have a natural curve. To find what feels natural for you, go to the extremes:

- Extreme 1: Tucking your pelvis too far forward—to do this think of bringing your glutes forward, like you are trying to eliminate the presence of your butt by bringing it forward without moving your hips or legs.
- Extreme 2: Completely release your abdominal muscles and stick your butt out. This is known as sway back, because you'll feel that your back is arching.

Hopefully neither of these positions feels natural for you. Instead, find the middle of your hip bone. Look down—you should be able to draw a straight line to the middle or your ankle. If the line is diagonal in either direction, you should investigate further.

Arms and Hands

Ideally, your arms and hands should be relaxed and resting at your sides. Go to a mirror and stand, facing your reflection. Are your arms resting against your torso? Are your palms turned inward (almost touching your thigh?) If so, fantastic. If not, the issue will most likely be tension in your shoulders or a misalignment of your pelvis, and correcting issues in those areas should, in most cases, fix any major issues you might be seeing with your arms and hand position.

Something to watch out for is tension. It is common to hold tension in your hands. This can lead to balling your hands into fists or unintentional hand movements, which can be distracting to your audience. **To release hand tension, try this exercise.**

Tense, hyperextend, release:

- With your arms hanging at your sides, form tight fists with both hands.
- Hold this position for eight seconds,
- Relax your hands and let them rest in neutral position for eight seconds,
- Hold your hand up and make the symbol for the number five (with your five fingers spread apart from one another).
- Keeping your fingers spread apart, stretch out your arm and fingers as far as you can, pretending that you are reaching for something just out of reach. Hold this position for eight seconds,
- Relax your hands and let them rest in neutral position for eight seconds,
- Repeat the sequence three times.

Neck and Head

The neck is a trouble zone for some people, often because one can become so used to holding their neck in a certain position and eventually no longer notice that it's suboptimal for comfort and efficient sound production. Since the neck supports the head, the easiest way to check to see if you have proper neck posture is by looking at the position of the head in relation to the shoulders. Ideally, the head should sit directly above the shoulders. Hours each day spent looking at a computer screen or down at our phones has left many of us with a head position that juts forward, meaning the head position lies slightly in front of the shoulders. This can cause tension and sometimes even pain. It can also make it harder to produce a free and easy tone, especially when speaking or singing higher in your range. The first step in working toward better alignment is releasing tension. **To release tension in your neck, try this exercise.**

The side stretch:

- Start with your head in an upright position. Slowly tilt your head to the right bringing your right ear toward your right shoulder. You should feel a slight stretch up the left side of the neck. To deepen this stretch, you may gently reach your right arm up and over your head, placing your right hand on your left ear.
- Hold this stretch for ten seconds.
- Return your head to a centered, upright position.
- Slowly tilt your head to the left, bringing your left ear toward your left shoulder. You should feel a slight stretch up the right side of the neck. To deepen this stretch, you may gently reach your left arm up and over your head, placing your left arm on your right ear.
- Hold this stretch for ten seconds.
- Return your head to a centered, upright position.

The Bobblehead

The bobblehead is much like the side stretch, but the degree of movement of the head is much smaller. Have you ever seen those bobbleheads? Sometimes people have them on their car dashboards, and they are common toys for children. They have plastic bodies with heads on a spring. These heads are often in motion, slightly wobbling back and forth, side to side.

To release tension while talking, you can imitate this toy, using this exercise:

- Gently tilt your head as if you were beginning to lower your right ear to your right shoulder.
- Repeat this motion in the other direction, beginning to lower your left ear to your left shoulder.
- Repeat this sequence on a continuous loop so your head is "bobbing" from side to side.
- Slowly count to ten, while continuing to bob your head. You might want to do this exercise in front of a mirror to make sure your head doesn't stop moving.
- Use this exercise as a tension release method while rapping, and as a first step toward proper head alignment.

If you find you have tension and posture issues, seeing your doctor might be helpful, as they can see if there are structural issues at play. There are also numerous practices and exercise methods that can dramatically improve posture and alignment, including, but not limited to, the Feldenkrais Method, Alexander Technique, body mapping, myofascial release, rolfing, yoga, and pilates.[9] Stretching each day as part of your warmup will help as well. Most importantly, finding what is most comfortable for you is key. Everybody is built differently, and the key for efficient, free sound production is practicing proper posture for you. These are guidelines, but ultimately, you need to trust and listen to your body. If something is constantly uncomfortable, odds are your body is trying to tell you to make some adjustments. Ultimately, it knows best!

Notes

1. Merriam-Webster Dictionary. (n.d.). Posture. https://www.merriam-webster.com/dictionary/posture

2. Vocabulary.com. (n.d.). Stance. https://www.vocabulary.com/dictionary/stance

3. Bone Health & Osteoporosis Foundation. (n.d.). Proper Body Alignment. https://www.bonehealthandosteoporosis.org/patients/treatment/exercise safe-movement/proper-body-alignment/#:~:text=Alignment%20refers%20to%20how%20the,a%20slumped%2C%20head%2Dforward%20posture

4. McKinney, William. (2005). *The Diagnosis and Correction of Vocal Faults.* Long Grove, IL: Waveland Press Inc., 33.

5. Merriam-Webster Dictionary. (n.d.). Projection. https://www.merriam-webster.com/dictionary/projection#:~:text=%3A%20the%20process%20or%20technique%20of,line%20by%20projecting%20its%20points

6. Barbershop Harmony Society. (2019, December 9). Better Body Alignment: Why and How. https://www.barbershop.org/better-body-alignment-why-and-how

7. Van Edwards, Vanessa. (n.d.). Look the Part: 8 Body Language Acting Tips. https://www.scienceofpeople.com/acting-tips/

8. Sage Music. (2015, January 28). Improving Your Singing Voice Part 1: Singing Posture. https://www.sagemusic.co/improving-singing-voice-part-1-singing-posture/

9. Leborgne, Wendy D., and Marci Rosenberg. (2019). *The Vocal Athlete*, second edition. London: Plural Publishing, 17–21.

Ten

"Lose My Breath" (Destiny's Child)

Breath, Inhalation, and Supporting Your Sound

You may ask yourself, why do I need to think about breathing? I've always known how to breathe without giving it a second thought. The American Lung Association says that the average human takes at least seventeen thousand breaths a day.[1] However, the breathing you do while singing or rapping is *very* different from the breathing you do while you are walking down the street or doing a HIIT cardio workout. Luckily, you already have all of the tools you need to master the art of breathing, so let's get to it.

Getting Your Body Ready for Singing

There are several moving pieces that must work together to create a healthy and efficient vocal performance. Fair warning: you'll often be asked to refer to other parts of this book in order to refresh your memory on key points that will help you to better understand the current topic. This is one of those times. Here are a few reminders.

Relaxation and Tension Release Are Critical

For example, people who play the violin store their violins in a protective case. This prevents the instrument from falling off the table and splintering, getting rained on, or warping in the sun. The case is one way to keep the violin in prime working condition. Before playing, the violinist usually tunes the strings, adjusts the music stand, and puts rosin on the bow. All of these things are necessary before a single sound comes out of the violin. Similarly, when your body is your instrument, you have to make sure it is ready to do the work. This means taking care of it by eating right, getting enough sleep, and taking proper care of your voice (see more on this in chapter 15). Before you can rap, it's also important that the body is loose and relatively free of tension, as that can impact the ability to breathe.

As we discussed in chapter 9, the body carries tension—there is no doubt about that. Just think of all of the idioms that utilize parts of the body to convey negative emotion: "shoulder the burden," "pain in the neck," "straw that broke the camel's back," "I can't stomach it," and so on. The most common places tension is stored in the body include:

- Neck
- Shoulders
- Hands
- Lower back
- Hips
- Feet

Tension is habitual and can be hard to eradicate. However, if you work to release tension before each performance and do exercises daily, you will slowly decrease the amount of tension carried in the areas most problematic to you. Even a simple stretch can work wonders. Here are three tension release exercises to use before you begin your breath work.

- **Rotations:**
    - *For the neck*: Gently let your neck relax and let your chin rest on the top of your chest. Then slowly roll your head (not letting your chin leave your chest) to the right, until your right ear is resting on your right shoulder. Hold there for five seconds and then slowly roll the neck in the other direction, back to center, so the chin rests on the upper chest. Then, slowly roll to the left until

the left ear rests on the left shoulder. Hold there for five seconds. Repeat this rotation three times.
  - *For the shoulders*: Starting with your shoulders dropped in a neutral position, slowly roll your shoulders in large forward circles (think big circular shoulder shrug). Do this several times and then switch directions, slowly rolling in backwards circles.
  - *For the hands*: Holding your hands at your side, move your wrists in small, clockwise circles, while simultaneously moving your fingers. Repeat this several times before switching the direction of the rotation.
  - *For the lower back and hips*: Stand up and spread your legs approximately shoulder distance apart. Place your hands on your hips and make large, clockwise circles as if you are hula hooping. Do this for ten seconds and then switch directions, making circles in a counterclockwise motion.
  - *For the feet*: (You can sit for this one.) Lift one foot so that it's slightly off of the ground and rotate it in clockwise circles five times (it will be your ankle that is actually rotating). Switch directions and repeat, moving in counterclockwise circles five times.
- **Tense and release**: You can isolate certain areas where you know you feel tension, or you can do this with your entire body. Starting with the feet, scrunch your toes up by curling them under and arch the feet. Feel that tension? If so, you're doing it correctly! Hold this position for five counts, and then release. Slowly move up the body repeating a five-second tension hold and a release making sure to isolate the legs, glutes, abdominals, hands, shoulders, and face. Once you've completed the process of tensing and holding each of the aforementioned body parts, tense everything in your body at once! Hold for ten seconds... hold... HOLD... aaaaand... relax.
- **Yoga inhalation**: Breathing is an essential part of every yoga practice. It's centering and it releases tension. Close your eyes. Take a deep, slow inhale for five counts through your nose. Then, hold for five seconds, and finally exhale for seven counts slowly through your mouth. Repeat this as many times as you'd like.

Don't Forget About Posture

"There are connections between posture + postural changes and the sound of singing in terms of vocal timbre (sound quality)."[2] Glance back at the chapter on posture. While you refresh, keep in mind that most of the time if you are being your authentic self and telling a story you believe in, your body will naturally move along with you. Just stay mindful of what can be compromised and what shouldn't be sacrificed regarding your posture when it comes to breath management. Everyone is different when it comes to what their body can handle regarding slouching/bending and the ability to control their air flow in order to make it to the end of a cadence.

Practice Breathing While Moving

The exercises in this chapter will have you standing, sitting, or even lying down. These positions will be helpful for your concentration and understanding, but once you feel comfortable it is imperative to practice this breath work while moving. Don't limit yourself! Practice moving across larger distances so you know you can maintain proper breath support while also performing live for your adoring fans.

> "When I'm playing the beat, I will actually stand in my mirror with that microphone and pretend I'm rapping to an audience. You know, the best way to create music is to try to replicate the environment you're going to be in, right? Kind of like, you know, how five-year-olds do it with a comb. But the reason I do that is so that when I'm writing my verse, I know exactly how wordy to make it."
>
> —Rama Kazi

Inhalation

Air as Fuel

Let's think about breathing using a metaphor of a car. Remember that a car needs a source (engine), something to power it, and several filters in order to be considered fully functioning. It has already been established that posture impacts the source (your body), so at this point of this analogy, all you have is the engine. You are now a shiny new (insert dream car here) sitting in the driveway, but you can't go anywhere. Why not? Because you need fuel. Cars need gas to run; that is their *power*. For singers, your fuel is *air*.

Airflow can be broken down into two simple actions: inhalation and exhalation.[3] Breathing in can be done either through the mouth or the nose. There are pros and cons to both, making it a widely debated topic among teaching professionals.

Inhalation Through the Nose

When you have a long recovery time between bars or when you aren't singing or rapping, inhalation through the nose may be the correct choice for a few reasons:

1. The nose is filled with two types of hair: cilia and vibrissae. These exist to catch particles in the air such as bacteria, pollen, and dust. Inhaling through the nose helps filter the air before it reaches your lungs.
2. Nasal inhalation helps moisten the air and keeps your throat from becoming dry.
3. Breathing in through the nose warms the air. Yoga and meditation practices believe that breathing in through your nose helps with relaxation and stress. When breathing through the nose, nitric oxide is produced. This helps to improve blood and oxygen circulation throughout the body.

Inhalation Through the Mouth

However, when you are actively rapping (and often singing), it's actually better to breathe in through the mouth. This has three crucial benefits:

1. More air can enter the lungs at a faster rate. The nasal passage is too small to intake enough air in the short amount of time between most rap phrases. Therefore, breathing in through the mouth will allow you to reach the end of each phrase successfully.
2. When done correctly, breathing in through the mouth is quiet. It can be a challenge for your listener to catch your words at the speed that you are saying them, so this helps eliminate any added distractions. A noisy inhale can also interrupt the mood you are trying to create and thus lessen the impact of your message.
3. Inhaling through the mouth can assist with the lift of the soft palate (otherwise known as the velum). This is the soft tissue found at the anterior roof of the mouth. (For more about the soft palate, see chapter 11, which discusses tone quality.)

How to Inhale

To recap, here are two takeaways we have learned thus far:

1. Our fuel is oxygen/air.
2. In the case of rapping, we will usually need to inhale through the mouth.

After inhaling, the air that we take in travels to the back of the mouth and down the throat. From there, it goes through your trachea and eventually flows into the lungs. Whether we are just "being" or we are actively singing, air flows into our lungs automatically. That's all thanks to a muscle called the diaphragm. The diaphragm is a muscle that looks a bit like a dented, dome-shaped forcefield covering a city in a sci-fi movie. It's located just below your chest cavity and is attached to your lower ribs. Below the ribs is your abdominal cavity as well as the rest of your organs and guts (i.e., the viscera). The diaphragm is often overlooked because, unlike some other muscles in the body, the diaphragm isn't something you can control. You can't go to the gym and get on the diaphragm machine—at least not implicitly speaking.

When you take an optimal inhale, the external intercostal muscles located in the space between your ribs work to lift and expand the ribcage. At the same time, the diaphragm contracts and lowers. The combination of these actions helps to expand the lungs. This expansion changes the pressure of the air and creates a vacuum effect. That vacuum "sucks" air into the lungs without you having to consciously think, "okay, I better breathe in now."

When the diaphragm contracts and lowers, it pushes on and slightly flattens all of the guts that are beneath it. This flattening causes your abdomen to expand slightly. Many singers try to push their stomach out when they breathe in, and this is not only unnecessary, but it also adds a lot of counterproductive tension. This should happen naturally without you having to push it out.

Now that you are an expert in relaxing into your breath, notice where else your body expands during inhalation. Actually, let's back up. Go to a mirror, and do a quick check. When you are taking the relaxed inhale, what do you notice? Your belly expands slightly because of the contraction and lowering of the diaphragm and the lungs are expanding in multiple directions. To be clear, you should *not* be noticing a lot of movement in your shoulders. If you are noticing that your abs are pulling in and/or that your shoulders are rising, then chances are your diaphragm isn't lowering. It may seem obsessive to be fixating on the diaphragm so intensely, but it really is vital to taking a proper breath. It will facilitate a relaxed inhale, but more importantly, it will allow you to easily control your exhale. A controlled exhale maintains an even flow of air, thus allowing you to reach the ends of your phrases without losing steam. You can trust that this work, though difficult, will be worthwhile. "Sing from your diaphragm!" is a term you might have heard in the past. Now feels like a good time to dispel this myth. Sure, if you connect the dots, you can probably see what they are getting at: relax your abdominal wall so the diaphragm can lower effectively and the lungs can efficiently fill with air. Okay, but "singing from your diaphragm" is nonsensical. You can't sing from your diaphragm. Period.

Once your shoulders are relaxed and you are seeing your belly expand, you are ready to shift your focus to the abdominal wall. Your abdominal wall goes all the way around your core, and when it expands you should notice the sensation in both the front and sides of your abdomen as well as in your back. It can be helpful to imagine that you have a pool inner tube around your waist. Inhale in a relaxed manner, feeling that you're expanding in all directions, thus making an airtight seal all the way around.

After you fully grasp the 360-degree abdominal wall expansion, you can begin to think about the expansion that happens in your ribcage. Since the ribs encase the lungs, it would only make sense that the ribcage expands when the lungs expand. This means you'll feel some expansion on the sides and back of your ribs, too.

EXERCISE: Six-sided inhale: It is crucial to remember that when you relax into your breath, you'll feel expansion in multiple directions at once. I heard a colleague of mine, Chris York, use the imagery of a box to imagine this expansion, and I think this image is incredibly helpful when trying to identify sensations that you feel. Let's go more in depth with our friend the box. Think back to your geometry class days—remember the three-dimensional shapes you had to measure? You do? Bet. Imagine a cube (or three-dimensional square). Now put that cube inside your core. Continuing with this imagery, try the following exercise:

- Side one and two expansion:
    - Place one hand on your belly button and the other hand on your upper back.
    - Take a relaxed inhale, remembering that you don't need to take an enormously large breath to feel these sensations.
    - See if you can feel expansion in your belly and upper back (i.e., does your belly go out, and do you feel the back of your lung move outward)?

- Practice this, playing around until you can feel these. Think of these as sides one and two of the box.
- Sides three and four:
  - Next, place one hand on each side of your ribs. Make sure they are high enough on your ribcage to feel the sensation—to do this, place your hands where (if you were wearing a bikini), your bikini strap would be.
  - Take a relaxed inhale, remembering that you don't need to take an enormously large breath to feel these sensations.
  - See if you can feel ribcage expansion on both sides.
  - Practice this, playing around until you can feel this expansion. Think of these as sides three and four of the box.
- Sides five and six: You have felt "front and back" and "side and side." Let's now feel the final two sides of the box: up and down.
  - Even though your diaphragm lowers and your lungs expand downward, you will still feel expansion in the upper abdomen. Think of this as the top (or side five) of the box.
  - Place one hand on the very top of your abdomen (i.e., the bottom of your ribcage) and the other hand with your thumb just underneath your belly button, and splay your hands so that your pinky is near your pelvic bone.
  - Take a relaxed inhale, remembering that you don't need to take an enormously large breath to feel these sensations.
  - See if you can feel the expansion of your lower abdomen. Students of mine have described this as the feeling of a drop of their belly button. To find this drop, imagine that you are a character in a movie relaxing your (imaginary) beer gut. Put your hand under the beer gut, where your button would be if you wore low rise jeans.
  - Practice this, playing around until you can feel these sensations. Think of these as sides five and six of the box.

The best possible thing you can do to get a good breath for rapping is relax. Yes, that's right. It might seem strange, but the diaphragm will lower easily and efficiently if your abdominal wall is relaxed. Think about what happens when a ball is flying toward your stomach, or if you trip and stumble on a crack in the sidewalk: your core engages and your abs tighten. If this happens, the diaphragm can't lower as swiftly, the vacuum is affected, and these things can result in a shallow breath.

Relaxing can also help you avoid the pitfall of trying to take in too much air/over-inhaling. You don't need to hyperextend the abdominal wall, suck all of the oxygen out of the room, or try to become as big as a balloon in the Macy's Day Thanksgiving Parade. Usually, a relaxed and efficient breath is effective and will get you through your bars. Over-breathing can create a lot of tension in the shoulders, neck, and false vocal folds.

Things to Watch Out For/Avoid When Inhaling for Singing:

- Your stomach pulling in during the inhale
- Holding/tightening your abs during the inhale
- Your shoulders rising dramatically during your inhale
- Taking in too much air: remember, no need to try and suck all of the oxygen out of the room
- Forgetting about posture: if your breath is affecting alignment, you might be working too hard or something might be off
- Only expanding in the front abdominal wall: remember, expansion happens all the way around your core, as well as in your ribcage
- Only expanding your ribs and not your abdominal wall
- Only expanding the abdominal wall and not your ribs

Things to Consider When Inhaling:

- **Quality over quantity**: Tempo, volume, number of syllables, and style of rap flow can affect how much air you'll need for a phrase. Taking in too much air for the phrase adds tension that can mess up your diction and tone. Keep in mind that not all phrases need huge breaths.

- **Make sure to leave yourself enough time to inhale**: It may be tempting to say a word until you think the beat ends, but if you are entering again on the next beat you may need to end your word a tiny bit early so you have time to inhale.

> **"In my earlier days, like I hated that I hated having to punch in for verse I just wanted to get through the whole thing in one take. . . . I think now that I've gotten older and well versed, I've realized that it's okay to punch in as long as you're able to still deliver what you're saying during a performance during a live performance."**
>
> —Ausar

- **Mark your breaths**: When writing out or printing your lyrics, make sure to write in where you are going to breathe. You can do this with tiny check marks, little slashes, or whatever makes sense to you.
- **Practice your inhales**: Taking calm breaths quickly is a skill that needs practicing as much as practicing crisp diction or varying up your volume.

Exhalation

You've gassed up your car (your body) with the fuel it needs (air) by taking a good breath. Now what? It's time to learn how to control your exhale. That way you can avoid running out of air, losing tone quality, or getting off beat by needing to sneak a breath at the wrong time. Eminem raps for almost thirty seconds without taking a breath in his song "Godzilla." Thirty seconds!!!! That's not just holding his breath for thirty seconds either—he's spitting consonants too. Controlling your exhale is about muscle coordination and balance. This can be referred to as breath support, breath control, or breath management.

What is happening during the exhale? Well, air exits the lungs, moves up the trachea past the vocal folds, and finally out either through the nose or mouth. Since you're speaking, you'll want to exhale through your mouth (that will happen automatically, although if you can rap through your nose, you'd probably become extremely famous on social media). The key is slowing down the rate that the internal intercostal muscles contract and slowing down the diaphragm's spring back to its original position. This muscle control gets better with practice over time. You might already do this! But here are some beginning breathing exercises to practice this coordination.

1. **Hiss like a snake**:
   - Breathe in for four beats, and then, hiss like an angry snake, exhaling slowly for eight beats
   - Breathe in for four beats, hiss out like an angry snake again, but this time, for twelve beats
   - Breathe in for four beats, hiss out for sixteen beats
   - Breathe in for four beats, hiss out for twenty beats
   - Breathe in for two beats, hiss out for eight beats
   - Breathe in for two beats, hiss out for twelve beats
   - Breathe in for two beats, hiss out for sixteen beats
   - Breathe in for two beats, hiss out for twenty beats
   - Breathe in for one beat, his out for eight beats
   - Breath in for one beat, hiss out for twelve beats
   - Breathe in for one beat, hiss out for sixteen beats
   - Breathe in for one beat, hiss out for twenty beats

   Exercise goal: Slowly increase stamina regarding breath control and speed of exhalation. As you work on this, notice what your abdominal area is doing. You should feel expansion in your ribcage and abdominal wall that remains during the exhale. The abdominal wall will probably engage/tighten during the hiss, and your goal is to slow down the deflation instead of exhaling all your air at once. If this isn't happening for you, go back and refresh your memory on the "inhalation" portion of this chapter. Just as with any muscle, it

begins to adjust the more you practice so be patient with yourself and keep working.
2. **Pant like a dog**:
   Stick out your tongue and imitate a dog panting because it's hot out. Feel your stomach moving? Great. Try to make sure your shoulders are not rising up and down with the panting.
   Exercise goal: To feel the abdominals working while trying to keep your shoulders relaxed and your ribcage expanded.
3. **Pulsing**:
   Similar to the angry snake exercises, you'll be breathing in for various counts, and exhaling for various counts. But this time, instead of exhaling on a hiss, try starting and stopping your air on a pulse (evenly distributed "S" sounds like "ts" "ts" "ts"):
   - Breathe in for four beats, pulse out for sixteen beats
   - Breathe in for four beats, pulse out for twenty beats
   - Breathe in for four beats, pulse out for twenty-four beats
   - Breathe in for two beats, pulse out for sixteen beats
   - Breathe in for two beats, pulse out for twenty beats
   - Breathe in for two beats, pulse out for twenty-four beats
   - Breathe in for one beat, pulse out for sixteen beats
   - Breathe in for one beat, pulse out for twenty beats
   - Breathe in for one beat, pulse out for twenty-four beats

   Exercise goal: To draw attention to the engagement of your abdominal cavity and your intercostal muscles (the ones near your ribs). Pay attention to the sensations you feel when you pulse, and then when you release, think about how things might feel differently. Where specifically?
4. **Consonant shuffle**:
   Repeat the following pattern at various speeds, and see how many times you can repeat it in one exhale:
   F, T, P, Ch, K, T, P, T, F, Ch, St, K, P, B, T, F, Sh, P, K, T, Ch, S, B, T
   Exercise goal: This is a fabulous segue into speaking. Certain consonants will naturally release more air than others, and this is fine. While you do this, pay attention to your abdominal cavity and

intercostals, and try not to work *too* hard. The key to this is being efficient—how much air do you need to make the sound? That's all you should use. Breathe for the needs of the phrase.

Factors in breathing:

1. *Stance is going to change how you breathe.* In any given performance you'll be squatting, bending, hell, even jumping around on stage. I just saw the rap duo AG CLUB live. They were moving constantly. They even stage dove into the crowd and rapped while laying horizontally and being suspended in the air by their fans. So trust me, you will be moving when you are rapping live. Just remember that those things will affect how you use your air. *The key to this is to practice rapping and breathing in these different postural stances.* It might change where and how often you'll need to breathe.
2. *Adrenaline will cause you to lose some of your support.* You will most likely use more air than when practicing in your room. Tip: Practice in front of groups of friends. It will drastically help lower the shock of adrenaline because you'll be used to doing the thing.
3. *Certain consonants use more air than others.* Just keep this in mind when practicing your diction. We'll get into specifics in chapter 13.
4. *Rapping loudly can use a lot of air.* No need to rap *too* loudly—you have a microphone. It can also lead to pushing and vocal strain.
5. *Stamina plays a huge role in successful rapping.* Try rapping while jogging or on the elliptical. It will help you work on stamina as well as cardiovascular efficiency.
6. *It's possible that you naturally use your air in an efficient and healthy way.* Don't become fixated on this if there isn't an issue. Doing so can cause unnecessary tension. These chapters are all here to help you with potential stumbling blocks, but you have certain things under control already before you picked up this book. In all of these chapters, use what you need and forget about what you don't need.

Okay I know that was a lot. If you suddenly felt like you were hanging out with Bill Nye the Science Guy, you wouldn't be completely wrong. But it's worth it! Trust me, you've got this.

Notes

1. Editorial Staff. (2017, July 20). How Your Lungs Get the Job Done. *American Lung Association*. https://www.lung.org/blog/how-your-lungs-work

2. Moreno, Amanda Marie. (2022). An Examination of the Effects of Body Mapping Instruction on Singers' Static Standing Posture and Posture While Singing. PhD dissertation, University of North Dakota, 14.

3. Merriam-Webster Dictionary. (n.d.). Inhalation. https://www.merriam-webster.com/dictionary/inhalation

Eleven

"Protecting My Energy" (Jackboy)

Pitch, Tone Quality, and Resonance

"The voice is a powerful tool that can be the most crucial element in making sure lyrics, flows, wordplay and delivery are savored by listeners."[1]

Yes, this is a book about rapping and not about singing. But I promise that this chapter is important to you, even if you don't strive to be the next Juice Wrld, Tems, Latto, or Drake. Did you know that your speaking voice has a pitch? Just knowing that empowers you because you know you can make a lot of different sounds. You have a variety of choices available to you that will help shape your delivery, all within your natural pitch range and tone quality. Let's dig into what that means, how you access it, and how you can use your pitch and tone in a sustainable way.

The Nitty-Gritty of Pitch and Tone

Pitch

So, what is "pitch" anyway? First, the scientific definition: *Encyclopedia Britannica* describes pitch in music as the "position of a single sound in the complete range of sound. Sounds are higher or lower in pitch according to the frequency of vibration of the sound waves producing them. A high frequency (e.g., 880 hertz [Hz; cycles per second]) is perceived as a high pitch and a low frequency (e.g., 55 Hz) as a low pitch."[2]

But for our purposes, pitch is basically how high or low your voice naturally sounds when you are speaking.

Your Rap Sound (Optimal Speaking Pitch)

The best thing you can do for yourself regarding pitch is to rap in the same pitch range that you speak. You can do this by finding your optimal speaking pitch and your habitual speaking pitch. Your optimal speaking pitch is "the level within a speaker's pitch range at which [they] can initiate vocalization with ease and effectiveness."[3] This can also be described as "the area in which the voice naturally lies. This area allows for optimal vocal quality, resonance, and comfort when speaking."[4] Speech and Voice Enterprises perhaps says it best, noting that "optimal pitch produces a rich and pure tone where the muscles of the vocal mechanism function at their best to produce an ideal quality voice with natural projection. Speaking in your optimal pitch range would be preferred for professional speech and voice since that is where the most vibrant tones are produced."[5]

This may or may not be the same as your habitual speaking pitch, which is the place where you usually talk. Most people don't use their optimal speaking pitch when they talk. There are a bunch of reasons for this, such as antiquated gender stereotypes, vocal fry (if you don't know what that means, think of that stereotypical "mean girl" in a sitcom: she often has a slight creak in her tone as she insults the protagonist. That, my friend, is vocal fry), lack of confidence, environment, and not realizing that what you hear when you speak isn't actually what your voice sounds like in a room. If you don't know if you have fry, try putting two books up against the front of your ears so that the spine of the book is against your head, and

> **"I'm pretty much who I am in my music . . . but there can be slight artistic exaggerations, times when I'm a bit more aggressive or bit more assertive or right-in-your-face with my content, but for the most part, like I always tell my manager, I'm a guy that wears a shirt and pants and I rap."**
>
> **—Cashus King**

the books are sticking out, perpendicular to your ear. Doing this creates a change in the way you hear your voice, and it more accurately reflects what you sound like to others.

You'll be able to rap for longer without tiring and will also be able to have more control and flexibility over your voice if you find your optimal speaking pitch.

To find your optimal speaking pitch, try the following exercise:

- Imagine that someone hands you a warm, delicious bowl of soup on a chilly day. Imagine that you eat a spoonful, and it's really *so* delicious. You must tell the nice person that gave you the soup that you love it. So, you say aloud "Mmmmm, this soup is yummmmmmmy," drawing out the MMM in the first word as well as in the word yummy. See where your voice naturally sits when you hum.
- Repeat this exercise, and this time, when you hum on the MMM, pay attention to where you feel the vibrations in your mouth: is it in the back of your throat? Is it in your lips? Or does it buzz elsewhere? If you are feeling buzz in your throat, play around with pitch, sliding higher and lower until you can feel a buzz in the front of your mouth, your lips, your nose, and/or your cheeks.
- Once you find that buzzy spot, repeat the MMMs several times, paying attention to the pitch at which you are landing.
- Then, hold the hum for four beats. Next, without changing anything else, open your mouth so that your MMM becomes an ahhhhhhhh sound.

Tip: Record yourself doing this either on your voice memo app or using the camera function of your phone. You'll probably be quite surprised at the sound of your voice. Remember, what you sound like inside your head isn't actually what you sound like in the room. Furthermore, your optimal speaking pitch is most likely a bit higher than your habitual pitch. But if you want to rap for two whole hours without a break, and if you want the freedom and ease to do this over and over, your optimal speaking pitch is going to be your best friend.

Here is another exercise to find your optimal speaking pitch as well as to feel sympathetic resonance: "Angry Cat."

- Put the middle of your tongue on the roof of your mouth, then say and hold out an "nnnnnnnnnnnnnnng" sound.
- Holding this "nnnnnnnnnnnnnnng" sound, make small sirens up and down. You'll notice that you sound like an angry cat who isn't hissing at you, but clearly isn't happy. Repeat these little sirens, experimenting until you find a comfortable range and tension-free approach. After some experimentation, extend the range slowly, sliding higher and lower. This doesn't need to be loud; in fact, if you are doing it correctly, it won't be loud at all. Your throat should feel relaxed, and nothing should feel strained.

Range

Your range is how high and low you can comfortably make sound without stress, fatigue, or strain. The simplest way to find this out is to test it out. Voice coach Cindy Hood offers a straightforward process: "You can determine your natural pitch range with the aid of a piano or guitar. Sing the sound 'ah' at a comfortable pitch. From that point, sing the next note downward on the musical scale. Continue to sing downward one note at a time until you cannot go lower without straining. Then sing your way upward until you reach the highest note possible without strain. The total number of notes from top to bottom represents your pitch range."[6] No worries if you don't have a voice or guitar, there are a plethora of piano apps on your phone (many are free), and your computer most likely comes with preloaded software that can play pitches (for example, Garageband, which is mentioned later in this book, when discussing recording methods for your songs). Remember that your optimal speaking pitch isn't fixed—it can change based on time of day, humidity, how much sleep you've gotten, how much you've used your voice that day, your health, and countless other factors. That said, it will usually be roughly the same. Your ultimate goal is to find the place that lets you speak most efficiently because that will allow you to play with tone.

Tone

While related, tone is different from pitch. Tone is the quality of sound. Other words people use to describe this concept are color or timbre. More specifically, tone is subjective, as it is a descriptive term to describe the sound of the voice. You might hear words to describe tone like warm, dark, bright, buzzy, rough, breathy, whiny, honking, airy, hooty, rich, sweet, young, full, thin, reedy, tight, etc. Or people might use emotions to describe tone, such as angry, aggressive, elated, excited, depressed, or mellow. Descriptive words can also be used to describe tone like eerie, spooky, sexy, sultry, or snobby. Muddy, sparkly, cloudy, and clear are even more ways to describe one's individual tone. While there would be categories that are generally agreed upon (bright versus dark, breathy versus non-breathy), the specific descriptors are personal to the listener. The takeaway for you, though, is that there are countless options available to you regarding adjusting and playing with your tone.

> "I actually really have wanted to embrace the youth of my voice, because I think it's something that I have in the space that I occupy in hip-hop that is pretty unique."
>
> —redveil

Importance of Pitch and Tone

Now that you know what pitch and tone are, you hopefully realize that you have all of the tools you could possibly need right inside your throat. Here is a quick recap of what we've learned so far:

- Speaking at your optimal speaking pitch is going to make it so much easier for you to prevent fatigue, and you'll be ready for that rap battle even at the end of a long day.
- You have the freedom to change your pitch when appropriate (we'll get into why this is important in a minute).

- You have the freedom to change your tone quality when appropriate (we're about to talk about why this matters as well).

How Do Pitch and Tone Affect Your Rapping?

1. It makes you as an MC *recognizable* and *iconic*:

    In a lot of ways, your voice *is* your rap identity. No one else sounds like you. Your healthy voice is terrific exactly the way it is. Don't fret if it doesn't sound like your favorite rappers. It's not supposed to sound like anything other than like *you*. Also, don't sweat it if it's not as deep, or not as high as you think it *should* be. There is room for *all* types of voices in rap. If you love Ol' Dirty Bastard, you might worry that your voice doesn't have that deep, rough quality. But Kemet High explains that there are pros to having a higher optimal speaking pitch as well. He explains, "a rapper's voice is just as important as the content of their music. When you think about the greatest rappers of all time, you can instantly mimic how they sound. While some voices are deep, raspy and rigid, like the DMX's and Biggie's of the world, the high-pitched voice in hip-hop has taken prominence over the years with the likes of Danny Brown, Young Thug, Swae Lee, 645AR and Playboi Carti."[7] There isn't one way to sound like a great rapper. But vocal tone qualities are memorable; when someone is folding their clothes and quietly rapping your rap, *your* voice would be inside their head. It's inseparable from the rest of the song. Author, professor, and podcast host Martin E. Connor really drives this home when he says that,

    > Every talented rapper has an extremely recognizable and unique voice. Earl Sweatshirt could never be confused with Kendrick Lamar, or Joey Bada$$ could never be confused with MGK. It is even those qualities, difficult to describe, that make people hear Notorious B.I.G. as a classic mafioso rapper, or Jay-Z as a celebrity that's bigger than rap. Pretty much every rapper who gets popular has a really unique

delivery, but some stand out more than others. Now, when the word "unique" is used, it doesn't always mean "best," as is the case here. If you look over this list of emcees, you'll notice that few of them have blown up as solo rappers on the level of someone like Jay-Z, besides Snoop Dogg. That's because as soon as a rapper reaches that high level of success, he spawns a legion of imitators who try and copy his style, including his delivery, which covers the way a rapper says his words in terms of pronunciation and pitch. But these emcees below have consistently stood out for their deliveries that haven't quite been replicated exactly anywhere else.[8]

So, if you've been changing your speaking voice on the regular, let's make this the moment you officially stop doing so.

2. It conveys *emotional intent*:

There are numerous debates over whether lyrical rap can be considered "singing." While that's interesting and all, it's beside the point. Rather than trying to fit inside the box of traditional pitches, rap's speech driven content frees you up to convey emotion.

One of my favorite acting exercises involves saying the same phrase numerous ways. Let's try it: Take a simple spoken phrase and see what happens to your vocal tone. Say the following phrase: "I said I'm going out." Repeat this simple phrase, but with the following emotional intents. As a bonus: record yourself while performing this exercise. Say the line:

- Furious
- Worried
- Relieved
- Weary
- Excited
- Joyful
- Timid

- Secretive
- Guiltily
- Encouraging

Now, go back and listen to your recording. How did your tone quality change with the change of emotional intent? Did your pitch change as well? Being able to convey emotion through tonal and pitch variations will drastically affect your delivery and will add texture to your flow. Listen to the following tracks to hear emotion conveyed in lyrical rap:

- "Hit Em Up" by Tupac and Outlawz
- "Checkmate" by Jadakiss
- "Lost Ones" by J. Cole
- "Nightmare on My Street" by DJ Jazzy Jeff and the Fresh Prince
- "Queen Bitch" by Lil' Kim
- "Art of War" by Jasiah, Denzel Curry, and Rico Nasty
- "Hotel Lobby" by Quavo and Takeoff

3. It makes you *compelling*:

    A common joke in movies about high school is the teacher who speaks in a monotone voice. Remember the teacher in the movie *Ferris Bueller's Day Off*? He's taking attendance, and he's repeating "Bueller... Bueller... Bueller." I'm falling asleep just imagining his voice in that scene. If you haven't seen that movie: go watch it, it's a classic. But I digress: in those scenes, this voice telegraphs to us the watcher that this class is immensely *borrrrrrrrr-iiiiinnnnnnnn-nnggggggggg*. That's the way people would receive your flows if they had a lack of pitch variance or lacked tonal coloring. Slight changes in pitch either upward or downward allow the listener to know if your sentence ends with a question mark, a period, or an exclamation point. If someone can tell that much with the direction of the final word, you can imagine all you can do with your complete vocal range.

Ways to Alter Your Pitch and/or Tone

1. Projection:

    This means making sure your voice is loud enough to be heard. This does not mean yelling. I repeat: *this does not mean yelling.* In fact, you'll rarely need to yell in rap. Let the mic do its job and work for you. But talking loud enough to be heard, in addition to, well, being heard, has multiple benefits:

    - It prevents you from rushing your speech and alliding important words.
    - It forces you to breathe, since louder volumes often use air at a faster rate than softer volumes.
    - It helps you to speak and enunciate clearly.
    - It inspires confidence, both in oneself and from your listener(s).
    - It commands authority and creates a sense of importance for your subject matter. Voice and Speech coach Jay Miller explains that "projecting your voice is an act of relaxed confidence rather than forceful exertion. It requires you to be fully engaged and fully available. The moment you tense up or pull back, the moment you become self-conscious or unsure voice projection will suffer."[9]

2. Talking quietly:

    Speaking as if someone is right next to you has many tonal influences, and positive results, including:

    - Air preservation. Assuming you aren't speaking with a breathy tone (i.e., assuming your vocal cords are fully closing to make sound), speaking softly will allow you to rap for a longer period of time before needing to take a breath.
    - Creating a sense of coziness or intimacy, which can calm your listener (imagine lo-fi or cloud rap when thinking of this benefit).

- Creating a sense of a casual atmosphere, lending itself to certain flows.
- Note: Just be careful of overusing this technique as there are pitfalls that include pushing too much air through the vocal cords via constriction of the false vocal folds, or, simply put, a tight throat (this will just make your throat hurt, and you'll feel tired). You also *really* have to balance with your track, or you'll get lost. It also can appear to be low energy, which is awesome if you're going for a lo-fi trance vibe, but just know what you are doing and why you are doing so.

3. Conversational volume:

    By far, without a shadow of a doubt, you are going to get the most bang for your buck at this volume. The volume is great because a conversational volume will allow for the most flexibility with both pitch and tone. This is because it's most in line with your day-to-day voice usage, and it's therefore muscles you've already flexed and vocal tract shapes that you already use as a part of your everyday speech. There are many other benefits to this volume:

    - Provides the most vocal stamina, since it's where you are used to speaking for most of your waking hours.
    - Vocal nuances: Just as with Goldilocks's porridge preference, this "just right" volume will allow for the most nuances to come through in your tone and pitch choices.
    - Lends itself to speed and agility. For speed rap, or extremely complex flows, conversational volume is *absolutely* going to be your best bet.
    - Allows for annunciation while conveying a wider variety of moods than amplified volumes.

4. Cursive rapping (vowel modification):

    Think of that old Britney Spears song "Oops I Did It Again"—when she starts that tune, she says, "oh baby baby." But she doesn't actually say "baby." It sounds more like "bayee-beh." This dramatic changing of vowel sounds, either by changing the last consonant (it's extremely common in pop to change the "ee" vowel to "ay" or "eh" if it ends a word), or changing almost all of the vowels, became popular in hip-hop in the late 2000s. Cursive rap got its name from good ol' Twitter. @TRACKDROPPA's viral tweet claimed, "voice so smooth its [sic] like I'm singing in cursive." Entertainment journalist Jumi Akinfenwa states,

> The term was interpreted to be in reference to Corinne Bailey Rae and Amy Winehouse, whose nostalgic but modern combination of jazz and vocal fry dominated the late 00s and has dominated pop music over the years since (think Sia, Lorde, Shawn Mendes and Billie Eilish). The final result is what we now know to be cursive singing or "indie singing"—a style characterized by diphthongization, wherein vowel sounds are stretched beyond what is necessary.[10]

While this quote discusses singing, the same result occurs with over diphthongization in rap (this is common in the more carefree songs of De La Soul and A Tribe Called Quest, as well as in novelty songs, including "Baby Got Back" by Sir Mix-A-Lot and "The Humpty Dance" by Digital Underground). It's a neat little tool that generally encourages vocal fry or nasality, both of which are tonal colors useful to word painting.

Exercise: The Cookie Monster:
The real term for this is pharyngeal wall vibration, but doesn't the Cookie Monster seem easier to do?

Try these steps:
Open your throat wide (remember this is not necessarily opening your mouth really wide, although sometimes doing that can help with the throat). You can find the wider space by either:

- The drink of water exercise (see inhalation in chapter 10)
- Laughing silently
- Panting like a dog

While the throat is wide, act like you are going to gently gargle. See if you can make a soft sound while you do this. *If you feel tightness/too much grip, STOP!* This should be done lightly.

You'll want to stay here, practicing this for no more than a few minutes at a time until it's quite easy to do. This might take weeks. When this is second nature, you can add sound. Now is when you get to imitate Cookie Monster, with a soft "Me Want Cookies" as the infamous character always says. Your pharyngeal walls are vibrating while your vocal folds are vibrating. So, your actual vocal folds are not what is making that growl. It might be easiest to separate the two, using the pharyngeal vibration to start your phrase, then relaxing and chilling that out when you start actually speaking. This is called an onset. That way, you had a growl (Cookie Monster) onset, and normal speaking.

5. Consonant Kicks:

   This is a great way to add energy to your tone without yelling, deciding which syllables are stressed (see chapter 13 for more about this) and choosing which consonants to spit within those stressed syllables can add a lot of energy to your tone quality without adding extra force.

6. Vestibular folds:

   Above your vocal folds (cords), you have a second set of folds often called the vestibular, or "false," vocal folds. They can constrict or retract, making your throat feel extra closed or extra open depending on their position. Adding slight constriction can add a lot of "grit," growl, or huskiness to your tone (think of Busta Rhymes), because when they constrict, they impede airflow, making the passageway smaller. This can cause vocal fatigue and even strain if you aren't careful, so use it slowly and sparingly please. Everyone is different. Some people can do this all day every day with no problem, and for some, this will feel unnatural and tense no matter how much you practice. Listen to your body and see if this works for you. If not, don't sweat it. Seriously!

The false vocal folds often constrict when we are lifting something heavy or are in a state of panic. Doing this slightly, however, can add sometimes the "noise"/"rasp"/"graininess" to your sound without tension.

To experiment with this, try the following:

Note: with all of these, use minimal exhalation, as pushing air will increase your chance for tension.

- Groaning in pain: While exhaling, tighten your abdominal wall, and say "ow ow ow," imitating someone who is in a lot of pain. This shouldn't be overly loud, but more of a voiced whisper.
- Menacing exhale: Imagine you are trying to scare your little sibling. Inhale regularly. On your exhale, pucker your lips, and make a "heh" sound while squeezing your abdominals. This should elicit a slight constriction of your false vocal folds, making that noisy exhale.
- Elderly voice: Voiceover artists often play numerous roles simultaneously in cartoons, etc. Movie actors sometimes play themselves as older: these are great places to look for people manufacturing false vocal fold constriction. Listen to Winona Ryder as an elderly version of herself in the movie *Edward Scissorhands* or Guy Pearce as Peter Weyland in *Prometheus* (I mean, at least that's a reason to watch an otherwise awful film). Mimic these sounds and see what your own voice sounds like. Then mimic these voices saying a line of your rap and see what you think.

> **"There's a wide range of things that you can do with a wide range of emotions; you can express just by making little changes in pitch and tone and, and cadence and like, volume. All of this makes a difference in terms of how it carries over to a listener."**
>
> **—Ausar**

Other Things to Consider

- Don't rely on volume. This was briefly mentioned earlier in the chapter, but it's worth mentioning again to drive the point home. One of the biggest pitfalls for a hip-hop artist is rapping too loudly: It makes sense: adrenaline is rushing, you might be trying to sound forceful or ominous to match the emotion you want to convey in lyrics, and it could seem like raising your voice beyond projection and into yelling is a solid choice to achieve your goals. However, rapping *too* loud Will. Do. You. In. Trust me on this one, folks. I would bet money that you're going to want to ignore this tip. So read this list several times to heed the warnings: Rapping too loudly:
  - Takes out overtones and harmonics in your speaking (and singing) pitches.
  - Can make you sound strained, thus being counterintuitive because it's limiting projection.
  - Can limit your control over pitch variance, and will cause vocal strain and fatigue (due to forced laryngeal lift and false vocal fold constriction).
  - If you don't believe me, listen to medical professionals. Ear, nose, and throat doctors in Charlotte, North Carolina, state, "normal loudness levels for speaking are around 70 dB. Yelling can result in over 100 dB. When you scream, the collision of the vocal folds as they vibrate against each other is much more forceful and damaging than normal speaking due to increased compression of the vocal folds against each other and reduced airflow as they vibrate."[11]
- Beware of pitches that are extremely low. "If your speaking pitch is too low, your voice won't project very well, and it will tend to trail off at the end of phrases. The tone of your voice will tend to be less clear, more prone to sounding scratchy and tense, with little depth and richness. If you're speaking at the bottom of your range, your delivery will tend to be flat and monotone because your voice has

no room to move around. Finally, a voice that's pitched too low will tend to tire quickly and feel uncomfortable."[12]

- Vocal fry is amazing for onsets, or for tonal effects, but be careful not to use it continuously, especially at a projected volume. "Another example of potential misuse is vocal fry (also called glottal fry), which is when a person speaks in a low, creaky tone. Vocal fry causes vibrations in the ventricular folds, rather than the true vocal folds. Vocal fry doesn't necessarily cause harm to the voice, however if a speaker tries to project a louder voice while maintaining vocal fry, then there is a higher risk for vocal injury. Chronic use of vocal fry could lead to laryngeal tension and vocal fatigue."[13]

Lastly, it wouldn't be a rap chapter about pitch and tone if we didn't discuss . . . you guessed it, autotuning.

The Autotune Phenomenon and How It Affects You as a Rapper

Remember the effects of autotuning when you are listening to rap. Autotune is a piece of computer software that can adjust the pitch you are singing so it exactly matches the intended pitch in the key you are singing. Basically, if you are a little sharp or a little flat when singing a tune, this can help smooth that over. But, in 1998, a pop singer named Cher released a song called "Believe" (if you haven't heard it, go check it out so you know what I'm talking about). On this track, Cher turned the dial of autotune *way* up so that she almost sounds robotic. Autotune slid into hip-hop thanks to T-Pain, who can be thanked (or punched in the face, depending how you feel about this whole autotune thing) for bringing autotune to the forefront of Rap (making it Rap&B); check out examples of this and listen to "Low" (Flo Rida and T-Pain), "Bartender" (T-Pain and Akon), and "Blame It" (with Jamie Foxx). If you listen to pop music, you probably know that everyone started using it at some point.

The first rappers to really make something artistic out of Auto-Tune seemed to pick up on the word "pain" in T-Pain (as opposed to his generally upbeat music). Something about the sound of Auto-Tune melted these rappers' hard hearts and opened up the possibility for tenderness and vulnerability: Lil Wayne's gooey ballad "How to Love," or his emo romp "Knockout," or his sensitive (despite its title) "Prostitute Flange" and its tidied-up remake, "Prostitute 2," on which Wayne's asthmatic croaks sound like his larynx is coated with writhing fluorescent nodes.[14]

Kanye West (yes, I talked about this earlier, and honestly, it pains me to do so. Therefore, I'm going to refrain from doing so again here—but if you skipped chapter 3, please go back and read about Ye as it's important that you recognize his contribution to the revolutionization of hip-hop as well as the downward spiral in his mental health resulting in hate speech) released his album *808s & Heartbreak* which was all about autotune, debuting at number one on 2008's Billboard charts. *Rolling Stone* named it one of the "40 most groundbreaking albums of all time." It seemed like for a good ten to fifteen years hip-hop and autotune were truly besties. If you've somehow managed to avoid this phenomenon, go check out Future or Lil Wayne. What you need to know is that a lot of rap artists that use autotune use it in their actual recordings. It isn't an effect that's added in by producers later. So, if you're into it, you'll need the software, and you'll need to know how to both use it in your recordings and live. Beware though: there are definite haters. Usher and Jay-Z, for example, well, they might come for you, just sayin'.

Notes

1. Zissok, Brian "Z." (2018, February 12). What Makes a Rapper Great? A DJBooth Squad Roundtable. *DJBooth*. https://djbooth.net/features/2017-05-23-what-makes-a-rapper-great
2. Britannica. (n.d.). Pitch. https://www.britannica.com/art/pitch-music
3. Eisenson Jon, and Arthur M. Eisenson. (1996). *Voice and Diction: A Program for Improvement*, seventh edition. London: Pearson, 93.

4. Hood, Cindy. (1994). Speaking and Singing: How Speaking on One's Optimal Pitch Affects the Singing Voice. Honors thesis, Ouachita Baptist University, 3.

5. Speech and Voice Enterprises. (2022, January 2). How to Improve the Pitch and Quality of Your Voice. https://speechandvoice.com/blog/1432/How-to-Improve-the-Pitch-and-Quality-of-Your-Voice#:~:text=Optimal%20pitch%20produces%20a%20rich,most%20vibrant%20tones%20are%20produced

6. ToastMasters International. (2011). Tips for Adding Strength and Authority to Your Voice. Retrieved March 1, 2023, https://toastmasterscdn.azureedge.net/medias/files/department-documents/education-documents/199-your-speaking-voice.pdf

7. High, Kemet. (2020, June 24). How High-Pitched Voices Found Their Way into Hip-Hop. *XXL*. https://www.xxlmag.com/high-pitch-voice-hip-hop/

8. Connor, Martin. (2014, May 28). Rap Analysis—10 Unique Rap Voices. *Rap Analysis*. https://www.rapanalysis.com/2014/05/rap-analysis-top-10-most-unique-rap/

9. Voice & Speech. (n.d.). Voice Projection. https://voiceandspeech.com/articles/voice-projection.html

10. Akinfenwa, Jumi. (2020, July 21). A Brief History of "Cursive Singing," From Amy Winehouse to TikTok. *Vice*. https://www.vice.com/en/article/pkyqkv/cursive-singing-tiktok-trend-explained

11. Charlotte Eye Ear Nose and Throat Associates, PA. (2021, May 25). Why Does Screaming Hurt My Voice? https://www.ceenta.com/news-blog/why-does-screaming-hurt-my-voice

12. Voice & Speech. (n.d.). Optimum Pitch for Speaking. Retrieved March 1, 2023, https://voiceandspeech.com/articles/Optimum-Pitch-for-Speaking.html

13. Baylor University. (2020, March 25). How to Prevent and Repair Vocal Damage. https://onlinegrad.baylor.edu/resources/how-to-prevent-and-repair-vocal-damage-for-teachers-fitness-instructors-podcast-hosts-more/

14. Reynolds, Simon. (2018, September 17). How Auto-Tune Revolutionized the Sound of Popular Music. *Pitchfork*. https://pitchfork.com/features/article/how-auto-tune-revolutionized-the-sound-of-popular-music/

Twelve

"Hustle & Flow" (Ro Diddy)
Rhythm and Flow

Before we start: have you downloaded a metronome app on your phone yet? You need one. This is non-negotiable. If not, put this book down and do that now. Seriously, right now—this chapter will wait for you. Okay, you, have it? Fabulous. You may read on.

Steady Beat

The term "beat" can mean two things:

1. The instrumental track created by the producer. This will have percussion as well as other instruments (bass, synth, keyboard, samples, etc.) layered on top of one another.
2. A steady pulse. The length of time between beats is consistent, meaning it repeats over and over at the same rate. To picture what a steady pulse sounds like, think of a heartbeat in your chest. The heart beats over, and over and over, and the length of time that there is silence between the beats is the same between each beat. You'll probably find yourself bobbing your head along with this steady beat. That repetition is fundamental in forming the groove of the song.

Now that we've covered that, let's first dive into a few quick exercises to help you further understand a steady beat as it relates to the main tenets of this chapter: rhythm and flow.

Exercise 1:

- Remember that metronome app you downloaded onto your phone earlier? Now is when that will really come in handy. A metronome is a *great* tool for you to find a steady beat, hear what it is, practice keeping it, change tempos, and avoid rushing or dragging in your raps. So, once you have your metronome app open, choose a slower tempo, for example, seventy-five beats per minute. Let it play and hear the steady, repeating cluck of the metronome. Using that steady cluck, walk around the room, marching in tempo. Don't rush. Next try simply tapping your foot, then clap, and finally nod your head. Test this out at different tempos. Look at that—you're keeping a steady beat.

Exercise 2:

- Now that we've gotten the steady beat into our body, let's take it one step further by trying to bring it into our voice.
- First, alternate a clap, snap, clap, snap pattern, trying to keep a steady beat.
- Next, replace the snaps with your voice. Every time you would have snapped previously, say "buh" instead. It would go something like this:
    - Beat one: *Clap*
    - Beat two: *Buh*
    - Beat three: *Clap*
    - Beat four: *Buh*
- Finally, layer your voice on top of the claps. On beat one and three: Clap and say the syllable "tuh," simultaneously!
    - Beat one: *Clap/Tuh*
    - Beat two: *Buh*
    - Beat three: *Clap/Tuh*
    - Beat four: *Buh*

Using movement in the body to find (and keep) a steady beat is very important when it comes to rap practice and performance. "The work of Émile Jaques-Dalcroze demonstrated the importance of movement in the development of musical understanding. Jaques-Dalcroze believed that whole body movement allowed the body to process and perceive rhythms more accurately. Using the body to feel rhythms rather than just counting them provides a more complete rhythmic understanding."[1] Jaques was (of course) correct.

> "When someone has a flow that kind of resembles a drum pattern or something like that, it makes it a lot easier to remember their verses and their words than if there wasn't anything that was distinct."
>
> —Rama Kazi

Rhythmic Patterns

Congratulations, you've now got a steady beat! Now let's move on to rhythm. Rhythm is the groove, pattern, scat, pulse, time, and periodicity of a song. It is the most important element of rap. Strung together rhythms form patterns, thus making the phrase, or cadence. Let's use the image of a nesting doll to help us better understand. Have you ever seen that old-fashioned toy/wooden figurine? You can open it up, and the same figurine is inside, only smaller. You may open it four or five times until you reach the smallest figurine. Relating it to rhythmic patterns, your rhythms go inside your beats just like these dolls fit into each other. In a rhythmic phrase there are a variety of notes that can be all different lengths (we'll get into that in a second) but for rap, you usually have notes that are held for a shorter amount of time than the beat. That's because you'll want to be able to include as many syllables as you need in order to get your message across to your listeners.

Syncopation

"Syncopation in music is the concept of playing rhythms that accent or emphasize the offbeats. It shifts or displaces a standard rhythm by stressing beats generally not stressed."[2] Hip-hop relies heavily on syncopation. In any given bar, a certain number of syllables are said, often with the stressed syllable not falling on the downbeat or even one of the four "main" beats. In order to understand how to organize these syllables and remember your flows, you must learn about different note values. The following pages will discuss the most common note values that, when combined, can help you formulate and clarify your rap phrases. Before we get to that, however, let's make sure that you understand how syncopation works in relation to rhythmic patterns.

Here's another exercise:

To better understand syncopation, listen to the chorus of Bootsy Collins's "Jingle Belz." Using that song as your example, utilize the step-by-step instructions borrowed from the wonderful The Musical U Team:

> As you listen to the music, use your ear training skills to:
>
> 1. Find the pulse of the song
> 2. Tap a basic four note rhythm
> 3. Identify the downbeats
> 4. Hear how the instruments and/or vocals deviate from the stronger beats
> 5. Listen for rhythms on the weaker beats
>
> If you are comfortable with syncopation, take out a pair of sticks and try to tap out the more difficult rhythmic beats.[3]

Bars

Music and math often work together because they both have so much counting involved. One of your most helpful tools in rap will be "bars." Counting bars is absolutely essential if you want to master a flow while also staying on beat. Bars are a way of measuring time in the music via the beats you were reading about earlier. Think of bars as breaking down something bigger into smaller segments. "In simple words, you can think of a . . . [bar] . . . in music theory just like a container that holds a certain number of beats."[4] Once that container is full, there will be another bar (or container) to hold the next set of beats. This repeats over and over for the entire song. By breaking things down into bars, you will be able to keep a steady rhythm as opposed to rushing or falling behind.

Notation

In most rap, there are four steady beats per bar. Thinking back to our nesting dolls analogy, there are four beats "nesting" inside a bar. This will make more sense if you can see it, which is one of the reasons why figuring out a way to notate/write down your raps is essential. I came across a brilliant thesis written by scholar Martin Connor in 2018 that compared five different ways to notate rap bars. Connor organizes them (and explains where he discovered each) as in the following:

1. **Flow diagrams**—an orthographic-focused system underpinned by a 16th note grid. In this system, words are vertically arranged over beats numbered 1-4 within the bar (Adams 2009, Krims 2000).
2. **Typographical charts**—created in a word processing program like Microsoft Word, these charts pay special attention to global motions like structure and texture (Miyakawa 2004).
3. **MIDI rolls**—outgrowths from the natural workflows of digital-audio workstations, these vertical representations of a simple piano keyboard can also be used to chart rap's pitch vertically and its rhythms horizontally.
4. **Arabic Maqam notations**—maqam theory posits that each note within a scale can be wider than the traditional acoustical definition of a semitone. As such, maqam may be suited to capturing the intonation of rap that falls outside the standard western twelve-tone system.
5. **Western musical notation**—Common western music notation.[5]

The takeaway is that there isn't necessarily a right way to notate your raps. A lot of folks believe that the "correct" way to write down music is common western music notation. If you order a piece of sheet music from music notes, you'll see the music written on groupings of five horizontal lines stacked on top of one another with a slight space in between each line. The lines tell you what pitch to sing, and the symbol tells you how long to hold the note. It's great. It's organized, effective, and conveys a lot of information. But rap has extremely specific needs, and it's important to note that common western music notation might not be the best way to write it down. Martin offers the aforementioned alternatives, and ultimately, you should write down your raps in using whatever system helps you remember what you create, and helps you communicate these thoughts to others. As soon as I write this down, two hundred rappers will disagree with me, but I'm going to go out on a limb and say that my preferred method of seeing rap notated is a flow diagram. Today, the industry commonly calls this notational system a bar chart.

Bar Charts

The following is a visual example of a bar chart. In this example I'm using a phrase from A Tribe Called Quest's song, "Scenario." Pull this up on Spotify, YouTube, Apple Music, or however you listen to your tunes. You can make a bar chart or get them online. The best bar charts I've seen in my research are by a rapper named ColeMize. This is a simplified version, but if you are writing out the entire song, I'd highly recommend you look into his bar charts to help you (Colemizestudios.com).

"Sit Back Relax and Let Yourself Go"

Bar 1								
Beat 1		Beat 2			Beat 3		Beat 4	
Sit	back	re	lax	and	let	your	self	go

As you can see, it's a box. The numbers along the top count the bars. The numbers inside the box going across represent the beats. Then there is room for you to write in your lyrics, putting them on the correct beat, in

"Hustle & Flow" (Ro Diddy)   207

the correct bar. If you look at the first example, you'll see that "Sit," "-lax," "your," and "go" are the syllables that land *on* the beats while the syllables "back," "re," "and," "let," and "self" are syllables found within the beats. The rhythmic syllables nest inside the beats, and the beats nest inside the bar, and a bunch of bars put together form the song.

You may be familiar with sheet music if you studied an instrument, were in a choir, or participated in a school musical. When it comes to a gig or a concert, you'll often be handed standard sheet music, which will look different from a bar sheet, so let's quickly decode that with some basic music theory terms. In Western European music, you'll find the following elements in your music:

1. **A Staff:** Five horizontal lines and the four spaces in between those lines. Each line and space represent a specific pitch. Because rap is spoken, this notation isn't incredibly useful for us.
2. **Time Signature:** A symbol in music that looks a lot like a fraction. However, in music, the top number indicates how many beats per bar there are, and the bottom number indicates the length of what constitutes a beat. In rap, if we were to use a time signature, ours would be 4/4: four beats per bar, and a quarter note being worth one beat.
3. **Measure Lines:** Vertical lines spaced evenly on the staff to separate each measure (or in rap, bar) from the next.

Here is what a staff looks like versus a bar sheet:

Beat 1	Beat 2	Beat 3	Beat 4

Note Values

By now, you know that rhythmic patterns will consist of notes of varying lengths. To better write, learn, and/or memorize your cadences, you'll benefit by understanding note values and what they mean. Remember our good friend math? It's time to put that math knowledge to the test in order to make the whole "counting out your rhythm" thing much easier. A bar is four beats long. This is the complete pie:

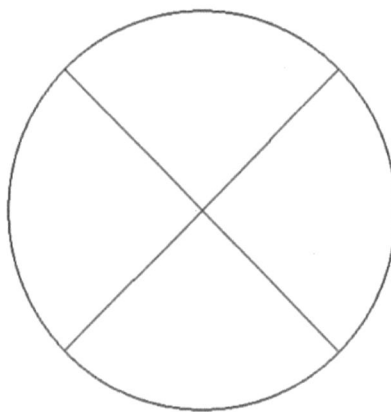

- **Quarter Notes:**
    - Each of the four beats that you've been reading about is one-fourth of the bar, or a quarter of the bar.
    - Counting that out sounds simply like this: 1, 2, 3, 4, 1, 2, 3, 4, 1, 2, 3, 4, and so on. In musical notation, this note value is called a quarter note.
    - On a bar sheet, it looks like this:

Beat 1	Beat 2	Beat 3	Beat 4

Before we discuss anything else, let's do another exercise:

Using your metronome to find your steady beat, count the quarter notes as follows:

"Hustle & Flow" (Ro Diddy)

Beat 1	Beat 2	Beat 3	Beat 4
1	2	3	4

Now, switch the numbers out for a neutral syllable. Still using your metronome, count the four beats for each bar, but instead of saying numbers, say Nah. Nah. Nah. Nah. Repeat this for four bars.

Beat 1	Beat 2	Beat 3	Beat 4
Nah	Nah	Nah	Nah

Practice this daily until both the quarter note and the steady beat are automatic to you.

- **Eighth Notes:**
  - Let's take another look at our pie. Remember that the bar is the entire pie. Each Beat is one-fourth of the bar, or one-quarter of the pie. An eighth note is . . . you guessed it, one-eighth of the pie and looks like this:

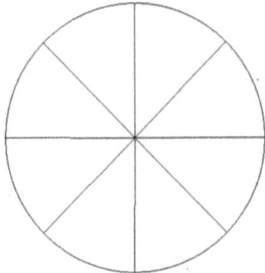

Or 1/8th of the bar and looks like this:

Beat 1		Beat 2		Beat 3		Beat 4	

Time for another exercise before we move on!

Insert this on a bar chart: 1 muh 2 muh 3 muh 4 muh. Say this four times, keeping your beat steady (use your metronome—think of it as your drum machine).

Beat 1		Beat 2		Beat 3		Beat 4	
1	Muh	2	Muh	3	Muh	4	Muh

- Substitute the syllable "Nah" for each number. Therefore, your pattern will look like this: Nah Muh Nah Muh Nah Muh Nah Muh

Beat 1		Beat 2		Beat 3		Beat 4	
Nah	Muh	Nah	Muh	Nah	Muh	Nah	Muh

- Alternate between quarter and eighth notes:
- Buh muh Nah Buh muh Nah

Beat 1		Beat 2	Beat 3		Beat 4
Buh	muh	Nah	Buh	muh	Nah

- Nah Buh muh Nah Buh muh

Beat 1	Beat 2		Beat 3	Beat 4	
Nah	Buh	muh	Nah	Buh	muh

- Buh muh Buh muh Buh Muh Nah

Beat 1		Beat 2		Beat 3		Beat 4
Buh	muh	Buh	muh	Buh	muh	Nah

- Nah Buh muh Buh muh Nah

Beat 1	Beat 2		Beat 3		Beat 4
Nah	Buh	muh	Buh	muh	Nah

Repeating these exercises daily will improve your ability to maintain a steady beat, count eighth notes, and begin to work on your diction and articulation.

- **Sixteenth Notes:**
  - Wow! This pie is really being cut up by this point. If this were Thanksgiving, I'd be annoyed that my piece of sweet potato pie was this tiny, but I digress. Here is the pie divided into sixteen pieces:

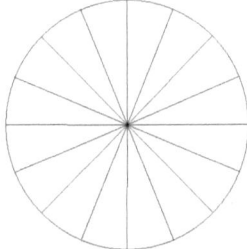

If we are cutting the bar up, we are not just splitting it into quarters, or eighths, but now, sixteenth notes. On a bar sheet, that is going to look like this:

Beat 1				Beat 2				Beat 3				Beat 4			

You guessed it . . . we're doing another exercise

Using your numbers as anchors, say the following: 1 Nee and uh 2 Nee and uh 3 Nee and uh 4 Nee and uh

Beat 1				Beat 2				Beat 3				Beat 4			
1	nee	and	uh	2	nee	and	uh	3	nee	and	uh	4	nee	and	uh

As you can see, that is each beat, broken into four equal parts, or one-sixteenth of the bar.

See if you can say that twice in a row:

- 1 Nee and uh 2 muh 3 Nee and uh 4 Nee and uh
- 1 Nee and uh 2 muh 3 Nee and uh 4 Nee and uh

Now let's see if you can alternate between sixteenth notes and eighth notes. Try saying the pattern indicated in the next bar chart. You will notice that beat two consists of eighth notes while beats one, three, and four consist of sixteenth notes. Try it now:

Beat 1				Beat 2				Beat 3				Beat 4			
1	nee	and	uh	2		muh		3	nee	and	uh	4	nee	and	uh

Let's alternate that with eighth notes now:

- 1 nee and uh 2 Nah 3 Nee and uh 4 Nah
- 1 nee and uh 2 Nah 3 Nee and uh 4 Nah

Beat 1				Beat 2		Beat 3				Beat 4	
1	nee	and	uh	2	Nah	3	nee	and	uh	4	Nah

- **Thirty-Second Notes:**
  - Okay, fair warning: these might be tricky, but here goes: A thirty-second note means that each count/syllable is worth one-thirty-second of the bar. Since there are four beats in a bar, that means that eight of those counts/syllables have to fit inside every beat. That means your pie is divided into . . . you guessed it again: thirty-two pieces. At this point at my Thanksgiving table, I would just get up and go buy myself a pie, but in rap these thirty-second notes are going to be your best friend.

"Hustle & Flow" (Ro Diddy)

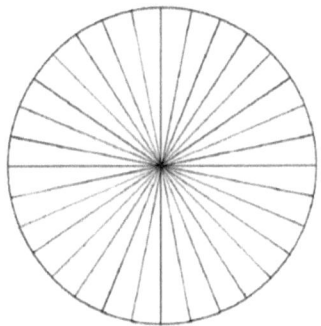

On a bar sheet, it would look like this:

How could we not do one last exercise for the thirty-second notes?

(For the sake of sanity, the numbers are removed from your vocabulary for this exercise.)

Beat 1								Beat 2							
BUH	duh	buh	duh	buh	duh	buh	duh	BUH	duh	buh	duh	buh	duh	buh	duh

Beat 3								Beat 4							
BUH	duh	buh	duh	buh	duh	buh	duh	BUH	duh	buh	duh	buh	duh	buh	duh

Choose a slow tempo for your metronome. Prioritize being able to say these syllables with clear diction, repeatedly. If you look at this exercise, notice that the first BUH of each beat is in all caps. This is done on purpose as a reminder to you to try to say that one slightly louder than the other seven syllables in the beat. This should help you keep track of where you are in a litany of buh duh buh duhs.

Slowly increase your speed, but only to the point where you can keep your diction clean.

Eventually, try to have the metronome speed that you had during your sixteenth-note exercise.

> **"There are definitely lot of technical elements that people don't really think about that go into trying to do a lot of these cleaner, faster versus that people don't realize how difficult they are until they try to rap them and go like 'wow this is actually crazy.'"**
>
> —femdot.

Triplets

Until now, you've been dividing notes evenly, cutting them into smaller and smaller pieces of the pie. Triplets are slightly different. A triplet is a three-note rhythmic pattern that fits into a typically two-note pattern. All the notes in the triplet pattern are the same (meaning that they have the same rhythmic value). They're very common in current rap because of the trap beat. "Trap music uses a 'halftime' drum pattern, usually with a kick on beat 1 and a snare on beat 3 in its simplest form."[6] In trap, you'll usually hear the hi-hat cymbal hitting sixteenth notes in rapid succession. To hear what this sounds like, listen to "Poppin' My Collar" by Three 6 Mafia. Trap uses a kick and snare pattern, with the kick on beats one and three and the snare on beats two and four. This drum pattern is referred to as "boom bap," which is a cool onomatopoeia: the BOOM is the sound that the bass drum makes the mallet "kicks" it and the BAP is the sound that you hear when the drumstick hits the snare drum.

The trap rhythmic pattern lends itself to the use of triplets in rap cadences. The triplet can be used on many different note values, but the most common is the eighth note triplet.

- **Eighth note triplet:** "An eighth note triplet rhythm is 3 notes played in the space of 2 eighth notes. You may find it easier to think of the eighth note triplet as being 3 notes dividing a quarter note (since 1 quarter note = 2 eighth notes)."[7]

You won't see this one quite as often, but occasionally you'll see the sixteenth note triplet in rap.

- **Sixteenth note triplet:** "A sixteenth note triplet contains three sixteenth notes over the span of two sixteenth notes or a single eighth note."[8]

Some more exercises following, focusing on the eighth note triplet (wow, we're really getting a lot of exercise, now aren't we . . . feel free to skip the elliptical today).

Triplet Exercise Part 1

Beat 1			Beat 2			Beat 3			Beat 4		
Straw	beh	ry	Straw	beh	ry	Straw	beh	ry	Straw	beh	ry

- Make sure that each of the syllables have the same rhythmic value. It might help to slightly stress the STRAW of the Straw-beh-ry to keep time.
- Tom Cullen (professor and blogger) takes this idea further by adding the challenge of moving the stress: "First try playing the triplet evenly from beat to beat with no accents. Once you get the hang of it try various speeds like 65bpm, 80bpm, 100bpm and 120bpm. Now, let's get a closer look at the triplet. This time play the same exercise but accent the first beat of each triplet. Continue to play the triplets but now accent the middle note of every triplet. Finally, accent the 3rd note of every triplet."[9]

Triplet Exercise Part 2

- Without music, let's imagine that we are waltzing (if you don't know what this is, go look up the dance they're all doing in the Netflix show Bridgerton), and say the following, giving each number equal duration, and stressing the 1 each time:
  - 1 2 3 / 1 2 3 / 1 2 3 / 1 2 3 / 1 2 3 / 1 2 3 / 1 2 3

Beat 1			Beat 2			Beat 3			Beat 4		
1	2	3	1	2	3	1	2	3	1	2	3

- Stop and analyze: did you stress the 1? That tends to be our natural instinct. You've practiced stressing the 2 and the 3 in a previous exercise. Let's make it a bit more complex. Say the number patterns again but let's stress every four beats. Say the following triplet pattern and stress/accent the **bold** numbers only:
  - **1** 2 3 / 1 **2** 3 / 1 2 **3** / 1 2 3 / **1** 2 3 / 1 **2** 3 / 1 2 **3** / 1 2 3

Beat 1			Beat 2			Beat 3			Beat 4			Beat 5			Beat 6			Beat 7			Beat 8		
1	2	3	1	**2**	3	1	2	**3**	1	2	3	**1**	2	3	1	**2**	3	1	2	**3**	1	2	3

- How did you do? Practice it slowly, and then you can slowly pick up speed. If you truly want a challenge, try this over a trap beat.
- Try the pattern once again, but stress every fifth note. Do this slowly enough that you can keep the triplets even and in tempo:
  - **1** 2 3 / 1 2 **3** / 1 2 3 / 1 **2** 3 / 1 2 3 **1** 2 3 / 1 2 **3** / 1 2 3

Beat 1			Beat 2			Beat 3			Beat 4			Beat 5			Beat 6			Beat 7			Beat 8		
1	2	3	1	2	**3**	1	2	3	1	**2**	3	1	2	3	**1**	2	3	1	2	**3**	1	2	3

Shifting the accent will make you feel like you are in a different time signature (i.e., it will make you feel like your bars start and end in a different place than when you were emphasizing the first beat of every triplet). Just remember that your metronome doesn't lie—what you've done is created a polyrhythm/cross rhythm. "A polyrhythm is the simultaneous combination of contrasting rhythms in music. Rhythmic conflicts, or cross-rhythms, may occur within a single meter (i.e., two eighth notes against triplet eighths)." Okay . . . off the music theory soapbox (for now).[10]

The Pocket

Simply put, to rap "in the pocket" is to rap on the beat . . . sort of. Perhaps a better definition or description of the pocket might be being within the groove of your track/beats. The meaning of this phrase is widely debated among rappers and rap lovers alike. To help us in this context, let's say that we are trying to figure out a simple pocket before moving on to more advanced flows that play with being slightly ahead of or behind the beat while still staying within the groove. That is still being in the pocket in rap, but for purposes of learning, we'll call that the advanced pocket. These are not official terms. We are just using them so that you can understand that you need to take one step at a time regarding staying within the rhythm of your track. As they say, walk before you run; for us, we'll say master staying in the simple pocket before mastering staying in an advanced pocket. To stay "in the simple pocket" does not mean that you can only say one syllable per beat, but rather that the beginning of a syllable or a purposeful rest coincide timing wise with the beats of the instrumental track, specifically beats one and four (of the four beats per bar). If we were thinking about advanced pockets, you can think about it as being more complex and dealing with the overall groove. Within the overall groove, there can be a push and pull within syncing up exactly with the beat. Being ever so slightly ahead of the beat can be seen as forward motion of sorts, while being ever so slightly behind can give a chill vibe, etc. Some people who prefer a more simplistic style might criticize this as being not "in the pocket." However, they'd often be incorrect. This purposeful non-alignment of the beat can work masterfully in creating an extremely complex and interesting flow. For example, Mitchell Ohriner's book *Flow—The Rhythmic Voice In Rap Music* utilizes Talib Kweli's "Get By" to demonstrate what Ohriner deftly names micro timing and/or expressive timing, saying "Any time listening to Kweli's flow reveals an unusual rhythmic style, one in which syllables often do not fall on expected parts of the beat. Yet neither 'complex' nor 'off-beat' adequately describes this style. 'Complex' is problematic because the style persists even in 'simpler' passages with fewer syllables. And the 'off-beat' label is problematic because it connotes incompetence."[11]

Rests

We've spent pages talking about note value and the combination of these values to form patterns. However, when creating cadences, the silent beats are just as important as the beats with syllables of your lyrics. Silence is an important part of rhythm and is crucial for impactful phrasing. You naturally take pauses when you speak, right? Therefore, it would make sense to take pauses when you rap. In music, pauses/beats of silence are notated using rests. If you look at a piece of music, you'll see the following symbols for rests of different lengths:

It might help you to use these same symbols when writing your rhythms out on your bar chart. This will help you remember not only to pause, but how long that pause should last. It will also remind you that this is where you want to take a breath. That said, use whatever symbol system that makes sense to you—you could use X's, slashes, etc., as long as they are clear, memorable, and repeatable to you.

Last exercise of the chapter, I swear!

This exercise combines rests into a simple rap flow using eighth notes and rests. Notice that there are rests of different lengths, thus determining what the rest of the bar looks like. For this exercise, and X indicates a rest.

Beat 1				Beat 2				Beat 3				Beat 4			
1	2	X	4	X	2	3	4	1	X	X	4	X	2	X	4

Combination

You've learned and mastered so many different rhythmic concepts in these pages. Way to go! You might be writing your own raps, practicing and analyzing popular rap songs already in existence, or rehearsing for a part in a hip-hop musical. Regardless, from now on, you will be learning your raps with rhythm as a priority. Hooray! When you put these rhythms together in various combinations, they create a rhythmic pattern. This rhythmic pattern would be the template for your lyrics. Think of it like layers of a cake. The first layer would be your instrumental beat/track/sample/accompaniment. The second layer would be the various rhythmic patterns that you create/learn, using combinations of quarter, eighth, sixteenth, thirty-second notes and rests. Now that you have a basic understanding of rhythm and how it works for you, you are ready to add another layer to your cake and dive into the concept of flow.

Flow

Before you continue, go back and read the paragraphs on flow from chapter 8. Flow is pivotal to your style and execution in rap, and the more you can learn about it the better. As previously stated, flow can mean so many things. Adam Krims defines it as "an MC's rhythmic delivery."[12] Sometimes people use flow in regard to encompassing a rapper's entire technical approach and capability. "Flow" may be thought of as the rap equivalent to what instrumentalists call "technique," a set of tools enabling the performer to most accurately convey their expressive meaning. In instrumental performance, these comprise the musician's approach to legato, breath control, pedaling, fingering, and other skills specific to the instrument.[13]

Flow is a rapper's "sound"—it's what distinguishes them and makes them unique. The way a rapper chooses to combine rhythmic patterns will shape their flow. The choice to have a phrase cross beyond the four bar (typical cadence length) will be another identifying flow trait. Other things that impact flow:

- Syllable count consistency
- Rhyme scheme
- Alignment with the instrumental beat (this includes making intentional decisions to be slightly ahead of or behind the beat as well)
- Dynamics
- Vocal tone creating the vibe
- Pitch variety
- Stressed syllable placement

Flows have become more complex over time. Early rap was often in duple meter, with simple rhyme structure. Eventually, more syllables were added, and phrases moved from two bars to four bars in length. Rhyme scheme evolved into sixteen bar cadences. Internal rhymes complicated the game further. Rhythmic patterns and syncopation became downright virtuosic. Multiple flows in one song became commonplace. The list goes on and on. This evolution allows for endless choices when it comes to flow and delivery. This is great news for you because . . . the sky's the limit!

> "I hate doing the same rhythm in a song, especially when it comes to my lyrics. That's how you lose the listener. You want to make sure, like, okay, this guy, he's serious. He knows what he's doing."
>
> —Lavon Bibb

Many of these elements are discussed in detail in other chapters. But it's important to see how they contribute to the final product—that they have an impact not only on proficiency but also your identity as an artist. The takeaway from this particular chapter is that rhythm, and your understanding of rhythm, is the foundation of unlocking your unique voice as a rapper. With a strong sense of rhythm comes a strong sense of flow, and that is the key to finding ownership in this artform.

Notes

1. Dell, Charlene. (2010). Strings Got Rhythm: A Guide to Developing Rhythmic Skills in Beginners. *Music Educators Journal*, 96: 31–34.

2. Levin, Harry. (2020, September 21). What Is Syncopation in Music and Why It Matters. *Icon Collective*. https://iconcollective.edu/what-is-syncopation-in-music/#:~:text=Syncopation%20in%20music%20is%20the,of%20strong%20and%20weak%20beats

3. Musical U. (n.d.). Get Rhythm: All About Syncopation. https://www.musical-u.com/learn/rhythm-training-101-study-syncopation/

4. Hip Hop Makers. (n.d.). What Is a Measure in Music. https://hiphopmakers.com/what-is-a-measure-in-music

5. Connor, Martin. (2018). The Notation of Rap Music. MFA dissertation, Brandeis University. https://scholarworks.brandeis.edu/esploro/outputs/graduate/The-Notation-Of-Rap-Music/9923880011801921#file-0

6. Russell, Aden. (2023, January 13). How To Make Trap Music: 7 Steps to Beats That Hit Hard. *Edmprod*. https://www.edmprod.com/how-to-make-trap-music/

7. Study Bass (2023). The Eighth Note Triplet Subdivision. https://www.studybass.com/lessons/rhythm/the-eighth-note-triplet-subdivision/

8. MasterClass. (2021, November 2). Guide to Triplets: How to Play and Count Triplets in Music. https://www.masterclass.com/articles/how-to-play-and-count-triplets-in-music

9. Philly Music Lessons. (2021, June 25). How Well Do You Know the Triplet? https://phillymusiclessons.com/how-well-do-you-know-the-triplet/

10. *Encyclopedia Britannica Online*. (n.d.). Polyrhythm. https://www.britannica.com/art/polyrhythm#:~:text=polyrhythm%2C%20also%20called%20Cross%2Drhythm,simultaneous%20combinations%20of%20conflicting%20metres

11. Ohriner, Mitchell. (2019). *The Rhythmic Voice in Rap Music*. New York: Oxford University Press, 183.

12. Krims, Adam. (2000). *Rap Music and the Poetics of Identity*. Cambridge: Cambridge University Press.

13. Adams, Kyle. (2009). On The Metrical Techniques of Flow in Rap Music. *MTO* 15 (5).

Thirteen

"Runnin' Your Mouth" (Notorious B.I.G.)
Diction—Articulators and Articulation

While many puzzle pieces must fit together simultaneously to make a rap successful, two of the most important pieces of the puzzle will be your lyrics and your flow. Your lyrics might be sick, but that won't be worth much if no one can understand you when you say them. "When rappers attempt to build worlds with their words, the voice is integral in giving the end product its hue. Once enunciation is botched, the rapper's flow loses pristineness, and the balance on the song is very likely to be thrown out of whack."[1] That, my friend, is why this chapter is dedicated to diction and articulation: what that means, why it's important, the key players that make them effective, and how you can master these things so that people can clearly understand the important words you are putting out into the universe.

The Intricacies of Diction and Articulation

Diction

"Diction can be simply defined as the pronunciation or enunciation of your vocal expression. In regards to singing, it is the clarity or particular way words are pronounced in a song,"[2] or the "pronunciation and enunciation of words in singing."[3] Beyond being comprehensible, diction choices (the way you form your vowels and consonants) will affect your tone and timbre. It's almost weird to think about speaking, since most of us do it frequently throughout each day. But speaking for rap is a bit more complex than the kind of speech you use when you're hanging out with friends. Common problems rappers run into include tripping over words (which knocks you out of the pocket), slurring words together, mumbling (when the genre is decidedly *not* mumble rap), losing volume or breath support, or feeling the enemy that is tension creeping into the throat, the jaw, or the tongue. "The most common causes of poor singing diction can be any or all of the following:

- Mouth shape while singing
- Tongue position
- Poor control of breathing
- Strong accents and dialects
- Poor mic technique"[4]

Articulation

People often use the terms diction and articulation interchangeably. The majority of this chapter will deal with diction. But understanding articulation adds an arsenal of tools to your toolbox. While diction deals with the formation of words, articulation deals with the stuff between the words. In other words, "the articulation is what happens in between the notes. The attack—the beginning of a note—and the amount of space in between the notes are particularly important."[5]

There are many articulation choices in music, but in rap, you'll find three of these choices to be both common and the most useful:

- **Staccato:** Notes are short and detached from other notes (this is really useful to make your flow extra percussive)
- **Legato:** Notes are connected and flow directly into one another, with no space/silence between notes (this is common in all genres, but is the standout tool utilized in lo-fi or melodic rap)
- **Accents:** *Encyclopedia Britannica* says that an "accent, also called Stress, in music, momentary emphasis on a particular rhythmic or

melodic detail."⁶ If you accent a note, it means you give it a little bit more oomph than the notes on either side of it—this is incredibly useful for both conveying emotion as well as improving listener comprehension.

> **"Emphasis on certain sounds function almost like kick drums and high hats that fit in open pockets of the beat."**
>
> —Rama Kazi

So by now, you might be saying, "Okay, I know I need good diction . . . but how do I fix my problem?" Have no fear! Your articulators have the solution. Let's get into what the articulators are.

The Lips, the Tongue, the Teeth, and the Jaw

The lips, the tongue, the teeth, and the jaw all work together to form different sounds and combinations of sounds. These are also known as your annunciators. An extremely common warmup actors use before going on stage is based simply on listing these, speaking as clearly as possible: "The lips, the teeth, the tip of the tongue" (repeated multiple times in quick, crisp succession). You speak every day, which means you know how to form words to be understood in everyday conversation. The downside is that you also have ingrained habits regarding the way you talk that might inhibit the word density necessary to rap. The following paragraphs are aimed at helping you identify your habits impacting crisp diction.

1. **The lips:**
    The lips are amazing at being the finishing touch to a killer outfit (we all know that the right shade of lipstick can make or break your final look). Wait, sorry, wrong book. Perhaps the most important function of the lips as articulators is to change the tone quality and resonance.

Lip Relaxation Exercises

- **The fish:** Pretending like you are a fish is a childlike but easy way of engaging the lip muscles and kicking them into high gear. Here's how you do it:
    1. Go in front of a mirror, and, while keeping your mouth closed, pucker your lips like you are going to blow someone a kiss.
    2. Keeping your lips in the pucker position, separate the top lip from the bottom lip. You won't be able to move them very far apart in the pucker position, which is the point, as this partially isolates the lip muscles so they, and not the jaw, are primarily moving.
- **Feeding the baby:** Here is another throwback to childhood. Now you get to make the sound of an airplane motor by doing the following:
    1. Pucker your lips very slightly.
    2. Take a calm, low inhale.
    3. Exhale while keeping your lips loosely together. Experiment with how much air to blow out and how forcefully to exhale this air until your lips are vibrating, making the sound of an airplane motor. This exercise is called feeding the baby because, sometimes, when a baby won't finish their food (imagine this baby, in their highchair, stubbornly refusing to eat that sweet potato mush baby food). You, the babysitter, are trying to get them to finish their meal. So you act like the spoon is an airplane. You lift the spoon high above their head and slowly fly it in zig zag positions, all while making this airplane motor sound with this lip buzz/trill.
    4. Ta-da! Now you've not only relaxed your lips, you've learned a tricky toddler tip.

Lip Positions Explanation and Exercises

Lips can move horizontally from a pucker to a smile, and this movement drastically changes the tone quality. One can think of the lips as having four main positions (remembering that there are numerous positions that exist on the sliding scale moving from one position to the next).

- **Puckered:** In this position, the lips are in an "oo" position, slightly parted, or an "oh" position, where the mouth is opened and the jaw is slightly dropped. Look at yourself saying these two vowels in a mirror. Notice your lip shape when you say these vowels. This lip shape will give you a darker, warmer tone quality.
- **Neutral/resting:** In this position, your lips are in their resting state: slightly open and not puckered, nor are you frowning or smiling. They are simply hanging out in their neutral position. Say "ah-ha," or, keeping your lips closed, say "hmm," while keeping your lips relaxed and in this neutral/resting position.
- **Smiling/spread:** In this position, your lips are pulled horizontally into a parted smile position. This position will give you a brighter tone quality.
- **Closed:** In this position, "the lips meet and touch to seal off the contents of the mouth from the outside. The position is attained through easy, non-forceful movement."[7]

Now, time for the exercise: **Imitating Aaron Neville**
1. Spread your lips into a smile. While smiling, say "AH."
2. Now move your lips into a neutral position and say "AH." Can you hear the difference in tone quality between the two of these? If not, record yourself saying the same vowel in these different lip positions. Finally, pucker your lips, and say "AH." Can you hear a change in tone quality now? If not, record yourself and listen back closely to the recording.
3. Practice these different lip positions on different words, noticing the changes in your tone quality.

Lip-Driven Consonants

Imagine you are a ventriloquist, and you are trying to say words without moving your lips. Try it. Say the sentence, "Wow it's difficult to say words clearly without moving my lips." Feel free to open and close the mouth, move the tongue, etc. But your lips should stay still ... were you able to speak clearly? Probably not. That is because your lips also help say certain consonants, especially P, B, W, F, and V.

To work on your diction for these consonants, practice with the following words and phrases:
- **B:** Bigger business isn't better business, but better business brings bigger bucks.
- **W:** Wanting won't win; winning ways are wacky ways.
- **F:** Feel free to follow funny fellows.
- **P:** If Peter Piper picked a peck of pickled peppers, where's the peck of pickled peppers Peter Piper picked?
- **V:** Vivian plays viola vivaciously.

2. **The jaw:**

When you think of your jaw ... actually, you probably don't think about your jaw very often. But, if asked why you need your jaw, you'd probably say that it's necessary to help your teeth bite and chew food. For speaking and diction, the jaw movement will affect the way your vowels and consonants sound. As far as vowels are concerned, how much your jaw opens will change vowel shape and sound. For consonants, a tight jaw can drastically affect consonant production, and your speech can become slurred.

Jaw Position Explanation and Exercises

There is no "correct" jaw position for singing—it changes for every word being said. That said, the primary goal should be to have a relaxed and free jaw. Sometimes in singing, you'll hear the phrase "drop your jaw," but a dropped jaw isn't extremely useful in speaking (and honestly, it's sometimes not as useful as people think for singing):

One of the best ways to achieve jaw mobility is to permit the sounds of language to be shaped according to their natural postures as determined by pitch and power. When we raise the pitch, we open the mouth more, but we retain relative relationships among the vowel shapes with regard to lip and tongue postures. . . . Emphasizing loose, flexible movement of the jaw is a more efficient solution to jaw tension.[8]

Releasing jaw tension usually does wonders for creating the optimal speaking position for a given word.

> **"When I rap a little faster, I don't open my mouth as much. A lot of the words are more like, joined together as opposed to me just enunciating every single word. With that . . . I might push my jaw up a little bit more forward than I would normally, and I just kind of like just go until I decide to take a breath or switch the flow up."**
>
> **—igobylc**

Now, time for an exercise. This one has a cutesy little name: **The Lemon and the Lion.**

1. Imagine biting into a lemon and how extremely sour it tastes in your mouth. Perhaps your lips and jaw are tightening and puckering just thinking about this (if so, fantastic!) Exaggerate this feeling and scrunch your face up, even closing your eyes.
2. Hold that tension position for at least five seconds.
3. Relax to a neutral position.
4. Now, imagine you are a lion and imitate the enormously open mouth position of them roaring. If you look up a video of this, you'll notice that the lion doesn't just open their jaw vertically, but rather there is movement of the bottom jaw slightly side to side as well.

5. Alternate your lemon and lion face, noticing the difference in jaw opening, movement, etc.

Another great exercise to try is called Thumbelina. Here's how it works:
1. Put the tip of your thumb between your top and bottom front teeth.
2. Holding your thumb in that position, say "the weather today is cloudy." Keep your teeth touching your thumb.
3. Remove your thumb, and say the same sentence, being careful not to open your mouth more than when you had your thumb in your mouth. This is a great approximation of a relaxed but not forcibly dropped jaw.

3. **The tongue:**
The tongue helps us taste food, starts the act of swallowing, and helps us speak. When the tongue is just chilling, assuming your mouth is closed, the tip of the tongue should be just behind the top teeth and lightly touching the roof of the mouth. This position also assists us in speaking clearly. "To articulate words or lyrics, the tip of the tongue should stay at or near the front teeth. Yes, certain vowels and pitches need different tongue involvement but the point is to operate the tongue in the front and keep the back of the tongue relaxed, not bunching or bulking up."[9]

Now, let's do a simple exercise to work this muscle: "try putting two fingers firmly up under your chin, pressing into the tongue base there. Purposefully intend/suggest that this area relax as you sing or talk. Expect the tongue muscle to obey and you'll be amazed at how it does."[10]

Preparing the Articulators for Rap

If you are a mumble rapper, you have probably already skipped this chapter. If you are not exclusively into mumble, this chapter might be the one of the most important contributors to your flow. Clear and tension-free diction helps people understand your lyrics, increases your stamina, and allows your intended nuances to shine through. However, before you hop into your cadences, take the time to develop an articulation warm up that you can do before you go on stage. The following are some simple exercises that you can do daily both to improve your diction and to warmup before your shows.

1. **For the tongue:**
   Against the Bottom Two Front Teeth
   - To practice this, curl your tongue upward so that the tip of the tongue touches the roof of the mouth.
   - Drag your tongue slowly backward along the roof of your mouth toward the back of the mouth. Remember, only curl your tongue as far as it will *comfortably* go.
   - Hold your tongue in the curled position for at least three seconds.
   - Slowly relax your tongue back to its resting position, checking to make sure the tip of the tongue rests against the bottom front teeth.

   Tongue Stretching
   - Stick your tongue out as far as it will go (imagine you are a little kid who is teasing another little kid because you got away with something and they didn't).
   - Gently close your teeth to hold the tongue in the stretched position.
   - Hold for ten seconds.
   - Release your tongue back to its normal resting position.

   This is, hands down, my favorite tongue release exercise. It's quick and easy, and can drastically improve the clarity of your words.

2. **For the jaw:**
   The Roll Down
   - With your hands, make two gentle fists, with your index and middle knuckles slightly protruded/sticking out.

- Place one hand on each side of the face in front of the earlobe.
- Using those two knuckles on each hand, slowly move them down your face, over your cheeks (aim for a diagonal line from the starting position next to the ear, to the outward corner of the mouth).
- At some point, you'll hit a spot where your jaw automatically opens slightly. Using your knuckles, gently press inward on the spot and hold that position for five seconds.
- Repeat this motion three to five times.

Try to avoid the following, as they increase habitual jaw tensing:
- "Cradling the telephone receiver between your shoulder and jaw."[11]
- Opening your mouth all the way, as when singing loudly or yawning (try dropping your head to your chest to stifle a yawn).
- Clenching or grinding your teeth, biting your lips, or chewing your fingernails. Try to recognize when you are clenching your teeth, then relax your jaw and separate your teeth.
- "Clenching things such as pens, pipes, or cigars between your teeth."[12]

3. **For the lips:**
   Slo-Mo
   - Choose one of your rap cadences. Casually say it as if it is a conversation to someone. Pay attention to your lips while you do this (you might want to stand in front of a mirror while doing this exercise).
   - Repeat the sentence but this time, speak in slow motion, while exaggerating every syllable. Chances are your mouth and lip movement increases dramatically.
   - Repeat the cadence once more, but once again speaking conversationally . . . do you notice any difference in lip movement (and jaw movement)?
   - Finally, say your cadence as if you are performing the actual rap verse. You'll be amazed at how your diction has improved.

Tongue Twisters for Each Consonant Sound (which will work your tongue, jaw, and your lips)

- For the letter **B**: Bitter Bobby bit a bit of barely baked brittle bread. But Bitter Bobby baked the barely baked brittle bread and baked brittle bread is better brittle bread.
- The letter C can either sound like the letter K or the letter S—this exercise treats the letter C like the letter **K**: Cal cooked chewy cobbed corn carefully.
- For the letter **D**: Deepa does dirty dishes while delightfully dancing dizzily.
- For the letter **F (and PH blend)**: Felicia fought feisty forewarned froggy fish before fighting five frantic festive phantoms for the fiery fuschia phone.
- For the letter **G**: Gus gagged and Gooey gook got on Gil's gorgeous green garage.
- For the letter **H**: Heaven helped Haley hook hefty halfway hungry halibut in Hartford Harrisburg and Hampshire.
- For the letter **J**: J'Siah joked gently about Jamie's jeweltone gel nails.
- For the letter **K**: Kissing cute cuddly kitties quickly quite carefully keeps Queen Kimmie calm.
- For the letter **L**: LaQuan laughed loudly, lingering longingly, looking at the last little letter.
- For the letter **M**: Many mumbling mice are making merry music in the moonlight. Mighty nice mighty minnie mice.
- For the letter **N**: Unique New York Unique New York Unique New York. You know you need unique New York.
- For the letter **P**: Penelope Pike picked purple peppers. But Penelope procrastinated pickling the peppers, and purposefully produced purple peppers.
- For the letter **Q**: Quiet queens quit quite quickly.
- For the letter **R**: Writing really round Rs, Roger wrote Rakeem rewarding reading.
- For the letter **S**: Sahana sells seashells by the sea shore.

- For the letter **T**: Thomas twerks and tells Talia terrible tales twice.
- For the letter **V**: Victorious venomous victory to vile Victor and Victoria.
- For the letter **W**: While wearing white, Wilma won't wet her whistle with wine.
- For the letter **Y**: Yelling at yellow yaks yields you yesterday's yarn.
- For the letter **Z**: Zelda zooms zippily. Zeke zaps zebras zig zagging in the zone.

Vowel Sounds

Now that you've mastered consonants, it's time to tackle the vowels. There are five(ish) vowel sounds (A, E, I, O, U, and sometimes Y), but there are twenty vowel *sounds*. Yeah, the English language is complicated. This toolbox of twenty sounds is vital to your diction and communication. Why, you ask? Well, my friend, vowels should matter to you for two reasons:

1. **Comprehension:** By now you are well aware that you'll be saying a lot of syllables quickly. This entire chapter is dedicated to the importance of your audience understanding you. Slight changes in your vowel can change the meaning of your word, and accidentally changing that meaning can result in a change of your entire sentence. For example: imagine that you need to say the word "beach" (meaning "the place where you go and forget what day of the week it is. You visit the beach only in the summer because that's when you get tan and have endless long nights. Your days at the beach consist of waking up, going on a bike ride, going to the beach, coming home with new tan lines and sandy hair then going to bed and repeating this process")[13] in a lyric. For example: "*And it's a fact I keep a gat in my arm reach, I charm freaks and bomb geeks from here to Palm Beach*" ("Put It On" by Big L).

    The "ee" sound in beach is crucial for you to know that Big L is referring to a place. If he was lazy with his vowel sounds and made the "ih" sound (i.e., fish), it would become "Palm Bitch," which takes on a completely different meaning.

2. **Rhyming:** You might *want* to change your vowels slightly in order to rhyme words that might not straight up rhyme. Knowing how to say the vowel correctly, and understanding what your jaw, tongue, and lips are doing to say that vowel, puts you in control of making tiny degrees of change—not so much that you're saying a different word (or suddenly saying a made-up word), but just enough to nail your rhyme.

   While you know these vowel sounds, regional dialects, or merely the need for speed in some cadences, might cause things to get a bit fuzzy. Therefore, it's probably a good idea to be intentional about your vowel shape by practicing. You can organize your mind by splitting vowels into three categories: short vowel sounds, long vowel sounds, and other vowel sounds (if this is giving you flashbacks to third grade, you are spot on and, by the way, your third-grade teacher is proud of you right now). You can use the following word list to organize, understand, categorize, and practice each sound. It's now when I need to make the disclaimer: there could be entire books on vowels, and we could make this whole vowel breakdown much more complex. Vowels can be categorized by how they are formed with the tongue and mouth, or using a symbol system called International Phonetic Alphabet. Still another way to categorize vowels is by the degree of muscle tension or laxness it takes to form the vowel. But the bottom line is making rapping easier for you. So, with that goal in mind, the following is a way to get you to clearer rap phrases without making you feel like you are studying for a final exam. Honestly, even with this basic breakdown, it's still a lot of information. This portion will be helpful to come back to when you need something, or when you are finding that you are having trouble with certain words in your raps. For now, look over it so you remember the categories, and just know that if you want to delve deeper into vowels, there are many nuances and deeper categorizations you can explore.

Types of Vowels

- **Long vowel sounds:** Before we get into these, let's be clear, this doesn't mean that it takes longer to say these vowels, or that you should hold these vowels out for a longer period of time. The easiest way for you to think about "long vowels" is that they sound the same way you'd pronounce the letter (if you want to geek out with me, these are often actually categorized by tongue position needed to form the vowel and/or the degree of muscle tension or laxness to form the vowel).

    There are five long vowel sounds:
- **A:** Cake, mane, base, brake, replay (note: this section is dangerously close to becoming overwhelming, so I'm just going to say this, when you read the paragraph about diphthongs/glides, remember this vowel)
    - Phrases:
        - Hazy lake
        - Lazy aim
- **E:** Eat, speed, feet, weed, cheap, feat
    - Phrases:
        - Easy and breezy
        - Wheezes and sneezes
- **I:** Iowa, fine, why, mile, bike, eye (note: when you read the paragraph about diphthongs/glides, remember this vowel too)
    - Phrases:
        - I like pie
        - Sky high
- **O:** Row, bogus, woke, open (note: when you read the paragraph about diphthongs/glides, remember this vowel too)
    - Phrases:
        - Low blow
        - Bow and arrow

- **U:** Booze, lose, blue, rude, knew
  - Phrases:
    - Cool clue, dude
    - Super sleuth
- And a special circumstance: The invisible **Y + U** combo sound. These words sound like there is the consonant Y present, but it isn't actually there: use, huge, cube, menu.
  - Phrases:
    - Cute unicorn
    - Beautiful music
- **Short vowel sounds:**
  There are five short vowel sounds:
- **A:** Cat, man, babble, rattle, sand
  - Phrases:
    - Rad pad
    - Bad apple
- **E:** Ever, red, said, pebble
  - Phrases:
    - Effortless elegance
    - Extra credit
- **I:** Fish, big, lived, river
  - Phrases:
    - Pitiful kitten
    - Little nibbles
- **O:** On, wobble, pond, lobby
  - Phrases:
    - Odd jobs
    - Hot pocket
- **U:** Bus, rumble, under, cut
  - Phrases:
    - Comfortably numb
    - Wonderful umpire

The Schwa

Then, there are other vowels (because, of course, the English language is ridiculously complex). The most commonly used vowel is the sound you hear in crook and look:

- "OO": Book, pull, stood, cookie, crooked
  - Phrases:
    - Wooden bookshelf
    - Good rookie

Diphthongs/Glides

These are vowels where two vowel sounds happen on one syllable (they glide quickly from one to the next, but the tongue and sometimes lips change shape within that single vowel). Remember the long A and the long I sounds from before? Sometimes (and almost always, depending on where you live) those lend themselves to being diphthongs. Say some of these words in slow motion and notice how your tongue/mouth move:

- **The "eye" sound:** (eye-ee) (remember: you saw this in its pure vowel form earlier . . . it's the same as the long vowel "i"). Here are some to practice and have fun exaggerating the diphthong. Notice that the first vowel (of the two that are squished together to form one syllable) gets more time and attention than the second vowel, which is almost like a tag.
  - Buy, my, cry, bye, sigh, lie, kite, lime, fight, alibi, fright, sight, might, wry, rye, spider, style, vitamin
- **The "aaaaaeee" sound:** (remember, you saw this earlier as well, as the long "a" vowel).
  - Rain, pail, make, same, late, snake, eight, snail, mail, bail, fake, break, dismay, awake, failure, neighbor, chaos, weight, savior, steak

- The "ow" sound: this is most often spelled with an ow combination or an ou combination.
    - Cloud, powder, allow, round, ouch, wow, brown, bow, however, clown, drown, sound, pound, mouse, growl
- The "ohhhooo" sound: this too, can be the pure long vowel sound, or the diphthong, depending on where you call home. Loan, mow, slow, enroll, toe, tow, stowaway, though, oh, no, poke, focus, broken, cyclone, sew, boat
- The "ooooee" sound: this is usually spelled with either an oy or an oi sound.
    - Oil, disappoint, boy, foil, coil, paranoid, toilet, spoil, voice, noise, destroy, poison, coy, coil, pointing, soy, employed, tabloid

The Bossy "R" Vowels and Diphthongs

This is an odd one, but you use vowels this way all of the time. Sometimes when a vowel and the letter R are next to each other, they make a new sound. The easiest way to understand this is to think of words that fit this description: church, bird, and feather, for example. Note that all of these are spelled differently, but all have the same sound. The interesting thing about this is that whether this applies to you drastically changes depending on where you live: people in some parts of the country/world utilize the R sound differently, and sometimes drop the sound completely. For example, the bossy R is frequently dropped in the northeast—if you visit Boston, pay attention to the pronunciation of words like park or car. You can feel empowered by this sound, because whether you choose to use it gives it a different vowel sound, and vowels are generally what you use to determine rhyme. Therefore, you can determine whether using this sound creates two words that rhyme. These R vowels also fall into categories. (Whew! Okay, we're almost done, I promise). One last thing though:

There Are Five Bossy "R" Regular Vowels

- **Ar:** Bark, car, marker
- **Er:** Slumber, feather, paper
- **Ir:** Whirl, bird, smirk
- **Or:** For, torn, border
- **Ur:** Further, turtle, surf
- Two examples of bossy "R" diphthongs:
    - **The "air" sound:** (can have different spellings—for this sound, the important thing to recognize is the vowel + R combination results in this sound): compare, flair, dare, beware, hair.
    - **The "ear" sound:** (can have different spellings—for this sound, the important thing to recognize is the vowel + R combination results in this sound): fear, beer, pier.

Thoughts on Practicing

Practice, practice, practice. Practice makes perfect. Don't practice until you get it right, practice until you can't get it wrong. You've probably heard these sayings before, and that's because they're true. But sometimes knowing how to practice is as important as the practice itself. For effective practice, follow the steps outlined here. This will initially work on your diction and articulation, but continuation of this practice will improve your word stress (and deciding what the stressed and unstressed syllables should be). It will improve your dynamics, your rhythmic accuracy, and your breath support. Practicing will help you memorize, and all of that will improve and solidify your flow. Breaking down practicing for diction:

- Practicing the sounds, making sure that you can say each consonant and vowel easily, is vital. For each consonant/vowel/diphthong, begin by saying the sound by itself. Look in a mirror at your mouth and your tongue. Repeat the sound ten times, slowly at first, and then increase speed.
- When that becomes easy, practice the sample words provided, again, seeing what they feel like in your mouth, in your jaw, and on your

tongue. Next, say the string of words as if they are a sentence. Begin slowly, and then speed up. Do the same with the practice phrases provided. Not only will this work on your articulation and agility, you'll also be practicing different consonants/vowels back to back, meaning that your mouth will be making different shapes in rapid succession. Perhaps the best bonus is that you'll also often be practicing something called consonant blends: this is when two consonants next to each other form a new sound (i.e., the ch in choose, or the fl in flower).
- When all of these become easy, go back and practice the tongue twisters provided earlier in the chapter, thinking about your newfound clarity and ease.
- Finally, record yourself and listen. Can you understand yourself, and, more importantly, do you sound the way you want to sound saying the words? If you can't, repeat the exercises until you are happy with what you are listening to!
- Try memorizing some of the phrases. Getting off of the page will let you practice word stress, add punctuation, and insert dynamics.

Other Essentials

1. **Playing with Voiced and Voiceless Consonants**
   While each consonant and sound is unique and its own special little snowflake, there are things that groups of consonants have in common. Knowing how to make these commonalities work in your favor might be the final key to unlocking your speed rap so you can be the next JID.

   Consonants are either voiced or voiceless.

   - **Voiced:** If consonants are voiced, it means that the sound comes from vibration of the vocal cords. The upside to this is that very little is happening in your lips, teeth, tongue, and jaw. Odds are they'll be more relaxed since they aren't needing to move around quickly! The combination of relaxation and lack of needing to

change shape means that words can flow more efficiently (with more ease, and faster). The naturally voiced consonants are B, D, G, J, L, M, N, R, V, W, Y, and Z.

- **Voiceless:** Voiceless consonants, on the other hand, do not use the vocal cords to make sound. So while they chill out, the articulators get to work. These consonants are formed by the use of the tongue, teeth, lips, and jaw. The great thing about voiceless consonants is that, if said without push (excess effort), they'll use less air, letting you get through longer phrases before needing to breathe. Voiceless consonants are also much more percussive, which helps you stay in the pocket and set the groove in the flow for your listeners. Finally, voiceless consonants can convey emotion when punched for effect. The naturally voiceless consonants are F, K, P, S, and T.
  - **Replacing voiceless consonants with voiced consonants:** Each voiceless consonant has a voiced consonant that sounds similar (easing up on the articulator movement will increase your speed and agility). Therefore, it makes sense that swapping out some voiceless consonants for its voiced partner will help you speed up, without sacrificing clarity. Here is the consonant partner chart:[14]

VOICELESS		VOICED	
/p/	park	/b/	bark
/t/	town	/d/	down
/k/	coat	/g/	goat
/f/	fan	/v/	van
/s/	sip	/z/	zip
"sh"	sure	"zh"	treasure
"ch"	chain	"j"	Jane
"th"	thigh	"th"	thy

"Runnin' Your Mouth" (Notorious B.I.G.) 243

Try it with a couple of words and see how the movement changes in your mouth and if it's easier to speak faster. Now try the following sentence from J. Cole's "No Role Modelz":

I'm writin' down names, I'm makin' a list

1. Get a piece of paper and pen, or use the space provided.
2. Write this phrase on your paper.
3. Now, looking at this phrase, identify and circle the voiceless consonants.
4. Cross out the voiceless consonant and replace it with its voiced partner.
5. Say the sentence using only voiced consonants.

Workspace:
I'm writin' down names, I'm makin' a list
It would look something like this:

I ' m w r i t i n' d o w n n a m e s,
       O   O
I' m m a k̶ i n' a l i s̶ t
      O   Ⓞ
↓
I' m w r i d̲ i n' d o w n n a m e z̲,
I' m m a g̲ i n' a l i z̲ d̲

Key of Voiceless → Voiced
F → V
K → G
P → B
S → Z
T → D

Assessment: could you speed up? Once you got used to the swaps, was it easier to say? How noticeable was it? Could you meet in between the two and "sort of" swap them out (i.e., move those voiceless closer to voiced but don't completely switch them)? Try this and see if it works for you.

2. **Using "light and bright" to your advantage:**
Listen to the following:

- Li'l Wayne's verse in Tyler the Creator's "Hot Wind Blows"
- Nicki Minaj in "Barbie Dreams"
- Twista in "Runnin off at Da Mouth"
- Eminem in pretty much anything Eminem does (but to choose one for the purposes of this, let's go with "Rap God")
- Daveed Diggs in "Guns and Ships"
- Tonedeff in "Velocity"

It must be stated that the organization of consonants and vowels in these flows are genius because the allocation of movement in the tongue and mouth constantly shifts to prevent the overuse of one tongue/jaw/lip position, thus preventing over-taxation. But, beyond that, listen to the tone and pitch of these rappers—they are all "up and out" (i.e., not dark and in the back of the mouth with a flattened tongue). There are multiple ways to do this: you can use slight nasality, you can add a smile, which slightly raises the dorsum (middle of the tongue). You can raise your pitch slightly (and for all of these, you're controlling breath, using very little air). Regardless, all of these methods create an up and out/light and bright quality, and that helps with both clarity, as well as with speed.

3. **Practice your bars in small sections:**
It's easy to get overwhelmed with twenty-five hundred words to articulate. But if you practice four bars, and you think, "I'm going to articulate purposefully on these four bars; which might mean that I'm going to mumble slightly because I'm into lo-fi, or it might mean that I'm going to have crisp annunciation because I'm in practicing for a rap battle and I need the crowd to hear every word. I'm going to make decisions on word stress for these four bars, and I'm going to memorize these four bars," it seems *much* more manageable.

4. **Softening and alliding:**
Remember, speaking clearly and effortlessly doesn't mean that you have to over-enunciate beyond that of conversational diction. It also doesn't mean that you can't "cheat" a bit on the beginning or ends of words. This may mean that you soften ending consonants or eliminate them completely.

This might also mean that you allide words. For example: "You never turned down nothing" might smoosh together/allide to sound like: "You never turnedownothin"

Notice how the word turned ends in the letter "d," and the word down starts with the letter "d." There is no need for the listener to hear that D sound twice. Notice the N at the end of down, and how it can run together into the start of the word nothin'. If you listen more intently to your conversations with other people, this is actually common practice; however, when you look at words like this on paper, it can seem daunting. Try saying the sentence both ways:

You never turneD DowN Nothin'

versus

You never turneDowNothin'

Which one is easier? These points may seem counterintuitive at first, but hopefully after putting this into practice, you'll find that your diction improves.

5. **Return to neutral:**
Remember the exercise where you rapped with your tongue sticking out? Do you remember why that was effective? As the tongue muscles become stressed, they "bunch up" and the tongue tends to want to pull slightly backward. Finding tongue relaxation is crucial to great rap diction. Forcing yourself to return to a neutral tongue position on the regular should help you prevent that tongue bunching. To do this, try inserting the word "a" between each syllable of a lyric. For example, look at the following lyric from "Best Friend" by Saweetie:

- Say the lyric: "Got me steppin' out that Jeep, got Manolo's"
- Insert the word "a" between each syllable (you might want to write this out as well for reference): "Got a Me a Step a Pin' a Out a That a Jeep a Got a Man a O a Lo's."
- Say the lyric as is written here.
- Slowly increase the tempo.
- Remove the extra a's and see if it's easier for the lyric to roll off of your tongue.

Whether you are working on lyrical or melodic bars, diction and articulation will set you apart from the crowd, as it will not only help your flow, but it will help you connect with your audience. It takes practice, but it does get easier, and you *will* improve. Everyone is different, and speed isn't necessarily the goal. You know what is important? Comprehensibility. Like that train from your childhood books, start slow, slowly increase your speed, stay on track, and nothing will be able to stop you.

Notes

1. Teenstar. (2020, November 6). Diction in Singing | What Is Diction in Music. https://teenstarcompetition.co.uk/advice/diction-in-singing-music
2. Teenstar. (2020, November 6). Diction in Singing | What Is Diction in Music. https://teenstarcompetition.co.uk/advice/diction-in-singing-music
3. *Merriam-Webster Online.* (n.d.). Diction. https://www.merriam-webster.com/dictionary/diction
4. Successful Singing. (n.d.). Diction for Singers. https://successfulsinging.com/diction-for-singers/
5. Schmidt-Jones, Catherine. (2005). *Understanding Basic Music Theory.* Suwanee, GA: 12th Media Services.
6. *Encyclopedia Britannica Online.* (n.d.). Accent. https://www.britannica.com/art/accent-rhythm
7. Beckman Oral Motor. (n.d.). Normal Lip Patterns. https://www.beckmanoralmotor.com/impairments/lip-patterns.php
8. Miller, Richard. (2015). *On the Art of Singing.* Cambridge: Oxford Academic.

9. Rodman, Judy. "All Things Vocal Blog & Podcast by Judy Rodman: Tongue Tips for Singing and Speaking—Updated 2020." All Things Vocal Blog & Podcast by Judy Rodman: Tongue Tips for Singing and Speaking—Updated 2020. Accessed August 30, 2023. https://blog.judyrodman.com/2011/05/tongue-tips-for-singing-and-speaking.html.

10. Rodman, Judy. (2020, April 7). Tongue Tips for Singing and Speaking. *All Things Vocal* (blog). https://blog.judyrodman.com/2011/05/tongue-tips-for-singing-and-speaking.html#:~:text=To%20articulate%20words%20or%20lyrics,not%20bunching%20or%20bulking%20up

11. "Jaw Problems: Exercise and Relaxation." MyHealth.Alberta.ca Government of Alberta Personal Health Portal. Accessed August 30, 2023. https://myhealth.alberta.ca/Health/Pages/conditions.aspx?hwid=hw209204.

12. MyHealth.Alberta.ca. (2022, March 9). Jaw Problems: Exercise and Relaxation. https://myhealth.alberta.ca/Health/Pages/conditions.aspx?hwid=hw209204

13. *Urban Dictionary*. (n.d.). Beach. https://www.urbandictionary.com/define.php?term=beach

14. Dahl, Natalie J. (n.d.). Voiceless vs Voiced Sounds. https://www.handyhandouts.com/viewHandout.aspx?hh_number=460

Fourteen

"Express Yourself" (Ice Cube)
The Art and Authenticity of Storytelling

First things first, let's begin with a huge shout out to someone truly remarkable . . . you! If you've reached this part of the book, you've worked on your rap technique in so many different ways. You've taken the time to become familiar and/or deepen your knowledge of hip-hop history, study different genres of rap, and listen to some of the iconic music that has influenced the rap of today. From a technical standpoint, your breathing and your posture are improving each day; you're thinking about the ways diction, articulation, pitch, and tone add to your toolbox; and you're able to use those tools in both your practice and performance. Now, my friend, it's time to think about your delivery. Many rappers make the mistake of skipping right to this point. If this is you, and you opened the book straight to this chapter, it's cool, but you have been caught with your hand inside the metaphorical cookie jar. Feeling a little guilty? Good—now I'm going to encourage you to go back and read the chapters leading up to this point. They are there to help you lay a strong foundation before you jump to this section. I promise it'll be worth it. For those of you that read this in order and have been practicing some technique, it's time to take the plunge into delivery.

Delivery

You've worked so hard on your rap technique, and now people need to hear your stories. Like all music, rap is intended to stir up a variety of feelings in the listener. All of the things you've been practicing are necessary because as a rapper, you want to connect with your audience. To be clear, both your flow and your delivery are important to conveying your message in a clear and meaningful way. Your flow will be the vessel in which you are able to say these (crucially important) lyrics in a way that will make your audience pay attention and actually listen. The flow sets the vibe for your song, which will drastically impact how the listener receives the lyrics. While we build our unique flow, we cannot forget that storytelling is really, *really* (and I mean *really*) important as well, okay?

"The slang term 'Delivery' is a noun which is used by rappers in rap/hip-hop music to represent how they say, pronounce or articulate their words and lyrics."[1] The *Cambridge Dictionary* defines storytelling as "the activity of writing, telling, or reading stories."[2] Let's combine the two meanings to define "delivery" as *how you utilize the tools in your technique toolbox to communicate the meaning of your lyrics*. In other words, your goal is to express the lyrics in such a way that the listener understands the meaning, story, context, and how you feel about it, while also being moved, changed, or affected in some way.

Purpose—The What

What are you talking about in your song? Knowing that will point you in a direction that will help guide mood, vibe, tone, dynamics, and other elements that affect delivery. Popular subjects include[3]:

- School
- Love
- Life
- Depression
- Fake friends
- Food
- Racism
- Money

This list is just the tip of the iceberg. You can rap about absolutely anything (coffee creamer, couch cushions, etc.), but the bottom line is that if you connect to it, you can rap about it. When I'm working with my students on songs, they often are performing a role in a show and the songs they're singing/rapping are directly connected to a character. That character has an identity, and a want, intent, or a reason for saying whatever it is they are saying in their lyrics. The same is true for you in your raps, even when they're not a part of a show.

Subject Matter

Not only is it crucial that you are specific and understand every nuance of your song's meaning, but it's also helpful to categorize your rap. If you know what category of rap your song lives in, you can listen to other songs that live within that category for guidance. That isn't to say copy these artists (please do *not* copy these artists), but using them as reference points can be extremely useful. There are several broader categories of rap content.

> "When I'm trying to make a song, like I need something that inspires me to write. Something that makes me want to even you know, add something, something that moves me."
>
> —Joseph Chilliams

Personal Experience Rap

This is rap that is based on your authentic, personal experiences (things that have happened to you, that you've done or witnessed, or situations that you yourself have encountered). If it's happening to you, it's probably happening to others, and therefore it will be compelling. In the event that it is not happening to others (perhaps you have seen an alien life form and you are the only person that has seen these aliens), that personal experience will still be fascinating to your listeners because you are sharing a part of yourself, and vulnerability encourages empathy. The bulk of rap falls into this category.

Polarizing Rap

Polarizing rap is rap that is shocking and/or is about shocking subject matter such as violence, drugs, or sex. It enrages some listeners and hooks other listeners from the jump. Often this disquieting subject matter is authentic to the experience of the artist and/or is a vehicle for spotlighting the difficulties that plague a culture's experience. "So, hip hop's extensive repertoire of stories about violence, guns, drugs, crime, and prison is compounded by everyday life for those who have little or no option but to reside in the poorest and most troubled neighborhoods and communities. Such stories become more powerful in this context, providing an image of everyday realities that can overemphasize the worst of what young people in these places face."[4]

When reading about polarizing, or shocking, rap, many people will immediately think of gangsta rap or drill. You will find countless articles and conversations outlining the pros and cons of hip-hop's influence on society. This in itself proves the point, yes? If everyone is talking about it . . . it means everyone is talking about it.

Conscious Rap

This rap category usually has a political view and calls for awareness, activism, or unity. It originated with the OG Afrika Bambaataa and was then followed by the Native Tongues, Common, and Kendrick Lamar. This rap also talks about real-life issues, but it also typically includes a call to action/call for change.

Humorous Rap

This one is pretty self-explanatory, but this would be subject matter that has a primary goal of being funny. It can also cross-categorize and be about real life or be shocking. The difference here would be that humor is the primary mode of connecting with the listener and/or grabbing their attention.

Party Rap

Party rap could be considered a genre itself, but it is best used as a subject category because multiple genres (bling era, crunk, etc.) primarily use subject matter about partying in "da club." Deee-Lite's "Groove is in the Heart"; Nelly's "Hot in Here"; Usher, Lil Jon, and Ludacris' "Yeah"; Flo Rida's "Good Feeling"; or Don Toliver's "After Party" could all be considered party "let's a have a good time" rap.

Storytelling and/or Fantasy Rap

Storytelling and/or fantasy-based rap is rare, but not irrelevant. If you are rapping in a performance art piece or a musical, this is the category you would be working under. Storytelling rap has a clear narrative with a beginning, middle, and end. Famous story-based raps include Slick Rick's "Children's Story," "Kick, Push" by Lupe Fiasco, "You Got Me" by The Roots and Erikah Badu, The Beastie Boys' "Paul Revere," and Jay-Z's "Friend or Foe."

Purpose—The Why

You've figured out what you are rapping about, so the first step to making decisions about your delivery is to figure out your purpose. Why does your audience need to hear this? Why are you talking about your subject matter? What do you want them to know? Why? *Why? Why?!* The answers to this question should always be specific and personal to you as the artist. However, here are some guideposts for you, as well as a few examples of different purposes for rap.

Culture and History

Rap helps the listener learn about, experience, or understand your culture and personal history. Rap has become a supersized megaphone and an extremely successful platform to inform the world of cultural experience. A prime example being socio-economic and race-based marginalization. "So, hip hop's extensive repertoire of stories about violence, guns, drugs, crime, and prison is compounded by everyday life for those who have little or no option but to reside in the poorest and most troubled neighborhoods and communities. Such stories become more powerful in this context, providing an image of everyday realities."[5] Another strong example of this is the mental health crisis in America (Joyner Lucas's powerful song "I'm Sorry").

Escapism

Music is often used to tune out the troubles or problems we're facing in our everyday lives. Rap is very much included under the umbrella of escapism. Party rap is one of the largest grossing genres of rap music. Whether it is the beats that convey a "pick me up vibe" or the storytelling of a happy evening out, party rap can create endorphins that help both the listener, and potentially the artist as well, in "escaping" life's issues, no matter how big or small. In an interview, C.A.M. discusses this concept saying, "I started writing songs with a good feel to them. I like songs like that. I like songs that can take you from here to there. So, I made music just like that."[6] Multiple studies have shown that music can influence the creation and release of dopamine in the brain. "The foundation of hip-hop is grounded in African drums, jazz, blues, R&B, reggae, funk, and soul, and therefore it embodies the pain, struggle, innovation, and triumphs that the listener is having a visceral reaction to."[7] So the next time you are stressed, turn up the volume and see what happens.

> **"Whenever I over exaggerate, it's kind of me just like manifesting a future lifestyle, or what I've seen on a TV screen. I wouldn't consider it being fabricating, but maybe like an over exaggeration or something."**
>
> —Kinga World

Healing

If this were a game of poker, healing would say to escapism "I'll see your mood boost and raise you with therapeutic effect." Through showing vulnerability, hip-hop is decimating the one-dimensional image of the "badman myth form" that politicians Dan Quayle (the US vice president in 1992), Tipper Gore, and C. Delores Tucker would want you to see:

> Dr. Dre dedicated "The Message" to his brother, Tyree Du Sean Crayon, who was killed in a street fight. One of the most iconic rap songs, "They Reminisce Over You (T.R.O.Y.)" by Pete Rock and CL Smooth was inspired by the death of their close friend, Troy Dixon. In "Life Goes On," Tupac eulogizes numerous friends who died or went to jail saying, "But now that you're gone, I'm in the zone / Thinking I don't wanna die all alone, but now you gone."[8]

This vulnerability creates community and serves as a buoy and aural support system for listeners.

Rap can also serve as a salve for isolation and loneliness. Emo rap is an entire genre dedicated to this purpose. But subgenres aside,

> after a painful social experience people usually seek an empathic friend to share their negative feelings and receive comfort. At the same time, a preference for mood-congruent, sad music has been observed in this kind of socially distressing situations. Due to these findings, it stands to reason that affect-congruent musical pieces may act as a surrogate for an empathic friend after experiencing a social loss.[9]

Rappers shouldn't necessarily feel saddled with the burden of being role models, although this is often expected of them. There is a strong connection between rappers and their listeners, and this makes it easy for them to have a positive impact on the world around them.

> "I really don't talk about a lot of personal things. But if I make it into a song, that's where I can best, you know, vent, or describe what I'm feeling, or just thoughts that's been on my mind in that time."
>
> —Lavon Bibb

The Need for Authenticity

If you take nothing else away from this book, I hope you fully understand the necessity of authenticity in rap. You should only rap about things you can relate to and things you care about. If you don't relate to the lyrics through lived experience in a personal way, you are doing a disservice to the poetry. That doesn't mean it needs to be a firsthand lived experience. As seen in our earlier discussion, there are many purposes that call for fictitious rap, but that doesn't equate with authenticity or lack thereof. "Put simply, authenticity means you're true to your own personality, values, and spirit, regardless of the pressure that you're under to act otherwise. You're honest with yourself and with others, and you take responsibility for your mistakes. Your values, ideals, and actions align."[10] Finding yourself in your performance paves the way for an ease of expression and emotion because it will naturally come from within. If your delivery is inauthentic, you run the risk of your emotion being false. This will make it hard for you to truly and organically *care* about your story. If you don't care, how can you move others in the way your art intended?

> "I think sometimes we reach different sounds, stuff that's really not as authentic as other sounds are. Because, you know, I think the stuff that's really the most what you are, is going to come very easily—it's going to come very naturally, very fluidly."
>
> —redveil

Story Deconstruction

"Stories give one the choice to work in a laboratory of imagination to sort out values and issues relating to trust, integrity, self-respect, and so forth in a place where no physical danger is involved."[11] There are many wonderful sources for writing rap lyrics; however, this book is not one of them. That subject needs a book's complete dedication, and to insert a snippet of advice in passing would be disrespectful to the artform of lyric writing. So that, my friend, will mean another trip to the library for a book on how to write lyrics. Once you have grabbed a book (or five) on the subject, there will be a few overlapping thoughts and ideas. This section will be helpful to you to reflect upon after you've studied lyric writing.

When approaching delivery, you should ask yourself the following questions:

- To whom am I speaking/Who am I talking to?
- What am I talking about?
- Where am I during this conversation?
- What has happened that leads me to say what I'm saying?
- What happened just before I started talking? (in acting, this is often referred to as "the moment before")
- What do I want?
- How am I going to go about getting what I want?

By answering these questions, you'll hopefully find authentic entries into choices about dynamics, tempo, word stress, and other tools (which we'll dig into in a minute).

Helpful Tip

Conflict is a playwright's best friend and should be the actor's as well. Too often, unfortunately, particularly in the United States, young performers think that emotion is where their acting energy should go, and that the storytelling aspect of a script is the province of the playwright only. They often believe that when they are in a play, a film, or even a commercial, the story will simply take care of itself.[12]

> **"Many people have stated that my target or analysis comes off as if I'm spitting a verse to them and I really liked that. This art helps me organize and synthesize my thoughts, process, my experience, and summarize it."**
>
> **—Koifish**

If your lyrics are a mini play, keep the problem at the forefront of your mind. What is the problem? How are you trying to work that out in your head to solve it, to change it, or whatever you are doing? Knowing this storytelling tactic will be invaluable, I promise.

After identifying the problem, it is equally important to become familiar with the obstacle. If there wasn't something in your way, there wouldn't be an issue to be talking about in the first place, right? Something is causing the problem and is simultaneously blocking the path to a solution:

> What is keeping my protagonist from achieving his or her desire? Forces within? Doubt? Fear? Confusion? Personal conflicts with friends, family, lovers? Social conflicts arising in the various institutions in society? Physical conflicts? The forces of Mother Nature? Lethal diseases in the air? Not enough time to get things done? The damned automobile that won't start? Antagonists come from people, society, time, space, and every object in it, or any combination of these forces at once.[13]

Storytelling Toolbox

By this point, you've done quite a bit of analysis to get to the heart of understanding the meaning of your lyrics, your point of view, and your goals. The next step is to practice your delivery. Here are some simple but important tools that will help you successfully convey your thoughts and emotions to your listeners, and then hopefully, *they'll* think and feel things as well.

Remember That You Have a Microphone

It's only natural that you will feel a deep emotional connection to what you are saying—that's the goal! But often when that deep emotional connection meets adrenaline, the result is something called vocal pushing. Vocal pushing is talking too loudly and pushing too much air through the vocal tract/vocal cords. Doing this will have the opposite of the desired effect. Instead of having more power, you'll sound strained and often won't be any louder. Now is the perfect time to remember that you have a microphone. The mic is your best friend (assuming you use it correctly, which is why you'll read chapter 16). The mic will give you the amplification you want, so that you don't need to push. That will allow you to have the vocal nuances that are coming up next on this list.

Trust a conversational volume. Peek at chapter 11 (pitch and tone) for a more in-depth discussion about conversational volume.

Here is an exercise to use while practicing your delivery:

- Get an object like a water bottle or a pen—anything that you can see and easily hold. Hold it out in front directly in front of you with a straight arm. Imagine that object is a person, and you are having a conversation with that person in your living room. How loudly would you speak to a person right in front of you? Try delivering your lyrics to this object, and notice the comfortable volume utilized.
- Sometimes your lyrics will stir up authentic fury inside of you, but I still want you to try to use this conversational volume, remembering that *you have a mic*. For this, imagine that you are in an argument or debate with someone, and they are being quite stubborn (we all have that one friend or family member that never lets up). However, the location of your argument is the library. You can't scream in a library, right? How can you convey your emotion without yelling? Practice

your delivery in this imagined scenario and see what happens. Hopefully, the results will include maintaining a relaxed throat and larynx, and with that, the ability to keep your tone quality in check.

Remember to Be Aware of Resonance

> Resonance is key to avoiding vocal fold fatigue. The air inside the vocal tract does not get tired, vocal fold tissue does. Maximizing resonance to create volume is key to not adding excess collision or pressure to the vocal folds. The majority of acoustic information from the vocal tract feeds back to the vocal folds.[14]

What exactly is resonance? Let's picture a guitar. It has a hollow body and strings on the outside that are attached at one end to a long neck. The strings then travel down to the body of the guitar, passing over a hole located in the body of the guitar. Looking inside this hole lets you see the hollow inside of the guitar. If you pluck a string on this guitar, the string will vibrate (move quickly in tiny movements back and forth). The vibrations create sound waves, and those waves bounce around against the hollow inside of the guitar, and that bouncing around amplifies the sound (makes it louder). That amplification is what we are referring to when we discuss resonance.

Resonance is going to be your friend and will help with both volume as well as tone quality. This alone should help you resist the urge to vocally push. "In speech and singing, vocal tract resonances usually determine the spectral envelope and usually have a smaller influence on the operating frequency. The resonances are important not only for the phonemic information they produce, but also because of their contribution to voice timbre, loudness, and efficiency."[15]

Remember to Utilize Sentence Structural Patterns

First and foremost, organize your speech patterns rhythmically. I think that's been well covered by now, but once you have your rhythms and lyrics nailed down, then what? This is where diction and choices of word stress make things really interesting. Word stress means just what it sounds like—which words are you going to give extra energy/punch/zest? Beyond that, you'll make decisions about which syllables to stress within those words, and you'll decide which consonant within that syllable should get the most oomph. There are several ways to approach this:

- Monologue driven (sounding like a conversation)
- Rhyme driven (you'll see this a lot in Old School rap, which is in duple meter, and thus stressing the simple rhymes)
- Beat driven (choosing to stress certain beats and prioritize that over what word might be said at any given time)
- Bookending (choosing to stress the first and last word of a phrase or cadence)

STOP! Let's do a quick word stress exercise here:

1. Take the following sentence and memorize it: "I thought she told you to get out."
2. Next say the sentence stressing a different word each time.
3. Individual words to stress each time you say the sentence:
   a. "I"
   b. "Thought"
   c. "She"
   d. "Told"
   e. "You"
   f. "To"
   g. "Get"
   h. "Out"

How did the meaning of the sentence change when you stressed each word? How did your inflection change? Did your emotions change? Volume? Reflect on how much word stress impacts your delivery.

Try Thinking About Your Lyrics as a Monologue

In theatre, actors often monologue, which is "an extended speech by one person." In a way, your lyrics are a monologue. Therefore, some of the practice techniques overlap:

- Practice your lyrics out loud.
    - How they sound in your head will be different from how they'll sound out in the room. In order to make choices, you'll need to say your lyrics out loud.
- Practice at performance volume.
    - It's easy to mumble, or practice lyrics in a "to yourself" volume, but you won't be able to properly work on tone, resonance, or diction unless you practice at performance volume.
        - Memorize your lyrics in sections.
    - Making the assumption that you know your lyrics because you wrote them or because it's a song you love will get you into trouble when you have adrenaline and nerves swirling in front of an audience. Just like multiplication tables, you *have* to drill them. Memorize one verse at a time or memorize your chorus first, whatever system works for you. Be sure to test yourself in order to make sure you are memorized.
- Be confident and have fun.
    - Remember, you have something special to say and to share. Have faith in yourself. You've put in the work, and you should trust in that. Be your biggest fan. That will give you energy, which will inspire your audience to feel energized by you.

If it's important to you, it *is* important. If it's worth saying, say it like you mean it. Above all else, choose material that you *love*. If you love it, it will show and it will be more meaningful to your audience. "The main drivers of authenticity . . . are the values people place on themselves, which may be motivated by a given social construction, and the resulting feeling of authenticity results from a determination of whether these values hold true."[16] This is the fun part—you get to show your audience who you are and what you care about. Trust that it is awesome, because, most likely, it really is.

> "I can't even deliver it as masterfully if I myself don't believe it. And I think you can hear a lot of rappers you know, when they don't believe what they're saying. It shows in their deliveries. So I'd say as far as bringing that authenticity to the table, just make sure you're drawing from your life and you know, even the lives of people around you."
>
> —Noah

Notes

1. DailyRapFacts. (2020). What Does "Delivery" Mean? Retrieved February 23, 2023, from https://dailyrapfacts.com/17415/what-does-delivery-mean/

2. *Cambridge Dictionary*. (n.d.). Storytelling. Retrieved February 23, 2023, from https://dictionary.cambridge.org/us/dictionary/english/storytelling

3. Edwards, Edison. (n.d.). 9 Most Searched Topics to Rap About. *Rhyme Makers*. Retrieved February 23, 2023, from https://rhymemakers.com/topics-to-rap-about/

4. Rose, Tricia. (2008). *The Hip Hop Wars: What We Talk About When We Talk About Hip Hop-And Why It Matters*. New York: Basic Civitas Books, 53.

5. Rose, Tricia. (2008). *The Hip Hop Wars: What We Talk About When We Talk About Hip Hop-And Why It Matters*. New York: Basic Civitas Books, 53.

6. Petronio, Kristen. (2022, May 17). The Escapism of Music in Its the Words We Give. *Savage Content*. Retrieved February 23, 2023, from https://www.savagecontent.com/post/the-escapism-of-music-in-it-s-in-the-words-we-give

7. Chesman, Donna-Claire. (2017, October 16). Hip Hop as Therapy: The Healing Qualities of Rap. *Complex*. Retrieved February 23, 2023, from https://www.complex.com/pigeons-and-planes/2017/10/hip-hop-therapy-healing-qualities-rap

8. Madu, Zito. (2021). The Great Escape: For Those Trapped in the Violence of Poverty, Rap Tells Heroic Stories of Breaking Free. *Plough Quarterly*, 27. https://www.plough.com/en/topics/justice/social-justice/racial-justice/the-great-escape

9. Schäfer, Katharina, Suvi Saarikallio, and Tuomas Eerola. (2020, June 25). Music May Reduce Loneliness and Act as Social Surrogate for a Friend: Evidence from an Experimental Listening Study. *Music & Science*. Retrieved February 23, 2023, from https://journals.sagepub.com/doi/full/10.1177/2059204320935709/

10. MindTools. (n.d.). Authenticity: How to Be True to Yourself. Retrieved February 23, 2023, from https://www.mindtools.com/pages/article/authenticity.htm/

11. Spaulding, Amy E. (2011). *The Art of Storytelling: Telling Truths Through Telling Stories*. Lanham, MD: Scarecrow Press, 136.

12. Miller, Bruce J. (2000). *The Actor as Storyteller*. Mountainview, CA: Mayfield Pub.

13. Fryer, Bronwyn. (2003). Storytelling That Moves People. *The Harvard Business Review*. Retrieved February 23, 2023, from https://hbr.org/2003/06/storytelling-that-moves-people/

14. Voice Science Works. (n.d.). Resonance. Retrieved February 23, 2023, from https://www.voicescienceworks.org/resonance.html/

15. Wolfe, Joe, Maëva Garnier, and John Smith. (2008). Vocal Tract Resonances in Speech, Singing, and Playing Musical Instruments. *HSFP Journal*, 3 (1): 6–23.

16. Allam, Amin. (2021). Real Rap, Does Authenticity Even Matter in Hip Hop? Bachelor's thesis, Arcadia University. https://scholarworks.arcadia.edu/cgi/viewcontent.cgi?article=1401&context=showcas/

Fifteen

"Protect Ya Neck" (Wu-Tang Clan)
Vocal Health

Picture this: You are added to the bill for the Lil Tour, featuring Lil Baby, Lil Durk, Lil Wayne, Lil Tecca, Lil' Kim, Lil B, Lil Yachty, and Lil Uzi Vert. (I really hope your rap name is Lil something, or this daydream isn't going to make a lot of sense.) On the first day of your contract, you wake up with a horrible sore throat. Talking is difficult. What do you do? Honestly, you probably panic. However, freaking out and canceling your biggest gig yet can potentially be avoided if you prioritize your vocal health, both in this daydream and in your real life.

Vocal health (also referred to as vocal hygiene) is "a daily regimen of good habits to maintain the health of your vocal folds. These include eliminating inappropriate vocal habits and situations that place unnecessary wear and tear on the voice and common-sense behaviors which contribute to efficient voice production and overall vocal health."[1] Keeping your voice healthy involves taking care of your voice and your body. This takes diligence and consistency, which can be a drag at times, but it's absolutely worth it. Think of it this way: if you owned Jimi Hendrix's guitar (a 1968 Fender Stratocaster valued at two million dollars), would you use it as a table for your hot coffee or leave it out in the rain all night? My guess is no for both—you'd probably store it in a protective case or mount it safely on a wall.

Why Is This Important?

You might be saying "okay, yeah, but I talk all day, and I don't worry about this, so why do I have to worry about it for performing rap?" The answer to that lies in the previous fourteen chapters. You as a rap artist know that rapping, especially when dealing with crowds and lots of adrenaline pumping through your veins, is an artform that takes practice and a rock-solid technical foundation. While rapping does utilize the speaking voice, the pitfalls of overuse, wear and tear, and improper use are still quite possible. Yes, you did just read an entire book to build technique. Solid technique is paramount to maintain vocal health. But even with great technique, vocal injuries can still occur. Put simply, you want to prevent vocal misuse because it can lead to serious vocal injuries. In a 2019 Instagram post, rapper JID announced that he needed to postpone a rap battle with Denzel Curry due to vocal health issues: "On da big God ever since I got off tour I been in pain and nervous af about my voice." JID continues in his Instagram caption: "I toured 10 months of the 12 last year and I've essentially been touring every year since 2014 and it took a toll, positively and negatively but all in all I should be fine, I'm on vocal rest for 2 weeks (vow of silence) with meds and steroids and shit. Also have to reschedule the battle vs. Denzel that was this weekend but I promise we will make it up to u guys very soon."[2]

It's not just JID. Rapper Machine Gun Kelly was sidelined early on in his career. "A polyp developed on his vocal cord which kept him offstage and out of the studio for six months." Without health insurance for surgery, MGK worked off the polyp by himself with tireless vocal exercises. "Every night I'd wake up at 4 o'clock in the morning wanting to blow my brains out," says MGK, "That was one of the most depressing periods of my life."[3]

Vocal injuries are scary, but they *are* fixable (just ask MGK, who worked his butt off, got rid of that polyp, and signed with Diddy a year later). These stories are not included to scare you into reading on. To be clear, vocal injuries do not mean that a rapper doesn't have good technique because, just as with life, sometimes things happen. But, as a performer, you must consider yourself an athlete and treat yourself like one, taking care of yourself every single day. How to do that for your voice? Just like posture, pitch, and rhythm, practicing vocal health and maintenance is a skill that can be learned.

What Is the Voice?

In earlier chapters, you spent a lot of time hanging out with the lungs (breathing); lips, teeth, jaw, and tongue (diction); and the spine, head, and neck (posture). This chapter is about your vocal cords, which is, specifically a "muscular body with a mucosal cover. When we force air through these structures, they vibrate, producing sound. The vocal folds are located inside the larynx, an organ inside the trachea ('windpipe')."[4] The vibration caused by the opening and closing of the vocal cords aid in the production of sound. When the vocal cords aren't vibrating, they are open, allowing us to breathe.

When it's time to speak, however, the brain orchestrates a series of events. The vocal folds open and close while air from the lungs blows past, making them vibrate. The vibrations produce sound waves that travel through the throat, nose, and mouth, which act as resonating cavities to modulate the sound. The quality of your voice—its pitch, volume, and tone—is determined by the size and shape of the vocal folds and the resonating cavities.[5]

Because everyone's shape and size of their vocal tract, vocal cords, and cavities that make up the sinuses and mouth are unique in and unto themselves, everyone also sounds unique. (This is a good reminder that your natural vocal tone is usually your best bet at your default rap sound because no one is going to sound like you . . . literally, no one).

How to Keep Your Voice Healthy

The following is a list of the top eight must do's to keep your voice and body healthy:

1. **Hydration:**
   You *must* drink water. A lot of my students have taken to carrying around enormous water bottles so they can make sure they have

enough water every day. (I mean . . . unbelievably enormous. I'm pro water, but they do look really heavy.) If you want to simultaneously get your water intake and get a bit of an upper body workout, these are a great solution. You can also bring a refillable water bottle around in your bag and fill it up constantly. But you can get your water intake however you wish. Just get enough. What is enough? At *minimum* you need eight glasses of water per day. That is sixty-four ounces of water.

Does all liquid count as water? No. This cannot be substituted with soda, iced tea, or coffee, as those dehydrate (i.e., dry you out). This means that you have to drink extra water to make up for the fact that you needed that caffeine. Sorry not sorry. You should also use a humidifier in your room if you live in a drier climate (or if it's winter, etc.). Why is hydration important? The vocal cords have this thin layer of lubricating mucus on them, and the water keeps this whole system functioning.

2. **Rest:**

When referring to rest and the voice, people could be discussing three different approaches:

- **Sleep:** Remember, we determined that you as a singer are an athlete. Just like athletes, you need to treat your body with the care it requires. To do this, you should try to get at least seven to nine hours of sleep per night. Yes, that is a lot, especially with all of the addictive shows streaming on Netflix. But resist the urge to let that next episode auto start and go to bed.
- Simply put, sleep affects everything. Getting a good night's sleep:
    - Assists in memory formation and general cognitive functioning
    - Supports your immune system
    - Aids in muscle recovery (including the muscles involving vocal production). "Sleep is the body's chance to rebuild cells and organs, replace worn-out tissues, and restore both mental

and metabolic equilibrium. Your voice benefits from all of this."[6]
- Lowers stress which can cause tension

If you are having trouble getting this sleep, you can try things like meditation, figuring out the ideal room temperature for your best night's sleep, and stopping any screens (yup, no late-night Snapchat for you) for an hour before bed.

When talking about rest, we can also mean vocal rest. This can mean total silence for several days or more, but it can also mean pacing yourself throughout a day and giving your voice breaks. If you are a social butterfly, this will be a challenge for you. If you have a demanding show schedule, look at your day ahead and write in several times at regular intervals where you can be silent for thirty to sixty minutes. During this time, you might not be sleeping, but you are resting the vocal apparatus.

3. **Diet:**

You are what you eat, right? Giving your body the fuel it needs also helps your system run smoothly, which helps in a similar capacity to sleep. Some top tips in regard to eating:
- Remember to avoid caffeine.
- Some people are also sensitive to dairy products, and if so, it can cause excess mucus to build up in the back of your throat, making things feel phlegmy and gunky.
- You will find that certain foods affect you and certain foods do not. Pay attention and see if you notice patterns—it doesn't mean you have to steer clear of those kinds of foods at all times, but you'll know to avoid it when you have a gig or recording session looming.

4. **Exercise:**

Exercise improves your muscle tone and cardiovascular system. This helps the machine you call your body run efficiently. It also helps you get a better night's sleep. When I'm thinking of exercise for singing, I'm first and foremost thinking of cardio, but having a balanced workout regimen that includes resistance training, weight training, and—my favorite (because I'm a ridiculous multitasker)—compound exercises, which work multiple muscle groups at the same time and often also raise your heart rate. But honestly, any movement you choose to do and like doing is great. Oh, oh oh oh—and you should move while rapping sometimes too—sometimes incorporating some exercises into your warmups (i.e., squats, planks, and warrior pose in yoga) will improve support. Walking while rapping can release tension, which can help articulation and decrease overall effort.

5. **Avoidance:**
   There are certain known irritants. It's best to limit the following:
   - Smoking (good thing edibles have become legal in most states)
   - Over-the-counter medications that contain decongestants, as the primary function of these medications are to dry you out. (Not gonna lie: Sudafed can potentially take you from a snotty mess to almost normal, until it wears off, of course). It will also make you as dry as the Sahara Desert. I mean, get ready to drink three of those enormous water bottles I mentioned earlier just to compensate. Sudafed is one of the more extreme over-the-counter decongestants regarding drying, but even your innocent-seeming Dayquil is going to dry you out.

6. **Warming Up and Cooling Down:**
   Be sure to do some strategic warmups before practicing or performing. When done, it's important to also cool down the voice.
   - **Warmups** take the voice from its normal "chill" state to one that is ready for the challenges of rapping.
   - **Cool downs**, on the other hand, take the voice in the opposite direction, helping the voice return to its chill, relaxed state.
   - Voice expert Kari Ragan states that, "implications about a vocal cooldown regime are that it can lead to a faster recovery time (especially if a singer is in the middle of a heavy voice load), the

speaking voice more quickly returns to baseline, and there is a significant improved overall sense of vocal well-being."[7]

7. **Non-Steroidal Anti-Inflammatory Drugs:**
Though the causes may vary, vocal swelling is often a symptom of a serious vocal issue. When we have a swollen ankle, the doctor usually prescribes anti-inflammatories (these are also referred to as non-steroidal anti-inflammatory drugs [NSAIDs] such as aspirin [i.e., Bayer or Ecotrin], ibuprofen [i.e., Advil or Motrin], or naproxen [i.e., Aleve or Anaprox]). If you read the fine print on the side of the bottle, one of the side effects is an increased risk for bleeding. That is because NSAIDs have blood-thinning properties. There are blood vessels in the vocal cords, and taking NSAIDs while singing can increase your risk of one bursting one of those blood vessels.

8. **Shouting and Screaming:**
You are smart. Therefore, you probably know that screaming and talking over loud noise can cause vocal strain. Try to protect yourself. Voice professional and otolaryngologist Dr. Robert Sataloff says, "The 'Lombard Effect' is the tendency to speak more loudly in the presence of background noise. At parties, we shout. Under these circumstances, we are rarely aware of good abdominal support and voice conservation techniques. Such abuse can wreak havoc on a voice, particularly when it is already tired after an evening of singing performance."[8]

Honorable mention: If you are performing after a flight (i.e., you're heading to the Lil Tour), you should try to wait several hours before performing and spend that time moving around and rehydrating your body, since planes are notorious for drying us out.

Vocal Dysfunction

Hopefully, you have a fifty-year span as a happy and healthy rapper. However, sometimes things aren't hunky dory in voice land. How do you know if there is a problem that you need to get checked out? What do you do if there is a problem? I'm going to say this many times, so it sinks in: please don't panic. Most issues can be fixed. In the following, you can learn about signs to look out for in order to spot potential trouble, as well as about some of the common issues singers and rappers encounter.

Signs of Vocal Fatigue or Strain

It's best to catch these issues early. Now please read this next statement repeatedly: *do not panic!* You are paying attention so you can prevent vocal damage, remember? However, if you do find yourself in trouble, you should make an appointment with an otolaryngologist (that is an ear, nose, and throat doctor that specializes in the voice). Make the appointment if you have any of the following symptoms persist after two weeks:

- Hoarseness or raspiness
- Loss of part of your range
- Feeling a need to constantly clear your throat or cough (if you don't have a cold)
- Feeling that it's generally harder to talk
- A sore throat of any kind
- Tightness in the muscles surrounding the throat
- Weakness in tone quality that wasn't previously present

Common Causes for Vocal Fatigue/Strain

Again, do not panic. Do not panic. *Do not panic!* There are many common sources of vocal fatigue that are easily corrected. These can include:

- **Allergies:** seasonal or environmental allergies can do a number on your voice because of the mucus build up and the increased coughing.
- **GERD or acid reflux:** if you've ever had heartburn, you've dealt with stomach acid. Acid reflux means that stomach acid has backed up

into your esophagus and chronic occurrences of this can cause vocal issues. Strategies to combat this include:
    - Change in diet to reduce/eliminate foods with high acidity (including but not limited to coffee, soda, garlic, citrus fruits, tomatoes, and chocolate)
    - Have your last meal at least three hours before you plan on going to sleep
    - Lying/sleeping on an incline
    - Medications
- You have a **virus** (i.e., you are sick/have a cold): sometimes your throat hurts as part of illness. A scratchy or sore throat is often the first sign of that dreaded cold. Other symptoms usually follow congestion, headache, cough, and/or fever, along with a myriad of other symptoms. While this can last for ten or more days, sore throats for this reason generally don't indicate a vocal issue.
- **Vocal damage:** vocal issues are sometimes more severe in nature than the aforementioned issues. They can include:
    - **Vocal hemorrhage:** remember reading about that blood vessel bursting earlier in this chapter? This is the official name for that phenomenon.
    - **Vocal fold/cord lesions (polyps, cysts, or nodules):** vocal folds can develop different kinds of lesions depending on the circumstances. All three of these interfere with the vocal folds' ability to function properly and can result in hoarseness, breathiness, fatigue, or pain.

Resources

If you are swallowing, humming, or talking right now to see if you feel anything slightly funky, you're in the majority. This topic often brings our anxieties to the surface. After all, our voices are the way we share our art with the world. But I will say it again, *please* do not panic under any circumstances. If you have taken preventative measures, and you have tried vocal rest, yet you still feel vocal strain for a sustained period of time without improvement, remember that there are tools for you. Remember too that you are building a solid technique. You will practice the prevention strategies laid out in this chapter. There are medications you can take and environmental changes you can make if needed. Finally, there are medical professionals to help you if you need it, like otolaryngologists or laryngologists, speech language pathologists, and coaches. Knowledge is power, and you've now added countless tools to your arsenal to keep yourself healthy.

Notes

1. University of North Carolina. (n.d.). Taking Care of Your Voice. https://www.med.unc.edu/ent/uncvoicecenter/wp-content/uploads/sites/516/2017/11/vocal-hygiene.pdf

2. J.I.D [@jidsv]. (2020, January 15). "On da big God . . ." *Instagram*. https://www.instagram.com/p/B7W_kb9FBIT/?igshid=NTc4MTIwNjQ2YQ==

3. First Avenue. (2015). Machine Gun Kelly. https://first-avenue.com/performer/machine-gun-kelly/#:~:text=A%20polyp%20developed%20on%20his,brains%20out%2C%22%20says%20MGK

4. University of St Augustine for Health Sciences. (2019, August 2). 10 Do's and Don'ts for Maintaining Good Vocal Health. Retrieved March 1, 2023, from https://www.usa.edu/blog/10-dos-and-donts-for-good-vocal-health/

5. National Institute on Deafness and Other Communication Disorders. (2021, April 15). Taking Care of Your Voice. Retrieved February 1, 2023, from https://www.nidcd.nih.gov/health/taking-care-your-voice

6. Musician Health and Wellness, St Olaf. College (2023). Resting Your Voice. Retrieved February 5, 2023, from https://wp.stolaf.edu/musician-health/resting-your-voice/

7. Ragan, Kari. (2016). The Impact of Vocal Cool-down Exercises: A Subjective Study of Singers' and Listeners' Perceptions. *J Voice*, 30 (6): 764.e1–764.e9.

8. Sataloff, Robert T. (1985). Ten Good Ways to Abuse Your Voice: A Singer's Guide to a Short Career, Part I. *National Association of Teachers of Singing Journal*, 42 (1): 24.

Sixteen

"Roc the Mic" (Freeway, Beanie Sigel, Nelly, Murphy Lee)
Microphone Techniques

If you plan on performing in front of an audience, your microphone is going to become your best friend. For hip-hop, mics have always been essential. Long before hip-hop became the highest grossing genre of popular music, in fact, before rap had even come into the mainstream, there were MC's. The MC's priority was to hype up the crowd. If they were doing their job correctly, the crowd would already be on the dance floor, having a great time. Because of how loud it would be, the MC would need to amplify their voice to be heard. Today, rappers still need the mic given that they need to be heard over ambient noise, especially by those sitting in the "cheap seats." However, now the microphone does more than just that: it also helps the rapper maintain the nuances of their individual artistry. They can have the flexibility to choose what pitch, tone quality, and dynamics to use, because, although they are making these pitches and tones themselves, the mic can pick up subtleties that would have to be eliminated if they had to scream to be heard over crowds. Most importantly, the amplification of the modern-day microphone allows for their words to be heard clearly and helps them maintain this clarity without causing vocal damage to themselves.

A Deeper Dive into Microphones

How Do Microphones Work?

At first, you might think this doesn't matter . . . you just need to know how to work the mic, right? Well, yes, but understanding the microphone's function should prevent some simple mistakes and miscommunications between you and your sound engineer.

You probably learned in science class that a power source is necessary to create sound. For a rapper, that is airflow. The air moves through the vocal cords, and they oscillate, making vibrations. The vibrations create a buzzy sound which gets louder as those vibrations bounce off of the resonators (the parts of the body such as the throat, nose, sinuses, etc.) and then travel outside of the body as sound waves. The soundwaves are awesome and all, but they have to be converted into electrical waves in order to be amplified. "Every microphone has two basic actions: first to convert the acoustic vibrations of the air into mechanical vibrations by having the air move a diaphragm—a light stiff surface; second, it must act as a transducer, and convert this movement of the diaphragm into electrical currents or voltages."[1] Those electrical currents will be sent via an output signal to another device. In short, a microphone converts energy from one form to another. It alone doesn't make you louder, but it is a crucial piece to that puzzle.

On Stage Versus Recording

The bulk of this chapter will discuss microphone use in live performance. However, some of you might want to record your vocals, either professionally or at home as a means of practicing. In either scenario, your use of a microphone is essential, but the benefits in each scenario are different.

On Stage (Live)

- To amplify over cheering crowds or background noise
- To maintain your natural vocal quality
- To allow for nuanced cadences (i.e., shifts in dynamics, word stress, pitch, and tone)
- To amplify effects such as echo and reverb

In the Recording Studio

- To maintain your natural vocal quality
- To pick up and accentuate subtle nuances in tone quality
- To assist in storytelling via use of dynamics

Types of Microphones

Microphones have become a highly specialized industry. There are microphones for Zoom sessions, podcasts, and choir singing. There are headsets, handsfree Bluetooth mics in car stereo systems, and gaming mics; the list goes on and on. Each and every make and model of microphone that has characteristics of its construction will elicit a different outcome when used by the rapper. Though there are countless brands, styles, and models, all microphones fall into three types/categories:

1. **Dynamic microphones**
2. **Condenser microphones**
3. **Ribbon microphones**

Dynamic, condenser, and ribbon microphones are all transducers (an instrument or device that converts energy from one form to another form), and they all work in roughly the same way. Despite the general similarities, each has a different method of converting sound waves into electrical currents. Because of this, different types of microphones are better for different situations. You'll need to understand which mic you'll want to use when performing live versus the mic you'll want to use when recording your vocals. Knowing this will help you get the best sound effectively and efficiently.

Dynamic Microphones

If you've sung live on stage with a mic, chances are you've used a dynamic microphone. There are many reasons for this:

- **Durability:** can take a lot of wear and tear
- **High tolerance for loudness** (distortion is a lot less likely)
- Specifically designed to **handle higher sound pressure levels**
- Resistant to feedback (i.e., helps reduce your chances of getting feedback)
- **Versatility:** great for use for voices, but also other instruments and forms of entertainment like drums, guitars, stand-up comedy, etc.[2]

Dynamic mics tend to make instruments (including your voice) sound warmer and more present. That, paired with their durability and their ability to resist feedback, make them ideal for the stage. However, dynamic microphones have some drawbacks. "Reach" is a term used to quantify a microphone's ability to pull in/amplify sounds from a distance. Dynamic microphones don't have great "reach." This works in your favor on stage, because your mic won't pick up noise from the crowd, from the band, or from your tracks in your mixer. Dynamic microphones also have trouble with high frequencies, which won't be a problem live either. Dynamic microphones are fantastic for a live stage (assuming you hold them and use them correctly). They are fantastic at getting the gist, or broad strokes, of your performance. But some of the nuances of your brilliant cadence might go unnoticed with a dynamic mic. That's okay with the adrenaline of live performance being the priority. But for the times when you need something a little more, you might want to look at the condenser mic.[3]

Condenser Microphones

Condenser mics will be your go-to mic if you are in the recording studio. Why?

- **High sensitivity:** can pick up subtle nuances in your voice as well as softer frequencies
- Produces a **clearer sound** than its counterparts[4]

If you are using a condenser mic, you'll want to purchase a "pop filter," which is a small mesh or metal screen that you place between you and the mic. A pop filter eliminates the popping sound (burst of air) that occurs when you say certain consonants, such as P, B, G, T, K, and G. A pop filter also catches your saliva when singing or rapping. We all know how important diction is—and hey, spit those bars, bruh—but all of that saliva can damage the sensitive condenser mic, and a pop filter helps prevent that damage from occurring. After reading this, you might feel like the condenser mic is annoyingly high maintenance, and you wouldn't be entirely wrong. Trust me, the sound quality you'll get when recording, however, will make this a worthy investment.

> "The whole point of a pop filter is to minimize the pop that comes with certain letters like a P or a B. And so if you're just doing it on the mic and someone says 'preparing to get paper,' you're gonna hear 'puh puh puh' and it literally sounds immature. So I've actually had to learn how to kind of minimize that pop on the P when I'm recording."
>
> —Rama Kazi

Ribbon Microphones

Ribbon microphones are from the 1950s and 1960s. They are technically dynamic mics, but they work and sound quite different from the dynamic microphones we know and love today. This would be a mic that you'd potentially use for a tune or two, but it definitely wouldn't be a go-to for rap, as you'll probably be looking for something that can capture the crispness and zap of your aggressive rhythmic attacks. The benefits of a mic like this though include:

- Producing a warm, satin like tone (great for jazz, crooning, and your best Norah Jones imitation)
- Very cool collectors' items (because they are fragile and quite expensive)
- Useful in recording studios where they can be optimally positioned for sound to expertly capture the nuances of certain timbres[5]

Polar Pattern

When considering what microphone to use, the other main factor lies in determining your priorities for a polar pattern. Polar patterns are also referred to as "pick up patterns." This makes sense because the polar pattern basically lets you know which part of the mic is "picking up" your sound. "Microphones capture sound differently based on the source of the sound in relation to the head of the microphone. The area in which it captures sound is known as the polar pattern. These polar patterns show the regions around the microphone where the microphone will detect sound. The reason for these different types of patterns is to provide microphones that work best in specific environments or to get a specific sound."[6] Polar patterns become important to you on stage when you are deciding how to hold your microphone (see the following section about microphone grip). How do you decide which polar pattern is best for you? Once again, it often deals with where you are and what you are using the microphone to do (i.e., performing live in front of a crowd versus in a recording studio). There are four basic polar patterns you might encounter in life, especially when recording rap: **omnidirectional, cardioid, hyper-cardioid,** and **shotgun**. Some condenser mics can switch modes to have different polar patterns. Each pattern is useful for different things (e.g., the omnidirectional mic is great if you want to pick up a group of people in different spots, since it picks up sound from all directions). But, for a rapper, the cardioid pickup will be most useful in both live and recording sessions. Some important things to know:

- A cardioid mic is designed to pick up sounds from the front and sides of the mic but does not pick up sound well from the rear of the microphone. The pickup (polar) pattern resembles the shape of a heart, hence the name "cardioid."
- The dynamic microphone someone hands you on stage is most likely going to have a cardioid pickup pattern. This helps you because it will pick up your voice, but not the crowd in front of you. "Cardioid microphones in particular are known for their tendency to boost lower frequencies at close proximity to the sound source while

attenuating those same frequencies as the distance increases. This is known as the 'proximity effect.'"[7] Remember when we said dynamic mics are great for live performance because they'll pick up your sound but not the crowds? You can thank the cardioid pattern.[8]

Microphone Stands

Picture yourself rapping live, on stage, in front of an audience. No seriously: close your eyes and imagine what it would look like (or what you would *want* it to look like). Did you picture standing and rapping in front of a mic stand? Chances are, you didn't. Most of the time, rappers need to move, and they'll prefer a handheld mic in order to have the freedom to do so. This is because rap is communication, it's telling a story, and it's connecting with the audience through spoken word. When thinking about hyping up the audience, it's hard to imagine standing still, but if you have a mic stand, you'd primarily be stationary because the mic would be on the stand, and you'd need to be near the microphone . You can't move around the stage; you can't stage dive (When Denzel Curry performed at the Observatory OC, he stage dove and rode the crowd *while rapping*. . . . You can't do that with a stand). However, there are some pros to using a mic stand:

- In melodic rap, you're singing. In this scenario, mic stands can be useful because they keep the microphone stationary, and, as long as you are standing relatively still, you know that you are staying roughly in line with the mic, meaning that it's not dropping so far away from your mouth that people lose your words. (Check out Young Thug's NPR Tiny Desk concert for a great example of when using a mic stand can be advantageous to the rapper.[9])
- Your hands are free, which helps some rappers emote and keep the groove in their flows, especially if they are purposefully slightly ahead or behind the beat.
- You can use the stand as a prop. It can almost become a dance partner of sorts. For inspiration, look at performers like Michael Jackson, Justin Timberlake, and Bruno Mars.

If you are using a mic stand, make sure the mic stand is low enough so that it doesn't block your face. For a rule of thumb, lower the mic stand so that the mic, if perpendicular to the floor, sits just under your chin. With the stand in that position, angle the mic upwards toward your mouth. This way, the mic easily catches your sound while still blocking out ambient noise. Finally, please, please, *please* find times to remove the mic from the stand so that you can move around the stage.

Handheld Corded/Wired Mics

In reality, most of the time, you will not be using a mic stand when rapping. I mean, how can you have a "mic drop" moment if it's stuck on a stand? (Deepest apologies for that dad joke). Since you won't have a stand, you'll be holding the mic instead, which is why these mics are often referred to as "handhelds." Generally speaking, these microphones will be cordless. But before that technology was invented, mics had long cords that connected directly to the speaker system. Once in a while you'll still encounter a corded mic, so it's best to know that they exist and how to use them properly. There are some pros to using corded microphones:

- **Sound quality:** Corded mics sometimes produce a better sound because they're plugged directly into the system.
- **Reliability:** You'll have fewer technological snafus with a corded mic because you won't have batteries dying on you and you won't have interference. If there are issues, they're easier to diagnose and fix in a corded mic system.

But, as with everything, there are also cons:

- **Limited range of motion:** With a corded mic, you'll be limited in the amount of distance you can travel. When trying to connect to your entire audience, traveling to the far sides of the stage and sometimes up into the audience is key.

- The other con is that you can trip over the cord. This can cause it to become detached from the amplification system, and no one will hear you. Furthermore, you could actually hurt yourself. It's probably safe to say that face planting is not how you plan to entertain the crowd.

A handheld, cordless microphone will be your primary mode of amplification at live shows. The combination of a sophisticated wireless microphone, a good in-ear monitor, and a good sound person is a tough combo to beat. Now let's talk through the pros and cons:

Pros	Cons
- **Freedom** of movement. - **Convenient** (you can literally put it in your pocket). - **Removal of a barrier:** just as removing the mic stand removes a barrier between you and your audience (both visually and symbolically speaking). - Many would say that it looks **"cooler"** (it's definitely in vogue to have a wireless mic these days).	- **Distance limitations:** while better than most wired microphones, there will reach a point where you are out of reception range (the distance depends on your mic and your sound system, but there is a limit, regardless). - **Expensive:** these are generally more expensive than their wired cousins (especially because of the batteries you'll need to replace), plus you'll need a good sound system to pair with the mic or you'll likely get . . . - **Interference (not to be confused with feedback):** outside radio signals or even physical objects (depending on the system) can cause spotty reception. This can impair, or completely eliminate, your mic's effectiveness in a show.

Regardless of the type of mic you choose, it's *imperative* to have a backup . . . or three with you at every show. You can never be too overprepared.[10]

Owning Your Own Mic

If you are serious about rapping, and think you'll frequently want to rap in front of a crowd, then purchasing your own mic is worth the investment. There are so many reasons you'll be glad you made this investment, such as:

- You'll know the sound of your mic. Because you chose it, you'll get to choose the polar pattern, the shape, the size, and the size of the components inside the mic that alter the sound and pick up.
- You'll be prepared. If you arrive and the microphones provided for you are crap, you don't have to worry about it.
- It's sanitary: I know, I know; I sound like a mom. I am a mom, so, deal. But seriously though, the mic is supposed to be close to your mouth. The term "spitting bars" comes from a true place. Think about how much saliva, and therefore the number of germs, that are going to end up on that mic. Maybe you don't care, and if so, you do you. But when I think about that, and when I think about how much a rapper has to breathe, that means that you aren't just near germs, you are potentially breathing in germs. I'm literally gagging a little bit thinking about this scenario.
- You'll know your battery life and charge. Being responsible about this can save you from tech headaches during your set.

Microphone Technique

How to Hold Your Microphone

There are so many conflicting viewpoints about this. The sound engineers most definitely have an opinion, and most rappers tend to disagree. Because this book is for you, the rapper, the approach is going to be to tell it like it is, approaching the biggest issue head on. So here are my thoughts on cupping the mic.

Every sound engineer would love you to pieces if you did *not* cup the mic. What is "cupping"? Simply put, it is the "holding one or two hands around the grid of a vocal microphone. This grip causes coloration of the

"Roc the Mic" (Freeway, Beanie Sigel, Nelly, Murphy Lee) 285

frequency response, basically due to the cavity/cavities created."[11] A mic has two main parts: the metal/mesh grille and the shaft, or handle. The microphones design intends you, the user, to hold it near the top of the handle/shaft. This keeps the mic stable in your hands but doesn't block any of the components of the microphone that actually pick up your sound. When you cup the mic, you are preventing those carefully designed parts in the grid from doing their intended job.[12] The results are:

- Cons
    - Changing the mic pickup pattern from dynamic (i.e., toward you) to omnidirectional (i.e., picking up sounds from everywhere). This can lead to a lot of ambient noise and, even worse, feedback.
    - Losing the "proximity effect," which will in turn change your tone quality, and risk losing the warmer bass colors of your sound.
    - A muffled sound: all of that work you did on articulation could go out of the window.
    - Potential affectations regarding what you hear in the in-ear monitor.
- Pros:
    - Percussive diction is crucial to flow and delivery. The proximity that cupping provides does accentuate this percussive diction.
    - Shaft position: Cupping the mic creates the ability to hold the mic shaft parallel to the floor. The hip-hop vibe is real; it isn't performed with the intention of looking stuffy, bubble gum pop, or sleek. Altering the mic so it's aimed straight out at the audience eliminates that unwanted slick sheen.
    - Sometimes the adjusted sound is intentional—again, to eliminate the amplified, clean sound to which a mic can sometimes allude.
- Control: I was asking various rappers about this, and okay—I've got to admit—one answer made me stop and really think about this entire cupping thing with *much* less judgment:

> "Though there are many reasons an artist might want to hold their performance mic differently, one common reason is the ease of control—the higher up on the barrel you hold a dynamic microphone, the easier it becomes to know where the microphone is at all times. The closer your hand to the top, the more consistent your grip on the microphone."
>
> —Jay Towns

Chances are, you've seen most of your favorite rappers cup the mic. Which means that you are probably going to ignore this advice and cup the mic when you perform. If you choose to do that, fine, but buy your sound engineer some Starbucks (and not just a tall hot plain tea . . . you need to go venti mocha with extra whipped cream). *If* they feel like helping you out, they can work their magic and balance some of this out, if their system, and skillset, are equipped to do so.

If you cup the mic, please cup the bottom half only, as a lot of mics have a metal ring around the center of the grille. Again, if you are going to ignore me (which, let's face it, you are going to ignore me) and cup the mic, please cup from the metal ring downward. The aforementioned effects will still exist, but the muffling issue is much less dire.

Arm Position

Have you ever lifted and then held your arms out at shoulder height? Do this for thirty seconds. Are your shoulders tired? Probably a bit, yes? To hold the mic close to your mouth (which you will), you'll need to preserve your arm strength.

> "Whenever I record or like, have done more performances, I just make sure that my mouth is as close to that microphone as possible. And that's one of the most important parts of your performance. If you don't have a good performance, like vocal performance, even in the studio booth, it's not gonna sound right like."
>
> —Kinga World

Exercise time:

- Pretend your elbow is "glued" to your side.
- With your forearm remaining "glued," bend your arm so that, if looking at you from the side, your arm would be in the position of the letter "V."
- The exact positioning should have the grille of the microphone no more than two inches from your face.
- You might need to move your arm to find your optimal mic position (perhaps you'd like the mic parallel to the floor instead of angled downward). Use this as a starting point and adjust until you feel comfortable.

Steadying the Mic

It's deceptively difficult to keep the microphone in front of your mouth, at the proper distance from your mouth. A combination of adrenaline, endorphins, commitment to communication, and work to hype up the crowd will cause you to move quite a bit. As you move, it's easy to go to one of two extremes:

1. The microphone will drift away from your face. Imagine you waving your hands in the air, waving them like you just don't care . . . and oops, your arm, and your microphone are waving above your head. No one is going to hear you with your mic that far away from your face.
2. That same rush of endorphins, adrenaline rush, or energetic storytelling can bring your microphone too close to your mouth, so close that you smack yourself in the teeth or lips. Um, yeah . . . ouch. Remember, that grille is metal, and that's going to hurt.

To combat these errors, a tried-and-true method is to use a finger to steady your microphone placement.

Here's another exercise to help you out:

Position 1

- Grip your microphone and bring it one to two inches from your face in speaking position.
- Bend your index finger in the "come hither" position, yet with the palm facing sideways instead of toward the sky.
- Using the other three fingers to hold the mic, take your bent index finger, and place it just below your nostrils.
- Check to see if your mic is still one to two inches from your face.

Position 2

- As an alternate position, the index finger can be replaced with a thumb: take your thumb and make a thumbs up sign.
- Keeping your thumb straight, use your four fingers to hold your mic.
- Place the tip of your thumb on your chin, directly underneath your mic.
- *Note:* This position can provide slightly more distance from the mic itself (depending on the position of your grip).

Either position should keep the microphone in a position that prevents self-injury and also eliminates (or greatly reduces) mic drift.

Movement and Audience Engagement

There is nothing quite like a live hip-hop show; the energy of the crowd is infectious, and you as a rapper will often find yourself feeling a sensation of euphoria as you witness the effect your thoughts and words have on your fans. Naturally, this energy will cause you, the rapper, to want to move around. Please, please, please listen to this instinct. The crowd wants you to move. Move your hands, much like we do when we talk. Move around the stage. Stand and, hell, even sit in different positions. While you do this, it's important that the mic stays glued in its position . . . which is right in front of your mouth.

> "When I'm doing cardio, I try to rap while I'm doing cardio just to make sure when I'm on stage I can move back and forth and still have a similar tone to what I have on the song on stage because my lung capacity is there."
>
> —femdot.

Other Tips

- Do not blow off the sound check. This is your vital time with your engineer to work out the plan of attack, to make sure there is no interference, and to check levels so you can hear yourself.
- Establish your form of communication with your engineer. This person is your best friend during the performance. If something is off, you need to quickly look at your sound person during the show, often mid-song, with a request or question. Some of this communication might need to be nonverbal.
- Beware of speaker proximity. Check your distance and don't let the mic get too close to a speaker since it will cause deafening feedback.
- Beware of making the volume in your in-ear monitor too loud; it might seem comforting but it can result in you pushing your voice to be louder because your brain wants to hear both your voice and the beats. This can result in fatigue, vocal nuance distortion, and, eventually, vocal health impairment.
- On a related note, make sure you can hear yourself in your monitor (in-ear or external), which can help prevent vocal pushing and strain. The balance of this is crucial. It's important to hear yourself, but the answer isn't always to ask for your vocals to be louder or for you to sing louder. It's about striking the right balance. Remember, it might even be that your in-ear monitor is *too* loud, which can cause you to push unnecessarily. Again, getting the right balance is crucial.
- Be confident! Hearing yourself amplified is overwhelming at first. But you've practiced and practiced and practiced for this gig. You've got this my friend. But in case you haven't practiced...

> "On stage it's fun to experiment and really just see how delivering the track differently can give people a different experience live, because the goal is to just get the crowd involved and give them a new experience."
>
> —Ausar

- Practice with a mic. I can't emphasize this enough. Practice. Practice. *Practice.* This is a skillset that needed a chapter dedicated to it just like breath support and diction. It can be tricky at first, so give yourself the advantage of practicing until you feel like rocking the mic is second nature.

This might seem like a lot of information to take in, but this is one of those cases where putting these techniques into practice makes things click. After spending some time with a mic, you'll learn what works for you, and you'll be able to see and hear the topics discussed in this chapter. There is a saying that says, "you learn best by doing." It's quite possible they were talking about mic technique when the saying was invented.

Notes

1. Crowhurt, N.H. (n.d.). The Purposes of Microphones. *Basic Audio.* http://www.vias.org/crowhurstba/crowhurst_basic_audio_vol1_030.html

2. *Teach Me Audio.* (n.d.). Dynamic Microphone. https://www.teachmeaudio.com/recording/microphones/dynamic-microphone

3. *Musician on a Mission.* (n.d.). The Different Types of Microphones: Home Studio Essentials. https://www.musicianonamission.com/types-of-microphones/

4. *Behind the Mixer.* (n.d.). Vocal Microphone Guide. https://www.behindthemixer.com/vocal-microphone-guide/

5. Levine, Mike (2022, December 28). Different Types of Microphones and When to Use Them: The Shape of Things to Come. *Popular Science.* https://www.popsci.com/reviews/types-of-microphones/

6. *Behind the Mixer.* (n.d.). Vocal Microphone Guide. https://www.behindthemixer.com/vocal-microphone-guide/

7. Edwards, Matthew. (2014). *So You Want to Sing Rock 'n' Roll: A Guide for Professionals*. Lanham, MD: Rowman & Littlefield Publishing Group, 174.

8. *Sound Technology*. (n.d.). Microphone Polar Patterns—Part 1: Omnidirectional. https://www.soundtech.co.uk/akg/news/microphone-polar-patterns-part-1-omnidirectional#:~:text="Polar%20pattern"%20refers%20to%20a,directional%20and%20figure%20of%208

9. NPR Music. (2012, July 27). Young Thug: Tiny Desk (Home) Concert. *YouTube*. https://www.youtube.com/watch?v=SAROJPnd_s8

10. *Musician Port*. (2019, May 2). Wired Microphone vs Wireless Microphone (OnStage). https://musicianport.com/wired-microphone-vs-wireless-microphone/

11. *DPAO Microphones*. (n.d.). What is "Cupping"? https://www.dpamicrophones.com/mic-dictionary/cupping#:~:text=Holding%20one%20or%20two%20hands,to%20the%20cavity%2Fcavities%20created

12. *OpenMic*. (2020, December 8). Microphone Technique for Singers: How to Sing Better with a Mic. https://www.openmicuk.co.uk/advice/microphone-technique-for-singers/

Seventeen

Beats, Rhymes, and Life (A Tribe Called Quest)

What to Prioritize and Other Things to Consider

By now, you've taken hip-hop history from its origins and followed the winding timeline through the decades to catch up to where we are today. Hip-hop has gone from Kool Herc and Coke La Rock to Post Malone, Lil Dirk, Ice Spice, Tyler, the Creator, Lil Baby, GloRilla, and Denzel Curry. You've also amassed an arsenal of exercises to build your technique. You are well on your way, young jedi. It is time to put your newfound book smarts into practice. But, how to practice?

The Ins and Outs of Practicing

Organizing Your Practice

Like everything else, this whole rapping thing takes a lot of practice and a lot of patience. Also, like everything else, doing things consistently, and in small increments, will reap the best results. Have you ever crammed for a test? You might have done well on the test (I mean, hopefully you did), but chances are, you don't remember a lot of the information you were cramming in your brain at three AM the night before the exam. The same applies for this: there are way too many components to juggle to cram and learn them all at once. These skills also require repetition for muscle memory and growth. Deciding on a systematic method of practice will get you to your goal faster, and the journey will be a heck of a lot more fun.

Preparing for the Journey

As you prepare to practice, you will need to make space and acquire a few tools. Don't worry, you don't have to build a three-hundred-square-foot, soundproof home recording studio. But you should set up a simple system so you can record your songs. This goes beyond quickly recording a new flow idea in your phone's voice memos app. Making a designated space prepares you to lay down your songs onto your beats. Start to think about the following:

- **Where to record:** You'll want a room in your house that is quietest and eliminates echo by absorbing sounds. This would mean there are a lot of soft goods, like carpet, bedspreads, and couches—a lot of my students record in their closets, since it's quiet and the clothes surrounding them dampen their sound.
- **Basic equipment:** If you are just starting out, and these recordings are primarily for yourself and your friends, you can get away with a bare bone set up consisting of:
    - A computer
    - A microphone
    - A pop filter
    - A microphone stand
    - Headphones
    - A digital audio workstation (more on this later in the chapter)
- **A practice room:** Where will you practice? Most rooms in your house are possibilities to practice, but you need to consider the following:
    - Is it quiet?
    - Is it free of distractions (as much as possible)?
    - Do you feel comfortable working on your technique or practicing your delivery in the space?
- **Writing materials:** How will you write your lyrics? Paper like Eminem? Phone like Drake or Logic? Keeping everything stored in your memory? (I don't recommend this, but there are rappers, i.e.

supposedly Jay-Z, who never write anything down). Where will you store your bar sheets? In a designated folder on your desktop? Screenshots in your phone? A messy pile on your bedroom floor? Hey—I don't judge. Whatever helps you stay organized and creative is the best system for you.

- **Miscellaneous:** Subscriptions to some streaming apps and a budget allotment for going to see other rappers' shows and sending out marketing materials should be set aside each month so that you have an outlet and external motivation to keep you chugging along.

> "When I first started rapping and started recording, maybe like eight years ago, [I was] recording in my house and getting a friend to master it. And, you know, it doesn't sound like the same quality as a radio . . . we're just constantly trying to work to get closer to that sound. And it's something that I'm still trying to, you know, find because getting that really crystal clear sound is an art of its own."
>
> —Swabski

Categorizing Your Practice

What to practice? When you try to answer that question in micro terms, your mind can start swimming. It's probably easier to organize your practice into larger categories, and then you can easily arrange your task list into its proper section. To do this, try thinking of things in one of these three broad categories:

- **The voice as an instrument:** Anything that builds your rap voice would fall under this category. This would include working on your breathing, your posture, your diction, your tone quality toolbox, your storytelling via delivery, understanding rhythmic concepts, counting beats, and execution of your flows.

- **Writing:** As previously stated, this is not a book on lyric writing or song structure. But, if you are an aspiring rapper, chances are you are writing, or hoping to write, your own raps. There are tons of resources to help you work on developing this skill, and you should definitely take some time to look into those tools. Once you are writing, this will also be something that you need to practice, and anything that can fall under the writing umbrella, whether it be coming up with rhythmic patterns, cadences, or lyrics should all fall into this category.
- **Performing/showbiz:** This is where mic technique, figuring out your crowd hype style, your audience interaction tactics, your stage posture, and, as you grow in confidence, determining set lists and transitions all come into play. This category can also include the business side of things, such as figuring out your rap name, what you want your social media presence to be like, your marketing strategy, and your business plan.

Determining Your Practice Structure

Are you the type of person who wants to delve into the technical aspects of rapping first, using your favorite rap songs as material? If so, terrific. Then you'd start off working on each element within the vocal technique category. It would probably be wise to spend five to seven dedicated practice sessions just thinking about one element, such as posture, before switching to another element, such as tone. These sessions should be between thirty and sixty minutes. If you don't have the stamina for that, you can work your way up to those longer sessions. If you don't have time for a thirty-minute session, five minutes is five minutes more than nothing, and five minutes every day will slowly but surely help you improve. Everyone is busy, and only you know how much time you can set aside for practice. Don't let these guidelines of practice length intimidate you. There is a saying, "don't let perfect be the enemy of the good," and that applies here. Just practice.

Once you feel you've got a good handle on one element, move on to another . . . but every few days, circle back and give yourself a refresher to make sure you've retained the muscle memory you built learning the skill in the first place. Eventually, you can begin to multitask and work on two to three (previously worked on skills) simultaneously. This might happen organically, and if so, great. Keep systematically working on these skills until they start to mesh, and eventually you will find that one skill helps another. For example, good posture makes breathing easier, which allows for easier diction. Mastering your pitch and tone toolbox helps your storytelling, which helps your flow, etc. Your skillset will ultimately build upon itself.

Once you've done a deep dive into building your rap technique, you might take a break from that and work on your songwriting and recording. You might want to record yourself, or you might want to team up with a producer. You might build a home studio, or you could go to a studio and rent recording time. You could purchase or lease beats or make your own. There are many ways to skin this particular cat, and it comes down to your money, time, skill, and preference. All of this is quite a deep dive of its own, so you'd want to have regular technique checkups during the period of time you are focusing on songwriting and recording. This can be as simple as rapping along with your favorite new release by NBA Youngboy or Lizzo while consciously thinking about the aspects of your technique.

Another vital component of your practice is creating and working on your public presence. This could be working on your TikTok, YouTube, or Instagram presence. Social media is an incredible way to build a following. Becoming part of the scene is also crucial to both your development as an artist and your training. This can manifest in multiple ways: attending shows and being an active part of the hip-hop community, both live in local clubs and in chat rooms. Uploading your music to an independent streaming platform is not only a way for you to put your music out there, but also lets you hear and

> "Being from the West side, I just practice a lot of things that I grew up around, and inspired and helped me to become a rapper. So like Twista, Do or Die, those guys . . . I want to show folks what that sounds like in present day."
>
> —Frsh Waters

> "You can get hot, you can start dropping records, and you can kind of build your own self up to the point where you don't need the big labels to come."
>
> —AC Tatum

connect with other artists. Spotify is spectacular, sure, but there is also MixCloud, Funk Whale, SoundCloud, Deezer, BandCamp, and Audius.

Eventually, working on these three categories of practice will triangulate and the result will be getting in front of people and doing your thing. Do this often, and as soon as you possibly can. You don't have to be perfect. Start by performing in front of a few friends. You'll get performance practice and will also get valuable feedback. That feedback helps take your work to the next level. So often we are working in isolation, and there is only so much an artist can do in a vacuum.

The most important practice tip of all is a simple one: try to do a little bit each day. You'll be amazed at your growth if you dedicate just a few minutes a day to getting better and working on you. Obviously, if you can do more every day (and you should do more than a few minutes several times a week), great, but the key to muscle memory is frequent repetition.

Further Study

You invested the time into reading this book, and hopefully you feel a bit more equipped to continue on in your rap journey. But as you know, this book focuses on history, finding your way into your authentic rap voice, and vocal technique. It does not focus on songwriting or entrepreneurship, for example. You know what I'm going to say next: just as you took the time to read this, you should take some time to read and study songwriting and the business of being a hip-hop artist. There are so many great books and resources out there, most of which you can get for free from your local library. At the bare minimum, please invest in a rhyming dictionary and/or a word rhythm dictionary. Some options include:

- *Hip-Hop Rhyming Dictionary*, by Kevin M. Mitchel
- *The Complete Rhyming Dictionary, Including the Poet's Craft Book*, by Clement Wood
- *The Extensive Hip Hop Rhyming Dictionary: Hip Hop Rhyming Dictionary: The Extensive Hip Hop & Rap Rhyming Dictionary*, by Gio Williams
- *The Word Rhythm Dictionary: A Resource for Writers, Rappers, Poets, and Lyricists*, by Timothy Polashek

Essential Vocabulary

Ultimately, you should write lyrics with the words you use in your everyday speech. Unless you are writing as an alternate persona or you are focusing on story rap, your material should be centered on your thoughts, feelings, and experiences. Those thoughts don't need to be put through a language filter that makes you sound like someone else. That said, when studying the GOATs (defined in the following), you will probably come across words and phrases that are perplexing to you. The best way to handle that is to look up those phrases in an urban dictionary or to have a rhyming dictionary on hand (there are many online, free resources for your consumption).

Beyond writing, there are a handful of essential definitions that might not have been previously discussed. Here are ten, need-to-know vocabulary words for the new rap artist:

DAW: Digital audio workstation. You'll come across this term when discussing recording your music. It's not an actual workstation (you're obviously not going to your office cubicle or whatnot), but rather, it's software. Features usually include recording, adding sound effects (for example, reverb, echo, delay) editing, mixing, determining the balance, compression, etc. Some examples of digital audio workstations include Reason Studios, FL Studio, MixCraft Pro, Ableton, Magix Music Maker, Garageband, CakeWalk, ProTools, Apple Logic Pro (Logic), PreSonus, Steinberg Cubase, and Audacity. These have different pros and cons, different price points, and different features. You can choose the right one for you based on your priorities.

FREESTYLE: People often think freestyle rap means rap that is completely made up on the spot. However, this isn't necessarily true. The definition has evolved over the decades: "In his 2003 book, *There's a God on the Mic*, rapper Kool Moe Dee writes, 'There are two types of freestyle. There's an old-school freestyle that basically rhymes that you've written that may not have anything to do with any subject or that goes all over the place. Then there's freestyle where you come off the top of the head.'"[1] There is a third definition in which things can be previously written but haven't been heard before and aren't yet codified. When discussing freestyling, it's important to mention the rap battle—this can happen on albums (listen to 50 Cent's cold justice on "Piggy Bank"), but started in the streets decades earlier, where the prize was often bragging rights. In these situations (i.e., in street and small club rap battles), the goal is to size up your opponent and/or cut down whatever claim they made in their rap moments earlier . . . this rap is improvised. Over the years, people have come to use the term freestyle to mean improvised, but it still does not have to be thought of on the spot to count as freestyle. So, if you hear your favorite rapper "freestyle," please know that might have been worked out long before you hear it.

G.O.A.T. or GOAT: This is another acronym that stands for greatest of all time. This term originated with the boxer Muhammad Ali's "I Am The Greatest. . . . In Sept. 1992, Lonnie Ali, Muhammad Ali's wife, incorporated G.O.A.T. Inc. This company was used as an umbrella for all of the former boxer's intellectual properties being used for commercial purposes."[2] The term became hip-hop focused with LL Cool J's 2000 album entitled *G.O.A.T.* But LL in turn credits Ali, "Without Muhammad Ali, there would be no 'Mama Said Knock You Out,' and the term G.O.A.T. would have never been coined."[3]

INTRO: Imagine listening to a song for the first time: have you ever hit "next" or "skip" before ever hearing a vocal? If that answer is yes, it can serve as a testament to the importance of the intro of your song. The intro is found at the beginning and sets up the song, establishing many of the song's important elements, such as the key, tempo, rhythmic feel, and even its energy and attitude. You will find that the intro is often the same music without singing over it as the verse or even the chorus. Sometimes, however, a song's intro will not have any material found later in the song. In this scenario, the goal is to create interest for the listener and encourage them to keep playing it. Either way, an intro typically lasts up to four bars.[4]

For a truly sick intro, listen to Chance the Rapper's "All We Got," "Spread The Opps" by LaCrae, or "Passin' Me By" by Pharcyde.

HOOK: This could arguably be the most important part of your song. It's that part you remember, the part that sticks with you long after you hear the song. People use this term to mean a lot of things, so for clarity purposes, let's use a definition used in an NPR article: "The term 'hook' likely goes back to the earliest days of songwriting because it refers to the part of the song intended to 'hook' the listener: a catchy combination of melody, lyrics and rhythm that stays in the listener's head—something that songwriters from the dawn of time have wanted to achieve."[5] In rap, a hook is often sung by a singer, who is given credit as a contributor to the song (for this think of Jay-Z and Alicia Keys's earworm, "Empire State of Mind"). But, if you're thinking of a rapper performed hook, listen to one of the following:

- Chamillionaire's "Ridin"
- Wu-Tang Clan's "C.R.E.A.M"
- A$AP Ferg's "Hood Pope"
- Ms. Lauryn Hill's "Doo Wop (That Thing)"
- Nate Dogg's "Regulate"
- Janelle Monae's "Django Jane"
- Mac Miller's "Objects in the Mirror"
- Mos Def's "UMI Says"

A hook usually repeats two to three times in a song. Check out the hook in $NOT's "Whipski" (featuring Lil Skies and Internet Money), which repeats twice:

> She gon' be a savage (whoa), bad bitch (yeah)Ridin' 'round in a new whipski (whipski)
> Pour the two cups (two cups) of the whiskey (whiskey)
> She gon' get lit comin' through your city (uh-huh)
> She gon' be a savage (savage), bad bitch (yeah)
> Ridin' 'round in a new whipski (yeah)
> Pour the two cups (yeah) of the whiskey (yeah)
> She gon' get lit comin' through your city (yeah, ayy, ayy, yeah)

KICK/SNARE/HI-HAT: These are three different drum beats, made by different drums in a drum kit. Each has a distinct sound.

- **Kick:** This has the deepest sound, and often falls on beats one and three of the bar in the boom bap genre. In boom bap (see chapter 3), the kick is the "boom," named for the sound the drum makes.
- **Snare:** This has a higher sound than the kick. It often falls on beats two and four of the bar in the boom bap genre, named because it makes a "bap" sound.
- **Hi-Hat:** This has the highest sound of the three famous drum sounds. The hi-hat is common in the trap genre and makes a "Tss-Tss-Tss" sound.

OG: The OGs refers to the founders, the originals, the firsts, the pioneers. This term is usually used in a complimentary fashion.

RAP: Rap is actually an acronym that stands for rhythm and poetry.

SAMPLE: In short, a sample is part of the beat (track) that is taken from a song that already exists. The history of the sample in hip-hop is important, especially if you are making your own music. NYU music technology professor Ethan Hein defines a sample as an audio excerpt from an existing recording, repurposed in a new context. In the early years of hip-hop, producers freely sampled from copyrighted recordings without permission, but a series of lawsuits in the 1990s put an end to this practice in commercial releases. Nevertheless, sampling continues to be central to hip-hop aesthetics, especially at the underground level. In commercial releases, samples are usually either cleared, or replaced before release. It has become common for producers to use royalty-free sample libraries, but the ability to creatively repurpose (flip) an existing piece of culturally significant music remains a respected skill. In casual usage, it is common to use the word "sample" to also refer to a quotation or interpolation, but legally, they are quite different.[6]

For a great example, listen to Missy Elliot's "I Can't Stand the Rain," which is arguably the best use of a sample ever to sample (sampling Ann Peebles).

VERSE: In song structure, a verse in a rap is where the narrative takes place and where you learn the point of view of the rapper. There are many ways to organize your song, so there is no hard rule requiring a song to have multiple verses, however most rappers have two to three verses in which they deliver their expert flow. For great examples of verses at work, listen to the lyrics of "Y.O.U." by Luh Kei, "Can't Hold Us" by Macklemore, and "Q.U.E.E.N." by Janelle Monae (this song is part sung, with the last verse rapped), to see the painting of the picture through multiple verses.

Well, my friend, we are almost at the end of our journey together, but it's only the beginning of your personal journey, and the starting line is such a cool place to be because each day you get to move forward. You've now got history to

> "The genre is something that will always continue to evolve as long as there are new up and coming artists willing to explore that type of sound and already established household names who through their existence will always keep the genre alive."
>
> —Cozy Kiyo

reflect upon, exercises to practice, and technique to strengthen. You've got the tools, you've got the desire, and you've got the talent. Most importantly, you have you and your story to tell. It's time for the world to hear that story. It will be our honor and privilege to do so.

Resource List

- *Hip-Hop Music: History and Culture*, Terence Elliot
- *The History of Gangster Rap From Schoolly D to Kendrick Lamar, the Rise of a Great American Art Form*, Soren Baker and Xzibit
- *Chuck D Presents This Day in Rap and Hip-Hop History*, Chuck D and Shepard Fairey
- *The Big Payback: The History of the Business of Hip-Hop*, Dan Charmas
- *The G.O.A.T Samples: Roots of Hip-Hop Music*, Michael E. King
- *The Cambridge Companion to Hip-Hop*, Justin A. Williams
- *"And It Don't Stop!": The Best American Hip-Hop Journalism of the Last 25 Years*, Rachel Cepeda
- *The Hip Hop Wars*, Tricia Rose
- *Hip Hop's Amnesia: From Blues and the Black Women's Club Movement To Rap and The Hip Hop Movement*, Reiland Rabaka
- *Can't Stop Won't Stop*, Jeff Chang
- *Why Are All the Black Kids Sitting Together in the Cafeteria? And Other Conversations About Race*, Beverly Daniel Tatum
- *The Rap Year Book: The Most Important Rap Song Every Year Since 1979, Discussed, Debated, and Deconstructed*, Shea Serrano, Arturo Torres, Ice-T
- *The Hip Hop Movement: From R&B and The Civil Rights Movement to Rap and the Hip Hop Generation*, Reiland Rabaka
- *The Concise Guide to Hip-Hop Music: A Fresh Look at the Art of Hip-Hop From Old-School Beats to Freestyle Rap*, Paul Edwards

Notes

1. *Bandlab | Blog.* (2021, March 18). The Origins and Evolution of Freestyle Rap. https://blog.bandlab.com/the-origins-and-evolution-of-freestyle-rap/

2. Bird, Hayden. (2018, September 7). A Merriam-Webster Editor Explained Tom Brady's Role in "GOAT" Entering the Dictionary. *Boston.com.* https://www.boston.com/sports/new-england-patriots/2018/09/07/tom-brady-goat-dictionary/

3. Reeves, Mosi. (2016, June 4). Muhammad Ali: World's Greatest Boxer Was Also Hip-Hop Pioneer. *Rolling Stone.* https://www.rollingstone.com/music/music-news/muhammad-ali-worlds-greatest-boxer-was-also-hip-hop-pioneer-152560/

4. Stoubis, Nick. (n.d.). Basic Song Structure Explained. *Fender.* https://www.fender.com/articles/techniques/parts-of-a-song-keep-it-straight#:~:text=song%20building%20blocks.-,Intro,verse%20or%20even%20the%20chorus

5. Cole, Tom. (2010, October 15). You Ask, We Answer: What's a Hook? *NPR.* https://www.npr.org/sections/therecord/2010/10/15/130588663/you-ask-we-answer-what-s-a-hook#:~:text=The%20term%20%22hook%22%20likely%20goes,time%20have%20wanted%20to%20achieve

6. *The Ethan Hein Blog.* (2020, April 22). Hip-Hop Glossary. https://www.ethanhein.com/wp/2020/hip-hop-glossary/

Eighteen

Shoot for the Stars, Aim for the Moon (Pop Smoke)

Interviews

1. Mavi
2. AC Tatum
3. TeaMarrr
4. AKTHESAVIOR
5. Noah
6. Joseph Chilliams
7. Anonymuz
8. redveil
9. femdot.
10. Black Prez
11. Ausar
12. Kinga World
13. Swabski
14. daedae

Mavi

Interviewer: The first thing I'm always going to ask a rapper about is their flow, and yours specifically is so unique compared to most of what we see in rap today. I just wanted to know your process of how you choose your flow.

Mavi: Alright, so for rhythm, the flow is usually the first thing I choose. And I feel like if I don't know exactly how to rap over a beat, I shouldn't rap over it. Eight times out of ten. You know what I'm saying? Like, if I don't hear the first flow or the central flow whether that be the final refrain or major chorus, or just the first movement or phrase in terms of the first few bars. I feel like you bein' kind of aimless. So I like to stay rooted into the drums. So I just immediately, when I first get a beat, I try to make up like the most interesting interplay with the drums, you know, before I have the words.

Interviewer: Got it, but I thought I heard once that you sometimes choose your lyrics first. So then, I wanted to know . . .

Mavi: So yeah, in those instances, so sometimes, right, I'll write a flow to a song. Like, especially like if I do it inaudibly, or sometimes it can happen when I have to do it really quiet, right? How it sounds in my head, and how like my actual voice, like the physical thing that I'm assigned, actually sounds different. So when that happens, usually that'd be my favorite thing when I have a rap that I really like and I don't know the beat for it because that's when I feel like, okay, it's classic making time. Like we finna really build the thing. Not into itself, but of parts that are not, you know what I'm saying. When I have songs with no beats, I try to choose BPMs that feel aggressive, and that feel a little difficult to rap. Just in terms of keeping on rhythm and stuff like that. I feel like, I don't know. It's just a taste thing. I be liking labored performances in rap. And like, when you can tell it's like they're working hard, you know?

Interviewer: Well, that's a good segue to my next question for you. And it's about your sort of delivery technique. Your music is really lyrical. But as opposed to other rappers who get placed in that lyrical category, you seem to have more of a legato through line in your diction. Your words flow together, and they're way more—

Mavi: Slurred sometimes, even. Even to the point of a slur sometimes.
Interviewer: Yes! I mean, I assume that was on purpose?
Mavi: No, so sometimes when I'm being languid on songs like "Moonfire," like "Chiasma," you know, those really slow waltzy kind of songs. Where I like to use that, sometimes we call it my sleepy voice. So again, going back to the tonality thing. Depending on how loud I am when I'm writing a song. It might be an upper register song. It might be a spoken register song, or it might be a sleepy boy song. So your voice is like you rolled out of bed. Speaking voice is like how you sound in the middle of a high school day. Excited voice is like how you sound at the school, what's the shit called, the school assembly. So I was saying that to say the slurring comes, it comes two-fold. So sometimes it could come stylistically to engage the audience, and I'm a firm believer—and I was listening to a Nina Simone song in the car, right? I forget the fucking name of it. She was singing in French though. It's called *near*, I can't even pronounce it, *chi* or some shit like that, it basically mean like, "don't leave me," but I don't even know how to pronounce the words to the song, but based on the delivery, I can tell that it's a mournful and heartbroken and collapsing song. You know what I'm saying? So when it's prudent to the emotion of the song for the slur, the sleepiness, even the drunkenness, even the deliriousness that come through, I try to always put that front and center. But beyond that, sometimes it be a cultural artifact just from being from the South. And even as opposed to public speaking, right? The kind of enunciation required for rapping where, okay, your, what's them shits called? Your sibilants, right. And your end sounds? Not only do they have to be fucking accurate, like, let me see, let me give an example of a rap I said, um, damn. I'm gonna say this first thing then I'm gonna give an example, so like, not only do your sibilants have to be pronounced like "s" and your "t" have to be really audible against the backdrop of all the other words that you're saying. They also have to be timed perfectly. Sometimes on a drum and sometimes in the exact spot in between drums, you know what I'm saying? And so, adjusting the in and out of that enunciation while being a southern nigga who's speaking AAVE [African American Vernacular English]. Sometimes, it get

a little tricky because I can say I speak AAVE, but I be rapping with words that's not AAVE. It's not AAVE sometimes because I'm trying hard.

Interviewer: These might be some of the most fascinating answers I've gotten from an interview. I haven't thought about it like that. I love it because you're trying to try hard. In a lot of your songs, you seem to sort of change your pitch. Way up and down. But somehow it seems to match the instrumental backing. I'm wondering if you're doing that intentionally, or does your pitch just migrate or navigate to that?

Mavi: It used to be a migration, but now in an effort to make my studio time more productive I try to be super intentional about understanding. I even write it in the song lyrics now. Like, okay, this needs to be a low tempered, you need to be damn near shouting. I write that, just in case it's a long time before I come across the piece of writing again, and I don't know how to deliver it, you know?

So that's musically based and that really correlates beyond going to the content level that we talked about before. Like where it's these long bars, and I usually to do long bars in between the key changes. So the word that the key change is on is emphasized and emphatic within the lyrical context of the song. But the reason I do those is for musicality sake, like sometimes—I came from playing instruments, so sometimes I'll be feeling inferior because of the fact that I'm a rapper, even as opposed to a singer or a spoken word artist, and so the space for my voice to be a dynamic instrument, it's something that I have to reimagine and push the envelope on to myself even as I continue to grow, you know?

Interviewer: Yeah, wow. I'm just so interested that you feel inferior. I mean, you are the reason why people are turning the music on, you know what I mean?

Mavi: But it's just like, as opposed to—you can listen to me or you can listen to Motown, you know, so at some point, I gotta have my musicality somewhere, you know.

Interviewer: Yes. I get that. And I also love the answer. So I have one last question. It's about how you fell into your specific avenue of rap. I don't want to say branded, like you're stuck there. But you're really associated with Earl Sweatshirt and Mike. Was that your goal all along, or did something happen along the way?

Mavi: I guess the coolest question you asked was, was that your goal all along? Because I feel like nobody asked me shit like that. Like, do you want this, do you accept this? Do you acknowledge this? But no. I do love, let me say—because it was one thing in that lane that they tried to put us with early on, that did a sexual assault. I don't associate with that. My tip a lot of niggas, I really do appreciate them and my way of coming into knowing them. They actually reached out to me. So it was my first trip up to New York City. By myself in life. And Nova Blu DMed me, and they FaceTime me and invite me to a studio the next day in Brooklyn. I went there and I met Mike. We all made a song that night. We did a show the next day. And then you know, I started—every time I come to New York now I just be linked in. But oh, definitely not. I kind of never, as weird as it sounds—I lowkey never expected to be really . . . or at least not for a long while, you know, having made himself so—it kinda fucked up my brain a little bit. Because it wasn't—I didn't get to have the fan combination. Because just how organically I came into admiring him as a friend. Completely separate from my admiration for music. When I was a kid, you know what I'm saying? So when we came to being friends and when my music came to be a process that he's present for or things like this, right, the main thing that revolutionized our relationship was that he gave me advice on the theory of rapping, I went there, he told me go slow down, even though I disagree all the time. Are you telling me how rapping works, you know? But definitely not something I did on purpose, but it's not that I'm not super grateful for it because I'm fucking with them niggas and kind of before because I was rapping on them knowledge base and shit like that. Before I had ever met them. I was doing a lot of things that they were doing in a slightly different way. Before I had known them or their music, just because of where rap was growing in the post Grizelda era and all of that shit, right, so they were able to expand my horizon as far as what fits within that lane. Count is beautiful, like how far experimental you could take it, how far you can take it.

Interviewer: Wow, that's great. Thank you.

Mavi: But oh, can I say one more thing though? That's kind of off topic? Hip-hop is so important because hip-hop was invented by DJs. Yes. And it was one of the first jobs to be invented alongside bedroom pop and honestly, right, UK garage. So hip-hop speaks to the fucking—the eligibility, all music and especially music with a family. So then the Black music family, like the West African, the West music family. From jazz to funk, to blues, to fucking New York, true to Chicago true to Texas true to Detroit rap to soul to R&B, it's all co-intelligible.

Interviewer: You are so right, that's what I'm going to Alabama to talk about for a few days as that's my whole life, is basically how Black music is pop rock styles and they're all connecting, showing people how to connect the dots between that and showing people how things call back to gospel, and also the history of the African American and why this music sounds like this, so that's what I'm flying out to do. So I really feel you.

Mavi: Thank you.

Interviewer: Oh my gosh, you see the pleasure is mine. So I thank you so much.

AC Tatum

Interviewer: The first question I'd love to ask is: a big part of this book is recognizing how pop music has been heavily influenced by hip-hop. So I'm curious, what do you think hip-hop's influence on pop music has been? And then to supplement that, when do you think that influence started to happen?

AC Tatum: So let me get this straight. You're asking pop's influence on hip-hop or vice versa?

Interviewer: Vice versa, although if you have thoughts on either I'd love to hear them.

AC Tatum: So hip-hop's influence on . . . yes. Okay. So from what I understand, this dates back to—you saw flashes of it in the late 1990s kind of when it wasn't quite pop yet, but you started to see the emergence of rappers doing collaborations with R&B stars. So, you know, you had your Method Man and Mary J. Blige, but those were largely considered either rap or R&B records, but the pop really started to take off in the early 2000s. I remember platforms like *106 & Park* and things like that started to catalyze because what happened is—for the longest time the pop executives over at the major labels, they didn't want to touch rap or gangster rap or anything like that, because they wanted to keep their pop artists, you know, pristine and all that. But when they started to see that rap was becoming the predominant genre, you started looking at *106 & Park*, started looking at all these stars. That's when you started to see a lot of collaborations. So you started to see Britney Spears reaching out to rappers and you started to see the Fergies of the world, things like that, Christina Aguilera doing pop/rap records. So from my perspective, it was like pop had got to a point where it was—we tried to keep rap as our kind of little brother, kind of keep rap under, but now that rap is starting to become hip-hop or whatever you call it—it has become the predominant culture. We have to almost go against what we've been doing for so long. So I think that was the inflection point for me. In terms of the influence, I mean, you can see it as like, you turn on the radio, and, you know, pop content is hip-hop content, and almost vice versa now too—pop influenced rap to the point where it's almost blending together now. So that's how I see it.

Interviewer: Okay, blending together. Can you maybe give an example you might be able to think of this kind of blending of styles?

AC Tatum: I think Post Malone is a perfect example. You know, he's hip-hop. He has hip-hop content, but he's kind of transcended that into being a pop star. Or like, Doja Cat is 100 percent a pop star but she's definitely—if you listen to her rap I mean, her cadence or voice control—all that is up there with any of the top rappers in the game. So you got pop stars who are hip-hop, and you got hip-hop stars who are more pop now. Drake is really the definition I think—I think Drake is probably the pinnacle of, you know, the marriage between pop and rap. Because he can do "Hold On, We're Going Home," then he can also do the tougher rap records, and then he can do records that are a blend of both to the point where he'll be rapping for four bars and then he'll break into traditional pop melody and then go back into a rap, so I think he's almost mastered it. That style.

Interviewer: Okay, wow. Thank you, so awesome. Yeah, I think we had definitely seen Drake's versatility seeing the difference of albums like *If You're Reading This It's Too Late* versus *Take Care* or something like that. So then, another area that's in line with hip-hop's influence—I'm curious what you think hip-hop's influence on social justice and especially the recent social justice movement has been, as well as hip-hop's longer history with social justice too.

AC Tatum: So my kind of introduction to rap was in the early 1990s, mid-1990s, but when I discovered rap music it was big to go back and do the research on artists that came before, right. So I was going back even to KRS-One or Public Enemy, or other rappers in that same lane who came before me—I went back and listened to them because I started to figure out, okay, in order to understand what rap is now, I'll kind of want to understand the evolution of it. So in going back—also N.W.A., you know—I just started listening to these records that were much more centered on social justice, much more centered on how do we as a people, you know, fight back against an unjust system. Or how do we understand even the more gangster rap records were more of an introspective look at what's going on in the neighborhood, as opposed to showing you how tough or how gangster I am, it was more a journal of what was going on. And then when you started seeing the real big money start to come into rap music, you know, around the late 1990s, early 2000s, the content really shifted, man. And this is a theme of rap music—there are millions of rap artists, so we can't count out the conscious rap artists of today because you have a bunch of them. There's Noname. There's, you know, Tech N9ne, there's—I think even to a certain extent, J. Cole and Kendrick have a lot of concerts. But what you see is the big money makers are the ones that get pushed to the forefront. So the content is very surface level—it just disregards social justice altogether. So I think what happened is you had the late 1980s, early 1990s, where social justice was a focal point of rap music, or at least a very controlling part of it. You had a lot more conscious rappers. We had conscious labels like Raucous Records, you had people that were specifically pushing conscious rap music. And then that kind of got weeded out in the big money era of music. And if you asked me, I think that in the mainstream there are very few who have the big machine behind them to be heard. Because that's the thing—there's millions of rappers. I rap. I feel like I'm better than a lot of people that are out, but I don't have a major label. I don't have money, you know? So we can point out a lot of constants, rappers, but in reality, they really don't have any influence on the game. Right? So we have to look at Kendrick and we have to look at J. Cole and man, Common whenever he puts out stuff, or I think NAS still has a very conscious level aspect to his music. But if you just look at what's dominating—if you look at the big money earners—the content is very shallow, very devoid of any social message. So I think that compared to the late 1980s, early 1990s, we probably have 20 percent of the mainstream rappers who are conscious or even seeking from a social justice perspective. So yeah, that's kind of unfortunate, but I do think on the flip side, the people who are doing it are doing it well and doing it in a way that can kind of be consumed by the masses. Because if you look at the kind of rap or what people think is social justice music or conscious music—there's a trope behind it, that it's not for the masses, you know, and I think Kendrick and J. Cole have kind of transcended that. They found a way to make that type of music palatable to everyone. And that's really—to me it's a feat, because it's hard to do. It's hard to do because people don't want to party to social justice music. That's the problem. So you have to kind of figure out a way to even market it to get people to listen to it. So yeah, it's tough, man. It's very tough.

Interviewer: Okay, cool. Now I'm curious, what do you think has made J. Cole and Kendrick able to make social justice music appealing to so many people? I mean, we're looking at Kendrick right now. You know, all eyes in the hip-hop world are on him. What do you think? Is there anything you can think of that has made them able to be popular while having this message?

AC Tatum: Yeah, I think they were able to establish themselves outside of the conscious music realm, so if you go look at their biggest records, you know, a lot of them are more upbeat, more clubby records, like Kendrick's "HUMBLE." or "Poetic Justice" is more of a club record or whatever. So if you can get in that space where you have smash records then that kind of frees you up to be able to promote and just basically do what you want, because then you can't be really told you don't know what you're doing or this isn't gonna work. So now you have the leverage, because you got to think like these people—even though Kendrick and J. Cole and them, they have a lot of creative control, they're still going in terms of approval, like if we're gonna spend thirty thousand or a million dollars on this marketing budget, then let's pick the right record. You know, traditional artists coming in the game. A label is not going to put a big budget behind the record. Because they're just not going to see the ROI—their return on investment is not going to be obvious, because it's just not—the demographics aren't there for it. And so you kind of have to build the leverage. And also, I think Kendrick is smart enough to know, okay, this record might be a loss, that I might put out this record and it might not make the money, but it's going to stamp me among the people that are culture makers or, you know, this record is going to give me critical acclaim. So while it might not bring me a lot of money, this was going to put me in a different space artistically. So people are gonna look at me differently like people look at Kendrick like a Marvin Gaye or transcendent artists, not just a surface-level rapper. So he's an artist and I was like, damn. Then I was like, everybody's waiting on that because we haven't heard anything from him. And we also know he's gonna give us something that has substance to it. So people are listening to Kendrick's music with a different ear. Whereas if a new artist was to put that out, they're not going to get the same ear because people, the mainstream music consumer, is not trained to hear conscious music. That's the thing. And so Kendrick is actually doing a lot for conscious artists because he's almost keeping the lane open for them because the more that that music kind of filters into the public, then it becomes more accepted. But the less of that music exists, the more and more it gets pushed out and not heard, so it's really tough. So I actually give him a lot of credit for doing what he's doing. And the crazy part is he's probably going to sell the most records out of anybody this year.

Interviewer: Yeah, no, I think so too. I think it's gonna be really interesting. The numbers he's about to put up.

AC Tatum: It's gonna be crazy. Yes, I think people resonate with authentic music, but people are scared to do that type of music because it just doesn't sell. Kendrick can sell with it, but there's kind of a unwritten thing that, okay, are you really gonna jump out there and do that, but I think from an independent perspective if you're an independent artist, I think that's all you should be doing, is doing conceptual records and stuff that kind of at least is some type of artistic work, because that's how you're going to cut through. I think just copying and pasting the popular sound, it's just pointless at this point, because it's so oversaturated—there's so much of it. It's just pointless. But yeah, I think what allows Kendrick and J. Cole to do that stuff is just having massive success off of other records and then being comfortable enough to say, you know, if I never sold another record again, that doesn't matter. I'm more concerned with putting out something that I can stand on. I think if you add Jay-Z, his *4:44* album was so much more mature than anything else you'd ever put out. But you get to a point where the money means less, and then your legacy starts to mean more. So it's like, okay, I need to put together something that I can stand on and be happy with thirty, forty years from now, not just music that I didn't even want to perform. I might be embarrassed by it, but I know it's gonna give me some money—these guys are tens, hundreds of millionaires. Jay-Z's a billionaire. You get to a space where it's like, alright, I don't have to rap for money anymore. I'm not rapping for survival. I'm rapping to convey that message. And I think that's when you see a change as artists.

Interviewer: Okay, that's really interesting. So you basically said that a lot of artists have to wait until they have a platform before they can start to do things that are more adventurous, which embarking in trying to make a record they can stand on advocating for social justice can be a part of. Do you think—

AC Tatum: Well, let me amend that because I don't think you have to do that. I think that they have artists that will have a variety of records, and I think that it's just easier to put a budget behind something if you've already had success, because it's just harder to break through with conscious records.

Interviewer: That makes sense. So I have a question, though. Where do you think the social justice movement in hip-hop is being driven by? Do you think it is being driven by people that are more underground making these records because there are some people like that, or do you think it is being driven by people at the top like Jay-Z or Common or somebody who has this platform and then they inspire more underground people to do that? Where do you think the cause is? I'm curious what you might think.

AC Tatum: It's always been underground since the beginning. And it filters up. So the message will filter up, and then the artist will filter up—so you'll see certain conscious artists will catch a hit record and then that will propel them, then you'll go back and look at their content. And they've always been doing some level of conscious music, but it's like, oh, this record that blew up, nine times out of ten that record that blows up isn't their traditional conscious music. I remember I was a fan of Dead Prez back in the day and Dead Prez was the ultimate conscious—like, they even go into conspiracy. Some of the stuff I might not agree with, but I just find it to be interesting music, but they had the song "It's Bigger Than Hip-Hop" and that was a smash for them. And then once that smashed everybody was like, oh, let me go get the album, let's see what they're about. So I think sometimes they just need to cut through with a big record. And then I do think there's a decision to make, because it's like, do I stay kind of underground? Or do I follow up on these smash records and just try to do more singles . . . so you'll see artists go, and then they'll transcend conscious music and do more mainstream stuff, or you see people just stick to what they do. And they might not have the mega success, but they're very proud of the work they do and they make a good living, a lot of these people have cult followings. So you'll see like—I'm not a huge fan of Tech N9ne, but Tech N9ne will go on tour. And he's an independent artist, never been signed to a major, but he has a cult following and his stuff is very deep introspective music. I don't know. I don't know if he's classified as a conscious rapper. I know he has conscious songs but he's just more of just a real guy, and so I think there's a route to do it. But it's just way more difficult. So you see a lot of people just trying to swing for the fences with hit records and stuff like that.

Interviewer: That's some very interesting thoughts, man. Thank you so much. This is kind of unrelated, but I was looking at your Twitter and it seems like you have other connections in the world of hip-hop, right? I'm just curious, can you tell me what they are? I would love to know—I'm just very fascinated because I think you're saying some incredibly important things here now.

AC Tatum: Yeah. So I grew up in LA [Los Angeles]. I signed a deal. I was at a high school, going to college. I never signed a record deal. It was an independent record deal. But I was in a group, we did a bunch of music and then we—it wasn't big or anything, right. So we were just trying to get it on the radio. We had a couple of songs on the radio and then back then I just made connections. I started writing for people. I got a call from Will Smith's people to come in and help write for him on a couple of things, and then that kind of propelled into other relationships with other artists and stuff like that. So I got to work with Too Short and Ty Dolla $ign, I have some stuff with him. Back in the day, even before he blew up, I was working with him. My first mixtape was produced by Ty and Hit-Boy. Years later they go on to be mega producers. So what happened is the group I was in, long story short, the people that signed us, they were just these rich guys that we were just like, oh, they're gonna pay for our music, whatever. And they turned out to be super shady individuals. And we basically had to leave the label, start all over. So I started off as a solo artist, and then life kind of happens, I'm like, oh shit, I gotta figure things out. So I went back to school. And I was always interested in contracts, right? Because my first contract was super fucked up. I gave away a lot of my publishing. I didn't know any better. So when I went back to school, I was like, man, let me figure out—because I want to do something in music still, and I just took a break from creating it. Let me figure out the legal side in case I want to work with a label or if I want to represent people. So I went to undergrad out here in Santa Barbara and then went to law school at Notre Dame. Once I graduated from Notre Dame, I practiced law in New York for a little bit, moved to Chicago, and then moved back to LA and then when I got back to LA a couple years ago, man, like you said, I had connections from back in the day and producers and engineers were hitting me up like man, you need to get back in the studio. But I was just so jaded with the music industry that I had to take a long break from it, but when I came back, I had everything there. So I was able to use a lot of those connections that I established back in the day to kind of get going again, whether I needed to produce it adding beats or if I needed studio time, I can just hit up somebody if I needed to get it mixed and mastered. I could send it out to somebody. Basically, my first project I put together was all favors—I had no budget whatsoever. I just used all favors. And the interesting part is these were favors that were returned to me because when I was in law school, and after I graduated people would call me for like, hey, could you just take a look at this contract, or hey, I'm about to do this deal. I just want to make sure I'm straight. I would just look out for people. So when I came back out here it was like nothing to get back started again. But yeah, that's kind of my story, man. And then Snoop did an intro to one of my records. And that's kind of how I started. Got back going again to now and I plan to put out an album or two every year, but then I'm also doing writing and doing a bunch of stuff in the culture to prepare myself after, because I feel like I'm not going to be doing this for too much longer. You know what I mean? So, but yeah, and then it helps. It definitely helps to have some friends in the industry for sure.

Interviewer: Wow, thank you for giving me that background. You're the perfect person that can answer this next question—what do you think is next for hip-hop? You know so much kind of about what the field looks like. How do you see it continuing to evolve?

AC Tatum: Yeah, this is something I think about a lot. I think that a lot of the power that was controlled by the top is now being a lot more decentralized. So not only do you see people foregoing deals, just going independent, but then you also just know you have people that know more about their rights. You have people that know, okay, I shouldn't just give all this away. And now you also have platforms that a lot of artists didn't have back in the day. So for one you have social media, so you have TikTok, Instagram, even Twitter or something that you have a way to distribute. You have a way to establish your own audience. And then you have real distribution. So you can basically pay a very small fee and get all your music distributed everywhere, but back in the day, you would literally have to have industry relationships. Because there's no way to get in Walmart or

Target or get your actual CD on the shelf. Right? Unless you have those connections. But now the game has completely changed. You can build a community online. You can get hot, you can start dropping records, and you can kind of build your own self up to the point where you don't need the big labels to come. I think if you're trying to be a superstar, you always need the big machines behind you—you at least need a partnership or a Spotify or something like that, because there's no way to reach millions and millions of people consistently without huge budgets. Or relationships. But I think music—or rap music, specifically—I think it's going to get better in terms of content because money is starting to come. It's starting to come back into the game. There was a lot—there was a time between, I would say, the 2010s to 2020, even the late 2000s, when the money was drying up out of the space because people were just streaming music illegally or just finding a way to get it. But now the game is changing so a lot of money is coming back in. And it's not just top heavy. It's just not at the major labels. You see regular everyday artists being able to make a living. So I think with that said, it's going to make the content better because you don't have to necessarily fit into a mold to have some success in the music industry. And that's going to free people up artistically, especially if they see more people start to make it or have better content and be like, yo, this person is able to make a couple hundred thousand or a million dollars. And they have their own business going. I think more people are starting to look at it as a business and that can be good and bad. But I think artists like myself, we're kind of figuring out how to make it happen without the big machine, which is tough, man, but I think that's gonna help the game out. And I don't know, I'm interested to see where it heads, man, because I think people are growing tired of—because music is cyclical, we have our party phases and then we have our more introspective times. I think we're moving out of the show-off-how-much-money-you-got, like XYZ, to okay, what are you talking about? I think more artists are going to be pushed to create music that's actually saying something. And I think that's a good thing for rap music. So I think that's where it's headed if you ask me.

TeaMarrr

Interviewer: I loved that you made a comment that you think that if Amy Winehouse and Biggie Smalls had a baby, it would be you. That's amazing. I'm wondering if you could talk a little bit about the components of your voice and sound that you feel parallel these artists. If it's your sound that you're talking about or if you're talking about your lyrics, or both?

TeaMarrr: Yes, definitely a combination of everything. Amy—I definitely feel like, "Rehab," "One Job," "Back to Black," there's a very raw, jazzy approach that I think she and I share. And with Biggie, it's definitely more of my unreleased stuff, but I like to rap a lot. And I think my flow pockets resemble the time capsule of the time when Biggie was here, and I try to play with my voice and make different tones and sounds—I can sound like a baby, sound like a woman, sound like a sixteen-year-old girl with certain flows and sometimes I do it intentionally . . . sometimes, it's all just flowing out of me and when I play it back, I'm like, oh, she shouldn't be there, and—but yeah, definitely a mix of everything.

Interviewer: In "One Job" and a lot of your songs, your voice is really—I don't know if it's okay to describe it like this—but sort of light in tone, it's bright, but it's sharp and daring in its expression. I'd love to hear about your conceptualization of your unique sound, as well as your technique for creating that sound. We were talking just a minute ago about sounding all different ages and everything. Do you think about the timbre of your tone? Or is it more just the lyrics sort of influence what comes out?

TeaMarrr: I definitely think the lyrics influence, and how I'm feeling comes out. I noticed that I can only sound like the record once the record is basically established—yeah, like "One Job" and "In My Mind," like . . . I know to automatically do those things, but when I am creating it, it is a zoo trying to figure out how to lay this down. And I'm losing track of your question because there's so many things going through my head as I answer the questions. But one of the tonality things I noticed is when I am going through a breakup, or going through some sort of event in my life, that's a big transition—mostly bad, you know, sad, mostly in that, but when I'm going through those things, and I take myself to the studio, the reference to freestyle is—usually there's a good 80 percent of that gets left into the comping before we start writing. Because there's something about my initial—I can't hold every feeling, it's like I gotta, I don't know, I just put all my emotions into the very first take. And as I, you know, as I warm up, I get, you know, better, and then after that, we have to stop it at two takes because I could flow for eleven minutes, and that's a lot to go through and figure out, and then you go through it for eleven minutes and there's like four different song contents on there—you don't know which one's stronger, which one to pick—because my mind is going at a mile a minute whether it's a ballad, a melody, a freestyle, a rap, when my brain waves are open and I'm just really ready to receive and give my music, I find out about my song after the fact. I have a freestyle called "Black is Blue" and when I play it back, I'm like, "Whoa, who the hell is that?" Because there's certain parts that just amaze you . . . and mind you, I just finished watching Billie Holiday's movie—that movie about her—*The United States vs. Billie Holiday*. And then the next day, I go to the studio and then all of a sudden I hear scat in the song that just sounds like—I'm like, "Whoa, that sounds really like her." And when I tried to recut it, I could not get that same tone, same nasal . . . I couldn't get it. I have two versions of me trying to me freestyling it and then me on a regular night after I've written it, lay it down. And some tones, it's like, you better get it while you can or it's gone forever.

AKTHESAVIOR

Interviewer: How do you balance the process of pairing a flow (or flows) with a beat without compromising the authenticity of his lyrics?

AKTHESAVIOR: Whenever I approach writing music before I choose the flow, I usually have an idea of what subject or concept the lyrics would be about, but sometimes I don't and I'm just going off vibes. In those times I try not to stress about the lyrics too much or try to be anything but myself and what the beat makes me feel and let things come out organically in a sense. Overall, when I do write music, staying true to myself comes natural because I'm usually just sharing personal experiences or my perspective on things.

Interviewer: Do you have any practice techniques to master your flow when recording a new song such as practicing on a neutral syllable, especially for those that are incredibly intricate such as "Philanthropist" or "The Redemption"?

AKTHESAVIOR: I do practice different techniques when writing . . . most recently for my song "The Remedy," I heard the beat first and recorded a melody that I wanted it to flow like and listened to it over and over and filled in that flow with words. This technique is one of my favorites because it keeps the initial vibe that I felt when I first heard the beat and also gives me direction for the entire track so I don't stress about flow switches or anything else.

Noah

Interviewer: So being inauthentic, boasting, people saying they represent things they don't actually. Do you think with the rise of social media and the internet, that has increased or changed in any way?

Noah: Oh, 100 percent increase. I talk to my friends about it. Sometimes I think social media in my mind as it pertains to rap, it killed the regional effect of rap. It's harder and harder and harder to know what a region sounds like, because everybody knows what's hot on social media. If Atlanta music is hot on social media, there's going to be a bunch of people trying to make something that sounds like that, and not to say that there wasn't always an element of that, if something blows up into the number one song in the country, maybe before social media, of course, you're gonna have copycats and stuff like that. But not everything that comes out of Atlanta or Detroit or Memphis or any other popping music scene right now is a number one record, but it's hot in the streets. So you got people from Jersey, New York, maybe not in New York, that—they have the whole drill scene or whatever. But you know, Jersey and other places that aren't as on the map sounding like Detroit rappers, sounding like Atlanta rappers and like this, that and the third. I think social media has taken away that regional element of hip-hop to an extent and kind of made it more of a melting pot of things that are just flows and ideas and beats and concepts and pockets and patterns that are all mixed, blended together. And you can see on any hip-hop=related tweet, you have Kendrick, I've seen you know nothing, but you know posts about Kendrick latest video, but what do you have right under that? It's a YoungBoy fan right under it saying YoungBoy clears or some shit like that. Social media is the place where those two entities can even exist in the same realm. There was a point in time where if you were just going outside and you found a Kendrick fan, you guys weren't going to be bombarded with NBA YoungBoy troll accounts or something like that. So I definitely think that in that happening, everybody also feels a lot more comfortable and entitled to other people's culture. Which isn't even always necessarily a bad thing, because culture is interesting, but you always just want to make sure that you're digesting and going about it in a respectful manner. And I think the thing though, social media is just—it's a free for all, we're doing what the fuck we want with whatever the fuck we want. They're just words. They're just accents. They're just songs, whatever, whatever, whatever. And we're all here to have fun. So you know, do what you will about it. I mean, social media and hip-hop in general, they're two places, they're two entities that I believe are just imperfect for each other. A lot of hip-hop culture is built off of street culture. And what's every street guy's favorite thing to say, you know, we don't do the internet. We don't blah, blah, blah, and this that and the third. But now, our livelihood is kind of directly impacted by social media. So I think of Freddie Gibbs and Akademiks beefing all the time. I'm like, bro, there's no way for Freddie Gibbs to win this back and forth. Because his thing at the end days is gonna be like, everybody's just me looking at him like oh, aren't you supposed to be the street dude, why are you arguing with his internet troll? And everybody that's Akademiks' fan, you know, his content and loves his content is just gonna be like, oh, you own Freddie Gibbs. Oh, my God, you either got him pissed, or you got it or you looked up something on Google that makes him look like not as much of a thug or, oh my God, his family's belief. How did you dig that up? Social media is uncovering the veil on, it's lifting the veil on things that should have—I don't want to say shouldn't, it's lifting the veil on things that traditionally before social media came about were done and moved on from. Now the way it's impacting everybody, you probably have a lot of rappers that are here today and breathing and alive and well if not for social media. Somebody in their entourage is posting their every location when they're in a city or something like that. And now the people that want to bring you harm know where you are, because they're looking at your homie's Instagram, and he posted that you guys were at the mall two hours ago. You're at the club tonight. You're going to be leaving the club at 4 AM, they know exactly where you are. I just think they're two entities that should have remained separate.

Interviewer: Wow, that's a lot to think about. But I definitely see what you're saying. I mean, the example I think of was Pop Smoke, you know?

Noah: Exactly. I think we all remember, and this isn't to blame anything on anybody because social media is the catalyst. So I don't like blaming things on people. I don't like blaming people for how the system turns them out. I'd rather look at the system and say, what about this system prompted this action? But I think we all remember seeing after Pop Smoke unfortunately passed away, people were posting that his homie had been posting his address and stuff, where he was gonna be, and then Pop Smoke dies during a home invasion. It's fucked up. And it's something that, if that kid didn't have an Instagram, I doubt he'd be just out here being like, yo, we're at 7737 Hidden Hills, pull up like that. That's not something that would have happened. But social media has effects on people. And us logging on Instagram and seeing everybody living the life that they want to portray to us. And wanting to be the cool person. You get to doing things that are out of your element and out of your character. And unfortunately, those things can result in things like Pop Smoke dying.

Interviewer: Yeah, I never thought of the idea of these two different entities not being meant for each other, because I think you could probably say that social media is a part of the reason that hip-hop has grown to the huge amount of popularity it has. But also with that, hip-hop has changed too. So that's definitely a lot to think about, then.

Noah: There's give and take to everything. It's grown hip-hop. It's also made it more accessible, like I don't think we can even quantify at this point what SoundCloud did for hip-hop, how many acts are—whether we're talking about Uzi or Carti or Uno, or any of those guys, X before he passed, Yachty, that was all SoundCloud era, that was all just anybody being able to have the freedom to make and release music. And I think there's a lot of beauty in that because music should be this thing that we can just do. There shouldn't be this elitist glass ceiling above anybody that just wants to rap about their story on a nice beat, that should be accessible to everybody. I always say everybody can rap. It's just a matter of if you want to make a career out of it. So it has helped in a huge way as far as growing its popularity like you said, and just the accessibility of it. But the thing about accessibility is it brings entitlement, and a lot of times people can't separate the music from the culture. So not to say that there isn't an issue with people feeling entitled to the music, but it's a even larger issue if you feel entitled to the culture as a whole. And that's kind of one of the dark sides of what social media merging with rap music has brought about and just street culture in general.

Interviewer: Okay, wow, man. What you're hitting on right now is exactly why I want to write this book, because I felt like a lot of people were discrediting hip-hop's roots, and people need to know where these things come from.

Noah: Ah, everybody does. Nobody, you know. It's another thing about social media. It's moving so fast. Nobody cares about history. People don't care about what happened a month ago in hip-hop because the news cycle, it's not twenty-four hours anymore. It's minute by minute. You scroll and you see some new outrageous thing whether it's true or not, and it just keeps going all day.

Joseph Chilliams

Joseph Chilliams: What brought me to hip-hop really was mainly Eminem and OutKast at the time. They both were so different from everything else. As a kid there was a lot of rap that I really couldn't, like—it really didn't do anything for me, it didn't register. He talked about love and dealing drugs or hardships you're going through. I didn't understand at the time, however old I am, I'm a kid. But Eminem felt like watching a movie, or a TV show or something. All my friends would come over and just listen. And we'd be like, "What in the world? What is this?" You know, it's like an episode of South Park or, you know, a crazy movie. And OutKast was so otherworldly. Like "B.O.B. (Bombs Over Baghdad)," "Rosa Parks," all of it was just—I'd never heard anything like this. They stood out so much, and they sounded so over the top in a great way. You know, they got choirs. They got spaceships. They talk about Rosa Parks, I know who Rosa Parks is at the time. So a lot more of it could actually register and I could relate to at my life at the time. So I would say those two artists. It gave me a space where I was like, "Oh, cool. This is cool that you could do this," you know?

Interviewer: Okay, I have a question about your actual technique when you think about rapping. I don't know how much you think about it—does it all just come naturally to you? Or do you think about, for instance, what goes into choosing the tone quality of your voice in each cadence? Do you consciously decide to change it depending on the pitch and volume, depending on what you're talking about, or does that just naturally happen?

Joseph Chilliams: Yeah, that's a really cool question. Something that I'm always like, huh? Because a lot of people, well not a lot of people, but sometimes people comment on my voice like, "Hey, you have a great voice," or like, "I really liked what you did here." And I'm like, "Really? Really?" I don't even—because I'm still trying to master my voice. I feel like there's so much that I don't know yet. There's a lot of music that I'm working on where I'm really experimental in my voice, but not a lot of that is out, so it's really cool with what does exist people can get something from my vocal performance. But pretty much it's the same thing. It's just what sounds good. There's no real right or wrong way to do stuff. There's stuff that sounds bad, but that's subjective. So, I guess, like, "Colbert"—there's a song called "Colbert" that we have. And it was just playing on a loop and I was just like, we've been in the studio for a while. So the longer I'm in the studio, the more comfortable I feel with my voice and with the whole recording process, I don't feel rusty. And it's this one line. I'm like, you know, "Let me check that flight at O'Hare. Know you feel the same cause we both got a great mind." And I'm like, if I wasn't in the studio for hella hours, hella long, I wouldn't have felt comfortable really projecting on some sing-song types. When I'm able to put the hours in I really feel comfortable experimenting, and then that's what gives me those moments where it's like, "Oh, damn, he's doing something cool with his voice," you know? Yeah. You know when singers are like, "Oh, damn, I didn't warm up my voice yet," and it's gonna sound like—recording often gets you in the habit of this—is where you, this is where you need your voice to sit. My voice is deep, but it's also kind of a nasally thing going on. So it cuts through in a certain way. You know, and it's really good for sitting on top of the beats a lot of times, like how Q-Tip, or you know just high pitch weird-sounding voice dudes. But like—

Interviewer: I want to turn my screen around because I have a framed *Midnight Marauders* record—like, I'm looking at it.

Joseph Chilliams: Yeah, yeah. I just try to do what would actually sound good with my voice and try to just emulate some things I've heard in the past. Some things I thought were cool that someone did and hope for the best.

Anonymuz

Interviewer: So in your opinion, what has been the influence of Japanese pop culture elements on hip-hop in recent years?

Anonymuz: What's the influence? I mean, I think a lot of kids in the 1990s grew up watching Toonami, watching a lot of cool animes like *DBZ*, and I feel like it's been transferred, you know—*Naruto* got really popular, now *Demon Slayer* is really popular, and *My Hero* is very popular—I just think people realized anime is cool, it's the same thing as cartoons. I think anime is just a little bit more adult, you know what I'm saying, is the answer—and certain themes and things it deals with. And I think that on top of that the art style just really captured a whole bunch of kids, and when you grow up and you fuck with shit like that you're gonna talk about it, you know what I'm saying, like that's what you're supposed to do in this rap shit, you're supposed to talk about your life and what you're going through.

Interviewer: Awesome, thank you so much. I also just wanted to shout out your Pokémon cypher from 2019. I'm a huge fan of that verse.

Anonymuz: Oh, shit, thank you. Shout out to Shofu.

Interviewer: Your flow is really something, and you make really interesting cadence choices. And what I'm really impressed with is your breath control, like your speed rapping, you've got tons of consonants flowing. And you really do go forever before you take a breath. I mean, it's really impressive, I've even tried to do it and can't do it. And so I'm wondering if you ever think about it—like have you thought about breath control or breathing work, or just naturally? And if so, what do you think about or what have you done to work on it?

Anonymuz: Ironically, I just started doing breathing techniques recently—I mean really recently, like the past month or so. But really, the best way to describe it is like—so for me, I don't think it's really about the breathing in between the verses. It's kind of how you—I don't want to say enunciate, but it's more so about how it's performed. So I'll give you an example, like in "Hiei" or "Gundam Wing," there's a portion where I really don't breathe for thirty seconds. Instead of when I'm talking to you guys right now, I'm using a lot of breath. I'm using a lot of air to talk to you guys, but if I were to talk to you like I was rapping, then—right now I'm already out of breath, but I'm still talking to you guys. So it's one of those things where I just kind of project from my diaphragm instead of actually projecting from my lungs, which is something that I feel like a lot of people don't really talk about. Because when you—it's really weird. I don't know how—it's hard to describe it. But when you talk using your lungs, you just use a lot of air, and when you talk using your diaphragm I just feel like you just use less of it—your diaphragm, and crazy enough, might be my stomach too. But yeah, I just got it basically holding my breath while still being able to talk. I think what contributed to it is martial arts, really. I would exercise when I was younger and then when I got into martial arts, that's a real big thing—core strength. Especially because that's where most of your—I mean, striking all comes from the core, you know, punch, kicks, all that sort of stuff. So I guess that just helped me get a stronger core and made it easier for me to rap. Because I definitely feel like when I'm working out, I mean on top of obviously just having better cardio and things like that, just having a stronger core makes it easier to do these long phrases. You know, stretches of a verse where I'm not breathing.

redveil

Interviewer: From my perspective, one of the most interesting things about your sound is the timbre of your voice—have you ever heard that before? Or is that, am I coming from outer space?

redveil: No, I have heard that before definitely, about enjoying the sound of my voice, which I think is interesting. I think it's interesting because I feel like my voice hasn't fully matured yet cuz I'm still eighteen and when I put out the first stuff that people will like, I was sixteen and I was fifteen working on it, it was really interesting.

Interviewer: Well, and that was my question—I was gonna say given how young you are, and how young you started—and maybe you haven't noticed as much because it's you, but in what ways has your voice and your tone changed from when you first started rapping to now?

redveil: It's completely changed. I definitely noticed that—it's completely changed. When I first started recording music just for fun, I was a baby, right? And then I hit about fifteen and my voice got to where it is now, and it hasn't really changed, and it really changed significantly since then. But from it hitting this level and this pitch, I've learned how to use it in more impactful ways since then. Yeah, I think it's definitely impacted a lot. It's definitely been cool to listen to old stuff and hear the development.

Interviewer: How has that led to changes in your vocal technique, or things you do differently? Like, can you give me an example of something that you've changed as you've gotten older? I think that's so cool.

redveil: I actually really have wanted to embrace the youth of my voice because I think it's something that I have. I think it's something that I have and the space that I occupy in hip-hop is pretty unique. You know, having that youthful sound in my voice . . . and I try to embrace it more and hit higher registers and have more energetic deliveries and stuff. And it had to really feel like it's coming from a young, probably eighteen-year-old—whereas before, when I was a little younger, like fifteen or sixteen, I was trying to sound as old as I possibly could. And so, I think as a result of that, I made more impact in the music game.

Interviewer: Cool. So you end by trying to sound older, so then—does that mean trying to get deeper and lower? Because I heard you say when you are in your registers.

redveil: Yes.

Interviewer: That's great. That's what I was wondering if you'd say so. I'm glad I guessed right. That's cool. I was listening to "Fastlane," and something that stood out to me is that low-key and calm vibe in the whole sound, and it's so successful in making the listener feel that way. So how do you maintain your articulation and flow while keeping such a chill vibe?

redveil: I found out that's how I talk normally anyways, so I think it's authentic. It's authentic when I'm doing that and it doesn't take a whole lot of . . . I don't really have to manipulate how I'm talking at all. Like, how I deliver something on a song, "Fastlane" . . . [it's] like how I would tell you if you were in front of me type thing. So, I think because of that, me normally having a lower register and how I speak and stuff and just a more chill way in how I speak. I kind of feel like, it's like how regularly, if were literally having a conversation. So it felt natural, that's why it's so calm.

Interviewer: Awesome. Thank you. So I've read interviews where you discuss learning to work on being more open about demons and struggles and basically being yourself, right? So, what advice would you give to a young rapper that's trying to find their authentic voice in this world?

redveil: I would say whatever you make that feels the best to write, that feels the best record, that feels the easiest to record . . . because I think one thing that people when trying too hard are less authentic, or they're trying to really be versatile as they can and stuff, is that I think sometimes we reach different sounds, stuff that's really not as authentic as other sounds are. Because I think the stuff that's really the most what you are, is going to come very easily—it's going to come very naturally, very fluidly. Recording it, writing it—it's just about the words, and rap is like that because most is more like this.

femdot.

Interviewer: What are the biggest ways you've seen hip-hop influence pop culture today?

femdot.: I think the biggest ways I've seen hip-hop influence pop culture... if you look at sports, if you look at fashion, if you look at really any element of entertainment even outside of music, it's just hip-hop has leaked in. A lot of what—every, you know, basketball player wants to be a rapper, every rapper wants to be a basketball player, or you look at even certain stories that weren't told in film for a long time, like movies like *Juice*, you start looking at movies like *The Woods*, things that are sort of like as Black people are starting to hold space in different mediums. It's very interesting to watch how hip-hop itself then finds a way into those spaces because it ends up being the soundtrack for the life that they live so when they want to showcase that it shows up, like film, any type of media, and even just any casual conversation—there are so many phrases now and things of that sort that weren't considered normal that are very normal now. That all stems from rappers or just the cultures that hip-hop talks about.

Interviewer: So when you're rapping, either during performances or when you're recording, do you think about breathing at all? And if so, how do you think about it?

femdot.: Absolutely, I think about breathing a lot, actually. When recording I think starting out a lot of times you like to breathe from your mouth and things of that sort and you start hearing it, you hear these deep breaths on records, and then when you want to change flows, or you want to find a new pocket or—it's not much different from singing where you have to start using different muscles to get different tones and different voices, but it all comes back to breathing. So I've learned to breathe through my nose so it doesn't show up as much on the record so it's a cleaner take. Or if I know I'm about to do a very long-winded verse or long-winded part of a verse, I may take a deeper breath right before I go to try to exhale as many words as possible. On stage—even working out, I try to—when I'm doing cardio, I try to rap while I'm doing cardio just to make sure when I'm on stage I can move back and forth and still have a similar tone to what I have on the song on stage because my lung capacity is there. If you look at rappers like Kendrick, like Twista, even if you look at people that don't necessarily rap as fast or even older rappers like Rakim or look at a lot of these types. Or a lot of these different [rappers] where their flow is very distinct, their breathing patterns are very distinct too because it has to be in order to find a pocket that previously didn't exist. So breathing is something I think about actually too much at this point, but it's a real thing.

Interviewer: How do you approach the faster verses in your flow, like the speed rap that you were just referencing? Do you do anything different? Do you think about your mouth at all? Do you just do it because it's all on the breath? Or do you also have to think about other things like how you say something differently because it's a speed rap?

femdot.: Yeah I think the thing is when you're rapping faster, obviously there's less room for words. So, I think if you're taking account of what you're talking about, each word becomes more important to me. Not necessarily … in two different ways. Because when it's a slower rap, each of the words is more important because you can hear everything clearer, but when you're rapping a bit faster, at least in my head, each word is important, but because of placement, because one line will set up another line, and it only sounds good in this flow, or now you have to really think about inflections to keep it moving, and a lot of times when somebody is rapping fast it's probably in a specific part of the beat whether that's the hi-hat or the kick or something like that, they are rapping to try and fit everything within a certain pocket and the pocket is following one element of an instrument or in the song. So you're trying to squeeze as much as you can in, so if you need to drag a syllable or if you need to put a lot of emphasis on a certain word where you have to do that, and a lot of times that requires you to play with your voice a little bit. So you may make a little ugly face when you rapping. Or you may try to reach down in your diaphragm or something like that. Or if you want it to be more conversational, then you may have to really focus on how you talk regularly and see how fast you talk regularly. So there are definitely a lot of technical elements, I think, that people don't really think about that go into trying to do a lot of these cleaner faster verses. People don't realize how difficult they are until they try to rap them and go like, "Wow, this is actually crazy."

Black Prez

Interviewer: What are your go-to techniques that you use to create your upbeat and highly motivational sound? Not lyrics—do you think about pitch, do you think about tone quality? Do you think about resonance or placement or any of those things? Or diction? Is it just really a result of your mindset? Or do you think about things like that?

Black Prez: No, I'm very conscious. I'm very, very conscious about that. I know when I first started rapping, and I think it was because I was a kid. I was like thirteen or something. And I was under this false . . . I thought that alright, Imma rapper. I gotta sound tough, you know, so I would rap into this kind of fake . . . I was of course thirteen. So I obviously didn't have a man voice. I had a kid voice. So I would try to put on almost a fake deeper voice but I was like, I don't know, that's my rap voice, that's fine. Then that kind of progressed into this more nasally high-pitch thing that I started doing. I don't know why but it just kind of was my thing. And then, this guy I was working with, he was like, "Bro, you should do a song with a super smooth sexy D voice." And I did this song with his dude. And it was like, oh, this actually sounds dope. I like this. So then I started experimenting with that. And then obviously as the years go on, I've experimented and tried different things. And also still today depending on the type of song I'll use a different voice if that makes sense. Okay, cool. I'm gonna do the deep deep chill flow or deep chill voice for this one. Or, oh, no—I want to go a little more higher on this one. Or this one is kind of just more like my speaking voice, like "Riding the Wave" is a song I have, and that one I'm rapping like how I talk. It's just my normal talking voice basically. But then I have other songs like "Ha Ha Hey Hey" where it's a little more higher, just more energy, you know? But I have . . . and it's funny too, because I didn't know this about myself until a couple of years ago. Because people were making fun of me, my friends were making fun of me. Like my friend. She's like, "Oh, I'm gonna talk like Josh." And it was going up and down. And I was like, "What do you mean?" She's like, "Oh, like when you speak. You're all over the place, you'll be low then you'll be high." And I didn't know that because I don't hear my voice. But I guess it is how I talk naturally, I go high and low and whatever. But also, what I think is very important, what I also tried to do, I really tried to enunciate when I'm rapping, and one thing that I do when I'm in the booth recording—I over-exaggerate, like I consciously open my mouth more than I would when I'm speaking basically. So if I said in a rap, I don't know, if I said like, "Alright, here we go, I'm going with the flow. Here we go. I'm going with the flow," but when I record it, I would move my mouth like [*changes enunciation and mouth shape*] "I'm going with the flow" because I just feel like it sounds cleaner and clearer, crisper. And it's just easier for people to understand. I don't want to be too mumbly I guess. Obviously, it depends on the song too, because there's some times, okay, now this gonna be a little more mumbly or a little more "cursivey" or whatever. But yeah, it just kind of depends on the song.

Ausar

Interviewer: For sure. Are there any big changes you have to make when you're performing as opposed to recording in a booth?

Ausar: For sure. I mean, I'm still learning this myself. It's like there's a different energy from when you go out and perform that you don't usually have in the booth. I think also when you're given a performance that breathing and that breath control you had in the studio is going to be a lot different because on stage you're jumping around interacting with the crowd, like it requires you to be in great physical condition in order to bring those tracks to life the way that you want them to on stage versus what you do in the studio. I think that's the biggest difference. Also on stage it's fun to experiment and really just see how delivering the track differently can give people a different experience live, you know what I'm saying, because the goal is to just get the crowd involved and give them a new experience watching it live. So sometimes you do deviate from what you may hear on the track and just try different things.

Kinga World

Interviewer: Thanks for sharing your thoughts on that. Another question—when either recording or performing, are there any techniques you have with the microphone to achieve the sound that you're looking for?

Kinga World: Whenever I record or have done more performances, I just make sure that my mouth is as close to that microphone as possible. And that's one of the most important parts of your performance, though if you don't have a good performance, like vocal performance, even in the studio booth, it's not gonna sound right for the final product, so you just want to make sure, at least for me. I'm giving my all and speaking from my diaphragm and then just speaking close to the mic, even if I'm just either rapping or just singing words.

Interviewer: Alright cool. My last question kind of relates to hip-hop and the wider scope of things—when you look at hip-hop as a genre, as still continuing to grow and develop, is there anything that you think is next for hip-hop?

Kinga World: I feel like there's a rise of different—I don't even know how to describe it, just different subgenres of rap. Obviously, we have mainstream influences, like Young Thug or maybe Playboi Carti, and there are rising artists trying to kind of emulate them, but I feel like there's also a resurgence in kind of a need, more lyrical, right. I feel like that was more present in the 1990s and maybe even the 2000s but I just feel like there's gonna be more lyrical rap on the radio in the next five years or people wanting to hear that type of stuff and maybe those monthly listeners on their Spotify or something will get into the millions instead of them just being underground or necessarily considered underrated or something like that, but I think definitely influences right now, and lyrical, underground rappers will be making a resurgence the next five years.

Swabski

Interviewer: Can you tell me if there's anything you do, like practice your articulation, like practicing on the same syllable or something like that? Do you have any techniques like that?

Swabski: Yeah. I'm sure there's people who have certain bars and stuff that they constantly practice, you know, or maybe, what is it, like . . . ? You know, one of those, what do you call those? Like you know, "Sally by the seashore"—the tongue twisters and stuff like that, that people can practice especially if they're going to go, you know, really crazy in a bar. If they have some kind of alliteration setup. Yeah, for me personally, I like to just write the bar. And I just keep practicing it until I get it. And I guess that helps me for future things, just the more you practice, the more comfortable you get saying certain words and saying them really fast. So you're working out and training your muscle or reading books to train your mind. You also just gotta be—I think the more you started reading lyrics and start writing lyrics, just keep spitting them, the better you're gonna get in terms of being fast, being able to read fast and comprehend how you're going to do it. And you know, it's quite interesting because you can, have the same sentence, but based on how fast it is and how people are gonna say certain words, slow down on certain words and complete the rest of the sentence—you can get so many different flows off of that. So it really depends how you're gonna articulate and that's why it's really cool to see all these different styles because people are gonna articulate in different ways, or they might not even articulate at all and that makes it sound even slower. You know? I mean, that's the thing with mumble rap, are you going to articulate the words more, are you going to articulate the flow, but you leave—the Migos, they're known for the triplets, you know? And, yeah, I think articulation is very important. And that's why I like rap, and hip-hop, because all these different genres have their own pros and pros, right? Like, what makes them stand out. And for rap, I like it because you can say a lot of things more than other genres, in terms of the words you have, but the way you're saying, the cadence of the articulation and stuff like that, so yeah, for me, I'm always just trying to practice by spending the ones that I've already written. There's also ciphers that go around in the city to freestyling where you go and there's just a bunch of people freestyling, and I used to go a lot more—I haven't, as after I started working, but prompter I hit it up. But it's always good because you're training the mind. Freestyling is a whole nother thing. But you know, to be able to just put words together—and once you start getting better at freestyling you're not able to just put words together but you have to rap faster and articulate. Because your mind—I guess when you're unsure of what you're rapping about, you're not going to be articulating as much, but yeah, just stuff like that. I think all those things kind of help with that.

Interviewer: Yeah, for sure. What you said there with being sure of what you're articulating, and also how you said that you need to enunciate more than you actually think—could you break down that process of knowing how much to enunciate your words?

Swabski: Yeah, I think so. I mean, especially on the recording. You want to make it so everyone can hear what you're saying. And yeah, I mean, the recording part is complicated, and honestly it's something that I'm trying to figure out as an independent artist. You know, when I first started rapping and started recording maybe eight years ago, and recording in my house and getting a friend to make some, master it. It doesn't sound like the same quality as a radio, and then I take it to another engineer and we're just constantly trying to work to get closer to that sound. And it's something that I'm still trying to find, because getting that really crystal-clear sound is an art of its own, it really just makes everything sound good. Because to be honest, I was listening to "Dead President" yesterday, I was comparing it to one of my friends who's also an artist and he's been doing it as long as I have, and you know, his sounded a bit clearer just in terms of how everything was in unison. When I listened to "Dead President," I love the song but it's a bit like the instrument tools and the vote with the vocals are separate, it doesn't sound like 100 percent in unison in terms of the mix. And so there's all these sort of things in terms of unseating words or even notes in the background, it is good to be clear, just so maybe it's easier to work with. But like I said, every artist is different, not everyone's going to want to enunciate because it really just depends on how they want to do it. You look at Young Thug, I don't know if that's enunciate maybe, but that's a whole nother thing, this depends what kind of flow you want to go with. For me, I had an NCAA because there were just so many social political things that I wanted to bring up, and I didn't, I really wanted to talk about it, you know, and it's just something and it wouldn't make sense for me to write to talk about all those things. Like, make it into a mumble rap style. Also, it's just not my style. I think it'd be very weird if I just tried to mumble rapping.

daedae

Interviewer: You're a Northwestern grad. I'm a Bienen grad, too. So what an interesting trajectory you've had—what led you to hip-hop and producing?

daedae: To be more specific about me with going to Northwestern, being a classical percussionist, growing up as a drummer and percussionist, all over I have a very rhythmic mind. Also I have a very mathematically musical mind. The way that I listen to music is very different than the way that a lot of other people listen to music. It's not really on purpose. I actually hear things. I hear vocals as melodies, rhythms, articulations, consonants, and vowels. I don't really hear the words that are being said. For the most part I have to listen again. To be able to take that in. And that's a big part of what I contribute to a lot of what I work on with people, if I'm executive producing something. For the most part a rapper is thinking about the words, because they're a rapper, they're writing words.

Interviewer: Right.

daedae: I'm not really thinking about that as a human, I'm more thinking about that as an instrument that—does this whole thing sound good? Is the vibe here feeling what it should feel like, and how do I reverse engineer that? Which is something that I especially . . . working with Cory, going back to that, learning how to make beats while I was still going to school for percussion and taking orchestra auditions and stuff. I had to learn how to reverse engineer that shit because I didn't know how to use FruityLoops, but I would hear something, I'd be like, "Oh, listen to this backwards reverb thing they did. Wow, how did they do that." And I would figure out how to do it myself. I wouldn't go on YouTube. You know what I'm saying, that shit wasn't as big of a thing in 2009, YouTube and Twitter and Instagram. I couldn't just go and be like, "I'm gonna learn how to do this reverse engineer, I'm going to learn how to do this reverse reverb," for example, right now in five seconds by watching a YouTube video. I would make up how to do it. So I think a lot of starting with that and a lot of what I do now comes from having to reverse engineer shit back then and having to figure shit out for myself, but also being a person who does figure shit out for myself, being a percussionist and being someone who came from a very, very different background. So the way that I think about rap and hip-hop music is just very, very—or even just music in general, like rhythmically, it's just very, very different than most people. I think I bring that perspective. That's important to a lot of people I work with, because they don't think about it like this.

So did we—because we know how to reverse engineer what's going on that we're seeing or that we're hearing. It's like our brain just takes it and automatically chops it up like, "We could do this and this. This is how this could be better. This could be this and this could be this." You don't have to fix everything. You don't have to have perfect tech—you don't have to, Travis Barker has terrible technique. You don't have to have good technique. In fact, a lot of the best musicians sound the best because they have bad technique, because that's their—that's unique. That's their sound. It's like over the years after getting out of classical percussion school realizing that sometimes quote unquote bad things are the best things.

Interviewer: That's very well said. I hear you and I get it because I'm the same and I wish that I could just go have fun, and I—it's not that I'm not having fun. It's just that I'm working. My brain's working.

daedae: It's hard to turn off. . . .

Oh man, pop music is probably the worst for me. I'm like, "Okay, what did Max Martin do here, what is this? What's going on?" And pop music is really like, that's just at the end of the day the producers making pop music, that shit is mathematics.

Interviewer: It works. I have one more question for you—you mentioned it briefly a few minutes ago with YouTube and Twitter and everything. I was wondering, how have you seen the role of hip-hop change with all of this presence of social media?

daedae: This is a very deep topic. Because it's changed in so many ways and there's so many different parts of it that have changed and people don't have a long attention span, people's attention spans are so short, something comes out and it's gone. Like *Few Good Things* is damn near old now. Now it came out what, two weeks ago. Things come out and they're just—people have no attention spans especially now with just access to anything at their fingertips in ten seconds. Like I was just saying, I couldn't go on YouTube, really. And I mean, maybe I could, but this wasn't the thought process in 2009, 2010. This wasn't a part of your thought process, really, you wouldn't be like, "Oh, I just go and do this." These things hadn't blown up this fast.

Now if I want to know what the word "superfluous" means, I can hold the side of my phone down for three seconds and say, "What does 'superfluous' mean?" And my phone will just tell me. But that's way different. I didn't grow up with any of that. I grew up with—I had to go find a *Webster's Dictionary* and look it up, you know what I'm saying, it's not that one thing, like a huge example of all of it, it's just everything is so saturated now. So you have to think about how that's going to work with when you're putting out music, when you're doing a rollout of an album and stuff, like *Few Good Things*—they just did a whole documentary thing, they did a whole film. They did all this other shit, you know what I'm saying, he's doing all these interviews and all this shit. I think that I have so much to say about this. Even just from the beginning, even from 2009, 2010, it's the same. But if you go back even farther, the 1990s, the early 2000s. Famous people were icons in a different way than they are now. You didn't have access to them. And Denzel Washington is still very much on this. I've read a couple of things that he's talked about this where he's like, I think he said something like if people have access to you all week they're not going to go see you on the weekend. Or something like that. They're not going to pay to go see him, you know what I'm saying, why, why, why. . . . How are you still making revenue? How are you still making a living, if everyone already can just see anything you're doing every day? This is not something that famous people were doing, they be living their lives and then when they leave their house it blows—everyone's like, "Oh my God, it's Brad Pitt." You know, they can't go anywhere, but at the same time they're not on TikTok. They're not on these things all day. They're not forced to sit by their managers or their publishers or whatever to do, "Hey, we need you to do three TikToks every day, the next day," and they don't have to do any of that. It was very different. Like if you text me and then you think if I don't respond to you, it's like this—you know what I'm saying—there's this whole new slew of negative possibilities in life and judgments in life based off of this immediate access that everyone has now to everything, and they expect to be able to have it to you as well. I hate that. I hate using the word hate, but it's like if you have a spiderweb of life, and now there's a whole new opening of this part of the web now, that's what's so—all this shit is now—all these new possibilities of people being mad at you. It's all these things, people judging you and all these things, and even you taking things the wrong way, like Instagram—if someone didn't like your Instagram posts it's like, damn, you know what I'm saying, and that's something that maybe even four years ago, I'd be like, "Oh, it's stupid, like why am I even thinking about someone not liking my shit," like, whatever. But now it's like, this shit kind of matters. You can scroll Instagram and see that, maybe one of my friends, you know what I'm saying, because we're all a little, what, H-list famous or whatever. So you can scroll and see, you know, it'll show you "Saba Pivot" liked Daoud's thing. That's a big supporting thing. So I think it's important for people to be able to scroll and see daedaePIVOT liked Saba's—I try to have post notifications on for all the people that I think it's important for me to be like, whenever they post some shit, I'm trying to like it and comment on it, you know what I'm saying, and that's some shit that was stupid before. Like who cares. But now, 2022, this shit is part of the business 100 percent.

Interviewer: Yeah, no, this is—you've given me a lot to think about. I could quote you fourteen times in my book and might. Thank you for these incredible thoughts. This conversation has truly made my day.

Select Bibliography

Adams, Kyle. 2009. "On the Metrical Techniques of Flow in Rap Music." *Music Theory Online 15*, no. 5. Accessed March 12, 2023. https://www.mtosmt.org/issues/mto.09.15.5/mto.09.15.5.adams.html.

Ali, Lorraine, and Eryn Brown. 2015, May 9. "Hip-Hop, Not Beatles, Had Greatest Influence on Pop Music, Study Says." *Los Angeles Times*. https://graphics.latimes.com/music-evolution-hip-hop-rap/.

Bailey, J. 2014. *The Cultural Impact of Kanye West*. New York: Palgrave Macmillan.

Baker, Soren. 2019. *The History of Gangster Rap: From Schoolly D to Kendrick Lamar, the Rise of a Great American Art Form*. New York: Abrams Image.

Barker, Hugh, and Yuval Taylor. 2007. *Faking It: The Quest for Authenticity in Popular Music*. New York: W. W. Norton & Company.

Bruner, Raisa. 2018, January 25. "How Rap Became the Sound of the Mainstream." *Time*. https://time.com/5118041/rap-music-mainstream/.

Caramanica, Jon. 2016, August 18. "White Rappers, Clear of a Black Planet." *The New York Times*. https://www.nytimes.com/2016/08/21/arts/music/white-rappers-geazy-mike-stud.html.

Cepeda, Raquel. 2004. *And It Don't Stop: The Best American Hip-Hop Journalism of the Last 25 Years*. New York: Farrar, Straus and Giroux.

Chang, Jeff. 2005. *Can't Stop Won't Stop: A History of the Hip Hop Generation*. New York: St. Martin's Press.

Charnas, Dan. 2011. *The Big Payback: The History of the Business of Hip-Hop*. New York: New American Library.

Chuck D. 2019. *Chuck D Presents This Day in Rap and Hip-Hop History*. New York: Black Dog & Leventhal.

Cochrane, Naima. 2019, October 2. "The History of Hip-Hop Going Gospel, From MC Hammer to Sunday Service." *Billboard*. https://www.billboard.com/music/rb-hip-hop/hip-hop-gospel-kanye-west-jesus-is-coming-8531931/.

Connor, Martin. "Rap Analysis—10 Unique Rap Voices." Rap Analysis. May 28, 2014. https://www.rapanalysis.com/2014/05/rap-analysis-top-10-most-unique-rap/.

Connor, Martin. 2019. "The Notation of Rap Music." Master's Thesis, Brandeis University.

Djavadzadeh, Keivan. 2011. "Blacking Up: Une Histoire Du Rock Aur Prisme Du Blackface." *Transatlantica: American Studies Journal*, no. 2. Accessed March 22, 2023. https://journals.openedition.org/transatlantica/6553#tocfrom1n3.

Duinker, Ben, and Denis Martin. 2015. "In Search of the Golden Age Hip-Hop Sound (1986-1996)." *Empirical Musicology Review 12*, no. 1. https://emusicology.org/article/view/5410/4799.

DX Staff. 2021, February 19. "The Complicated Black History of Billboard's Hip Hop & R&B Charts." *HipHopDX*. https://hiphopdx.com/news/id.60686/title.the-complicated-black-history-of-billboards-hip-hop-rb-charts.

Edwards, Matthew. 2014. *So You Want to Sing Rock 'n' Roll: A Guide for Professionals*. Lanham: Rowman & Littlefield.

Edwards, Paul. 2009. *How to Rap: The Art and Science of the Hip-Hop MC*. Chicago: Chicago Review Press.

Edwards, Paul. 2015. *The Concise Guide to Hip-Hop Music: A Fresh Look at the Art of Hip-Hop, from Old-School Beats to Freestyle Rap*. New York: St. Martin's Griffin.

Elliott, Terence. 2021. *Hip Hop Music: History and Culture*. Solana Beach: Cognella Academic Publishing.

Ewoodzie, Joseph C. 2017. *Break Beats in the Bronx: Rediscovering Hip-Hop's Early Years*. Chapel Hill: The University of North Carolina Press.

Grem, Darren E. 2006. "'The South Got Something to Say': Atlanta's Dirty South and the Southernization of Hip-Hop America." *Southern Cultures 12*, no. 4: 55–73.

King, Michael E. 2021. *The G.O.A.T. Samples: Roots of Hip Hop Music.* Infinity Aquarius Entertainment.

Kitwana, Bakari. 2002. *The Hip-Hop Generation: Young Blacks and the Crisis in African-American Culture.* New York: Civitas Books.

Krims, Adam. 2000. *Rap Music and the Poetics of Identity.* New York: Cambridge University Press.

LeBorgne, Wendy D., and Marci D. Rosenberg. 2019. *The Vocal Athlete.* Second edition. San Diego: Plural Publishing.

Leight, Elias. 2020, June 17. "'Separate and Unequal': How 'Pop' Music Holds Black Artists Back." *Time.* https://www.rollingstone.com/music/music-features/the-problem-with-pop-1013534/.

Mamo, Heran. 2020, July 7. "Lin-Manuel Miranda Explains How 'Hamilton' Serves as a 'Love Letter to Hip-Hop' That He Grew Up On." *Billboard.* https://www.billboard.com/music/rb-hip-hop/lin-manuel-miranda-apple-music-interview-9414834/.

Miller, Richard. 1996. "The Role of the Jaw in Singing." *On the Art of Singing.* New York: Oxford Academic.

Morris, Wesley. 2019, August 4. "Why Is Everyone Always Stealing Black Music?" *The New York Times.* https://www.nytimes.com/interactive/2019/08/14/magazine/music-black-culture-appropriation.html.

National Institute on Deafness and Other Communication Disorders. 2023, April 15. "Taking Care of Your Voice." https://www.nidcd.nih.gov/health/taking-care-your-voice.

Ohriner, Mitchell. 2019. *Flow: The Rhythmic Voice in Rap Music.* New York: Oxford University Press.

Open Mic UK. 2018, January 10. "Microphone Technique for Singers: How to Sing Better with a Mic." https://www.openmicuk.co.uk/advice/microphone-technique-for-singers/.

Perry Films Inc. 2019, December 2. "And You Don't Stop: 30 Years of Hip Hop—Episode 1 Library # 9051." https://vimeo.com/376910942.

Quinn, Eithne. 2004. *Nuthin' but a "G" Thang: The Culture and Commerce of Gangsta Rap.* New York: Columbia University Press.

Rabaka, Reiland. 2012. *Hip Hop's Amnesia: From Blues and the Black Women's Club Movement to Rap and the Hip Hop Movement*. Lanham: Lexington Books.

Rabaka, Reiland. 2013. *The Hip Hop Movement: From R&B and the Civil Rights Movement to Rap and the Hip Hop Generation*. Lanham: Lexington Books.

Rodman, Judy. 2020, April 7. "Tongue Tips for Singing and Speaking." *All Things Vocal*. https://blog.judyrodman.com/2011/05/tongue-tips-for-singing-and-speaking.html#:~:text=To%20articulate%20words%20or%20lyrics,not%20bunching%20or%20bulking%20up.

Romero, Elena. 2012. *Free Stylin': How Hip Hop Changed the Fashion Industry*. Santa Barbara: Praeger.

Rose, Tricia. 1991. "'Fear of a Black Planet': Rap Music and Black Cultural Politics in the 1990s." *The Journal of Negro Education 60*, no. 3: 276–90.

Rose, Tricia. 2008. *The Hip Hop Wars: What We Talk About When We Talk About Hip Hop-and Why It Matters*. New York: Civitas Books.

Serrano, Shea, Torres, Arturo, and Ice-T. 2015. *The Rap Year Book: The Most Important Rap Song from Every Year Since 1979, Discussed, Debated, and Deconstructed*. New York: Abrams Image.

Titze, Ingo. 2021. "Is Rap Music or Speech?" *Journal of Singing 77*, no. 4: 519–20.

Wickman, Forrest. 2015, September 24. "All the Hip-Hop References in Hamilton: A Track-by-Track Guide." *Slate*. https://www.slate.com/blogs/browbeat/2015/09/24/hamilton_s_hip_hop_references_all_the_rap_and_r_b_allusions_in_lin_manuel.html.

Williams, C. L. 2020, June 24. "How the New Jack Swing Movement Redefined an Era, PopMatters." *PopMatters*. Accessed May 5, 2021. https://www.popmatters.com/new-jack-swing-1991-2495947856.html.

Williams, Justin A. 2015. *The Cambridge Companion to Hip-Hop*. New York: Cambridge University Press.

Wimsatt, William U. 2017. *Bomb the Suburbs: Graffiti, Race, Freight-Hopping and the Search for Hip-Hop's Moral Center*. Berkeley: Soft Skull.

Wolfe, Joe, Maëva Garnier, and John Smith. 2008. "Vocal Tract Resonances in Speech, Singing, and Playing Musical Instruments." *HFSP Journal 3*, no. 1: 6–23.

Index

Aaliyah, 71–72
AAVE. *See* African American Vernacular English
accents, 224–25
acid reflux: vocal fatigue/strain and, 272–73
Adams, Kyle, 150
Adele, 81
Adidas, 36, 42
adrenaline, 180
Ad-Rock, 43
Aerosmith, 69
African American Vernacular English (AAVE), 309–10
African music, 22
Afrika Bambaataa, 33, 36, 81, 91
Afrocentricism, 48
Afrofuturism, 48
Aftermath Entertainment, 72
Aguilera, Christina, 313
a-ha, 81
air sound, 240
air travel: vocal health and, 271
Akademiks, 325
Akinfenwa, Jumi, 193
Akon, 197
AKTHESAVIOR, 323–24
Al B. Sure!, 46
Ali, Muhammad, 300

alignment: defining, 155
allergies: vocal fatigue/strain and, 272–73
All That, 47
"All We Got," 301
"Amen, Brother," 25
Amen breakbeat, 25
American Bandstand, 42
American Lung Association, 167
amplification, 259–60
angry cat, 186
anime, 329
annunciators, 225
Anonymuz: on breathing, 330; interview with, 329–30
Apple Music, 206
appropriation, 135–39
Arabian Prince, 72
Arabic Maqam notations, 205
Arbery, Ahmaud, 3
arm position, 162; in microphone use, 286–87
Arrested Development, 99
articulation: defining, 151–52, 224–25
articulators: preparation of, 230–34
As Nasty as They Wanna Be, 61
Atlanta, 57–58
audience engagement: microphones and, 288–89

Audius, 298
Augustyn, Heather, 20–21
Ausar, 28, 177, 195, 290; interview with, 336
authenticity, 139, 316–17; as brand, 130–31; categories of, 128–30; cultural, 129; importance of, 256; personal, 129–30; representational, 129; value of, 131–32
autotune, 76; rapping and, 197–98
avoidance, 270
Azalea, Iggy, 132, 138

Babyface, 47
"Baby Got Back," 193
background noise, 271
Backstreet Boys, 46
"Back to Black," 322
Bad Boy Records, 56, 75
Bade, Rob, 25
Badu, Erykah, 49, 62
Baker, Hugh, 128
"Bamm," 119
Bandcamp, 298
"Bank Account," 151
Baraka, Amiri, 28–29
The Barber of Seville, 116
bar charts, 206–7
Barnum, P. T., 117
bars, 204–5; practicing, 243–44
"Bartender," 197
Basquiat, Jean-Michel, 35, 37–38
B-boying and B-girling, as pillar of hip-hop, 18–19
Beach Boys, 72
the Beastie Boys, 43, 136
Beat Butcha, 77
the Beatles, 11
beats: beat driven structures, 261; defining, 144–45, 201–2; making, 297; steady, 201–3
Beats (brand), 84
beats per minute (BPM), 147
"Beautiful," 74
"Believe," 197
Bell Biv Devoe, 46
Belle Meade, 22
Benny the Butcher, 4
"Be Our Guest," 119
"Best Friend," 245
Beyonce, 58, 61, 72, 76–77, 85, 132
B.G., 84
Bibb, Lavon, 220, 256
Big Daddy Kane, 44, 54
Big Freedia, 61
Bigg, 44
"The Bigger Picture," 4
Biggie Smalls, 24, 27–28, 54, 55, 96, 121–22, 322; death of, 56, 101–2
"Big Poppa," 54
Big Sean, 62
Billboard, 79–80
"Billie Jean," 35
Biz Markie, 107
Bizzy Bone, 107–8
The Black Album, 74
Black Arts Movement, 28–29
Blackface, 133
Black is Beautiful movement, 28–29
"Black is Blue," 323
Black Lives Matter, 3
Black music: representation of, on *Billboard*, 79–80
Black nationalism, 29
Black Prez: interview with, 334–36
Black Sheep, 5
Blackstar, 4
Blackstreet, 46, 74
"Blame It," 197
Blanchard, Terence, 69

Blige, Mary J., 312
"Bling Bling," 84
Bling Era, 84
Blondie, 37–38, 118, 136
"Blurred Lines," 73
"B.O.B. (Bombs Over Baghdad)," 328
bobblehead, 163–64
Bomb the Suburbs (Wimsett), 33
Bone Thugs and Harmony, 82, 107
Boogie Down Productions, 44
bookending, 261
boom bap, 38, 46, 94–96, 102, 214
bossy R diphthongs, 240
bossy R vowels, 239–40
Boston Globe, 20
"Both Sides of the Coin," 117
bounce, 61
"Bow Down," 86
Boyz II Men, 46, 82
BPM. *See* beats per minute
Brand Nubian, 44, 48
brands: authenticity as, 130–31
breakdancing, 5. *See also* B-boying and B-girling
breaks: in DJing, 17
"The Breaks," 36–37, 81
breathing, 167; air as fuel, 171; Anonymuz on, 330; factors in, 180; femdot. on, 333; through nose, 171–72; posture and, 156–57, 170; stance and, 180; while moving, 170; yoga inhalation, 169. *See also* inhalation
Bring It On, 119–20
Bronx, 13; crime in, 14–15; fires, 15–16
Bronx Historical Society, 5
Brooklyn, 54–55
Brooks, Gwendolyn, 29
Brother D and Collective Effort, 39, 48

Brown, Bobby, 46
Brown, Danny, 62, 188
Brown, James, 43–44, 118
Bruno Mars, 281
BTS, 12
"Buffalo Gals," 136
"Bussin!," 11
Busta Rhymes, 44, 54, 117, 120
Busy Bee Starski, 40

cadence, 145, 149
caffeine, 268, 269
C.A.M., 254
Campbell, Clive. *See* DJ Kool Herc
"Can't Hold Us," 303
Cardi B, 84, 87
cardioid microphones, 280
"Careless Whisper," 81
Carmen, 119
Carson, David, 34
Carter, Shawn. *See* Jay-Z
Cash, Johnny, 71
Cassidy, George, 18
"Catch Me," 105
C&C Music Factory, 46
Chaka Khan, 75
Chance the Rapper, 86, 120, 301
"Change Clothes," 74
"Changes," 4
Cher, 197
"Chiasma," 309
Chic, 27
Chicago: redlining in, 14
Chicago Drill, 7
Chief Keef, 7, 111
Childish Gambino, 4
Chilliams, Joseph, 16, 252, 327–29
"The Choice is Yours," 5
Cholly Rock, 18
A Chorus Line, 117
The Chronic, 72, 121

Chuck D, 40, 50
church, 23–24
Civil Rights, 23, 49
Clams Casino, 110
Clark Kent, 21
Clayton, Merry, 136
Clinton, Bill, 48, 58
Clinton, George, 26, 73
cloud rap, 110–11
CL Smooth, 255
"Club Can't Handle Me," 147
"Colbert," 328
ColeMize, 206
The College Dropout, 75, 85
Collin, Lynn, 25
Collins, Bootsy, 204
Color Me Badd, 46
Combs, Sean. *See* Puff Daddy
Common, 1–2, 29, 48–49, 77, 99, 318
The Complete Rhyming Dictionary (Wood), 299
condenser microphones, 277; advantages of, 278–79
confidence, 262, 289; posture and, 158
conflict, 257–58
Connor, Martin E., 188, 205
conscious rap, 4, 47–48, 252
consonant kicks, 194
consonants: lip-driven, 227–28; replacement of, 242; voiced, 241–42; voiceless, 241–42
consonant shuffle, 179–80
conversational volume, 192
Cookie Monster, 193–94
"Cookie Puss," 43
Cooley High, 38
cooling down: vocal health and, 270–71
Coolio, 82

Cooper, Barry Michael, 46
Cornell, Chris, 71
COVID-19 pandemic, 3, 120–21
Cozy Kiyo, 302
"C.R.E.A.M.," 46
crime: in Bronx, 14–15
Crosby, Bing, 80
Cross Bronx Expressway, 14
Cross Colors, 47
"The Crossroads," 107
Crotona Park , 14
crunk, 60, 100–102
cultural authenticity, 129
culture of hip-hop, 253–54
cupping, microphones, 284–85
Curry, Denzel, 61, 266
cursive rapping, 192–93
Cyrus, Billy Ray, 86

DaBaby, 61
Da Brat, 82
daedae, 146; interview with, 339–43; on social media, 341–42
dairy, 269
Damien, 105
DAMN, 87
"Damn It Feels Good to Be a Gangster," 59
Daoud, 343
Davis, Miles, 69
DAW. *See* digital audio workstation
Daydream Sound, 94–95
"Dead President," 339
Dead Prez, 318
Death Row Records, 56, 72
DeBarge, 82
decongestants, 270
Deezer, 298
Def Jam Recordings, 42–43, 69
De La Soul, 48, 49, 62, 81, 96
"Deliver," 4

delivery: defining, 249–50; importance of, 249–50; Mavi on, 308–9; purpose of, 250–51; storytelling and, 250, 257
Detroit, 61–62
Dhaliwal, Rishma, 152
diaphragm, 173, 175, 330
diction, 279; defining, 151–52, 223–24; practicing, 240–41
dictionary: rhyming, 298
Diddy. *See* Puff Daddy
diet, vocal health and, 269–70
digital audio workstation (DAW), 299–300
Digital Underground, 51, 193
diphthongs, 238–39; bossy R, 240
dipthongization, 193
Dirty Rotten Scoundrels (film), 117
the Dirty South, 58–59
disco, 18, 36, 91, 135; hip-hop and, 26–27
Dixon, Troy, 255
DJ Count Matchuki, 21
DJ E-Z Rock, 25
DJing: breaks in, 17; invention of, 17; as pillar of hip-hop, 17
DJ Jazzy Jeff & the Fresh Prince, 55
DJ Khaled, 61
DJ Kool Herc, 17, 21, 91
DJ Premier, 68, 69–70
DJ Screw, 59
DJ Yella, 72
D.M.C., 41, 42
DMX, 121–22, 188
Doggystyle, 54
Doja Cat, 87, 313
"Don't Stop Til You Get Enough," 80
dorsiflexion, 160
downrocks, 18
The Dozens, 19–20
Drake, 11, 77, 83, 86, 106, 313, 314

Dr. Dre, 62–63, 72–73, 82, 84, 98, 121; as producer, 53–54
Dreamgirls, 118–19
Dreamville Records, 61
drill, 111–12; Chicago, 7; UK, 7
"Drop the Bomb," 48
drop the needle, 79, 81–82
drugs, 15
Duinker, Ben, 148
Duke Bootee, 39
dynamic microphones, 277–78; advantages of, 278

"Eagles Soar with Perfect Attendance," 108
Earl Sweatshirt, 188, 311
ear sound, 240
Earth, Wind, and Fire, 36
ear training, 204
East Coast hip hop, 54, 97; West Coast v., 55–56
Eazy-E, 72
Edwards, Matt, 22
"Ego Tripping," 28–29
8 Mile (film), 63
808s & Heartbreak, 75, 198
eighth notes, 209
elderly voice, 195
electro, 62
Emancipation, 23
Eminem, 96, 132, 137, 138, 152, 327–28; in pop culture, 62–63, 84
emo rap, 255
emotional intent, 189
"Empire State of Mind," 301
endorsement deals, 36–37, 42
engineers, 289
Eric B., 43–44
"Eric B. is President," 43–44
escapism, 254

Evans, Faith, 24
Eve, 87
Ewoodzie, Joseph C., 27
exercises: Aaron Neville, 227; exhalation, 178–80; inhalation, 174–75; jaw, 228–29; Lemon and the Lion, 229–30; lips, 226–27; for microphone use, 287–88; for pitch, 185; relaxation, 226–27; triplets, 215–16; vocal health and, 269–70
exhalation, 177–81; exercises, 178–80; menacing, 195; process, 178
The Extensive Hip Hop Rhyming Dictionary (Williams), 299
external monitors, 289

Fab Five Freddy, 37–38
Fabolous, 96
Fallon, Jimmy, 54
fantasy rap, 253
Farrakhan, Louis, 57
"Fastlane," 332
feedback, 298
feet: in posture, 160; rotation of, 169
Felix and Jarvis, 62
femdot., 214, 289; on breathing, 333; interview with, 332–34
Fergie, 313
50 Cent, 84–85, 131
"Fight for Your Right," 43
"Fight the Power," 4
fish, 226
Five-Percent Nation, 44, 48
floor-sweepers, 19, 203
Flo Rida, 61, 72, 105, 147
flow: complexity of, 220; defining, 149–50, 219–20; Mavi on, 308
Flow (Ohriner), 217
flow diagrams, 205
flow speed, 148

Floyd, George, 3
flyover country, 57–63
Foreigner, 81
Forever 21, 4
"Formation," 61
4:44, 317
Francis, Sherise, 23
Franklin, Kirk, 24
"Franklin Shepard, Inc.," 117
freestyle, 338; defining, 300; Kool Moe Dee on, 300
The Fresh Prince of Bel-Air, 47
"Friends," 107
Frsh Waters, 297
FruityLoop, 340
FUBU, 47
fun, 262
funk, 36; hip-hop and, 25–26
Funk (Vincent & Clinton), 26
Funk Whale, 298
"Funky President," 43–44
Future, 147, 198

gangs, 18, 49–50
gangsta rap, 49–57, 97–99
Gang Starr, 69
"Gangsta's Paradise," 82
Garageband, 186
Gaye, Marvin, 316
gender stereotypes, 184
GERD: vocal fatigue/strain and, 272–73
"Get By," 217–18
"Get Down," 119
"Get Lucky," 73
Geto Boys, 59, 69
Get Rich or Die Tryin', 84–85
G-funk, 7, 52–54, 97–98
Ghostface Killah, 24
Gibbs, Freddie, 325
Gilbert and Sullivan, 116

Gilette, 82
"Gimme Some More," 117
gimmicks, 45
"Gin and Juice," 54
Ginuwine, 71
Giovanni, Nikki, 28–29
glides, 238–39
glottal fry, 198
Glover, Donald, 58
GOAT, 300
G.O.A.T. (album), 300
"Goin' Bad," 11
gold chains, 36–37
Golden Age, 45–49, 96–97
Goodie Mob, 58
"Good Times," 27
"Good to Be Bad," 119
Gordy, Berry, 61–62, 134–35
Gore, Tipper, 255
gospel: hip-hop and, 23–24
The Graduation, 75
graffiti, 16; crews, 34–35; development of, 34–35
Grande, Ariana, 83, 86
Grandmaster Flash, 19, 48
Grandmaster Flash and the Furious Five, 36, 39, 81
Great Migration, 13, 59–60; Second, 52, 57
Greene, Tamar, 122
griots, 28
groaning, 195
Grob, Julie, 59
groove, 217–18
Gucci Mane, 13–14, 59
Guetta, David, 11–12, 147
"Gundam Wing," 330
GWAR, 132

"Ha Ha Hey Hey," 335
halftime, 214

Hamildrops, 120
Hamilton, 119–24
The Hamilton Mixtape, 120
handheld corded microphones, 282–83
hands: microphones and, 281–82; position in posture, 162; rotation of, 169
"Happy," 73
"Hard Times," 39
Harlem, 13
Harlem Gallery of Science, 16
Harlem Hit Parade, 80
Harlem Renaissance, 28
harmonics, 196
Harris, Jasper, 77
Harrison, Donald, 27–28
head position, 162–63
headspin, 18
healing, 255–56
Heatmakerz, 75
Heavy D, 44
Hein, Ethan, 301–2
hemorrhage, vocal, 273
Hendrix, Jimi, 265
"Hiei," 330
High, Kemet, 188
hi-hats, 301
Hill, Lauryn, 49, 87
hip-hop: African roots of, 22–23; B-boying as pillar of, 18–19; breakthrough of, 83–84; culture of, 253–54; disco and, 26–27; DJing as pillar of, 17; fashion, 36–37; funk and, 25–26; gospel and, 23–24; history of, 1–2, 6, 253–54; importance of history of, 1–2; injustice challenged by, 38–40; mainstreaming of, 37–38; Mavi on, 312; newness of, 6; *New York Times* on, 12–13;

origin of, 13–16; pedagogy of, 3; pillars of, 16–30; as pop culture, 3; pop music and, 11–12; popularity of, 11; rapping as pillar of, 19; R&B and, 24–25; stigmatization of, 6; women in, 86–87; women portrayed in, 51–52. *See also specific topics*
Hip-Hop Rhyming Dictionary (Mitchel), 299
hip-house, 62
hips: rotation of, 169
hissing, 178
Hit-Boy, 319
H&M, 4
"Hold On, We're Going Home," 313–14
Holiday, Billie, 323
"Hollaback Girl," 82–83
holy hip-hop, 104
Homeboys in Outer Space, 47
Hood, Cindy, 186
hooks, 301
horrorcore, 60
Hot Black Singles, 80
"Hot in Here," 74
Houston, 59
Houston, Whitney, 81–82
"How Much a Dollar Cost," 4
"How We Gonna Make the Black Nation Rise," 39, 48
Hughes, Langston, 28
"HUMBLE," 315–16
humidifiers, 268
humorous rap, 252
"The Humpty Dance," 51, 193
"Hurt," 71
Hustle and Flow (film), 60
Hutchinson, Gregory, 53
hydration: vocal health and, 267–68
hype man, 21

hyper-cardioid microphones, 280
hypermasculinity, 50–51
hyphy, 7
"Hypnotize," 54

"I Can't Stand the Rain," 302
Ice Cube, 50, 72
Ice T, 89
Idlewild, 119
"I Don't Like," 111
If You're Reading This It's Too Late, 314
igoblyc, 229
"I Got 5 On It," 82
"I'll Be Missing You," 24
"I'll Find You," 24
"I'll Fly Away," 24
"I'm Lovin It," 74
in-ear monitors, 283, 289
"I Need a Beat," 42, 69
"I Need Love," 81
"Informer," 138
inhalation: air as fuel, 171; considerations during, 176–77; correct, 172–73; exercises, 174–75; through mouth, 172; through nose, 171–72; things to avoid during, 176
injustice: hip-hop challenging, 38–40
In Living Color, 20, 47
"In My Mind," 322
Instagram, 266, 320, 340
instrumentation, 152
intercostal muscles, 173
interference, 282–83
International Phonetic Alphabet, 235
In the Heights, 119–20
Into the Woods, 118
intros, 300–301
isolation, 255
"It's Bigger Than Hip-Hop," 318

"It's Goin' Down," 119
"It's Hard Out Here for a Pimp," 60
"It's On," 119
"It Takes Two," 25
"I Want to Know What Love Is," 81
"I Wish," 82
Izzo, Stephanie, 161

Jackson, Janet, 46
Jackson, Michael, 35, 46, 80, 281
Jacobs, David, 13
Jahaan Sweet, 77
Jamaica, 17, 20–21
Jam Master Jay, 41
Jaques-Dalcroze, Émile, 203
jaw, 225; exercises, 228–29; position, 228–29; rolling down, 231–32; tension, 232
Jay-Z, 24, 54, 74, 85, 188, 301, 318
jazz, 27–28
J. Cole, 4, 61, 86, 243, 314–15
J Dilla, 62, 99
Jesus is King, 76
JID: on vocal health, 266
Jimmy Jam, 47
"Jingle Belz," 204
Joey Bada$$, 188
Johansen, David, 132
Juice WRLD, 109, 110
"Juicy," 54
Jung Kook, 12
the Jungle Brothers, 48
Junior M.A.F.I.A., 82
"Just a Friend," 107
Just Blaze, 75
J-Zone, 147

Kazi, Rama, 170, 203, 225, 279
Kei, Luh, 303
Keith, Tay, 77
Keni Can Fly, 152

Keys, Alicia, 77, 301
kick drum, 301
Kid and Play, 47
Kidd Ken, 151
Kid Rock, 62
Killer Mike, 58, 311
King, Cashus, 130, 184
King, Martin Luther, Jr., 51
King, Rodney, 52
Kinga World, 254, 286; interview with, 336
knees: in posture, 160–61
Knight, Marion "Suge," 56, 72
"Know Thyself," 4
Kodak Black, 109
Koifish, 258
Kool and the Gang, 82
Kool Moe Dee, 40, 44; on freestyle, 300
Krayzie, 107–8
Krims, Adam, 148, 219
Kris Kross, 96
KRS-One, 4, 44, 46, 95, 314
Kurtis Blow, 36–37, 38–39
Kweli, Talib, 4, 99, 122, 124, 217–18

LaCrae, 24, 301
Lady in the Dark, 117
Lady Pink, 35
Lamar, Kendrick, 4, 11, 99, 137, 188, 314–16, 325; Pulitzer Prize won by, 87
Landis, Noah, 123
The Last Poets, 29, 49
The Late Registration, 75
launch stance, 158–59
Lee, Kevin, 84
Lee, Spike, 38, 47, 69
legato, 224
Legend, John, 48–49
Lemon and the Lion exercise, 229–30

Lennon, John, 11
lesions, vocal cord/fold, 273
"Let Me Ride," 98
Lewis, Terry, 47
License to Ill, 43, 148
"Life Goes On," 255
light and bright, 244
Lil B, 265
Lil Baby, 4, 58, 265
Lil Dicky, 138
Lil Durk, 265
Lil Jon, 58
Lil Kim, 54, 265
Lil Nas X, 86
Lil Pump, 61
Lil Tecca, 265
Lil Uzi Vert, 265, 326
Lil Wayne, 61, 84, 86, 131, 198, 265
Lil Yachty, 58, 265, 327
lines, measuring, 207
lips, 225; closed, 227; consonants driven by, 227–28; exercises, 226–27; neutral, 227; positions, 226–27; preparation of, 232–33; puckered, 227; relaxation exercises, 226–27; smiling, 227
A Little Night Music, 117
Little Simz, 11
"Like a Virgin," 81
Lizzo, 28–29, 87, 297
LL Cool J, 36–37, 42–43, 69, 81, 300
Lombard Effect, 271
loneliness, 255
Los Angeles, 52–54
"Lose Yourself," 63
love, 262–63
"Low," 197
The Low-End Theory, 121
Ludacris, 58
Luniz, 82

Lupe Fiasco, 4
lyrics: memorization of, 262; as monologue, 262–63; practicing, 262; writing, 296

Machine Gun Kelly, 188; on vocal health, 266
Macklemore, 136–37, 303
Madonna, 43, 81
mainstreaming: of hip-hop, 37–38
"Mama Said Knock You Out," 300
"Manifest," 69
Marsalis, Branford, 69
The Marshall Mathers LP, 84
Martin, Denis, 148
Martin, Max, 341
masculinity, 50–51
Mase, 54
Master P, 61
Mathers, Marshall. *See* Eminem
Mavi: on delivery, 308–9; on flow, 308; on hip-hop, 312; interview with, 308–12
Max, Peter, 34
MCA, 43
MC Breed, 62
McCartney, Paul, 77
MC Coke La Rock, 17, 21
MC Hammer, 24
MCing. *See* rapping
McKinney, William, 156
McLaren, Malcolm, 136
MC Lyte, 44
MC Ren, 72
"Me, Myself, & I," 81
medications: for vocal health, 273–74
Meek Mill, 11
Megan Thee Stallion, 4–5, 87
Melle Mel, 39
melodic rap, 105–10, 281
melody, in rapping, 105–6

memorization: of lyrics, 262
Memphis, 59–60
Mercury Records, 37
Merrily We Roll Along, 117
"Me So Horny," 61
"The Message," 39, 48, 81, 91
Method Man, 82, 312
Metro Boomin, 77
metronome, 201, 202
Machine Gun Kelly. *See* MGK
Miami, 60–61
microphones, 259–60; arm position for, 286–87; audience engagement and, 288–89; cardioid, 280; condenser, 277, 278–79; cupping, 284–85; dynamic, 277–78; exercises for use of, 287–88; functioning of, 275–76; handheld corded, 282–83; hands and, 281–82; holding, 284–86; hyper-cardioid, 280; interference, 282–83; movement and, 288–89; omnidirectional, 280; ownership of, 284; polar patterns of, 280–81; positions, 288; practice with, 290; proximity effect, 285; range of motion, 282–83; rapping and, 275; in recording studio, 277; reliability of, 282; ribbon, 277, 279; shotgun, 280; on stage, 276–77; stands, 281–82; steadying, 287–88; technique, 284–89; types of, 277–79; wired, 282–83; wireless, 283
Middle School. *See* Golden Age
MIDI rolls, 205
Midnight Marauders, 329
Mike D, 43
"Milkshake," 74
Milli Vanilli, 132

minstrelsy, 133
Miranda, Lin-Manuel, 119–20, 121–22
Missy Elliot, 72, 302
Mitchel, Kevin M., 299
MixCloud, 298
Mobb Deep, 122
Mo' Better Blues, 69
Momodu, Nezi, 41
"Mo Money, Mo Problems," 54
Monae, Janelle, 303
monitors: external, 289; in-ear, 283, 289
monologue, 261; lyrics as, 262–63
"Moonfire," 309
Morrisiana, 14
Mos Def, 54
Moses, Robert, 14, 34
Mosley, Timothy Zachery, 71
Motown, 61–62, 134–35, 309
mouth: inhalation through, 172
movement: microphones and, 288–89
"Move that Dope," 147
MTV, 35
multitasking, 297
mumble rap, 107–9
murders, 44
musicals, 119–24
Musical U Team, 204
"My Adidas," 36, 42
The Mystery of Edwin Drood, 117

"N95," 11
Nas, 54, 68
Natas, 62
Nation of Islam, 44, 48
The Native Tongues, 7, 48, 99–100
Naughty by Nature, 82
NBA Youngboy, 297
neck: position in posture, 162–63; rotations, 168–69

Nelly, 74
the Neptunes, 74
N*E*R*D, 74
neutral, 245
Neville, Aaron, exercise, 227
New Jack Swing, 46–47
New Kids on the Block, 46
New Orleans, 61
New School, 41–44, 93–94. *See also* Golden Age
New York City, 4–5, 13; redlining in, 14
New York Times on hip-hop, 12–13
Nicki Minaj, 24, 28–29, 86, 105, 132
Nielsen Soundscan, 82, 83
"A Night in Tunisia," 69
Nine Inch Nails, 71
"99 Problems," 71
"No," 12
Noah, 263, 324–27; on social media, 325
"No Merci," 11
Noname, 314
non-steroidal anti-inflammatory drugs (NSAIDs), 271
"No Role Modelz," 243
North Carolina, 61
Northwestern University, 5
nose: inhalation through, 171–72
"No Sleep Till Brooklyn," 43
$not, 61
notation, 205–6
notes: eighth, 209; quarter, 208; sixteenth, 211–12; thirty-second, 212–13; values of, 208–14
"Not Getting Married," 117–18
Notorious B.I.G. *See* Biggie Smalls
Nova Blu, 311
"now," 117
NPR Tiny Desk, 281

NSAIDs. *See* non-steroidal anti-inflammatory drugs
NSYNC, 46
"Nuthin' But a G Thang," 54, 98
Nuyorican Poets Cafe, 29
NWA, 50–52, 56, 72, 314
"NY State of Mind," 68

obstacles, 258
Off the Wall, 80
"Off the Wall," 80
OG, 301
Ohriner, Mitchell, 149, 217
Ol' Dirty Bastard, 188
Old School, 38–41, 91–93
omnidirectional microphones, 280
106 & Park, 313
"One in a Million," 72
"One Job," 322
onsets, 197
otolaryngologists, 274
OutKast, 57–58, 85, 96, 119, 327–28
overtones, 196

panting, 179
Parker, Charlie, 69
Parliament-Funkadelic, 36, 73
party rap, 100, 148–49
"Passin' Me By," 301
patter songs, 115–18
pedagogy: of hip-hop, 3; rapping, 5; vocal, 7
Peebles, Ann, 302
pelvis position, 161
Pentecostalism, 24
percussion, 22–23
personal authenticity, 129–30
personal experience rap, 251–52
P-Funk, 53
Pharcyde, 301
pharyngeal wall vibration, 193–94

Phat Farm, 42
Philadelphia, 54
"Piggy Bank," 300
Pink Friday, 86
The Pirates of Penzance, 116
Pitbull, 61
pitch, 297; altering, 191–95; defining, 183–84; exercises for, 185; importance of, 187–88; optimal speaking, 184–86; in rapping, 188–90; tone v., 187
"Planet Rock," 81
plantarflexion, 160
plantations, 22–23
Playboi Carti, 58, 86, 188, 326, 337
playwrights, 258–59
the pocket, defining, 217–18
"Poetic Justice," 315–16
polarizing rap, 252
polar patterns of microphones, 280–81
Polashek, Timothy, 299
polyrhythms, 217
"Pony," 71
pop culture: dominance, 84; Eminem in, 62–63, 84; hip-hop as, 3
pop filters, 278 79
pop music: hip-hop and, 11–12; Tatum on, 312–13
"Poppin' My Collar," 214
pop rap, 105–10
Pop Smoke, 54, 326
Post Malone, 138, 313–14
posture: arm position in, 162; breathing and, 156–57, 170; confidence and, 158; defining, 155; elements of healthy, 159; feet in, 160; hand position in, 162; head position in, 162–63; importance of, 155–56; knees in, 160–61; neck position in, 162–63; pelvis position in, 161; projection and, 157–58; storytelling and, 158–59

Powell, Colin, 15
power moves, 18
practicing: bars, 243–44; delivery, 259–60; diction, 240–41; feedback and, 298; lyrics, 262; with microphones, 290; organizing, 293; structure, 296–98; Swabski on, 337–38; volume and, 262
"Pray," 24
"The Prayer," 24
producers: role of, 67–69
projection: benefits of, 191; defining, 157; posture and, 157–58
pronation, 160
Proof, 62
"The Proud," 4
proximity effect, 285
Pryor, Richard, 20
"P.S.K. What Does It Mean," 89
Public Enemy, 4, 40, 69, 314
public presence, 297–98
puckered lips, 227
Puff Daddy, 24, 54, 117
pulsing, 179
punk rock, 26–27, 130
Puth, Charlie, 12
"Putting it Together," 117

Q-Tip, 329
quarter notes, 208
Quayle, Dan, 255
"Q.U.E.E.N.," 303
Queen Latifah, 4, 48, 107
Queen Mary University, 11
Quiñones, Lee, 37–38

rabbits, 19
Race Records, 80
racism, 91
"Radio," 69
ragtime, 134–35
Raising Hell, 42, 148
Rakim, 28, 50, 107; as rapper, 43–44
range, 186
rap battles, 40–41, 93, 300
"Rapper's Delight," 27, 37, 81
rapping, 301; autotune and, 197–98; building blocks of, 144–52; loudly, 180; melody in, 105–6; microphones and, 275; pedagogy, 5; as pillar of hip-hop, 19; pitch in, 188–90; preparation of articulators for, 230–34; purpose of, 253–56; of Rakim, 43–44; roots of, 27–30; as singing, 188; technique, 297; tone in, 188–90. *See also specific topics*
Rap's Mama (Wald), 20
"Rapture," 37–38, 118, 136
The Rap Yearbook (Serrano), 94
Raucous Records, 314–15
Raymer, Miles, 108
R&B, 59–60, 79–80; hip-hop and, 24–25
realness, 50–51, 131. *See also* authenticity
Reckless Records, 72
recording studio, 294, 297; microphones in, 277
records, 17
redlining: in Chicago, 14; in New York, 14
redveil, 187, 256; interview with, 331–32
"Regulate," 54
"Rehab," 322

Reid, LA, 47
relaxation, 167–69; exercises, 226–27
"The Remedy," 324
Rent, 119
representational authenticity, 129
resonance: defining, 260
rest, vocal health and, 268–69
rests (musical), 218–19
"The Revolution Will Not Be Televised," 29, 48
Rexha, Bebe, 11–12
rhyming: dictionary, 298; rhyme driven structures, 261; vowels and, 235
rhythm, 22; combination, 219; defining, 145–46; patterns, 203; polyrhythms, 217; of trap, 214
ribbon microphones, 277; advantages of, 279–80
Richie, Lionel, 81–82
"Riding the Wave," 335
"Right Here," 74
Rihanna, 72, 77
Riley, Teddy, 46, 74
Rilke, Rainer Maria, 33
the Ringtone Era, 58, 85
Roc-A-Fella, 75
Rock, Pete, 255
rock and roll, 134–35
"Rock with You," 80
"Rock Your Body," 74
Roddy Ricch, 89, 109, 150
the Rolling Stones, 135–36
The Roots, 54, 96, 99
"Rosa Parks," 328
Rose, Tricia, 40
Ross, Dante, 93
Rubin, Rick, 42, 70
Run, 41, 42
Run DMC, 36–37, 41, 69, 94

"Saba Pivot," 343
sampling, 43–44, 45; defining, 301–2
Sataloff, Robert, 271
"Saving All My Love For You," 81–82
Saweetie, 87, 245
Scarano, Ross, 84
"Scenario," 46, 206
Schoolly D, 89
schwa, 238
Scott, Steve, 157–58
Scott, Travis, 59
Scott-Heron, Gil, 29, 48
Scott La Rock, 44
screaming, vocal health and, 271
segregation of music charts, 80
"Self-Destruction," 44
Selma, 48
sentence structural patterns, 260–61
Serrano, Shea, 94
"7 Rings," 86
Shady Records, 84–85
Shafer, John Candyman, III, 21
Shaggy, 82
Shakur, Tupac, 4, 44, 54, 65n21, 82, 255; death of, 101–2
Sheeran, Ed, 83
"She's Out of My Life," 80
shotgun microphones, 280
shoulders: rotation of, 169
shouting: vocal health and, 271
showbiz, 296
showtunes, 118–19
side stretch, 163
Simmons, Al, 29
Simmons, Russell, 42, 69, 94
Simone, Nina, 309
Simpson, Jessica, 72
"Sing," 117
singing: preparation for, 167–70; rapping as, 188
Singleton, John, 38, 47

Sir Mix-A-Lot, 193
Sister Souljah, 48
Six, 119
"6 in the Mornin'," 89
645AR, 188
sixteenth notes, 211–12
"60 Second Assassin," 117
69 Boyz, 82
Skee-Lo, 82
skillset, 297
"Slave 4U," 74
slavery, 22–23
Slayer, 70–71
Sleep, vocal health and, 268–69
slo-mo, 232–33
"SMH," 147
Smith, Marc, 29
Smith, Sam, 72
Smith, Will, 56
smoking, 270
snare drum, 301
Snoop Dogg, 24, 54, 74, 98, 320
Snow, 138
social consciousness, 38–39
social justice, 317–18
social media, 89; daedae on, 341–42; Noah on, 325; presence on, 297–98; Tatum on, 320–21
So Far Gone, 106
softening, 245
Soldier Boy, 86
Something Rotten!, 116
Sondheim, Stephen, 117, 118
"Song Cry," 24
Songs in the Key of Life, 73
songwriting, 297
The Sorcerer, 116
Soul, 80
Soulja Boy, 58
Soul Train, 56
sound check, 289

SoundCloud, 110, 298, 326–27
The Source, 38
Spears, Britney, 74, 313
Speech and Voice Enterprises, 184
speed, 146–47
spirituals, 23–24
spoken word, 28
Spotify, 143, 206, 298
"Spread the Opps," 301
staccato, 224
staff, 207
stage, microphones on, 276–77
stamina, 180
stance: breathing and, 180; defining, 155. *See also* posture
Stax Records, 59–60
Stefani, Gwen, 82–83
"Stomp," 24
storytelling, 104–5, 151, 253; deconstruction and, 257; defining, 250; delivery and, 250, 257; posture and, 158–59; toolbox, 258–59
Straight Outta Compton (film), 51, 56
Streep, Meryl, 118
streetwear, 36
stretching, 163–64
subgenre, 148–49
subject matter, categories, 251–53
"Sucker M.C.'s," 94
Sugar Hill Gang, 27, 37
Suicide Squad, 48–49
Sullivan, Jazmine, 81
Sunday in the Park with George, 117
"Supa Dupa Fly," 72
"Super Bass," 105
supination, 160
Swabski: interview with, 337–39; on practicing, 337–38
Sweat, Keith, 46
Swift, Taylor, 84

SWV, 74
syncopation, 204

Take A Day Trip, 77
Take Care, 314
"Take Care," 108
"Take on Me," 81
talking quietly, 191–92
Tatum, A. C., 33, 43, 132, 298; interview with, 312–21; on pop music, 312–13; on social media, 320–21
Taylor, Breonna, 3
Taylor, Yuval, 128
TeaMarrr, interview with, 322–23
Tech N9ne, 314, 318
teeth, 225
tempo: defining, 146–47
tension, 162; jaw, 232; release of, 167–69
There's a God on the Mic (Kool Moe Dee), 300
"They Reminisce Over You (T.R.O.Y.)," 255
"Thieves in the Night," 4
"Think (About It)," 25
thirty-second notes, 212–13
Thomas, Sven, 148
Three 6 Mafia, 60, 85, 214
"Through the Fire," 75
"Through the Wire," 75
Thumbelina, 230
T.I., 24, 59, 86
TikTok, 4, 297–98, 320, 342
Timbaland, 24, 71–72
Timberlake, Justin, 72, 74, 281
Tim Dog, 95
time signature, 207
Times Square, 5
Titze, Ingo R., 105–6
T La Rock, 95

TLC, 82, 96
toasting, 17, 19; history of, 20–21
"Today 4 U," 119
Tommy Hilfiger, 47
tone, 297; altering, 191–95; defining, 187; importance of, 187–88; pitch v., 187; in rapping, 188–90
tongue, 225, 230; preparation of, 231; stretching, 231; tongue twisters, 233
"Tonight's the Night," 74
Toonami, 329
Too Short, 319
"Tootsee Roll," 82
toprocks, 18
Total, 82
Towns, Jay, 286
T-Pain, 197
Trainor, Meghan, 12
trap, 59, 86, 103; rhythms of, 214
Traumazine, 4–5
A Tribe Called Quest, 4, 46, 48, 62, 74, 95, 121–22, 206
Trick Daddy, 61
triplets, 214–17; exercises, 215–16
"Truth is on Its Way," 28–29
Tucker, C. Delores, 255
Tupac. *See* Shakur, Tupac
Turner, Ike, 136
Turner, Tina, 81–82, 136
turntables, 17
21 Chump Street, 119
21 Savage, 151
twerking, 61
Twitter, 320, 340
2DopeBoyz, 85
2 Live Crew, 60–61
Ty Dolla $ign, 319
Tyler, the Creator, 150
typographical charts, 205

UK Drill, 7
"Ultralight Beam," 24
Underground Railroad, 23
"U.N.I.T.Y.," 4, 107
Universal Zulu Nation, 48
Uno, 326
UPN, 47
Utopia Ltd, 116

Van Edwards, Vanessa, 158–59
Vanilla Ice, 45, 132, 136–37, 138
verse, 302
vestibular folds, 194–95
vibrations, 276
"La Vie Boheme," 117
Village Voice, 46
Vincent, Ricky, 26
viruses, vocal fatigue/strain and, 273
vocabulary, 299–304
vocal cords, 267; lesions, 273
vocal damage, 273
vocal dysfunction, 271
vocal fatigue/strain: acid reflux and, 272–73; allergies and, 272–73; common causes, 272–73; GERD and, 272–73; signs of, 272; viruses and, 273
vocal folds, 267
vocal fry, 184–85, 197
vocal health, 265; air travel and, 271; avoidance tips for, 270; cooling down and, 270–71; diet and, 269–70; hydration and, 267–68; JID on, 266; Machine Gun Kelly on, 266; medications for, 273–74; rest and, 268–69; screaming and, 271; shouting and, 271; sleep and, 268–69; tips for, 267–71; warmups and, 270–71
vocal hemorrhage, 273

vocal injuries, fixing, 266–67
vocal pedagogy, 7
voice, understanding, 267
voiced consonants, 241; replacement with, 242
voiceless consonants, 241; replacement of, 242
volume: practicing, 262; relying on, 196; talking quietly, 191–92
vowels: aaaaaeee sound, 238; bossy R vowels, 239–40; comprehension of, 235–36; eye sound, 238; long sounds, 236; ohhhooo sound, 239; ooooee sound, 239; ow sound, 239; rhyming and, 235; short, 237; sounds, 234–35; types of, 236–37
Vulture, 124

Waka Flocka Flame, 58
Wald, Elijah, 20
"Walk This Way," 69
Wall Street Journal, 13
Warhol, Andy, 35
warmups, vocal health and, 270–71
Washington, Booker T., 51
Watts riots, 52
WB, 47
"We Are the World," 81
The Weeknd, 83
"We Real Cool," 29
West, Donda, 76, 85, 99, 198
West, Kanye, 24, 49, 59, 74, 75–77
West Coast hip-hop, 97–98; East Coast v., 55–56
Western musical notation, 205
Wham!, 81
"When I Am Gone," 152
"White Crosby," 80
white flight, 13
"Who am I? (What's my Name?)," 54
Whodini, 107

Who Sampled, 25
"Who Shot Ya," 56
"Wild Ones," 105
Williams, Gio, 299
Williams, Pharrell, 73–75, 99
Wimsett, William Upski, 33
windmill, 18
Winehouse, Amy, 322
The Winstons, 25
wired microphones, 282–83
wireless microphones, 283
Wiz Khalifa, 86, 120
women: gender stereotypes, 184; in hip-hop, 86–87; portrayals of, in hip-hop, 51–52
Wonder, Stevie, 73, 74
Wood, Clement, 299
The Word Rhythm Dictionary (Polashek), 299
World Class Wreckin' Cru, 72
WorldStarHipHop, 85
writing: lyrics, 296; songwriting, 297
Wu-Tang Clan, 29, 44, 54, 96

Xhosa, 28
"XXXX," 89

Yeezy. *See* West, Kanye
yoga inhalation, 169
Yo! MTV Raps, 35
Yoruba, 28
"Y.O.U.," 303
YouHeardThatNew, 85
YoungBoy, 325
Young Jeezy, 59, 86
Young Thug, 58, 86, 109, 188, 281, 337
YouTube, 206, 297–98, 340
Yuma, Eddie, 137
Yung Gravy, 11

Zulu, 28

About the Author

Melissa L. Foster is a professor of instruction in the Department of Theatre at Northwestern University, specifically teaching voice and topics in musical theatre such as pop/rock musicals. At Northwestern, she is the recipient of both the 2021 Galbut Outstanding Faculty Award and the 2022 Charles Deering McCormick Distinguished Professor of Instruction Award. She values her time inside the classroom just as much as she does outside, and simultaneously serves as one of five faculty-in-residence on Northwestern's campus, mentoring students via their residential experience. When not at Northwestern, Melissa has been a resident vocal consultant for LYRIC UNLIMITED (a division of the Lyric Opera of Chicago) and teaches for the CCM Vocal Pedagogy Institute at Shenandoah University. She has been guest faculty for Broadway Evolved, Artsbridge, Broadway Breakthru, IHSTA, and ArtsLink. She has also taught countless masterclasses around the world. Highlights include: co-teaching a live-streamed, sold out masterclass with world renowned opera legend Renee Fleming and recent talks at schools and conferences in San Diego, San Francisco, New York City, Ithaca, Pittsburgh, Philadelphia, Madison, South Bend, Goshen, Milwaukee, Detroit, Chicago, Birmingham, Palo Alto, Xi'an, Guang Zaiou, and Hong Kong. Foster has consulted for the companies of numerous national tours, including *Miss Saigon*, *Fiddler on the Roof*, and *A Bronx Tale* and has recently enjoyed consulting for pop/rock projects like the NPR Tiny Desk series and the multi-Grammy winning band *Coldplay*. Foster currently lives in Evanston, IL, with her husband Matt Boresi, their daughter Vivian, and their two adorable bunnies, Cinna and Rue.

www.ingramcontent.com/pod-product-compliance
Lightning Source LLC
Chambersburg PA
CBHW031703230426

43668CB00006B/91